THE LONDON TOWN MISCELLANY

Volume 2 1939–1990

Edited by
John Adamson and Len Hudson

THE ALEXIUS PRESS

A CIP catalogue record for this book is available
from the British Library

© *The Alexius Press Ltd.,*
50 South Parade, Mollison Way,
Edgware, Middlesex HA8 5QL.

ISBN: 0 9519886 0 3

Typeset by Susan Woolliams Desktop Publishing Services,
Woodbridge, Suffolk.

Printed and bound by The Lowfield Printing Company Ltd.,
Crayford, Dartford, Kent.

Published by

THE ALEXIUS PRESS LTD., 1993

The Cover Photograph: An aerial view of the Thames Barrier, possibly the most
enduring achievement of the GLC.
Reproduced by permission of the Thames Barrier Visitors Centre.

CONTENTS

Section 2: The Post-War World: Continuity and Change

Section 3: LCC into GLC/ILEA

Introduction

The *London Town Miscellany* grew out of Len Hudson's short history of *London Town* and its predecessor the *London County Council Staff Gazette*, entitled *Almost a century* and published by Alexius Press in February 1991. It grew, however, to be considerably bigger than *Almost a century*, to the extent that the Editors decided that only publication in two volumes would do justice to the wealth of material. The purpose of *Miscellany* has simply been to collect together in a convenient form as much as is practicable of the most lastingly interesting writing to appear in the *Staff Gazette* and in *London Town* over the period from January 1900 to March 1990, when the magazine closed. The choice of material has been that of we the Editors alone: and we are only too well aware that much excellent and representative work has had to be omitted. Our only defence is that no anthology can, by its very nature, achieve perfection: but we are convinced that we have made a fair and full selection from an often astonishing wealth of material.

We have chosen to present the material in, generally speaking, chronological order, though certain sections of the volumes have been devoted to specific topics, as we believe that this approach will assist the reader by bringing those topics into sharper focus. Two such sections in this volume, on the Staff Association and on Staff Association and *London Town* Notables, contain material from several decades, and lack a natural "home" in the chronological sequence. We have accordingly felt it best to place those sections at the end of this volume.

This volume of *Miscellany* begins with a section covering the period of the Second World War, and then follows the London government service as it met the new challenges of peace. Stability proved too much to hope for, however, and the service had to weather the abolition of the London County Council and the establishment in 1965 of the Greater London Council and the Inner London Education Authority. This new structure, inaugurated with high hopes, itself foundered for reasons which it is not the purpose of this book to attempt to explain, with the GLC being abolished in 1986 and the ILEA in 1990.

Much of *Miscellany* is however unrelated to political events. Within the various sections of this book the reader will find a great variety of material, illustrating the high standards which were reached in the pages of the magazine. Some categories of writing which figured very prominently in the journal (news of staff clubs, and monthly editorial comment, are the most obvious cases in point) are, however, only scantily represented as their interest has, in general, been diminished by time. While we have included some material of what might be called a political character because of its representative nature or its historical significance, it is, in our judgement, the "non-political" items which are of the most lasting interest and value, and most truly embody the spirit and purpose of *London Town*. The original spelling and punctuation of articles have been preserved throughout *Miscellany*, only manifest typographical errors having been corrected; hardly surprisingly, discrepancies from modern practice are less frequent in this volume than in the first.

The Editors were confronted by a perplexity in relation to this volume of *Miscellany* which did not arise in relation to the first, in that they had themselves been regular contributors to the magazine during the last twenty years of its existence. To include examples of their own articles might be thought to indicate some lack of modesty; but to exclude them would, we feel, introduce a distortion which former readers of the magazine would find odd. We hope that, in this as in other matters, we have achieved an acceptable degree of objectivity and balance.

Apart from the material taken directly from the journal itself we have provided introductory notes to each section and also individual notes - suitably concise, we trust - to specific items wherever these seem to be needed to render the text more accessible to the reader; and also a wide variety of illustrations, many of which are those which actually appeared in the magazine when the original articles were published. The illustrations will, we hope, illuminate and complement the text. The notes at times go beyond the provision of information into expressions of opinion, but not we hope in an intrusive way; it is the original material which is most important and the reader will, we are sure, interpret it as he or she wishes.

The one and only source for *Miscellany* has been, of course, the volumes of *London Town* for the years from 1900 to 1990; these exist in bound form up to the end of 1971. The volumes were readily available to the Editors. Thanks are due to the Greater London History Library (which houses an almost complete collection of the bound volumes, and also annual sets of the loose copies from 1972 onwards, amongst a wealth of other LCC/GLC/ILEA material) for never failing kindness and attention to our requirements; to the Greater London Photograph Library, the Imperial War Museum, the National Gallery, the Royal Commission on the Historic Monuments of England, London Regional Transport, Brighton Corporation, the J. Allan Cash Photolibrary and Thames Barrier Visitors Centre for providing such interesting and valuable illustrations for this volume; and to all those former members of the LCC, the GLC and the ILEA who have taken a lively and discriminating interest in this book and have, on occasion, suggested items for inclusion. They have helped to ease our work, never ending though it seemed at times. The Editors have been greatly assisted by the skill and patience of Susan Woolliams, who has typeset the book, and thanks are also due to Jeremy Adamson for his help with proof-reading.

Our final acknowledgement must be to the contributors to *London Town* who made this volume possible. We hope that we have done them justice, and that readers today and in the future will feel that the two volumes of *Miscellany* constitute a worthy record not only of those who wrote for and ran the *Staff Gazette/London Town* but also of the service which they represented.

JOHN ADAMSON and LEN HUDSON   *London, May 1993*

Section 1: Across the abyss: the Second World War

Introduction

Unlike the First World War, which came quite suddenly from a calm, summer sky, the even wider-ranging conflict which began on 1 September 1939 cast a long shadow before it. War might have come (for a while it seemed it would come) a year earlier than it did, in September 1938: the mood of that time is caught in some of the items in the last section of Volume 1. It was not long before it became all too evident that the Munich agreement of autumn 1938 had not purchased "peace in our time": in March 1939 the Germans occupied what had been left of Czechoslovakia after that agreement, and even in peaceful Britain war came to seem almost inevitable. The British guarantees to Poland and Rumania, in the spring of 1939, ensured that any further German aggression to the east would be met by war: and so, of course, it came about.

At first it was but a "phoney war" for Britain and France, with nothing doing on the western front, but the German onslaught on Holland and Belgium on 10 May 1940 changed all that: henceforth it was total war - a struggle for survival gradually changing to an equally hard struggle for total victory. The scope of the war widened greatly with the German invasion of the Soviet Union on 22 June 1941 and the Japanese attack on the United States base at Pearl Harbour on 7 December 1941. It was a war quite different from that of 1914-18, as was reflected in those letters home from the war fronts which, as in 1914-1918, filled the columns of *London Town*. Perhaps the most marked difference was that for almost four years (18 June 1940 until 6 June 1944) the western front did not exist: British forces were always in action during this period, in the air, at sea, and in ground warfare mainly in North Africa and Italy, and, following Japanese entry into the war, in the Far East; but it was not until the invasion of northern Europe which began with the Normandy landings in June 1944 that British troops were engaged en masse, on the western front, on a scale comparable to that of 1914-18. The stalemate of that war was happily avoided and letters written at that time evoke the euphoria of the liberation of France.

Although the war pervaded every aspect of the national life, from late 1942 onwards (when final victory seemed reasonably well assured) there was time for attention to turn increasingly to the shape of the post-war world. Plans were formulated covering every aspect of life from the rebuilding of "blitzed" London to the ending of mass unemployment, from vastly improved social security to the expansion of the arts. It was a time of "plain living and high thinking", of looking to the future with a determination to make it better than the recent past: and these preoccupations were reflected, to a great extent, in the columns of the journal.

Not always so clearly reflected, however, was the indomitable spirit with which the British people, in uniform or out of it, faced up to what was, from a global viewpoint, this most terrible of all wars. Other days, other ways: the fervour of 1914-1918 was no longer so apparent, even though the underlying determination to see it through was still there. The uninterrupted publication of

London Town during the war years in the face of difficulties such as those brought out in the contemporary diary edited by C. D. Andrews as his last contributions to the magazine (see page 17) was, in itself, an example of the determination at that time to keep things going in as normal a way as possible.

Evacuating Londoners.

(October 1939)

(About 1,000 members of the Council's office staff helped to carry out the evacuation scheme, mainly as leaders and escorts of parties of mothers and children under five. The operation was almost completed by Sunday, 3rd September. On Monday, 4th September, a number of stragglers were rounded up and despatched to the country. A leader of one of these improvised stragglers' parties sends us the following account of her experience. - Ed.)

Monday, 4th September, was one of the most exhausting and stimulating days I have ever spent. By nine o'clock I had arrived at a Deptford school, ready to register for evacuation that day an unknown number of mothers and small children. By eleven I and my two volunteer escorts (a charming mother and daughter, hastily mobilised by telephone from County Hall the night before) had collected about sixteen mothers and twenty-four children.

Train loads were collected on the 'snowball' principle. We were moved by school ambulance and private car to one school, and then another, linking up with other parties on the way. By almost superhuman efforts we managed to keep our own Deptford group together. By three o'clock we had reached our 'control point,' a side street near Waterloo Station. My escorts, unprepared for the rigours of an improvised evacuation, wavered in their well-doing, but decided to Go Through With It. At this stage I was fortunate enough to collect as assistant leader a young man colleague (henceforth known as M.), who had a wonderful way with babies.

Our party had behaved with amazing good humour and patience, but by the time we clambered wearily into the train we were all dying for a cup of tea. We got it at Salisbury two hours later. There we were decanted into buses. We anxiously inquired about the safety of the suitcases of which well-intentioned people had relieved us at Waterloo and were assured that we should get them at Pewsey.

Pewsey proved not to be our resting place for the night, but a distributing centre, and the authorities here dealt us a double blow. I had the unenviable task of breaking the news to my poor exhausted mothers that they would not get their luggage that night - it could not be sorted out in time. Moreover, said the billeting officer, no billets could be spared for leaders and escorts. Neither M. nor I contemplated with pleasure the prospect of seeking a hotel in Salisbury at midnight, sleeping in the station, or travelling back all night in a slow train, but the probable effect of this news on our two volunteer escorts appalled us.

At this point another six mothers with offspring were bundled into the bus. One of them handed me a struggling and screaming child of two, which she kindly exchanged a few minutes later for a three months' old baby lighter in weight, less strenuous, but equally vocal. 'If only,' said M., 'your section could see you now!'

We reached our remote Wiltshire village some time after nine, in pitch darkness. We hopped out and shamelessly demanded all the spare nappies and feeding bottles in the village, and suggested that strong brown paper was regarded by some as a useful substitute for mackintosh sheets.

The villagers (who were expecting school children) responded superbly. They knocked up the chemist and the dairyman, and made friends with the evacuees in the most delightful manner in the world.

I spent a hectic hour helping the billeting officers to fit families to billets, and finished about 10.30. Our own billeting problems were solved, after all. M. and I were most fortunate in our hosts (mine had a very good line in sherry), and mother and daughter were put up at the vicarage and given breakfast in bed.

Note: The LCC's scheme for the evacuation of children - and quite a large number of mothers - from London to what were thought to be places of relative safety all over the country proved to be a triumph of planning and organisation. The scheme went into operation as soon as the German invasion of Poland at dawn on 1 September 1939 made war inevitable, and within a few days some 650,000 children and mothers had been evacuated from London and safely billeted in their new wartime homes.

Fortunately, the expected massive aerial assault on London once war came did not materialise, so the mass evacuation was completed without any undue hindrance. The absence of air raids did, in fact, lead to the return of many evacuees to London and some were, unfortunately, to be killed when the air raids did begin, in 1940. However, a sizeable proportion remained in their new "temporary" homes throughout the war, and a few never came back, finding the attractions of a peaceful rural life too strong to be forsaken.

The Staff and the War.

(October 1939)

Under the stress of war all the normal activities of social life have to be re-assessed, and only those which are essential to the welfare of the community can continue. That test is easily passed by the Staff Association and by this journal. The first day of war saw the Council's staff scattered over the metropolitan area, many indeed far outside it, employed on unfamiliar tasks or standing in reserve awaiting the call to new duties. But, however dissimilar their conditions of life may be to those which existed in the less unhappy days before the war, they remain for the most part employees of the Council, serving common ends, and the need to preserve their communal life and protect their interests remains and may well become increasingly important.

The members of the Association, like other citizens, are willing to make every effort and to undergo many sacrifices in support of the cause of democracy against a policy of aggression in international relations. But, again in common with other members of the community, they will wish to assure themselves that every effort and every sacrifice is necessary and is directed to the best ends. They will not consent, for instance, to the overthrow of autocracy abroad at the price of seeing it established at home. For this, among other reasons, they will cherish in wartime those democratic organizations, of which the Staff Association is our domestic example, which are the guarantee that freedom and reasonable living conditions shall be preserved.

While the essential objectives of the Association remain unchanged, many old tasks must be set on one side and new ones taken up. For many months past the Association has been negotiating with the Council on the conditions of work of those who exchange their peacetime work for army life or for civil defence duties: many questions, such as those of accommodation, compensation for extra living costs, and hours of duty, are still under discussion, but much has been achieved already, and the Association is alive to the need for vigilance and prompt action on outstanding and future problems.

The welfare of those on active service will need careful consideration, for the absentee members of the Association have a special claim on our services. The cost of living will be watched, and, if a rise takes place, the Council will be asked to provide compensation. The risks of economic disturbance in wartime are manifest, but they are not more serious than those which may arise when peace is re-established; a powerful Association is an essential protection against the menace of a post-war slump.

London Town equally has its wartime function. It will continue to give publicity to the activities of the Association and the fullest possible news of service doings. Its columns remain open, as they have always been, for the expression of the views of the staff. Readers are invited to contribute material on wartime experiences, suggestions for improving staff conditions, and in general to maintain the flow of service news and views which it has always been our privilege to record.

Practical difficulties are serious, but they can be overcome. The Association has to rebuild its organization on a new and changing basis; departmental structure has largely gone, and new local forms (like the House Committee at Cooper's Hill) are growing up. The financial problem, both for the Association and for *London Town*, is severe; it is for members themselves to overcome it by sending their subscriptions direct to the Association office. Close co-operation between the Association and *London Town* has been assured, and with the friendly and active help of members the task of creating a new register and distributing *London Town* should be easy of achievement within a few months.

But the machine cannot be worked entirely from the centre. Members should read this issue of *London Town* carefully and study the Association's statement on page 353. This means that each individual member is asked to help in building the new organization; to volunteer to act as local agent or at least to take the initiative in linking up with a local agent. The job is one - like winning the war - that calls for a strong and united effort; we are confident that the effort will be successfully made.

Note: This is how *London Town* greeted the onset of war - sober indeed compared to the *Staff Gazette's* first editorial of the 1914-18 war given in Volume 1.

The Climactic Year.

C. D. Andrews
(September 1989)

We shall soon no doubt, be deluged with reminiscences of the war years - the thoughts and emotions of those years now remembered in tranquillity. Such recollections cannot match contemporary accounts: and few of those are as succinct as the often laconic diary kept by a young member of the LCC Chief Engineer's Department. That diary is now in the Tom Harrisson Mass Observation Archive of the University of Sussex - what follows are extracts covering the climactic year 1940.

Monday 22 January. It fell to 25 degrees below freezing on Saturday. It's worse on the western front - 42 below they say. A rush at the office as usual. We heard that C. had died in France. He can't have been there more than a fortnight. Pneumonia, they said - presumably meaning "exposure".

Wednesday 27 March. I breakfasted in sunshine in the canteen, and went out for a delightful walk around St. James's Park in the fresh morning air. I passed Mr and Mrs Neville Chamberlain doing the counter-clockwise circuit. The wind was cold. At home our coal is all finished again.

Tuesday 9 April. The day opened with rumours that Norway was at war. Then we learned that Germany had already invaded and occupied almost the whole of Denmark, and has this morning invaded Norway. This afternoon Oslo surrendered. People here seem quite cheerful about it all; they want movement, excitement and slaughter from this war.

Friday 10 May. At 8.00 am we heard that Germany had invaded Belgium, Holland and Luxembourg this morning, with mechanized columns and parachute troops ... At 9.00 pm Chamberlain broadcast his resignation. A Coalition Government is to be formed under Churchill. Allied troops are already in Belgium ... The weather was lovely. At the office we were very busy. The Government has cancelled the Whit Holiday.

Tuesday 21 May. We saw John Gielgud in Lear at the Old Vic - a rather searing experience of sound and fury and pity, behind which one was aware all the time of the furious battle raging in Flanders.

Monday 27 May. There was a hell of a rush at the office with measures for the new emergency - protection of bridges, tunnels, etc. We have barbed wire entanglements all round our building.

Throughout June, July and August the world watched with varying emotions while Britain coped alone with the triumphant Nazi state. The aerial assault on England began early in August: from 7 September it was concentrated upon London.

Monday 9 September. Yesterday's civilian casualties: 286 killed, 1400 wounded. After midnight the bombing increased in intensity and frequency .. I thought it was more sense to cycle to work. I was forced into a big diversion where they were waiting for a time bomb to explode. I was very late at the office. There was plenty of work, for both Greenwich Tunnel and Deptford Creek Bridge have copped it. Locally, most of St. Thomas's Hospital Nurses' Home is scattered over Westminster Bridge . . . After work the sirens sounded just as I started to cycle home. The streets cleared of traffic, and I had a fast run. A squadron of bombers sailed diagonally across the Old Kent Road, surprisingly low, as I pedalled down it, but I just reached home as the heavy stuff began to fall around me.

Bomb damage at County Hall, 1940.

Thursday 19 September. I slept like a log. Cycled to the office in a most bastard rainstorm and got very wet. We found County Hall in a mess. A land-mine had come down on the Members' Terrace, taking casualties from the canteen staff and doing a lot of damage, even in my office at the very end of the building and round the corner.

Friday 18 October. Having got to the office with some difficulty, I found that another bomb or parachute-mine on the foreshore had blown all the glass from my windows and door, not to mention throwing chalk slurry as far as York

Road and Westminster Bridge. We improvised screens and black-out blinds, but it is very draughty . . .

Monday 9 December. It took me a long time to get to the office. London was terribly congested. The reports were that last night's raid had been very heavy, with 700 tons of high explosive and 100,000 incendiaries. The estimate for the night is 250 killed. The weather was dull and damp, but in the late afternoon the sky cleared completely. I found it very difficult to get home to Blackheath. No trains were running. I managed it in stages by thumbing hitch-hikes on lorries. By the time I reached The Globe the moon, in its second quarter, was riding high . . . there was just moonlight and silence.

The writer joined the RAF on 13 January 1941 - "New Year, new life" as his diary concluded. One hopes he survived to see more peaceful days that in that year of "terrible beauty" - 1940.

On Guard – Forming the Battalions.

Miles Senior
(February 1941)

The story of the Home Guard will one day be written. That story will tell how nearly three million men sprang to arms overnight. It will match another epic - the defence of London. But the pages of *London Town*, which so rarely sings of arms and men, should not be turned in vain by our grandchildren for an account of how 5,000 men, servants of the London County Council, formed the L.C.C. Battalions of the Home Guard.

In May 1940 the London County Council and the War Office accepted an offer from the chairman, Mr. J. R. G. Williamson, and the vice-chairman, Mr. E. A. Hartill, of the County Hall branch of the British Legion, to recruit and train Local Defence Volunteers for the defence of County Hall. This rapidly merged into a much bigger idea - the defence of all the Council's properties. Companies grew into a battalion, and Mr. H. R. Oswald, M.C., an assistant clerk of the Council and security officer, was appointed, with the approval of all, as battalion commander. Seven companies, Cooper's Hill, County Hall, Fire Brigade, Parks, Public Health, Pumping Stations, and Supplies, formed this battalion, and the strength of each ranged from 200 to 3,000.

In December 1940 the units were grouped into two battalions, Mr. Oswald becoming the group commander. Colonel K. T. Lomas, D.S.O., of the Chief Engineer's Department, was appointed to the command of No. 1 Battalion and Mr. P. Gerrard, M.S.M., of the Public Health Department, was appointed to the command of No. 2 Battalion. No. 1 Battalion contained all the units except those in the Public Health Department.

There was, of course, a shortage of accoutrements (there always is in war-time, and the equipment of the Home Guards had to be done at the same time as the Regular Army had to be refitted after Dunkirk), but many ingenious devices were adopted to secure that 'deficiencies' should not interfere with training. By 1941 there were few men in the two battalions who could not be trusted with arms. Several hundred men of the battalions are now taking part regularly in mounting guard nightly over Council properties, the frequency of duty varying from about once in twelve days to once in four. The guard is mounted from Dartford to Wokingham and from Brentwood to Sutton, and the properties guarded vary from pumping stations to supply depots, from offices to hospitals and open spaces on which air-borne troops of the enemy might land; facing winter cold and wet and the Nazi fury from the air, the men on guard are often in the open without steel helmets. They do not expect prior notice of any emergency; 'incidents' may come upon them at any time. But they know at least that a rifle, like Ancient Gaul, is divided into three parts, and they are quite ready to apply the sharp end to the invader or the intruder.

The number of casualties has been remarkably low, although a few have proved serious. Sentries and patrols on duty have often prevented the spread of damage from fire or H.E. At least one enemy airman has been captured - and taken to hospital!

These brief notes cannot be closed without reference to the quartermaster, Mr. E. A. Hartill, and his assistants, Messrs. G. J. Ring and A. R. Vessey, interviewed by many and thanked by few. Problems of supply and distribution have had to be tackled over an area of nearly 1,500 square miles. Add to these difficulties the problem of securing what is needed against competition from other units - who are perhaps higher on the priority list - and some idea of the quartermaster's work can be gathered. It has been continued at a high pitch from the early days and is continuing. For the Home Guard, like all the other good soldiers, marches on its stomach, and when the stomach is the outsize of middle age or belongs to stalwarts of the Parks Department, quartermastering the L.C.C. battalions with battle dress may occasionally justify, off parade, some incoherence of speech or unsteadiness of gait.

But Hitler has welded the chain which binds us as servants and as citizens of no mean city. Some of us indeed are in danger of becoming proud of County Hall and the Council properties. We may before we leave them for good be able to show where this or that little 'incident' occurred. Amd those of us who have not left school for long may recall that Tacitus, when he mentioned London in history for the first time, said the 'sweetness of the place attracted its people' - *loci dolcedo nos attinuerat*. Thus shall our civic history march on as it began: we grouse, we improvize, we fight. Already the Home Guards can do all three indifferently. They are still learning.

Note: In May 1940 the newly installed coalition government in Britain, led by Winston Churchill, was both impressed and alarmed by the rapidity with which the Germans overran the Netherlands, that country being forced to surrender in less than five days. Paratroops, then almost untried in warfare, had much to do with this success: and it seemed all too likely that their next objective would be Britain, then virtually undefended in the absence of most of its trained troops in France and Flanders. On the day the Dutch surrendered, therefore (14 May) an appeal went out for volunteers for local defence. It met with a huge and enthusiastic response and before the month was out Local Defence Volunteer companies had been formed or were forming all over the country.

By the time of the surrender of France in late June, which left this country (with its

Commonwealth allies) alone against Nazi Germany, the new force - now called the Home Guard instead of the rather uninspiring LDVs - was formidable in numbers though not, as yet, in equipment or in training. The equipment was slow in coming along but the training, as the following item shows, was soon under way: there was no lack of veterans of the Spanish Civil War to put the new volunteers through their paces in guerrilla warfare (always, from the time of the Peninsula War in 1808-14, a Spanish speciality). By the summer of 1944 the Home Guard had a total strength of nearly 1 million. It was never, of course, called on to fight, and it may be that it would have fared disastrously against Hitler's Panzer divisions: but no-one ever had cause to doubt its spirit, whatever reservations might be felt as to its fighting ability.

The County Hall battalion of the Home Guard in training, 1940.

School for Guerrillas.

A correspondent describes a two-day course at the Osterley Park Training School for Home Guards

(August 1940)

This school is under the direction of Tom Wintringham, ex-commander of the British Battalion of the International Brigade, and is staffed mostly by ex-service men with experience of fighting in Spain. Other assistants include two young Spanish fighters, Ricardo and Felipe. No time is wasted on drill movements. In two crammed days the school answers such questions as these - How can tanks be stopped? What type of bomb can you make with materials from the chemist's shop, mine, and quarry? How do you use them? What can you do if cut off in enemy occupied country?

Mr. Wintringham started with a lecture on the characteristics of modern war as developed by the Nazis, and on the role of the Home Guards in defence. The great mobility and totalitarian character of German tactics were emphasized. The aim of the Home Guards is to be 'first class irregulars.' As well as defending their own localities they must go out to harass enemy troops in the vicinity. It is no use sitting on guns while mobile troops and weapons are moving on you. Stray tanks and other armoured vehicles, dispatch riders, airborne troops, and sentries, must be sought out and destroyed. Tanks must be made to 'keep the lid down all the time.'

On guerrilla tactics, Captain Crisp told us what was done in Spain. Some silent methods of killing sentries were illustrated - a 'cheese-cutter' round the throat, a knife in the back pushed upwards under the lung, and a lead pipe across the lumbar region. A wire across the road, 4 feet high, will stop a motor cyclist. A few lumps of sugar or some vinegar in the petrol tank will bring motor vehicles to a stop. Sticks of dynamite and a cartridge can be dressed up to look like coal and wreck a train.

In street fighting you work your way up the street inside the houses by breaking through party walls if possible. In crossing the open, an effective smoke screen can be made by throwing a jam jar filled with oily cotton waste on to the flame made by an inflammable grenade.

During a talk on stalking, scouting, and patrolling, six men in Home Guard uniform were posted on the edge of a wood about 120 yards across a field. We tried to spot them; the average number seen was two. Some conclusions are - do not move unless essential, and camouflage the face with branches or a net or a black stripe drawn diagonally across. When stalking, etc., avoid skylines, keep in the shade, and do not walk tiptoe, which is noisier than putting the feet down firmly. Crawling was demonstrated. In the 'Spanish crawl' you lie down half-left and push yourself along with the right foot. It looked like a swimming stroke, and as demonstrated by Ricardo was very fast.

Constant practice with any weapon you possess will give you confidence in facing more heavily armed men. This was the chief point of the musketry lesson, which dealt with revolvers, various types of rifle, the shot-gun, and the tommy-gun. Practice sighting in all possible positions - standing, kneeling, lying down, from a trench, behind a bush, or up a tree. In your garden you can practice throwing yourself flat and coming to the firing position. Keep your eyes on the target. Try to reload without moving, especially when sniping. Learn to gauge distances - every shot must tell.

In a talk on 'German tactics and what we may expect,' Home Guards were reminded again of the guiding formula of totalitarian war - *anything* goes. The use of British uniforms, the landing of air-borne troops and parachutists, air raids, and the activity of traitors will, the enemy hopes, bring about confusion and draw off reserves. If bridgeheads can be captured and held, armoured thrusts will search for weak spots. These were the tactics in Flanders and France in May and June 1940. If civilians do not panic and everybody means to resist, we need not fear the outcome. German tactics rely partly on loud noises and ugly faces.

An attack by a dummy dive-bomber demonstrated that the pilot or the part of the plane under the pilot's feet are the best targets to fire at.

A most popular lecture dealt with the manufacture of explosive bombs. No details are given here as I understand that full recipes will be set out in a sixpenny pamphlet, embodying the lectures, which will be published soon. Bomb-throwing demonstrations were given by Ricardo and Felipe, and a good deal of heaving and chuckling was subsequently done by those present. One point was rubbed in - as soon as the bomb has left your hands, lie down flat or get behind your cover at once. Do not stick your face up to see where the bomb is going.

The spirit of the school is well illustrated by the title of another lecture - 'Debunking the Tank.' The bowmen of England stopped the armoured knights at Crécy; and Captain Crisp asserted that Home Guards, without artillery and anti-tank guns, could stop tanks. The tank trap must be put in a place where there is no alternative route. In the trap shown, a camouflaged blockhouse to act as a tank bait was made at the bend of the road. Three or four hundred yards down the road were wire fences which could be placed across the road in a few seconds. Three men manned the wire and three the blockhouse. Each side of the road, near and in front of the blockhouse, were two small trenches shaped like a cross, for bombers. It was presumed that the tank would be preceded by motor cyclists. On the word from the look-out, the wire was put into position around the bend. Motor cyclists passed the bombers and the blockhouse and were dealt with by the men at the wire. When the tank came into view it was fired on by the riflemen in the blockhouse. The tank made towards them. On passing the bombers, grenades were thrown under the tracks. If all went well, the tracks would be injured and the grease and oil round the bogie wheels set on fire. The tankists would be feeling rattled, and a land mine nearby might finish the job.

Summer on the Green.

(August 1940)

The outcasts of the Council who have been sent to the far-flung Empire to shoot tigers (now substituted by parachute troops) are now reaping the reward for six wintry months' penance in the dreary wastes of Englefield Green.

Twice a week Captain Dale (Comptroller's) and his merry men may be seen disporting themselves on the green to the vociferous encouragement (or barracking if their game 'on the edge' is stopped) of swarms of evacuated East-Enders with a vocabulary that has to be heard to be believed and translated to be understood. On alternate Thursdays the village band, able to change from Beethoven to Benny Goodman with a wave of the baton, provides musical accompaniment. The wicket is of a sporting nature, with an outfield which at least gives an even chance of the ball breaking to your left or right. The sight screen at one end is the 'Barley Mow,' which has obligingly been painted white, and at the other end gorse bushes give the bowler a reasonable chance. The traditional village green is completed by the presence of a duck pond, from which the pitch is watered.

A Strong Team

The Cooper's Hill team consists mainly of youngsters and is of no mean strength, despite the continual call to arms. The star batsman is undoubtedly Cooksey (Public Control), while Fletcher (Comptroller's), a wicket-keeper-batsman of 16, shows promise of making his presence felt in any future departmental games. The War Office having been successfully petitioned to delay the calling-up of Blackhurst (Clerk's) almost until the end of the cricket season, we have had a fast bowler who would hold his own in any class of cricket. The occasional appearance of Lowe (Public Health) adds valuable experience to the team, and newcomer Ornellas (Comptroller's) should develop into a first-class spin bowler.

Over twenty games have been played in all, thirteen of them with outside teams, of which six have been won and three lost. The pick of the fixtures was against Holloway Sanatorium, a hospital at Virginia Water with a ground of county standard. Matches with the Signal Corps were very popular, and the local A.F.S. provided easy game.

Cricket undoubtedly holds sway, but tennis is very popular on a court in the village and at Egham Club. The river has also been a big attraction during the hot weather.

Letters from the Forces – Food and Billets.

(July 1941)

Food and billets seem most calculated to bring forth the latent humour of an aircraftman stationed at Blackpool, well known at County Hall before 'His Majesty decided that he had more need of his services than had the Staff Association,' to quote the chairman of the New Policy Campaign committee. The following description of the food and the landlady is one which, we hope, is not typical.

"About food. For breakfast we have a little porridge, followed sometimes by a little sausage, and then a little bread on which we spread at times something of the little portion of butter which must be shared by all nine, and now and again we see a little jam, but it's mostly stones. This is washed down by a little cup of tea. Little good does it do us. Dinner is usually very tasty, but as you have guessed, there's little of it and if I allow myself three minutes to get through it, there's usually a little time to spare. For tea, the early ones get perhaps a little fishcake, another little cup of tea, bread and butter but no jam, and a little slice of cake. There is no supper here, which is a little annoying. And if we return even the littlest part of our meals, the ration allowed is cut down the next day.

Five days have I been here, and five days have I been told by the lady of the house how inconsiderate the others are in not walking on the stairs in slippers (her way of saying how inconsiderate I am). The other evening the fire was almost out and I asked for some more coal. She pointed out the danger of allowing the room to get 'too close with all those airmen in it' and told the maid to give me just sufficient to keep the fire alight. ('That's too much. Put those big bits back.')

The maid here is a poor thin creature with deepset eyes and unkempt hair and she has one of the world's worst jobs. All day long she hears the perpetual drone. I chanced to come in this morning and she was brushing hard at the staircarpet. The charming one was standing over her and saying: 'Have you done the corners? I told you to do those corners. *This* is how to do corners.' Pause. 'Now look at those corners. What did I tell you about those corners?' and so on. Poor little kid."

Apparently things became too much for the 'poor little kid' for next we hear the following.

"I've just gone out into the kitchen to find the *Radio Times*. I had thought I was alone in the place, but sitting out there before the blazing fire is - the new maid. But rest assured! We had been debating her for some time, but only to-day has she turned up. If I tell you that she had come straight from attending children in a M.D. home and that she looks as though she must have done , you will understand why I prefer to continue with the letter."

The Powers That Be in the R.A.F. seem very keen on hygiene, apparently much to the disgust of their victims, for we learn that

"Inspections are very frequent and even more time than before has to be wasted on the various processes. We have even had two finger-nail inspections this week - just like the babies' class at school! . . . This evening we had a compulsory 'bath parade' - you should have heard the lads' comments! (perhaps it was better that you did not) - but I merely sat in my cubicle reading a letter, wetted the towel in a puddle, jumped on it, damped my hair - and that was that! I'm beginning to learn how things are done, you see. And talking of bathing reminds me that in the laundry lucky dip yesterday I came out well for a change. True, one of my handkerchiefs was swopped for a decidedly inferior one, but I did manage to obtain a change of underclothes which I certainly did not send."

Finally, on the bombing of County Hall, he says:-

"Poor old County Hall! Every time there's a blitz I have to write that. It seems that 'Brothers Boche, Hun and Antichrist' (to steal a beautiful expression from a friend of mine) are determined that it shall no longer house a mighty Y.A.C. movement."

Unkind critics may say that the 'Brothers' were not quite determined enough, since the Yacs are still housed here!

Note: "Letters from the Forces" became a regular and increasingly extensive feature of *London Town* as the war went on, occupying the place of "Letters to the Family" in First World War issues of the magazine.

Olga, Where Art Thou?

F. G. Gough Helps the Salvage Campaign by sending an Open Letter to THE DUSTMEN

(February 1942)

H.M.S. *Circassia*,
January 1942

To THE DUSTMEN
Gentlemen (?)
As a loyal Staff Association member I was overjoyed at receiving *London Town* for September, October, November and December. They came all in one large lump, it is true, but, nevertheless, they were welcome, they were welcome.

BUT, Gentlemen (?), BUT, my messmates and I wish to express our amazement, disgust, resentment and indignation at an insult to our ship which appears in your columns. That you should have singled out the noble *Circassia* for libel is something quite beyond the understanding of simple sailors.

In your otherwise enthralling serial you have as a principal character one Olga Kutuproff who is referred to as 'beautiful Circassian demi-mondaine and super-spy' (September); 'beautiful Circassian spy' with 'allure' and 'subtle fragrance' (October); in November she is merely 'spy and heart-breaker' but makes a come-back in December as 'lovely' and making 'heady advances' as a 'beautiful intruder.'

Now, Sirs, by special permission of the Admiralty, I am able to disclose that we have searched both high (mast-heads: you know - the big sticks that jut up here and there in a ship) and low (keel scraped personally by yours truly) and also from the bows (sharp end) to the stern (blunt end) and along the sides (where the fence goes), on the bridge where we closely questioned the officer of the watch, in the galley where we interviewed the chief cook, on whom we smiled for a change. We went to the sick bay where the attendant quite misunderstood our requirements, to the chart-room from which we were expelled by Navvy, to the canteen where the manager simply jutted his iron jaw and would repeat nothing but 'No tick!' to all our requests for information.

We asked Jimmy, Gunnery Jack, the Jaunty, the Buffer and the Crusher; the Yeoman, Sparks and Bunts; Nobby Clark, Dusty Miller and Knocker White; Jimmy Green, Tug Wilson and Pincher Martin; Chief P.Os., P.O.s and Killicks; Three-badgeman, Two-badgemen, One-badgemen and No-badgemen; A.Bs. and O.Ds.; Old Salts, Young Salts and Fruity Salts, but nowhere, nowhere was there the slightest trace of any person who might be described as a 'beautiful super-spy.'

We met many 'heart-breakers' quite capable of 'heady advances' but slipped up in 'demi-mondaine': most of us have been over at least half the world, so that was ruled out as having too universal an application.

We thought we had stumbled on the secret when interviewing the ship's cat. As the only female on board she ought to have known a thing or two, but as the surprised mother of many kittens all fathered in different ports, she obviously knew nothing and didn't mind admitting as much. 'Subtle fragrance' we met everywhere, but suspected the presence of bilge-water rather than Olga.

Now, Gentlemen (?), in face of this overwhelming accumulation of evidence, we feel sure you will see your way clear to removing this slur on our ship's fair name. After all, Olga might just as well have won Renown as one who was Valiant, Furious, or Formidable, but please, oh please, never let her have Implacable Revenge by being Victorious.

Thanking you in anticipation of Justice being Done, and this Awful Wrong being Righted, I remain, Gentlemen (?),

Your faithful Bunting-tosser,

F.C. Gough

Planning a New London.

Arthur Ling
(October 1942)

Plans for the redevelopment of London are on view at Burlington House until 28th November. They represent the interim report of the Royal Academy Planning Committee formed in 1940 with Sir Edwin Lutyens as chairman and Sir Charles Bressey as vice-chairman.

There can be no doubting the genuine desire of the Academician architects to see a better London, and with some of their proposals there can be little disagreement. Many of us may not like the emphasis which they lay on the vista, the geometric road patterning, or the spirit of a new classical renaissance which takes us into the past rather than the future, but the main question is, not what sort of new London we want, but how can we get a new London? We should be side-tracking the main issue if we allowed this exhibition to begin a controversy about whether a vista of St. Paul's should be obtained from Ludgate Circus or New Bridge Street; whether Piccadilly Circus should be round or rectangular.

I find it difficult therefore to praise or criticise the scheme; it is rather like answering the question at the present moment - 'Do you prefer pineapples or bananas?'

In the past, it has not been lack of plans or technical skill which has prevented London from being planned or reconstructed; it has been the straitjacket of our economic and social system. This system has either dictated impossible conditions to architects and townplanners or thrust them aside as unwanted - an unnecessary reduction on the profits.

Frustrated Architects

No architect in his right mind and with financial security would have designed Oxford Street as it is to-day with its change of height and style every twenty feet or so; nor would he have designed luxury flats (which have had to be boosted in the press in order to secure lettings) while thousands living in slums have cried out for his services. But architects, like the rest of us, have to earn a living, and to do so they have had to conform to conditions which demand the maximum exploitation of land and building space and disregard questions of co-ordinated design and elementary human requirements.

Who Will be Stimulated?

The Academy Plan is designed 'to stimulate interest and set a high standard.' One is tempted to ask whether it will stimulate the railway companies to move their stations back as proposed? Will it stimulate land property owners to waive their present rights to compensation? Will it stimulate the developer to demand well-designed buildings and co-operate with his adjoining owners to secure a co-ordinated plan which will be profitable in the national economy? I should be happy to believe that it would, but the consistency with which vested interests have frustrated reconstruction in the past makes me wonder what will save the Academy Plan from the fate of similar plans from Wren onwards.

The answer surely lies with the public. If their demand has sufficient strength the obstructing interests can be swept aside.

Will the Academy Plan stimulate the people to action?

In this respect it is unfortunate that the committee have concentrated their energies on the central area. To a considerable proportion of London's inhabitants the West End and the City are far-away places visited only on rare and special occasions - on Lord Mayor's Show Day or when Ma needs a new hat and Selfridges have a bargain basement-sale. The plan will not, I am afraid, stimulate the people of Poplar, Stepney, Islington, or Deptford. I doubt whether the East-ender will be able to work up much enthusiasm about an open space around St. Paul's or the duplication of the County Fire Offices north of a reconstructed Piccadilly Circus. He wants better housing, better schools, and somewhere for his children to play near at hand. In the Academy Plan he will have great difficulty in finding any proposals to satisfy these needs. A sound heart is no good without a body to function in, and London's heart is already sound in comparison with its diseased body.

Safer Ground

Moreover, planners are on safer ground in planning comprehensively for the working-class areas devasted by slum and bomb. Something will have to be done there, and the urgent requirements in housing, schools, community centres, etc., are already clear. Plans for the central area cannot under existing circumstances be anything but empty shells into which a new social system is expected to fit itself. And who can say whether this new social system will take heed of what is planned for it on paper? The design and arrangement of buildings are inevitably the reflection of the social and economic conditions of the times. Plans can help to inspire men to achieve new conditions, but they cannot bring changes in themselves.

We have yet to create the new world which will make a reconstructed London possible. The recent Uthwatt and Scott Committees' reports grope in the right direction, but it will be up to the people of London through their organisations to secure the changes which will put an end to London as a speculator's paradise and bring the opportunity of a new life and a new healthy environment to its several millions.

Meanwhile, we cannot allow our plans for the future to divert attention from the more urgent necessity of planning for the present or to obscure the first condition for reconstruction - that we win the war. If we do, we may find that the magnificent building planned for the north side of Piccadilly Circus is being built to house the Gestapo and that the avenue from the river to St. Paul's is but a triumphal entry for the swaggering Nazi.

Note: From late 1942 onwards it became more and more clear that the tide of German success in the war had passed its peak and was now ebbing fast: and minds turned increasingly to the shape of the post-war world. How and in what form London was to be reshaped and rebuilt was a question of particular interest to the readers of *London Town* as this article shows. Sir Patrick Abercrombie's plan, which caused a considerable stir during the first half of 1943, envisaged the realisation of Wren's plan for rebuilding London after the great fire of 1666, but on a much wider scale. Abercrombie visualised the sort of wide, sweeping avenues through the centre of London which were later, at his behest, laid out in the devastated centre of Plymouth. To see just how an Abercrombie planned London might have looked one need only consider Armada Way, Plymouth. It was not, of course, to be, but the idea that London should be rebuilt on altogether new and imaginative lines was very much part of the intellectual climate in 1943/45.

Women in the War.

Mrs. Kay J. Hammond

Mrs. Kay J. Hammond, perhaps better known to her colleagues in the Architect's Department as Miss Flack, sends her thanks from a W.R.N.S. Depot for the continued flow of *London Towns*. 'It is a welcome visitor . . . and apart from one or two stray visits to County Hall my only means of keeping in touch with the trend of events there . . .

'I am in the W.R.N.S. - and loving it. After being in the Service three months I changed from Signals Office to Regulating, and having completed my three months I applied for my "proficiency pay." To my surprise, I was given a "hook" instead - the anchor on the left arm, denoting a Leading Wren, and being the equivalent of a corporal in the A.T.S. or W.A.A.F. As it also entails a further 14s. a week you can imagine it was very welcome. A few weeks previously I had moved from the depot where I trained to this one. It is a vast building and when I came here there were three rooms habitable! For weeks we scrubbed, unloaded stores, put up beds, marked linen, scoured pots and pans, and then by way of a change scoured pots and pans, marked linen, put up beds, unloaded stores and scrubbed!

'However, the depot opened according to schedule and it is here that the increasing numbers of probationary Wrens report each week. It is a fascinating job, welcoming them in, and trying to make them feel at home - trying to teach them in the first fortnight, before they go out as enrolled Wrens, something of the traditions of the Navy.

'Regulating is receptionist-cum-enquiry bureau-cum-policeman, and demands a lot of one's free time and energy. But we all love it - as, in fact, all W.R.N.S. seem to love their jobs. Such care is taken to put round pegs into round holes! And the inner woman is looked after very well too; and though we don't march on out stomachs we certainly work on them. I think the natty new hats add a lot to our peace of mind, too! When I joined I did it *despite* the hats!

'I miss my colleagues at C.H., and should like to send them my regards . . . You may be sure, though, that those of us who have left County Hall will always follow its news with interest and affection - we spent may happy years there.

'My best regards to any who know us, from my husband and myself.'

(Mrs. Hammond is now a regulating petty officer.)

Women's Home Defence

The cookery section of the Women's Home Defence unit at County Hall are now having instruction in field cookery, under Lieut. Ballard. The syllabus is briefly as follows:- 1. Rations, how obtained, apportioned, etc. 2. Types of field and army kitchens - fuel - cleaning and firing. 3. Service of meals, dining hall discipline, washing up. 4. Preparation of meals. Duties of the master cook and assistants. Service under active service conditions; use of hay boxes and other containers. Kitchen routine. Description of the various cooking utensils allowed by equipment regulations. By-products and salvage. 5. Cooking for numbers. Types of standard meals. 6. Lecture by the Battalion Medical Officer on balanced meals, calories and vitamins, and suitable menus for service conditions.

In his first lecture, Mr. Ballard drew attention to the importance of satisfactory army cooking and said how grateful the Home Guard were that the W.H.D. were training to help them in these duties. The War Office were looking to women to furnish service of this kind and, if the occasion arose, the help of many more women would be required. Anyone interested may telephone Miss Marriott, Room 452, N. Block (extension 6108), who will be able to give exact information about the time and place of the lectures, which, subject to the exigencies of the Home Guard, will be held on Mondays at 6 o'clock in Room 151, North Block.

Note: From the very beginning, women played a prominent part in the war effort - a fact not always fully reflected in *London Town* even though, in these years, it was a woman, Joyce Eatherley, who perhaps did most to keep the journal going and another woman, Betty Turner, who became the leading figure in the Staff Association. In the First World War it was not until 1917 that womens' auxiliary services became fully established: in the Second World War they were functioning right from the start and by September 1944 there were well over half a million women in the ATS, WAAF and WRNS and the nursing services. A limited form of conscription for women had been introduced early in 1942 and apart from being taken into the uniformed services women were also directed into war work of all kinds.

A Fighter Pilot in North Africa.

(June 1943)

(The following is an extract from a letter from a member of the staff of the Education Officer's Department who is an R.A.F. fighter pilot in N. Africa. - Ed.)

Our squadron came out here with the first landings and after a week or so in Algiers moved up to Souk el Arba, only about 30 miles behind the lines. From our base we carried out all sorts of operation. I, myself, did 45 sweeps over the enemy held area, 40 escorts to bombers and reconnaissance aircraft, 30 defensive patrols over our own troops and positions: and dozens of other trips, such as ground strafing enemy transport on the roads and barges on the beaches. You can just imagine the excitement we had - it was terrific. Such names as Medjez el Bab, Pont du Fahs, Mateur, Bon Arada, Longstop Hill, as well as Tunis and Bizerta, of course, are merely place names to you as a distant observer, but I shall remember them much more vividly, as all our flying was done in that area and it was over these places that many of my pals went down in flames. We used to sweep over Tunis and Bizerta daily, but I'll never forget Medjez el Bab! A sorry sight now - a typical front-line town! I drove through it a week or so ago and all that's left of it is a deserted pile of bricks and stones with not a wall standing anywhere. Anyway, in the first weeks of the campaign we moved up to a hastily prepared airfield at Medjez, only two miles from the front. The first day we were there we were sniped at from the surrounding hills, shelled by the Hun artillery, spied on by Jerry tanks on the roads at either side of the valley and kept on the ground by a standing patrol of Messerschmitt 109s over our heads. We soon agreed that there was little future in that, so we moved back to Souk el Arba. That's just one reason why Medjez el Bab is so much more than just a name to me!

The words Pont du Fahs always remind me of a bomber escort job we did down there. Marching west from Pont de Fahs up to the front was a mass of German infantry. Our bombers crept up on them out of the sun and before they had time to disperse planted their bombs in their midst. Never had I seen such a massacre. Hun bodies and odd heads, arms, and legs went flying through the air in all directions. Mangled bodies covered the road and bordering fields, and it was estimated that over 1,000 fresh, front-line Hun troops were so successfully disposed of that he did not launch a counter attack, which our army was expecting. On another occasion while returning from a sweep over the Gulf of Tunis, looking for those big transport planes, we sighted a large Hun motor convoy on the road winding up the side of Longstop Hill. Nothing could have held us back and we went in with cannons and machine guns blazing, and raked the convoy from end to end. Petrol lorries exploded in terrific sheets of flame, others toppled over the cliff side, spewing bodies on the way down, while from others, full of infantry, German blood could be seen pouring over the tail-board into pools on the rocky road. What a scene of destruction when we left! As for the air fighting - well, we got into plenty of scraps as you can well imagine. It wasn't very funny at first, when we were outnumbered, but when we got equality and then superiority in numbers over the Hun, he wasn't keen to fight - in addition to which he has a very healthy respect for the Spitfire!

The incidents I have just related are typical of what we did to help bring the campaign to a successful conclusion and, though the going was tough and the life pretty grim, I can still look back on some pleasant memories of happy times, places visited, things achieved, and grand comradeship both in the air and on the ground. A couple of days after Tunis and Bizerta fell our squadron was moved up to the outskirts of Tunis, where we spent most of our time and where we were greeted by the inhabitants as deliverers. We collected enormous quantities of booty which the Jerries had abandoned in their flight, including numbers of cars which they left on the roadsides beside their burned-out tanks and knocked-out guns, so that each of the squadron's pilots has his own motor car - mine being a powerful Mercedes Benz! It was wonderful to be able to go into Tunis and civilisation again after spending six months surrounded by Arab squalor. To see pretty French girls nicely dressed - to hear music again, and to live between walls, for we did have to rough it during those six months in tents in a barren sweltering valley out of reach of any town - believe you me!

Now we are resting and waiting for the next campaign, which looks as if it should be the final one; then we shall have fought our way home through Europe, I expect, leaving in our wake the remains of a completely shattered Axis partnership.

Note: The war in North Africa began in the summer of 1940, after Italy's entry into the conflict (see note on page 51). The Italians had a large army in their colony of Libya, and during the late summer and early autumn this force moved cautiously forward into Egypt, which was held by only a small and poorly equipped British force - the 8th Army. The Italian advance ground to a halt at Mersa Matruh where, on 9 December 1940, 8th Army counter-attacked and routed the Italian army. The British swept on across the Libyan border and overran Cyrenaica, and on 7 February 1941 the entire Italian army, some 250,000 men, surrendered. Now, however, a German force led by General Erwin Rommel arrived upon the scene, and with Italian backing and by dint of brilliant manœuvering the British were "bounced" out of Cyrenaica and back into Egypt: but they held on to the harbour and fortress of Tobruk in Rommel's rear.

A stalemate ensued, for Rommel could not advance into Egypt with Tobruk untaken in his rear, while British attempts to break through the Axis lines were costly failures. On 18 November 1941, however, the 8th Army, now reinforced and re-equipped, at last broke through. The British had the better of a hard-fought tank battle in the desert south of Tobruk and Rommel fell back to El Agheila. Soon, however, he counter-attacked sharply, and 8th Army was obliged to retreat to defensive positions around Derma. Another stalemate ensued, until in late May 1942 Rommel again outmanoeuvred the British and forced 8th Army to retreat back to the very fringes of the Nile delta, taking Tobruk with a considerable number of prisoners in the process. From 31 August to 7 September 1942 a further German attack on the British positions around El Alamein failed to break through: and on 23 October 8th Army, now commanded by General Bernard Montgomery, attacked and rapidly broke into the German positions. By 4 November the German/Italian army had been totally defeated, and their retreat, which now began, did not end until they were safely behind the French fortifications of the Mareth line, on the border between Libya and Tunisia.

Meanwhile, Tunisia itself had become a theatre of war following the Allied (British and American) landings in French North Africa on 8 November 1942. These had been aimed at taking over the whole southern shore of the Mediterranean, but the Germans managed

A Hurricane fighter plane of the RAF's Desert Air Force on a captured Axis airfield in Libya, 1943.

to seize Tunisia and here the Allied armies were "bogged down" all through the winter. The coming of spring, coupled with the advance of 8th Army (which had successfully outflanked the Mareth line on 27 March 1943) into Tunisia broke the deadlock. The Axis forces were increasingly "squeezed" from both the south and the west. Co-ordinated attacks by the Allies, who now had control of the air, crowded the remaining Axis forces - about 240,000 men - into the Cape Bon peninsula. Their position was hopeless: they were bereft of Rommel, who had been invalided home; and on 13 May 1943 they surrendered unconditionally. Coming so soon after the far greater disaster of Stalingrad this was a tremendous blow to Axis strength and prestige.

Passenger to Teheran.

Leading Aircraftman C. D. Andrews
(February 1944)

Well, I've now turned my back definitely on Southern Arabia. No more tropic seas, sharks, and turtles brought ashore, no more Bedouins cutting the heads off our chickens by night. But I had a good year there, and I don't regret it. Now from a place that was roadless and cut off from even Arab 'Civilization', sea-washed, deserted, and almost unpopulated, I come to a cosmopolitan city in the northern Persian highlands, surrounded by snow-mountains, glittering with neon lights, noisy with almost every European and West Asian language, and fantastically expensive.

It took nearly six weeks to get here. We did the first four or five hundred miles in a little dhow (there were only a couple of us). Once we had got over the effects of the terrific farewell party we had had the night before, this was quite enjoyable. We took bags of rations for this stage because there was every probability of the crazy motor they had installed in this dhow breaking down. As a matter of fact, it did, and the dhow ran aground, but we were wise guys and had already transferred ourselves to another dhow before this happened. We made quite good progress, with favourable winds. We did another six or eight hundred miles by a more orthodox vessel, and the rest of the journey by army convoys and trains.

A Novel Bridge

Incidentally, I've read in the papers about the new bridge over the Shatt el Arab near Basra, so I expect you know about it too. It's the first moving bridge which allows river traffic to pass by depressing its centre span under the water to the river bed. We rattled over this bridge in the dark hours, past a couple of guards, and I found myself in Persia for the first time (if you don't count a quarter of an hour a year ago - just time to unload a case from a plane, smoke half a cigarette, and get back into the kite again). Through most of Persia we travelled on a railway, which is another great engineering feat, winding, tunnelling, bridging, and climbing its way among the great massif of the central Persian plateau. I forget how many tunnels, bridges, and culverts there are, but I know the railway covers twice its map length because of all the twisting and turning it has to do. It took years of building and rebuilding, absorbed the engineering brains of half-a-dozen countries, and cost thousands of lives - 2,000 in one landslide alone.

However, at last the locomotive shrieks triumphantly, and we roll along the stony plain to Teheran, capital of Persia. Far in the east the snow-streaked cone of Demavan, an extinct volcano, 18,500 ft. high, catches the last red rays of sunlight. Then we are in the station, a great austere modern building, erected by the Germans - they have craftily inserted white swastikas in the framing of the tall glass roof of the waiting hall. The German influence was very strong here until we kicked them out.

We are 4,000 ft. up to start with, and the cold strikes deep into our blood, watered by overlong sojourn down the Gulf. But the days are still sunny, the air marvellously clear. It is a pleasure to walk on a fine afternoon through the streets of the city. Gaily striped awnings protect the shops on the sunny side. Almost all streets are lined with trees, which are flaming with autumn colours. Along the avenues, separating the sidewalk from the carriageway, are deep and wide drainage trenches, which you cross by stone slabs. The buildings in the fashionable centre are all modern, and pleasingly designed. Behind you see the long range of the Elburz Range, 13,000 ft. high, and daily increasing and deepening its mantle of snow on the ridges.

A view of wartime Teheran, with British occupation forces (military police) conspicuously in view.

When night falls the city is a glittering spectacle. No blackout here. Tubular lighting in the expensive shops, lavish street lighting, neon signs flaring with the red and blue arabesques of Persian advertisements. In the restaurant windows signs in all languages invite your patronage, for there is a very fair representation of most of the United Nations here. Even without them the city would be cosmopolitan enough - Armenians, Turks, Syrians, the legation officials of Allies and neutrals, and a mass of Poles, settled in Teheran after being released over the border from the Russian camps. You can imagine that this is all highly fascinating to us who have spent twelve months without seeing a shop or a civvy suit (the Persians wear European clothes by the way); and, since in that time we barely saw half a dozen black women, what a revelation it is to see white women, freshly and slickly dressed. I shan't easily forget my first sight of a girl - a Polish assistant in the Naafi at Ahwaz. I sipped two bottles of beer very slowly, just staring and staring at this neat and smiling example of European femininity.

High Prices

Yes, there's something very nice to observe in civilization after all, once you come back to it. But everything is fantastically expensive. The great shortage of food is the chief cause. Other prices spiral to keep in proportion with food prices. And the advent of highly-paid troops of an Ally, troops who just pour money away, doesn't help things. Beer costs 3s. 8d. in town, vodka-and-vermouth (a thimbleful) 2s. 10d., a glass of coffee anything up to 1s. 10d., one dish in an ordinary restaurant will cost 4s. A photographic film is 12s., and each print you have will cost you 1s. 3d. If you can't get boot polish in the canteen it will cost you 5s. a tin in town. A secondhand bicycle was advertised for £40. How the civil population exist I can't imagine, but the rich must be very rich, for they are always well dressed, and the price of English cloth has advanced in the last nine months from 50s. to £10 per metre, while Persian cloth is nearly £6 a metre. Of course foodstuffs are severely rationed, but there is a lot of graft, hoarding, profiteering, and forging of ration coupons, etc., against which crimes new measures are announced almost daily by the Government. They now flog profiteers, with 50 to 200 lashes, not more than 50 in one day. But I think you can pay your way out of even that.

Cinema prices are about the only ones that haven't advanced at all. You can still get in for 1s. 8d. They aren't particularly good, however. They show American, French, and Russian pictures, but every 500 frames or so the sequence is interrupted while a written explanation and commentary in Persian is thrown on the screen; and the sound reproduction is poor. I saw *Gone with the Wind* - at least they only showed the first half - but I could only follow the action by reading the French sub-titles.

Most of the restaurants have orchestras, cabarets, and the like, and there are occasional gramophone concerts at the Services Club and the Anglo-Persian Institute. The Red Army occasionally gives very good concerts. I went to one recently by the Trans-Caucasian Red Army - just a concert by units who happened to be in the area - but it was smashing. The Russian dancing in particular would take London by storm. It was tremendous.

I have gone for tramps in the mountains, though they are rather far away without transport. The scenery is lovely, sometimes wild and rugged, sometimes very gracious, with valleys, thick with orchards of pomegranates, figs, grapes, mulberries, quinces, and what have you, and along the tumbling boulder-strewn streams slender lines of beeches and poplars. The rock is very rotten, often just slopes of scree, and we tramp rather than scramble.

I am pleased to say that I am now getting my mail pretty regularly. I hadn't a letter to speak of until the middle of November, but then I got nearly 50 in two deliveries, and after that I have had a fairly regular stream . . .

We had quite a do for Christmas, considering our remote and primitive life. At the last minute we got hold of some chickens and a little fruit and nuts. The rest of the stuff came out of tins, of course, but it was much superior to the usual tack - sweet green peas instead of yellow and black bullets, whole potatoes roasted instead of the sliced dried stuff we usually pulp up, sausage and onion stuffing, celery soup, and recognisable Christmas pudding. We were also very pleased to have a slice of bread each. We had enough beer over Christmas to enable us to buy seven bottles each. Since it was potent Canadian and Australian brew, and we had forgotten the taste of it, it was ample for Christmas Eve and for Christmas dinner itself - nobody seemed particularly enthusiastic about booze - in fact, it was a subdued gathering altogether.

Occasionally in my spare time I go for a tramp in the hills. The scenery is completely desolate of course, but quite romantic. For the rest, we pass our odd hours in swimming, reading, playing that highly skilled game of housey-housey, and indulging in interminable chatter about the most uninteresting things. In fact, this letter would probably be much brighter if I weren't trying to compete with this background all the time. And if I weren't writing I would probably be nattering quite as maddeningly . . .

Meanwhile, if you want to know the hundred most useful phrases in Arabic, Baluchi, or Hindustani, or the approved method of cutting hair with nail scissors, or a reasonable price to pay for Amarah silver work, or how to make pets of desert mice, write to me and I shall be your humble servant to command . . .

Note: During the summer of 1941 the British government, already very jittery over German activities in Iraq and Syria, became alarmed at the seemingly pro-German proclivities of the Shah of Persia, Reza Shah Pahlevi. The Russians, who had just been forced into the war by the German invasion of their country, were similarly alarmed. Both Britain and Russia had treaty rights, dating from the early twentieth century, to intervene in Persian affairs should their vital interests be threatened: and so joint intervention was quickly agreed upon. British troops began to advance northwards from Abadan on 25 August 1941 while Russian forces advanced southwards. There was little resistance: the British and Russians joined forces in central Persia: and on 16 September 1941 Reza Shah was forced to abdicate in favour of his son. Henceforth, until late 1945, Persia was under total military occupation, with US forces also involved after America's entry into the war. The Russians occupied the north of the country and the western allies the south and there was what seems, in the light of later events, a surprising lack of friction between them.

With the country so firmly under Allied control its capital, Teheran, seemed a good choice for the first wartime meeting of the so-called "Big Three" (Churchill, Roosevelt and Stalin) at the end of November 1943. It was at this conference that, apart from co-ordinating their military strategy for 1944, the three leaders agreed, to a very large extent, on the shape of post-war Europe, including the division of Germany into zones of occupation which was, a few years later, to give rise to the two rival German states. Stalin was very affable, in a tigerish sort of way (he made "jokes" about the number of Germans who would have to be "liquidated" at the end of the war) and it really did seem that a new and perhaps better world was emerging from this wartime domination by the "Big Three". We do not need to go into details as to what really happened in the aftermath . . .

Sport in the Desert.

(January 1944)

(We publish below an extract from a letter from Flying Officer Frank Clark, Public Health Department (Matron-in-Chief's section), who is serving with the M.E.F. - Ed.)

Cricket had now given place to soccer - and in my spare-time job as sports officer this has taken a lot of time. First of all we made a good pitch out of the desert - it is bare of grass and very hard but otherwise compares with any pitch at home. Our goalposts are a work of art - whitewashed metal tubing in best professional style, capacious nets (I never dared to ask how we came by them!), and from the amount of concrete we used to embed the posts I think they will stand as a memorial to all time. I sometimes think that future historians in North Africa will be able to trace the various occupations by different armies - the Italians by their inscriptions 'VV Duce,' the Germans by their jerricans (highly efficient mass-produced water carriers of which millions were left all over the desert), and the British by countless goalposts raised wherever a unit was forced into a long stay. And perhaps some philosophers will point out how typical these desert memorials are of the three nations concerned - how for twenty years the Italians strutted with fixed bayonets behind a bombastic Duce, and the Germans prepared ruthlessly and scientifically a splendid war machine; while the British, partly though laziness (we must admit), but mainly because they had seen the vision of a better world, were setting up goalposts on playing fields and recreation grounds and village greens. And then someone will point out how it was the goalposts that prevailed in the end.

Our football only started with the making of the pitch. Since then we have had a very full programme of games. These include a very keen inter-section league programme and weekly wing games - as well as all sorts of friendlies planned to cover all and sundry in the camp. For our policy is to cover physical exercise by organised games rather than P.T. I must say that the games are a great success - the friendlies produce great enthusiasm and fun (especially from the touchline), the league games are keenly contested on the field and afterwards and the standard of our wing team is high. We are very evenly matched with our neighbouring units, and have had some grand games. After Christmas, we start on an inter-unit competition for a Station Cup and that will be hotly contested.

As a footnote to this soccer gossip, I will mention that I have played occasionally myself in friendlies and have enjoyed it and done quite well. These games, and some regular refereeing keep me in exercise, and I am glad to say I feel quite fit again.

One other job I have done is to take a weekly class in English under the Educational Scheme. I don't vouch much for it from the educational standpoint, but I have had a very interesting time with a dozen airmen, and together we have got to understand a little more about our language and literature.

From the above you will gather that I have a good time and you may wonder why I want to move. This is mainly for a change of work and to get away for a bit from the emptiness of the desert. Unfortunately, I have to stay till I am relieved, and that is what has delayed me. I still have no definite date and in any case hope to spend Christmas here . . .

I shall not have the least regret when I am relieved of my commission and can resume normal civil life once more. This is not only for home reasons, but also because I think the L.C.C. is a far better *service* than the R.A.F. That is my opinion after two years' service in the R.A.F. Perhaps I haven't seen it at its best - most of it has been overseas and I never saw a big English station and, moreover, those of us who came in in 1941 missed the good jobs. I am speaking only of it as an administration. I take off my hat every time to the men who are doing the flying and the fighting. They are *sans peur et sans reproche*.

I get my *London Town* regularly. This is a great joy to get first-hand news

38

of the work and the people I know, and it is most interesting to keep in touch with current topics and problems. It is good to know what others are doing at home and in the services.

The return and reinstatement of all us wanderers is going to be a great problem. I don't think we can really envisage its details until we know how demobilisation is going to work. On the other hand, discussion of various aspects as they present themselves is going to help greatly and that is what *London Town* is doing.

From the Mediterranean.

(March 1944)

L.-Cpl. J. W. Shephard (Architect's), R.E., writes from Africa:- 'It was good to see the familiar *Gazette* once more and to read the Association news, and to know that we who are out here are being so fully considered by the Council and the Association. Welcome changes will have been made, and we can now look forward, having crossed the threshold of the year which promises us victory, to a speedy return, engaged in the Council's work of reconstruction, sitting once again in our own homes - some the model homes of the future - with our wives and families. I cannot tell you how much I am looking forward to this time. Prior to leaving England I was engaged as an R.E. draughtsman to an A.A. Defence H.Q. and I went with this unit to Sicily. Whilst at Siracusa I was able to visit many interesting buildings and monuments. If all had gone as expected I would now have been in Italy, but in the army one has to prepare for unexpected changes, and this finds me in N. Africa, where I have been stationed in Bizerta, Constantine, and Philippeville. Now I am somewhere else in Algeria, in an entirely new unit as R.E. draughtsman and H.C.O. Works. Our tents among the fir trees on the hillside overlook the blue Mediterranean, so near that I can hear the waves lapping on the sands. The weather remains fine, in fact most days are just like spring, hot and sunny. Daisies and various spring flowers decorate the countryside. Much of the worst weather seems to have passed; torrential rain and thunderstorms we had in plenty just about 'Xmas time and the New Year. On New Year's Eve terrific rains and a violent gale brought down tent after tent, great marquees lay strewn and twisted, all things strained and fell before the tempest. At dawn I crawled out with the others from under a mass of sodden canvas; during New Year's Day it was "All hands on deck!" in rain and storm to prevent further havoc. Such an immense camp of tentage I have not been sorry to leave, with its endless sands and the solitude of the cork forests and the lonely hills. You will be interested to hear that whilst there I met with the usual phrase, "So *you're* L.C.C. too!" from J. W. Taylor of the Supplies Department - we worked near one another for some time in the same company. Kind remembrances to all my colleagues at County Hall and in the Rescue Service.'

News from the Services, Summer 1944.

(July 1944)

Lieut. R. B. Broadbent (staff division) writes from Normandy:- 'I landed early on in the proceedings, but owing to the nature of my job have not moved very far inland. I am quite certain that Jerry is going to find things a bit hot when we really get going. The most satisfactory aspect at present is our complete air supremacy - so far we have only had two days on which any Jerries have polluted the sky by day, and one of those did not get home. At night we get small raids, the danger being mainly from falling shrapnel. The weather has been quite good, although very changeable. The day we came over it was terribly rough, and most of us were very glad to reach terra firma. Among the many things we captured in our area were the officers' and sergeants' messes, with all their rations. The butter they left behind is exceedingly good, but the wine and cigars are not so hot. Nearly all my lads have acquired souvenirs of all sorts, the favourites being pistols, bayonets, and steel helmets. Jerry left in such a hurry that all his ammunition and weapons were taken - really he was overrun by the assaulting infantry - a fine bunch of boys. All my chaps are doing their laundry, and we have fires and drying clothes everywhere. We are all in one large garden of a house which no longer exists, and really life is quite pleasant, although we have lots of work to do.'

Note: The British and American landings in Normandy on 6 June 1944 were made not without difficulties - in the western sector, in particular, US troops were pinned down on the beaches until nightfall. Nevertheless, on this vital first day of the campaign a series of beacheads were quite firmly established between the River Dives and Quinéville: and within a week these had been consolidated into one steadily expanding lodgement upon the coast and for up to eight miles inland. German failure to wipe out this Allied lodgement while it was still small and relatively weak was to cost them the whole campaign, as some of their commanders already recognised.

There followed six weeks of Allied build-up; with only slow progress against strong German resistance. Fighting was particularly fierce around Caen, on the British sector of the front, and the bulk of the German armoured forces were drawn into the battle in this area. This was to open the way for an American break-through (on 25 July) at the extreme western end of the front, on the coast near Coutances: from here the US armoured divisions raced southwards to the Loire and westwards across Brittany, but with their main strength wheeling eastwards towards the Seine and Paris. On 12 August a general German withdrawal from Normandy began, but it was too late to save those German troops who were by now trapped in a "pocket" around Falaise by the British grinding down through Caen and the Americans rushing up through Alençon. Their destruction, completed before the end of August, marked the end of the Normandy campaign.

(July 1944)

We have received the following news of Public Control Department staff:- The following extract from an airgraph to a colleague reveals that Lieut. R. Cameron, who was last reported as having been wounded during the Burma campaign, is now on the road to recovery. He says:- 'I'm writing from hospital near Secunderabad, where I am recovering (I hope) from wounds. I was hit at Kohima during the hectic fighting at the end of April, and have only just reached the stage where I can be propped up to write. I haven't had an airgraph from you since early April. It was impossible to reply then because I was in the thick of it. Then I got large chunks blown out of my thigh by a machine gun, and here I am. They tell me that with a little grafting and massage I should be as good as new, and I'm just longing to get back to the battalion.' We reiterate our wishes for his speedy and complete recovery.

Note: Burma (then a British possession) was occupied by the Japanese in April-May 1942 at the very end of their amazing career of conquest which had begun on 7 December 1941 with the occupation of Thailand and the landings in Malaya. The Japanese army deemed a further advance over the mountains into India to be impracticable: and for their part the British found it equally impracticable to make headway on this front. An offensive on the coast of Arakan in 1943 was a costly failure: only the forays behind Japanese lines by General Orde Wingate's "Chindits" met with any success. They also provoked the Japanese to go over to the offensive and advance into India, but they were halted, in the spring of 1944, by the British 14th Army and the Indian Army and around Imphal and Kohima they met with a serious defeat.

This opened the way, once the rainy season was over, for the British to go on to the offensive, which they did with increasing success from the end of 1944 onwards. The Japanese were defeated again at Meiktila in March 1945, and forced to evacuate Mandalay: and by late May, following the capture of Rangoon by an amphibious assault, the British were back in control of virtually the whole of Burma. The war ended, on 15 August 1945, with the 14th Army poised to advance into Thailand.

(July 1944)

L.A.C. L. Dixon (London Fire Force), R.A.F., writing from Ceylon, sends best wishes to all his old colleagues from himself and Flight Sergeant Navigator S. Kurta, another Fire Brigade man, whom he recently contacted. Kurta, who is now with a bomber squadron in India, congratulates the Association on the post-1939 entrants settlement, as does Dixon himself and other officers of the Council he has met in his part of the world. Dixon has been all over Ceylon, and spent some leave at Nuwara Eliya, 'a small town whose elevation of some 6,200 feet above sea level gives a temperate climate which seems impossible for a spot only about 400 miles from the equator. The enclosed photograph was taken there, and, while I was wearing tropical kit at the time, it is no uncommon thing - especially in December - to see airmen on leave wearing home kit, complete with greatcoat, and shivering to boot.' Dixon longs to get back to his comfortable chair at Fire Force Headquarters. 'Until then, *London Town*, which arrives with commendable regularity, will continue to be, as it has been until now, a valuable link with the life from which all of us in the forces are temporarily divorced.'

(August 1944)

Capt. A. C. Robb, R.A.O.C. (Comptroller's), writing from Normandy before the attack from Caen, says that 'apart from the rain, life here is quite

41

pleasant. Things have been pretty static up to the present, but we still find plenty to do - although considerably quieter than in England. We are, of course, under canvas, which isn't exactly ideal with this climate, but might be a lot worse. Food is plentiful, but rather monotonous - everything out of tins - it's a case of stew yesterday, stew to-morrow, and stew to-day. It will be a treat to taste bread again after all these army biscuits. We manage to buy a few things locally, such as butter and cream (real cream) - not to mention Camembert cheese. There is certainly no sign of poverty or starvation over here - the people look quite well fed, the cattle numerous and plump, and the grain crops seem quite good. The population are quite friendly, although their goodwill is mainly expressed in terms of roses, which don't really get you very far. There are exceptions, of course; for instance, I was out once and stopped to admire a rather picturesque old farmhouse (there is very little damage round here, by the way). The old peasantess dashed out, chatting away nineteen to the dozen (or perhaps in view of the rusty state of my French I should say at a thousand to one), and in due course proffered the inevitable bunch of roses (straight from the garden hedge), and also a dish of milk (straight from the cow) but none the less acceptable for that.' On pilotless planes he says: 'It would have done your heart good to have been with us, for example, last night, when a big force of our planes plastered the line quite near to us - a real tonic after reading about the "buzz bombs."

R.E. Haymes (Public Health) sends the following account of eight days' leave in Syria:- 'I determined to overcome the transport difficulties, and make the long journey to Syria, my prime objective being Damascus. The general lay-out is a narrow coastal plain, upon which Beirut stands, with two mountain ranges behind it and parallel with the coast. The plain is cultivated, possessing large orange and lemon groves, and many wild flowers. Beirut is picturesque, especially the harbour, if not slick in the glass-and-chromium-plate way. The journey from Beirut to Damascus, over two ranges and an intervening valley, must be one of the most attractive in the world. The road climbs the Lebanon range to about 3,000 feet, the Mediterranean sparkling and Beirut glittering below in the sunlight. Over the pass (about 5,000 feet) the road winds amongst snow-covered peaks, the crown of all being Hermon (9,000 feet). On its flanks some of the famous cedars can be seen. An incongruous note - a camel train padding along beside these snow-banks.

'The Anti-Lebanon range, by comparison, is not so fine. Here one passes the respective Lebanese and Syrian customs posts, pathetic - or valiant - reminders of the small group always striving to preserve intact a separate identity. Another sight, provoking thought in philosophic vein, was a combined cemetary for French and Druse killed in the latter's revolt in 1925. Here one saw, most unusually, Christian and Mohamedan graves side by side, one marked with the Cross, the other with the Crescent.

'The rushing mountain torrent of the River Barada (Abana of the Bible) heralds the approach of Damascus, which, indeed, it divides into two. The latter is a most fascinating city - really a huge oasis. The old walled city and surrounding newer portions are themselves enclosed by orchards, the celebrated "gardens." The city rests at the foot of barren Anti-Lebanon mountains, and on other sides one soon encounters the desert. With its abundant water, fertile "gardens," and flourishing commerce, it must have seemed a veritable paradise to the Bedouin caravans. It is claimed as the oldest still-inhabited city in the world, and an Arab name for it, most appropriate, is "the necklace on the throat of beauty." The bazaars are remarkable in extent and degree of specialisation; certainly the finest I have seen. In addition to masses of brocades, silks, inlaid woodwork, brass and copper engraved ware, gold and silver filigree, sweetmeats, and so on, one can see the little open-fronted shops of tinsmith, blacksmith, wood turner, leatherworker, ropemaker, and so on.'

Note: Under the Ottoman Empire the separate identity of Lebanon - resting in large part on the distinctive traditions of the Maronite Christians and of the Druzes, whose religion is an offshoot of Islam - was in large measure recognised. After the First World War, Lebanon and Syria came under a French mandate, and a Lebanese Republic was established in 1926. Following the fall of France in 1940, Lebanon and Syria were held initially by troops loyal to Vichy, the puppet régime in France supported by the Germans, but in the summer of 1941 these troops were defeated by Free French (Gaullist) and British forces. In 1944-1946 Lebanon and Syria emerged - not without difficulty - as independent states. The history of Lebanon since then has been a chequered one, and the country is now largely under Syrian influence.

(August 1944)

Sgt. L. Slavid (Education Officer's), R.A., writes from Normandy, where he has met Payne of Social Welfare:- 'There seems to be a temporary lull on this sector, and while I have been chasing around on my official business I have had the opportunity of contacting civilians in various parts. It appears that, although the Germans engaged in a lot of looting, official and free-lance, this area is such a rich agricultural country that there has never been any real shortage of vegetable and dairy produce. The trouble was that the Germans had almost unlimited money, and consequently sent the prices of everything soaring in an almost unlimited black market. Now that the Germans have gone, and that no part of the produce is requisitioned, there is plenty to spare for everyone and prices have come tumbling down. I have been given eggs, strawberries, cider, and other things with nothing asked in return, though cigarettes and chocolate are always gratefully accepted. The people are mostly delighted to see us, and the few ex-collaborators seem to be going about their business without anybody bothering much. We have been warned to expect a very different state of affairs when we move forward. The towns have always been short of food, and especially now that they have been cut off from this area. The Germans will have time to loot systematically. A million Frenchmen had been called up to work in Germany by the end of June, and, while the people round here have been saved in the nick of time, further forward they will have already been taken. It is fortunate that the French seem to have had an admirable organisation for faking identity papers and medical certificates. They have an exceedingly low opinion of the German's ability for "ruse," and generally seem to have made rings round them in such matters. Rumours purporting to originate from Caen allege that there the Germans have just been plain murderous, and, no matter how "rusé" the population may have been, there were large scale executions and deporta-

43

tions. It is encouraging to see how people, even when we have shelled and bombed their own houses, welcome us with open arms. The children especially are having one grand picnic, and are getting thoroughly spoiled by us. We are having a fairly good time in this part of the country, although the fellows up forward must be very much less fortunate. The weather is good, the food is good, except for the fact that we get no bread, only biscuits, and so long as this lull continues we have nothing to complain about around here.

Pictures from India.

(August 1944)

(The following impression of the Indian scene has been sent to *London Town* by Lieut. David Stamp, R.E., who is an assistant garrison engineer at Allahabad.- Ed.)

London Town arriving unexpectedly at infrequent intervals with the photograph of County Hall, etc., for the heading, rather has the effect of bringing the mountain to Mohammed, and each time makes me feel guilty of not having written before to my colleagues. I wonder whether, looking back over one and a half years, my kaleidoscopic recollections of impressions would convey anything. They may appear to you to go on and on and on. If so, then I have done well, for that is how it seems - for years it has been like that, for years it will be so.

The continuous sun with its intense heat (the really enjoyable winter we ignore, along with the summer break in the hills - if we can get it); the 'undressed' state of the masses, and the beautiful sarees of the better classes; the slow pace; bullock carts, donkeys, camels. and elephants for transport, just as in the old biblical pictures; the old single-decker buses, with as many brown bodies on top with the luggage as inside; the long train journeys, the sleeping berths and electric fans, the dustproof, flyproof, and sunproof windows and doors (but they're not!); the mêlée at all stations, with the many, many 'walas' selling most things from hot tea to an elephant; the washing and bathing on the platform during the stops; the lackadaisical shopkeepers who care not whether you purchase or not - rather do they seem to resent leaving their charpoy; the cinemas and their interval at the climax of the film; the tonga walas, bicycle rickshaw walas, dhobis, bearers, barbers, etc., etc., all waiting to 'do you now, sir'; the sacred cows lying on the pavement and in the road; the bazaar shops looking as if they have been 'tipped up' and all their contents had rolled to the front and on the pavement; the 'odour' from the bazaars and villages at meal times; the masses' lack of knowledge of their age (time no object would be very fitting); the keen little sepoys learning to swing right arm with left leg; their cleanliness on parade: the numerous castes, religions, languages, and dialects, and the lack of co-operation, perhaps due to these; the simple and seemingly insufficient food; the ekkas, the coolie rickshaws; the villagers' mud hut homes, serving as sleeping quarters for themselves and their cattle (or so it seems); the wells with bullocks drawing the water; the great pilgrimage to the River Ganges to bathe; the wedding festivals with their fifth-rate bands and elaborately decorated bridegroom going to the bride he has probably never seen, parading the streets in gaudy uniforms and beautiful dresses with bright lights carried on poles, and the carrying by the baboos (or clerks) of the Chamberlain umbrella to keep the sun off; the chattering, squawking birds; and the howling jackals.

All this amongst, around, and mixing with air-conditioned train coaches and cinemas, modern water supply, luxurious clubs, and good-class dance bands, fine modern buildings and large well-run shops, American super cars and lorries, modern Army vehicles, R.A.F. and American planes and transport, uniforms of all services, civilians in western clothes, ice cooled drinks, yachting, horse-riding, golf, taxis, hansom cabs . . . 'phew, what a country! And if someone should offer to explain it to you, beware, for it's just part of the mysterious East, as unfathomable and inexplicable as the famous rope-trick.

(October 1944)

(S.Q.M.S. Bignell (Public Health) sends the following letter from India, where he landed in May. - Ed.)

Imagine a narrowish main street, with buses, trams, 'gharis' (native horse-drawn taxis), jeeps, bullock-carts, army lorries all mixed in together, and all making their respective noises, plus natives shouting against each other, singing their very odd songs at the top of their voices, shopkeepers crying their wares or arguing with their customers about the prices; add the thick atmosphere compounded of numerous unimaginable smells; put the temperature up to round about 100 in the shade - and there you have our impression of the port of disembarkation. In quite a short time, though, we came to like this town. We were lodged in a transit camp in very comfortable quarters, and had nothing to do all day (pending receipt of posting instructions) but amuse ourselves. The authorities, unusually enough for the Army, didn't care whether we were in camp or not most of the time, with the consequence that we usually were anywhere but. We spent most mornings swimming, as there was sea bathing to be had within a very short distance of the camp, and in the afternoons we used to go into the town to collect mail, goods, and impressions.

The Washerman

The dhobi, or washerman, deserves a paragraph to himself. His method of operation is simplicity itself, and, if more generally known, would doubtless commend itself to many English ladies. He starts off with a large stone slab, rather like a miniature edition of a road block, but with a smooth surface. Having soaked the clothes in soapy water, he proceeds to beat the dirt out of them on the slab, much like an English roadman wielding his huge hammer. If articles have been returned for re-washing, as is often the case, he sings a natty little song as he beats them, a song very much to the detriment of the English sahib. When the washing process is complete the clothes are spread out on the ground, where they dry in a very short time under the Indian sun. When the rains come, drying is liable to be a problem, and I understand that it is then done by the dhobi

45

lighting a fire in his hut and hanging the washing around. Normally at this time of the year clothes given to the dhobi by 10 a.m. are washed, dried, ironed, and ready to wear by 5 p.m. the same day, which is pretty good going when you consider that each dhobi may wash for up to about 40 men. The charge for 'unofficial' washing (i.e. washing that goes direct instead of via the stores, and is back in 24 hours instead of 72) is 1 anna per article (i.e. just over 1d.) and this applies whether the article be a handkerchief, a pair of slacks, or a sheet.

We are now living in comparative comfort in modern barracks. They are so modern that they've not yet undergone a monsoon, and if the building work is of the usual Indian standard they will probably be washed away once the rains really start. I have secured a small room of my own, which enables me to be as unsociable as I like - apart from giving me a quiet place in which to write letters, read, and so on. It is taking a real effort on my part to get used to the idea of bearer, or personal servant, who does all the cleaning and polishing that are necessary, and can also be entrusted with sundry small errands. Never before in my Army career have I had my shoes and all my brass-work cleaned and polished so beautifully - in fact, one of the chaps in the office remarked on how good my badge was looking since my bearer had taken it over! Being in a comparatively civilized part of India - in fact in a very large city - which is not situated in a bad malarial belt, we are fairly free so far from mosquitoes and most other insects. A fast-running fly, rather like a small cricket in appearance, comes out into my room at nights, and interrupts my letter-writing by making me remove a stealthy slipper, give chase, and reduce the thing to a corpse; but apart from that we are remarkably free from livestock. Feeding is distinctly good. The one great shortage in the mess is beer.

News from France.

(October 1944)

(Another letter from France from Capt. A. C. Robb (Comptroller's). - Ed.)

We have been moving about every three days on the average, anything from fifty to eighty miles at a time! Our sites have been many and varied - at the moment I am living in a big moated chateau, quite the country gentleman! We have even got luxuries like electric light, so we are almost civilised again! This is the first time we have been under a roof since the beginning of this 'do,' however, so we are certainly not becoming soft!

Actually my colonel and I came up here on a 'recce' a couple of days ago, and picked out this as a highly desirable residence. It used to be the officers' mess of the Jerry air force, who had obviously got out in a bit of a hurry - there were still several photos of Hitler, Goering, and Co. hanging on the walls. There was a caretaker in residence, so he showed us over - we took good care to let him precede us into the rooms, just in case! - and then we went back to pick up our unit, leaving our 'reserved' signs prominently displayed.

When we got back the next day we learned that after we had left there had been a pitched battle between one of our 'divs.' and some Jerries still in the chateau! They must have been in the cellars all the time we were going over the place! As a mere detail, the photos of the 'Old Gang' were no longer recognisable! As you can guess, though, we went over the place very thoroughly after that - although it is impossible to comb the extensive woods behind the chateau. Anyhow, we have a 'mutual' aid system laid on with the local F.F.I., which is quite reassuring.

The people here are overwhelmingly friendly. There are really only a relatively small number of troops around here, and going anywhere is one triumphal procession along the roads - all the countryside is *en fête*, and everybody lines the road waving, cheering, giving the 'V' sign, shouting 'Vive les Anglais,' blowing kisses - even holding up babies to be kissed when the car stops. I suspect some of them may be Jerry babies - they probably think this helps to naturalise them!

On the other hand, when one of the many trucks of Jerries going back passes them no greater contrast is possible. If they ever had any illusions as to their popularity these must be completely dispelled by now! On one occasion when I was returning from a 'recce' I took back a couple of Jerry officers - they gave absolutely no trouble, their one desire being to get back to the safety of the P.O.W. cage; but the 'V' signs were so many and so emphatic that I began to get quite apprehensive lest they be goaded into something! Altogether I wasn't a bit sorry when they were safely handed over.

Needless to say, when the Jerries had this chateau the villagers were not allowed in. They have certainly made up for it since we came! There are always dozens of them in the park. It is impossible to do anything, even have a wash, without an audience. (We are only messing in the chateau, not actually living in it.) When my batman put up my tent and started to make my bed he was inundated by helpers, and I wasn't allowed to touch a thing in case I became 'fatigué.' My cook asked one of the youngsters for a few potatoes, but he soon regretted it, for after half-an-hour all the village began trooping up with potatoes - they were queueing up to go into the kitchen with them, and we couldn't stop them! In the end we had about three hundredweight - and we are only a very small unit! It was really one of the funniest things I ever saw; but the cook didn't see the funny side of it!

Now the villagers are turning their attention to eggs, which are a very different proposition. We are getting about two dozen a day here, a very welcome addition to the menu. We are also very fortunate in that mushrooms abound round here, so we don't do too badly.

The Liberation of Paris.

(October 1944)

(Capt. C. E. Nicholson, former president of the Staff Association, is with the American Civil Affairs branch in France. He is at present Chief Civil Defence Officer in Paris. The following extract from a letter to the secretary of the Association gives a vivid account of his experiences:- Ed.)

We landed in France on 18th July, when we still held only a small beachhead. We were at sea four days and three nights, finally coming ashore on landing barges, from which we waded to the beaches. The sea was rather spiteful, and soaked most of us to the skin before we reached dry land. We went inland a mile of two, and then went to sleep in an open field under the stars, and neither guns nor planes could awaken most of us that night - we were all so utterly weary and wet. We had had little sleep on the ship. From then we moved forward with the fighting troops for six weeks or so, living in little one-man tents (which the U.S. Army use) in fields, orchards, and foxholes. It was really a hard life, as the weather varied from almost tropical heat to thunderstorms and torrential rains lasting sometimes for days. At times life was dull and boring, and at others for short periods intensely exciting.

Then came our big thrill of a lifetime. One night, when we were camped in a big forest about 70 miles from here, we received orders to strike camp, put on our vehicles as much petrol, emergency rations, and water as we could possibly carry, and set out into the blue and reach our destination. We were told we should have to get through some strong German 'pockets of resistance,' but we had to make a 'do or die' sort of job. We removed all windscreens and hoods from our cars and lorries, so as to give a clear line of fire, and set off at midnight on a dark, cloudy, damp, cold night. Our convoy consisted of 1 heavy lorry, 2 small fast lorries, 2 jeeps, and 2 cars. One car led, my car followed, and the lorries tailed behind. We had about 18 officers and 22 men. Officers had revolvers only, men carbines, and we also had 5 tommy guns. We decided that we should need great luck to accomplish our mission. Suffice to say we had the luck. Only 10 miles from our destination we had to turn back and almost retrace our wheeltracks all the way because the Boche was reported to be too strong for us to force our way through. Eventually, by wandering across country (and incidentally, we subsequently found, coming through equally strong Boche forces), we reached our destination at 6.30 the next morning, parking in one of the most beautiful spots in Europe to see the sun rising gorgeously over the city.

We didn't have much time to admire the sunrise, as rifle and machine-gun fire opened up in every direction. We soon found out that the Boche was still in town, and was being chased out by the F.F.I. We could not take a hand in the game because both the F.F.I. and the Boche were in civilian clothes, and we were not sufficiently familiar with the position to picture friend from foe. Incidentally, we were not too comfortable, as our American allies, as you know, wear tin hats very similar to the Boche, and we were not sure whether the F.F.I. knew that! Anyway, nothing untoward happpened to us, and at about 8 a.m. we set off through the city to the square where we were to park until we had found billets. This took a long time, as we had not been announced or expected. So, while this was being arranged, we set off with our little convoy and drove all round the city to show the French the Allies had arrived. We were the first Allied troops to arrive. The inhabitants nearly went crazy. They shouted, they cheered, they stormed our cars, they threw bunches of flowers, bottles of champagne, cognac, etc., etc., into our cars, and generally went haywire.

After about an hour we returned to our parking spot to await billeting formalities to be concluded. This took about another four hours (i.e. till 3 p.m.). During that time, under a blazing sun, every single officer and soldier was subjected to every kind of endearment you can imagine. We were dirty, tired (we had had no sleep for 20 hours, and a rather nerve-racking journey of about 100 miles in the dark), and unshaven and dusty. Nevertheless, we were kissed and hugged - they kissed our dirty hands, our dirty faces, our dirty hair, they wept, they shook our hands. If we tried to get a little relief from the crowds and climbed into our cars they clambered in and draped themselves all over us. Never in all my life have I seen or experienced anything approaching it. Flags, bunting, and 'Welcome' posters appeared everywhere. Where they had come from or been hidden for four years I can't imagine. There was more champagne, cognac, wine, fruit, and flowers, and one dear old lady of about 80, after kissing me on both cheeks, and holding up her face for me to do the same, put her arms round my neck and wept quietly on my shoulder until she felt better. The crowd stood back for a moment till the poor old soul had recovered, when she took our of her bag a little religious medallion of the B.V.M., and asked me to keep it as a token of her gratitude. She said it was all she had to give. I tried not to accept, as she obviously valued it sentimentally, but she said she would be grieved if I did not accept. Another time a little kid of about 8 years climbed on to the footboards of the car, so as to reach me (I was standing beside the car), put her arms around me, and sobbed herself into laughter and then to tears again. If our coming meant so much to a little kiddie it is an indication of what life during the occupation must have been like.

When I tell you that during all this time street fighting was going on, sometimes near and sometimes far off, you can understand why I use the adjective crazy. Then the time came to move off to our billets. When we had got into our cars and had time to talk to each other we all realised at about the same moment that the dust off the roads had gone from our faces, which were now beautifully pink with rouge! Some of the fellows, who had never been to France before and did not know of the French habit for men to kiss men in moments of great emotion, were taken aback and at first rather shocked when they found themselves being embraced by men. I assured them it was quite all right, and that, as the women outnumbered the men about 10 to 1, they couldn't grumble if they were kissed by 100 men for every 1,000 women. They agreed it was a cheap price to pay. Incidentally, you will be interested to know that the women here are as smartly dressed and turned out generally as they have always been in the past. How they have managed it is one of the mysteries we have not yet solved. Since that day it has been much the same, except, of course, we are no longer manhandled or kissed - often.

There are very very few British here, but the Americans are now fairly thick on the ground, and the people are getting accustomed to the new conditions. But I still have not become accustomed to being smiled at by every man, woman, and child I pass in the street! Up to about three days ago if I and one or two British officers walked together through the town during the time of the afternoon *apéritif*, when everybody was sitting at the little tables on the pavement, and someone said 'Voyez les Anglais' (they seem to be uncertain about British uniforms), they would all rise at their tables and start clapping and shouting 'Merci,' 'Merci beaucoup.' It was a royal procession because, having started, the next crowd would take up the cry, and so it would go on all down the street. In the end we would flee to our hotel. Anyway, that has now all ended and,

Free French troops entering Paris, August 1944.

as I said before, it is just smiles all the way, with only an occasional stop by someone who is anxious to speak to the first 'Anglais' they have seen.

We have much to do, and what with work and excitement we are glad to get to our hotel at night for dinner and bed. We have taken over a well-known luxury hotel, where we have separate bedrooms with our own private bathrooms attached, chambermaids, valet-de-chambre, electric light, telephones, etc., etc. The other extreme from tents and foxholes.

Note: The liberation of Paris, an event of tremendous symbolic and psychological importance, was in military terms just an incident in the headlong advance of the Allied armies across France during August 1944. The Americans reached the Seine at Mantes, below Paris, on 19 August and pushed rapidly on beyond it: on the same day led by the

French Forces of the Interior (F.F. I.: the Resistance) Paris broke out in one of the many "eruptions" which have punctuated its history and for a few days it was the scene of savage street fighting until, on 25 August, a Free French division entered the city and evicted or captured what was left of the German garrison. A few Nazi fanatics (and some French collaborators who knew exactly what to expect from their infuriated countrymen) still held out: and when General de Gaulle, leader of the "Fighting French", who entered the city on 26 August, progressed in triumph - but with the usual de Gaulle *sang-froid* - to Notre Dame the next day snipers were still firing from the roofs. Nevertheless, Paris was free, and by its own efforts.

First Impressions of Italy.

(January 1945)

J.C. Craig (T.P.) has just arrived in Italy, and sends the following 'first impressions': 'You have got to see a country which has undergone the ravages of war to understand what it means. Civil administration on the Italian side I judge to be pretty chaotic, where it exists at all. A large town seems to resemble a very beautiful fruit which has gone bad. Tall buildings in a state of decay, which had obviously started before the war. Unshaven, unwashed people in rags, a big smelly huddle of them. Civil transport almost non-existent. Perhaps an occasional tram, packed to capacity, worse than travelling home in London during the blitz. As you pass, people either don't look at you, or if they do, glare sullenly. One of them shouts something, but whether of derision or greeting it is hard to say. Most Italian shouting seems to be derisive anyway. People living in decrepit buildings, the window frames torn out and the windows patched with dirty rags. A peculiar, all-pervading odour, in which one suddenly distinguishes the unmistakeable smell of goat. If one looks through the window of a hovel one sees men, women and children, cats, hens, goats, all living in the same room together. They converse stridently, their conversation somehow seems to explode in the air. From the balcony of a block of tenements a woman with greasy hair lowers a glass, which an old man puts under the udder of a goat and fills with milk. Chestnut stalls, their little fires glowing - and, as you pass, the call of "Chestanuts - Chestanuts -." Some gaudy magazine stalls.

'The country seems to be in a very wrecked state. One sees miles of railway lines torn up; repairs with odd bits and pieces. An adjoining power station bombed smack in the middle; trails of creeping wire everywhere. Twisted, distorted steel frames, which once were trucks and carriages. One has the feeling that here is something which is not only "down," but "out" as well.

'There are no pubs here, but little wine bars, and I must say that some of them are very clean and neat. The three main drinks seem to be cognac, Marsala and Vino Rossi; but the official beer ration was more than welcome.'

Note: Italy was the first, and for a decade the only, Fascist state in Europe and during the early years of Fascist (Nazi) rule in Germany the Italian leader (Duce), Benito Mussolini, was hostile to this new German variant of Fascism. By 1936/37, however, the two Fascist regimes had drawn closer together in the face of rising opposition to their expansionist policies: and by early 1939 this new relationship had been formalised by the so-called "pact of steel", more usually known as the Rome-Berlin Axis. When the war between Germany and the Franco-British alliance broke out in September 1939, however, Italy remained neutral: and it was not until France was on the verge of total collapse in June 1940 that Mussolini entered the war.

The ensuing three years saw one defeat and disaster after another for the Italians, even though their German allies were, for much of this time, going from strength to strength. The Italian army in Libya was completely defeated by the British by early 1941 (see note on page 32); the Italian empire in East Africa was overrun by May 1941; the Italian fleet badly damaged by air attack at Taranto in October 1940 and completely crippled off Cape Matapan in March 1941; an Italian invasion of Greece in late 1940 was routed; and by the summer of 1943 Italian cities were being bombed and the last remnants of a second North African army had surrendered to the Allies. Only an increasing amount of German support, and of German intervention in Italian affairs, kept Italy in the war.

Following the Italian invasion of Sicily, the Fascist Grand Council decided that "enough was enough", and on 25 July 1943 it deposed Mussolini and set up a new government (ostensibly still Fascist) led by Marshal Badoglio, which very quickly entered into secret negotiations with the Allies. On 3 September Allied forces crossed over to the Italian mainland, and on 8 September the Bagdolio government surrendered unconditionally. It was one thing to surrender and (as soon happened) actually to change sides in the war: quite another to make such decisions "stick". German troops had been present in Italy in considerable numbers for some time, and they rapidly occupied the whole country as far south as Salerno: Mussolini, who had been interned, was rescued and a German puppet state was established under his nominal rule.

There followed an agonising twenty months during which the rake of war was dragged up the Italian peninsula from Salerno almost to the Alps. The Germans stood on the defensive, making good use of the difficult Italian terrain, and they fairly soon established a line north of Naples. It was not until May 1944, after an attempt to turn the German line by a landing behind it at Anzio had failed to achieve its hoped-for objective, that British and American troops broke through and entered Rome on 5 June. The Germans conducted a fighting retreat north into Emilia and the Appenines, and by September they had once again established a defensive line across the "neck" of Italy. This they held until April 1945 when, with German resistance collapsing in the Fatherland itself, the final Allied offensive swept the Germans back to the Alps, where they surrendered unconditionally on 2 May. Meanwhile, Mussolini had been taken and executed by Italian partisans, who had been active ever since the German takeover of their country in 1943. The war in Italy was at last over - but at what a cost!

Ordeal By Royal Commission.

By Laurence Welsh
(May 1945)

Since I have ceased to be an active leader in Staff Association matters I have had the opportunity to sit back and watch the others. It is no new thing for me to realise what a great debt we all owe to those who look after our interests, but I am still sometimes surprised at the volume and variety of the jobs that fall on their shoulders. Here is an example.

I had read the memorandum containing the Association's evidence to be put before the Royal Commission on Equal Pay. It seemed to me to be a model of lucidity and cogent reasoning. I congratulated the Council's staff on having colleagues able and willing to prepare such a document. But it is one thing to sit down quietly at home, with reference books and unlimited time, to write out what one thinks on the subject; but its authors then had a far less enviable task - they had to appear in person before the Royal Commission, elaborate their written statement, and answer any question that any member of the commission chose to fire at them.

I went along on 23rd March to hear what took place. I went, if I may be forgiven for saying so, prepared to make allowances for our witnesses, for I knew the calibre of some of the commissioners. When it was over, if I was making any allowances at all, it was for the members of the commission.

Who are they - these commissioners? The chairman is an able lawyer, Mr. Justice Asquith - suave, courteous, kindly - but no logical flaw escapes his notice. There is Dr. Janet Vaughan, head of the Blood Transfusion Service, and Miss Nettlefold, managing director of a firm of wholesale ironmongers - two astute public women, who took nothing for granted. Lady Limerick was already something of a friend, for she is a member of the Council, and knows our conditions of service. The Hon. Jasper Ridley, a bank director, seemed a hard nut to crack, and so did Mr. Robinson, who is connected with I.C.I. in peace-time, and is Director-General of Filling Factories now; his innuendoes that women are all on the make, and have no sense of personal honour, must have been hard to bear without violent retorts. There is Mr. John Brown, a trade union secretary, and, last but by no means least, Professor D. H. Robertson, professor of economics at London University.

On the whole, you see, a fairly formidable bunch to appear before; not likely to be lacking in questions, friendly and unfriendly; and not easy to put off with woolly answers. And the range of questions was pretty wide. A lot of them were factual, and might have floored any less experienced staff experts than Miss Patricia Knox, Mr. H. G. Puddifoot, and Miss Betty Turner. Other questions raised issues of principle, on which the witnesses had to show perspicacity as well as discretion. I mention a few of these later.

Mr. Justice Asquith did a good job in making the atmosphere comfortable. There was nothing pompous or terrifying about the proceedings; but the intellectual standard, if I may use the phrase, was high. The members of the commission knew a lot about the subject, and they expected their witnesses to do so. Here are one or two matters which came up, and on which the witnesses had to speak outside of their written book.

Professor Robertson asked whether the witnesses agreed that the effect of the adoption of the principle of equal pay would be to redistribute the national income in favour of single women. It sounded like a trap - as though, somehow, single women were in some mysterious way an undeserving class of person; but the reply was not long in coming, and it was economically sound - that the real essence of the change (when combined with increased income tax allowances for dependants) would be to increase the purchasing power of lower-paid wage earners; and such people tend to concentrate their resources on necessary purchases.

Another question was whether the Association would favour a scheme of family allowances based on the 'occupation group.' This would mean that everyone in local government employment would contribute to a fund from which allowances would be paid to those with children on a more generous scale than (say) the Government's present proposals envisaged. The idea is that a national system is bound to be a flat rate, and cannot therefore be adequate to the needs of those whose standard of living is based on salaries of the middle or upper ranges. The witnesses (I thought wisely) said the Association had not considered such a scheme, but that they would prefer a national scheme, probably by way of more adequate allowances in respect of children for income tax purposes. They were then asked whether they thought that, under the income tax law, allowances for children, instead of being a flat £50, should be on a percentage basis of income, so that the better-off man would, as it were, have more money with which to maintain his family. To this the reply was guarded - that at any rate it sounded preferable to an occupational arrangement.

Miss Knox made the telling point that, if the Government wanted to help married people it might start by removing the penalty which the law lays on them: two single people are allowed £80 each free of tax, but if they marry they are allowed only £140, instead of £160, between them.

I instance these things to show the variety of topics with which our witnesses had to deal without notice, and I assure my readers that they did so with a commendable combination of assurance and discretion.

Two or three points which they added to their written statement are worth recording briefly. Referring to the illogical distinction between major establishment and general clerical class conditions in respect of equal pay, they remarked that if the criterion was to give equal pay to administrative workers the higher clerical class was obviously entitled to be included. Then, dealing with the legend that women are of less value to employers (and so should be paid less), because they tend to leave on marriage, the witnesses pointed out that the tendency of women to leave on marriage involves a financial saving (because they are replaced by others lower on the scale) which represents the employer's compensation for any lost training.

The chairman mentioned that Sir Eric Salmon's evidence about the relative sick leave of men and women suggested that, among the office staff, sick leave rates were higher for men than for women, whereas among teachers the converse was true. Sir Eric's figures for teachers showed an average of four days a year for men, eight for single women, and eleven for married women. Miss Knox used these figures very effectively. If a man teacher's salary was, say, for the sake of argument, £730 (i.e. £2 a day), and one day's pay was deducted for each day's absence, he would receive £722; a single woman, on the same basis, would get £714, and a married woman £708. But in fact (on the present basis of differentiation) all women teachers would get a maximum salary of £584 (i.e. 4/5ths of £730) - 'an extraordinary discrepancy, and quite out of proportion.'

My general impression was that the staff were being admirably served by their representatives. I was delighted by the aptness of their replies, and their presentation of their case; and I was constantly relieved that the questions were fired at them and not at me, sitting immune in the public gallery.

Note: The part played by women in the war (see note on page 30) gave great impetus to the campaign for equal pay but it was not to achieve any quick or easy successes. Equal pay for men and women within the LCC service was not attained until the summer of 1952, and many more years were to pass before the principle was anywhere near to being universally accepted.

End of the War in Europe.

(June 1945)

The Leader of the Council paid a handsome and a deserved tribute to the Council's staff in the following message issued on VE Day. We are glad to print it at the head of the first issue of *London Town* to be sent to press since the announcement of victory in Europe:-

'On this day of victory in Europe, I wish to express to all those in the Council's services, whether permanent or temporary, including the civil defence and other war-time services, whole-time and part-time, my sincere and heartfelt thanks for your splendid work during the difficult and dangerous days and nights of the past five years. Your courage and devotion to London and her people has been something of which every one of you can be greatly proud, as London is proud of you.

'As Leader of the London County Council, and Chairman of its Civil Defence and General Purposes Committee, I can find no words adequate to express my high appreciation of what you each and all have done. All London thanks you. - Latham.'

During the past five years we have published from time to time some interesting articles on different aspects of the Council's war work, and at a later date we hope to give a general review of the subject, which would, we believe, be of special value to our colleagues who have been on war service. But our chief purpose in looking back at this time should be to profit by our experience and by our mistakes. For the magnitude of our war-time tasks is exceeded by those which confront us if London is to be made a city worthy of her inhabitants. 'Yet much remains to conquer still: peace hath her victories no less renowned than war.'

Note: This is how *London Town* greeted the end of the war in Europe. Here again, the contrast with 1918 is illuminating and instructive.

Five Years a Prisoner.

Desmond Thain
(July 1945)

(We are happy to be able to print the following description by Private J.D. Thain (Social Welfare) of his life as a prisoner of war in German hands from June, 1940, when he was captured at St. Valéry, until his liberation in May, 1945. We take this opportunity to welcome him home, along with other colleagues recently repatriated. - Ed.)

This, briefly, is what happened after my capture at St. Valéry in June, 1940. We marched to Germany. The misery of that march is indescribable; torn clothing, next to no food, and the awful fatigue - all combined to weaken us. Then came the three-day train ride to Poland. Fifty or sixty men were packed in each cattle truck, many suffering from dysentery, and all of them lousy.

I was lucky in being already able to speak fluent German, and became an interpreter. For the next two years that was my job in various camps. It was a good one in so far as it meant that one did not need to do any manual labour, and in the early days one got better rations. However, this hardly made up for the responsibility, or for the running round the camp after commandants and people. In 1942 the food situation became so acute that I decided to have a shot at farm work, and in June went on the land in the Danzig district. I had never done any hard work before in my life, nor had I been acquainted with horses. Still, one gradually learned the work, and I even became a ploughman, driving a four-horse team. Conditions of life for P.O.W.s had greatly improved by this time. We received our letters and parcels regularly, and on the farms food was plentiful, if not very nourishing, consisting mainly of potatoes and rye bread. Still, with our Red Cross parcels we had enough. News of the war we got from German newspapers, and from anti-Nazi civilians, who listened behind barred doors and windows to the British radio news. We were fairly comfortable there. The work was hard in the summer - long hours in the hot sun; but the winters were not so bad, despite the severe cold.

Then early in January this year Joe made his big push, and we knew that we should be forcibly evacuated. Sure enough, on 24th January came the order for our working party to march. There were three inches of snow on the roads, and I had visions of a march worse than the one we had done in '40, so I decided that it wasn't good enough. Accordingly, at the first opportunity, I slipped off with three others, and returned to our village. Here we had every intention of staying until the Russians turned up. They were then only 30 kilometres away. (I should mention that I had learnt to speak Russian while working in the fields together with Russian men and girls employed more or less as slave labour.) Several farmers in our village had already evacuated, and the farmhouses were occupied by their erstwhile employees - the Russians and Poles. I therefore selected a comfortable billet, and settled down to await events, meanwhile consuming large quantities of food that the farmer had left behind. Our work was merely to feed the cattle and other livestock, chop wood for fuel, and keep enormous fires going.

However, this state of affairs couldn't last indefinitely. The Russian advance halted at Elbing and Marienburg, and some of the farmers began to return to fetch provisions, as they had not been able to get very far. I was then forced to return to my old farm, and once again work for my living. Of course, there was no guard, and I explained my presence by saying that I had lost the marching column, and had been wandering about ever since. The farmer was quite pleased to see me, and asked where I would sleep, as our camp had been plundered by civilians after our first departure. It was arranged that I should live with the Russians. My comrades (whom I seldom met) had also made arrangements for accommodation on or near their old farms. I lived very comfortably there for a month (there were no ration restrictions, and we helped ourselves to chickens, and so on), doing very little work.

Then, suddenly, we were rounded up, and taken to Danzig. After a short spell in the cells, we were put into huts in a French camp there, and when 230 British and American escapees had been collected, the party was marched to the docks. Here we went on board the *Lys*, a small Belgian vessel, which had been used for evacuating civilians. Among us were 180 Polish and 1,500 Russian prisoners, but we were put separately into a hold, which was at once battened down. The first week we were not allowed on deck to wash, and the hold was already crawling with lice when we entered it - we slept on the propeller shaft to avoid them). Worse things were to come, however. For the first five days we received no warm food, but a bread ration of 30 grammes per day and 30 grammes of horse-meat sausage. With this we were reasonably satisfied, but the bread ran out, and for the next eight days our daily ration was half a cupful of thin carrot soup. Despite Russian bombers and mines, we reached Lübeck on 26th March, and crawled off the boat in an emaciated condition. Now our troubles were practically at an end, for the Red Cross parcels we received there put us on our feet again.

British troops liberated us at Lübeck on 2nd May, and we were brought home in Lancaster bombers on the 10th from a near-by aerodrome.

Le Quatorze Juillet, 1945.

D. J. Moxley
(August 1945)

(Mr. Moxley acted as interpreter for the Council's representatives who recently visited Paris.)

The editor, at the suggestion of the Clerk of the Council, has asked me to write a few paragraphs on the recent visit to Paris by representatives of the Council for the first 14th July festivities since the liberation of France.

An official account of the visit - which was made at the invitation of the Paris municipal authorities - appears in the minutes of the Council of 31st July, and what is wanted here, I understand, is something more personal. What follows, therefore, is an impressionistic sketch of those aspects of four crowded days which linger most vividly in the mind of the delegation's humblest member.

Paris can be very hot in the summer, and throughout our visit the heat was overwhelming. During the great military review on the morning of 14th July - held for the first time in the Place de la Bastille instead of the Champs Elysées - the great columns of tanks and artillery thundering up from the rue du Faubourg St. Antoine had twice to be halted to let the dust settle. The working people of Paris, the women barelegged and in light frocks, the men in trousers and open-necked shirts, did not seem unduly uncomfortable. The French colonial troops seemed positively to thrive under the brazen sky. We, on the other hand, condemned to the respectability of lounge suits and collars and ties, wilted wretchedly at times. Yet there were compensations. An al fresco lunch on Sunday, 15th July, in a shady corner of the garden of the Restaurant Adrienne, in Montmartre, was one of them. A salad of tomatoes and lettuce, dressed as only the French know how, was delicious; so, incidentally, was the white wine, delicately dry and cold as ice.

No Hot Water
Life in Paris for the ordinary man and woman must be very grim at the present time. Our hosts, with traditional French hospitality, were determined that we ourselves should not suffer privations. We stayed at Claridge's. The cooking and accommodation were excellent, yet the private bathrooms with which each of us was provided were innocent of hot water; our breakfast coffee was black - milk is reserved for children - and throughout our stay we ate meat only twice, and on the second occasion - at a dinner at St. Germain-en-Laye - this was a gift to our local hosts from the American Army. It needs little imagination to grasp the implications of this for the daily life of the ordinary citizen. There were other signs also. French women go bare-legged because stockings are 600 francs a pair. Twice, at the entrance of our hotel, obviously educated and respectable Frenchmen asked me for a light from my cigarette, apologising for doing so, and saying that matches were unobtainable. People who certainly would not do so here bent to pick up cigarette ends dropped by American soldiers.

An amusing feature of our visit was the provision by the *Préfecture de Police* of what we were told were nicknamed *anges gardiens*. These were two policemen on motor-cycles, and with crash helmets, who escorted our cars wherever we went. In case of need, they cleared the roads by the simple process of riding full tilt at the crowd or the traffic, blowing continuously on their whistles. At other times they rode one ahead of us and one at the side, the one at the side occasionally dropping back to ensure that none of our cars lost the convoy.

This arrangement certainly ensured a maximum of interest on the part of passers-by. Crowds would collect whenever, for any reason, our cars slowed down. Interested faces peered in at the windows, *'Qui c'est?'* passed from mouth to mouth, to invoke, sooner or later, the reply *'C'est les personnalités anglaises.'* It was all extremely flattering, and we speculated more or less seriously - usually less - about the delights which might be derived from the introduction of guardian angels in London.

French politics to-day are a topic about which the foreigner who lays no claim to special knowledge - and I certainly do not - must be modest. Nevertheless, as a result of conversations with a number of men and women of widely differing political views, I personally have come home with a few tentative impressions which may be worth recording.

Our neighbours have not yet cured themselves of their old habit of forming a new political party on very slender provocation. They are well aware, however, that this does not make for stability in a Parliamentary democracy. They realise the harm it did to the Third Republic, and many of them regret its persistence.

Moreover - and this, I think, is important - common action and common

'Le Quatorze Juillet' parade in Paris, 1945.

sufferings within the resistance movement have softened in many ways the old acerbity of party divisions. There are limitations to this, of course; hostility to those tainted with collaboration with Fascism is implacable; there is no facile tendency in this respect to 'let bygones be bygones,' yet three men with whom I sat at lunch one day, all prominent members of the Paris Municipal Council, who admitted frankly that they belonged to different parties, and would, at one time, have regarded each other as on opposite sides of the barricades, used the familiar *tu* in conversation, were obviously profoundly attached to each other, and said repeatedly that while they would oppose each other if necessary in public debate on questions of principle, they understood and respected each other's integrity, and were quite determined to co-operate as far as possible.

'N. or M.?'

We heard many stories of the days of resistance and insurrection, told with that mixture of the commonplace and the dramatic which is the stamp of authenticity in these things. Of the little girl of five, for example, whose parents were travelling on a dangerous mission under an assumed name, and who, asked her name by a benevolent looking but unknown passer-by, hid her face with assumed shyness against her mother, while whispering 'Mummy, what is my name to-day?'

And of those unknown women and children of Paris, who many of them falling under machine gun fire, rode on General Leclercq's tanks as they swept down the Champ de Mars to storm the German strong point at the Ecole Militaire.

Of the affection and admiration of the Parisians for the people of London there is no doubt. We have earned it , perhaps, but they have also earned ours. There are men among them whom it is an honour to know. Old hook-nosed, tough-looking Marrance, the Communist President of the Seine Council, twenty years Mayor of Ivry, who, disguised with great flowing Gaulish moustaches and beard, which earned him the affectionate soubriquet of Vercingetorix, rode about on an old bicycle, organising and encouraging under the very noses of the Gestapo. Max André, Vice-President of the Seine Council, grey-haired, distinguished, cultured, and imperturbable, who, telling me of their lack of arms when they finally rose in Paris, said in his gentle voice, and with his charming smile, 'Ah! those were the days.' Priou-Valjean, young and fiery, a penetrating art critic, and now a Rapporteur du Budget de la Police, who took a prominent part in the capture of the *Préfecture de Police*. These we met and admired; how many hundreds are there whom we did not meet?

Unrra in Action.

(October 1945)

(The following article consists of extracts from letters written by Miss Laura Chamberlain, Social Welfare Department, now with U.N.R.R.A. in Germany.)

We (a team of eight people, two of whom are chauffeurs) were presented with an assembly centre containing 11,000 people - some 6,000 Russians, 3,000 Poles, and about 2,000 French, Belgians, Dutch, Yugo-slavs, Norwegians, Danes, Greeks, etc. A U.S. army team and a French team (about 30 people in all) were running it when we arrived. Two days later they cleared out, and left us to it. It seemed rather an overwhelming proposition at first, but, as the displaced persons (later referred to as D.P.s) do a lot of organisation for themselves, we have managed to keep our heads above water so far.

Our 'camps' are ex-German barracks - brick buildings, well fitted up with electricity and water supply. In our original camp we now (16th May) have over 9,000 Russians and about 2,500 Poles. Two weeks ago we inherited a third camp in the town, now holding about 2,500 people, most of whom are Poles. In many ways it is easier to run a camp of one nationality than one of varied nationalities, but the language difficulty is very great, as only one Russian and no Poles speak English. Fortunately, most of them can speak some German, and so we have to manage on that. As well as being principal welfare officer, I have been deputy director of the camps. It is not quite such a big task as it sounds, as the Russians have very definite ideas about welfare, and can organise things for themselves. The Poles also organise themselves, but not quite as well as the Russians. We have flourishing kindergartens, schools, and clubs of all kinds.

I am very impressed by the Russians and their admirable organisation. They have one great drawback, however. That is a tendency for looting - bicycles, pigs, and sheep are the favourite booty. The Poles also loot, but not so consistently or successfully as the Russians. I sympathise with them very largely, as they were uprooted from their own homes, and everything taken from them by the Germans. But order has to be kept in Germany, and if the looting goes on it will impede the Germans supplying the necessary food and services for the D.P.s themselves. Of course, all the Russians and all the Poles do not loot and kill, but, naturally, a community of 14,000 is a very mixed bag. On two occasions there was what our Russian leader called a 'scandale' - that is, some Russians found a dump of a kind of methylated spirit, and brought it into the camp and indulged in a drunken orgy. This resulted in a few dying and others going blind. The Russians appear to have dropped that pleasure now, but to my horror I discovered that the Poles had found a source of supply of the same delectable drink.

Eventually forty Poles died in two days from drinking methylated alcohol. The U.S. army are trying to find the source of supply, and so stop the trouble. It is my opinion that the Germans are supplying it to the D.P.s as a form of sabotage. So far the Russians do not appear to have had their share this time. In fact, our Russian camp for the last week has been a model of propriety. They are expecting a visit from a Russian general in a few days, and are probably keeping on their best behaviour.

We are very worried about the Poles at present. Up to ten days ago I should have said the Polish camp was going quite well, but they suddenly decided that they did not like their leader, and, after a very complicated form of plebiscite (instituted by themselves), they threw him out, and elected another leader and committee. The new regime has not quite found its feet yet. They are demanding all kinds of things which it is impossible to get. I am afraid the Poles are a psychologically sick people. They have had a very bad time in Germany, and cannot understand why at the moment, when the Germans are defeated, they cannot get all they want. At present we are trying to raise their morale by getting all we can to help them have a good Whitsun Festival. Also twenty-four couples are getting married on Whit Sunday, and we are having a wedding feast as well.

Each of our nationalities has a leader of its own, with whom we deal on matters of policy, and who administers his own camp. Our Russian leader, named Col. Kompaniels, is an extremely fine man. He is an ex-prisoner of war, captured by the Germans near Moscow in the autumn of 1941. (We have about 2,000 of these Russian P.O.W.s, including 400 officers - the remainder of the

9,000 are civilians.) He is 48-ish, and very Slav in appearance. For the first week we were regarded very coldly; his face was completely impassive, and we could get no inkling of what he was thinking. However, he apparently began to realise that although we might be fools we were well-meaning fools and well disposed towards the Russians, and a change took place. He began to smile when we greeted him at the morning conference, and now we are good friends and are even able to make jokes about the camp in our rather (on both sides) bad German. He is an artist, and an extremely well-read man, even in English literature, which language, however, he still insists that he cannot speak. Many of the Russians here are cultured people - doctors, teachers, etc. (I want to eradicate the impression that I might have given earlier that they are all looters.)

1st May was a great day in the Russian camp. I would have liked to have had a photograph of myself on the platform on the parade ground, with Col. Kompaniels on one side, Col. Shorthose (the U.N.R.R.A. team director) on the other, taking the salute from some 2,000 or so Russians as they marched by in a procession. There was one battalion of women, and these later gave a physical culture display of a very high standard. Our Russian camp is getting to be well known. We get a large number of visitors, who always appear to be impressed by it. Two American generals have also visited us, and expressed their opinion that it is the best camp they have seen. That cheers us up because we sometimes get a bit depressed about all the things we are unable to do because of the lack of staff and supplies.

Another general has come to live near the camp, and become very interested in it, and has promised to help us in getting the things we need. He kept his word with remarkable rapidity, for a few hours after we had seen him a U.S. army band came to play to the people, a radio and a loud-speaker installation appeared, uniforms for the Russian guards, and a new telephone! I have found the U.S. army very kind and easy to deal with on the whole.

We do not live in the camp altogether. We have a very charming house about two kilometres away; it used to belong to a well-known local Nazi. It is a good thing to be able to get away from the camp atmosphere in the evening. Our day is rather long, 8.30 a.m. to something between 6.0 p.m. and 7.0 p.m. Of course if there is what our Russian leader calls a 'scandale' we go up to the camp again; sometimes we also go back to concerts given by the camp Russian Arts Club (they are quite good - there are two ex-opera singers, and some very good Russian dancers). We (the team, not the D.P.s unfortunately) feed extremely well. U.S. army rations are amazingly good - we are extremely blasé about chickens, eggs, oranges, and fruit juices. Good wine is plentiful too.

Writing on 14th September, Miss Chamberlain says:-
At the end of June the 10,000 Russians went home; shortly after that our No. 3 Polish camp moved into better buildings, and out of our jurisdiction, and we were left with one camp of about 2,500 Poles. I enjoyed working with the Russians, but the Poles are very trying people. At first they all used to say that they would not go back to Poland. I think that was due partly to agitation by Polish liaison officers (appointed by the old London Polish Government), who used to visit the camps. After the new Polish Government was formed there was a change of opinion, and they started clamouring to go back to Poland. Official

repatriation of Poles was supposed to start in September, but so far it has not happened on a large scale.

At the end of July I went to another camp at Bebia, a small town in the middle of Germany, only a few miles from the border of the Russian zone. Unfortunately, I went sick after only four days. I have recovered now, and am at the U.N.R.R.A. staging centre at Karlsruhe, waiting for assignment to another team.

By the way, *London Town* is the only English literature that has reached me in Germany. I know people have sent newspapers and weeklies, but I have never had them; somehow *London Town* overcomes the obstacles, whatever they may be. Lack of reading material, news of what is happening in the outside world, and of any public means of entertainment is one of the great drawbacks of life here. However, the D.P.s never allow one dull moment.

Note: The United Nations Relief and Rehabilitation Agency (UNRRA) was one of the more successful United Nations Agencies - probably because it began its operations at a time when nations really were united by the need to overcome their common enemies. It was established in November 1943 to "provide a reserve of emergency supplies and services for the liberated countries." In fact it took a rather more active role that this remit indicates, and by the time it was wound up on 30 June 1947 it had carried out a great deal of much-needed relief work throughout liberated Europe.

Although the Poles may be very trying people, in this instance they had, so to speak, a lot to be trying about. Following the fall of Poland in 1939 a Government in Exile was set up in London - sometimes known as the London Poles. The Soviet Union initially maintained diplomatic relations with the London Poles but broke these off in July 1944 when it established, at Lublin south-east of Warsaw, the "Polish Committee of National Liberation" as a rival Polish government - the Lublin Poles. In January 1945 Stalin recognised the Lublin Committee as the legal government of Poland but in the following month, at the Yalta Conference where he met Roosevelt and Churchill, he accepted that some of the London Poles should join the Lublin Committee. Stalin's promise of free elections in Poland was not fulfilled and Poland became a satellite state of the Soviet Union, a curious result for Britain of a war which it entered in defence of the territorial integrity of Poland.

Section 2: The Post-War World: Continuity and Change

Introduction

The years from the end of the Second World War in 1945 until the onset of the "swinging sixties" (this well worn phrase is, unfortunately, hard to avoid) in 1962/63 were a time of both continuity and change, and as always *London Town* faithfully reflected the spirit and the aspirations of the times. The weariness and disillusion of the later forties, with the cold war rapidly ending all hopes of a secure peace and casting its long shadow over the staff of the LCC, were gradually succeeded by the return of prosperity in the fifties, and by occasional "thaws" in the cold war, though assured peace never did return during all these years. As the years wore on and the journal slowly returned to pre-war standards of size and presentation the old and well tested standbys came once again to the fore - remembrances of things past, very often of considerable interest and even historical value, informative or analytical articles on the Council's services; and much material on London, past and present. Under three very able Editors (Derrick Blackhurst, Pat Bacon and C. D. Andrews) *London Town* flourished as never before.

So continuity was always apparent, but change was also going on apace throughout those years, Change in the Council's services; change in the Staff Association - including what seemed the revolutionary step of affiliating to the TUC in 1956 - and change in everyday life as an age of affluence was ushered in and (by the late fifties) became firmly established. As the period ended still greater changes were looming up ever more clearly, for by 1962 it was all too clear that the LCC could not survive in its time honoured form: a Greater London Council was to be the shape of the future.

A Wanderer Returns.

(February 1946)

'So County Hall is still at war.' That was my first impression as I walked over Westminster Bridge and turned left into Belvedere Road, only to be confronted by a barbed-wire barricade. A great shock to one returning to Civvy Street's bleakness, after five years' sheltered existence in His Majesty's Forces! Tactful inquiries inside assured me that most of my colleagues realised the true significance of their VE and VJ days, so perhaps it was just a few of the Very High Ups, immersed in the problems, who had not yet heard the news that the war was over. In this, I reflected, they had much in common with the V.I.P.s who control demobilisation. So I decided to leave it at that, and reported for duty.

'Glad to be back?' 'What's it feel like to be out?' - so touching was the cordiality with which they welcomed me, and so great the relief at doffing that confounded uniform for good (though it does sometimes feel chilly without it), that I soon forgot the barbed wire and became immersed in much more vital things: finding my way to my new section, scrounging a desk and chair, getting myself a towel (three days' persistence that took), and trying to sum up my thoughts and feelings for the benefit of old acquaintances. Sometimes my feelings were like those of a ghost returning to the scene of a former existence; and always my bewilderment reminded me of my first days in County Hall, nearly twenty years ago, as a very green young thing straight from school.

Now that I've been back a month this novelty has worn off, and I can more rationally analyse my first impressions. I'm still quite embarrassed by the relief with which the veterans keep on welcoming us back, as though we were long-awaited reinforcements come to relieve the old citadel. Many of those veterans (old men and maidens alike) seem not a little tired and irritable. One of them warned me that I'd find a great deal of discontent amongst the staff - a sense of frustration, impatience, and short temper, he called it. Sure enough, I did sense something of the kind, and tried to analyse the reasons. It couldn't be the bombing; they'd taken that very well, and had nine months to get over it. Lack of food or varied diet, perhaps? No, I could smell little else all day in at least half of County Hall. Financial worries? Surely not, for everyone seemed to be an Acting Something or a Substitute Something Else, and they must have saved some of their commuted overtime. At last I had it - it all goes back to that confounded barbed-wire business, with its various counterparts inside the building. They've all had to suffer it so long that they've got used to the general air of squalor and no longer notice it.

I mean the blacked-out corridors, the bricked and sandbagged windows, the musty ground floor, the draughty, windowless staircases. Everywhere I find ancient and dilapidated notices pasted on walls, directing me to shelters for 50, fireguard points, first-aid posts, exhorting me not help the enemy, and warning me what will happen if a 'responsible officer' (have we any irresponsible ones?) does not draw the blackout. Now I know there are house to be built, and a grand renovation scheme at County Hall would not be popular with the public just now. But why go to the other extreme? The really decent London citizen used to be rather proud of County Hall - nowadays he must be ashamed of large parts of it. I know how proud you all are of having 'taken it,' and the honourable scars will remain for a long time; but, for crying our loud, let's have rid of those grim, obsolete notices, the sandbags and bricks, and blackout paint. And let the glaziers spend just a day or so in replacing the cardboard and whatnot with real glass windows. Even the railways, who don't pamper their customers, have been re-glazing station roofs!

Sweetness and light are what we need in County Hall - it might even appeal to the sense of economy of the Ministry of Fuel and Power if those everlasting lamps were switched off; certainly it would brighten up the browned-off veterans.

One morning my eyes popped when I saw a window-cleaner, clad in pin-stripe trousers and spats, operating on a fifth-floor window ledge. 'My gosh,' thinks I, 'they have improved the social status of the minor and manipulative grades!' Only when he turned and climbed back into the room did I realise that he was no window cleaner, but a colleague who had taken the wash-leather into his own hands. Sweetness and light - that man had the right idea.

Yes, it *is* nice to be back, though not so terribly different from working in the R.A.F. - a question which you all seem to ask. To work in County Hall's less penetrable rooms is not vastly different from working in the old hangar or the open air, though rather more draughty and rather less healthy. Again, the better rooms are not unlike Station H.Q. - though not so clean or tidy. Fate plays strange tricks, yet I never thought the day would come when I would long for a bit more 'spit and polish' (just plain 'bull' to my old comrades!).

There are many more first impressions of these last few weeks: trains even more crowded than in the good old days when the railways wanted 'a square deal'; restaurants, almost impossible - 10.30 to 11 a.m. seems a fairly good time for lunch nowadays; the weird and wonderful collection of home-made notices on office doors, in the most outrageous varieties of calligraphy and lettering; is your Saturday morning journey really necessary? . . . But I must not bind too much, or you will feel more browned-off than ever, and then it won't be quite so nice to be back.

Top Level.

A. C. Thomas
(November 1948)

As is well known, all conferences are conducted at their appropriate levels, which vary from the austere and monkish secrecy of chief officers down to the jovial and chatty informality of senior assistants. Below this point there are of course no levels - merely a morass of sprawling anonymity.

Admittedly there is a certain amount of overlapping. A super principal, or even a deputy chief officer, will sometimes shed a benign lustre upon the rather dingy deliberations of lower principals; and the latter permit, and even encourage, the occasional presence of a suitably obsequious senior assistant, who is to be heard on these occasions clearing his throat with imagination and *élan*. But really sweeping departures from the caste system are rare. A salutary object lesson was provided by the temporary technical assistant who was unmasked at a conference of chief assistants, which he had in fact been running with great efficiency up to the moment of exposure. He was, of course, publicly stripped and driven from the room with execration. It is gratifying to recall that he made some slight amends by jumping our of a top-floor window into the Thames; his body was found floating off Shoebury three days later.

But I digress. My purpose is to deal with the occasion when I myself breathed this rarefied top level atmosphere. A conference had been called to discuss the high altitude bridge which the Metropolitan Borough of Batterwell have been considering throwing across the river since about the turn of the century. High dignitaries converged upon County Hall, as they or their predecessors had done for the last 40 years, to discuss this mighty edifice (I speak metaphorically of course; the bridge is naturally still in the blueprint stage). There were the Town Clerk and Borough Engineer of Batterwell; the Borough Engineers of the adjoining boroughs of Wandswich and Woolworth; the Chief Engineer, the Architect, the Clerk, and the Comptroller were all worthily represented.

But who was to represent the Valuer? The conference was during the summer recess. The Valuer was on leave; most of the A.V.s were climbing Ben Nevis or immersing in brine veins made varicose by trudging the County Hall corridors; the remainder were engaged upon conferences as weighty and pressing as that of the bridge. Principals were at a discount; even the rarely-to-be-found seniors wore a harassed and preoccupied air.

It was a senior who found me. I was playing shove ha'penny with some members of the messenger service in a quiet part of the basement. He dusted me down, straightened my tie, combed my hair, thrust a vast bulk of documents, plans, and working drawings under my arm, hissed a command to keep my ears open and my mouth shut, and sent me on my way!

It was a lovely conference. First we moved the bridge up river, to meet a 'B' ring road at its southern end; then we moved it down river to meet an 'A' ring road at its northern end; then we moved the river. When the Borough Engineer talked in a Hiroshima whisper of strategic considerations, we thought seriously of turning the bridge into a tunnel; and once, in a moment of depression, we contemplated scrapping the whole thing in favour of a statue of Mr. Churchill.

When I say 'we,' I of course use the work only figuratively. My own contribution was nil. I did try to get in with a story of the time my father took me to Tower Bridge as a little boy: but apparently no one wanted to listen. So I sat back and watched the Town Clerk's Adam's apple.

As minutes, hours, possibly days, went wheeling by, my interest, both in the bridge and the cartilaginous protuberance, began to flag. I was dozing lightly when I heard the suave voice of the chairman ask, 'What are the Valuer's views?' With eyes closed I pursued this interesting if somewhat academic line of thought. What were the Valuer's views? For example, on the New Look? Or equal pay? Or five-figure transfer fees? Or the materialist conception of history? Had he weighed the pros and cons of the ground nuts scheme? Was he perhaps a pseudo? Or even a crypto?

At this point the chairman said again, no longer suavely, with something indeed of asperity, 'What are the Valuer's views?' I opened my eyes to see whose tardiness was introducing this note of disharmony into the proceedings . . .

He was looking at me! They were all looking at me! Suddenly I became aware of the hideous truth - for the purposes of the meeting I was the Valuer. It was a nightmare moment (I say it of course with all possible respect). I hadn't an idea in the world. The only thing I wanted to do with the bridge was to push them all off it, and I couldn't be sure if the Valuer would agree with me.

'The Valuer,' I said at last, with about the firmness of a Lee Oma, 'reserves his position.'

The effect of this inanity was quite extraordinary. My stock soared. It has gone on soaring ever since. I am now the recognised expert on the Batterwell high-altitude bridge. People ring me daily to ask if I have made up my mind about it. I never have, of course. A bridge like that is too good a thing to hurry over. I had to speak quite sharply to the Batterwell Town Clerk the other day for wanting to get a move on. With any luck I expect the bridge to last till I retire.

If you are finding life difficult, take my advice and get yourself a bridge. And then, when you've got it, reserve your position.

Real Estate.

(January 1949)

On a foggy Friday evening at the end of November, a fireside night if ever one was, the estates staff assembled in force at County Hall from all parts of London and beyond. They had come to discuss their experiences in the famous 'reorganisation.' First they heard Miss Turner, chairman of the Staff Side, outline the Staff Association's proposals for fair rates for the new jobs, fair treatment for those whose jobs have gone. Then they began, and for two hours they described what has been happening since the new era began in October.

In former days some estates superintendents were responsible for perhaps 2,000 homes. They lived in free quarters on their estate and took part in its community life; tenants with a problem, at work all day, 'could call and see the Super' in the evening. Now, some are area officers, getting much the same pay with 27s. 3d. a week instead of their quarters. They may still be living in the same place, paying perhaps 30s. in rent and spending as much as 15s. a week to travel to the other side of London. When they get there they have to do most of what they used to do, but do it for several estates, as many as 6,000 homes. They no longer live on the job; nominally, they have a 38$\frac{1}{2}$-hour week; 'but they must still assist tenants with their problems as required' and 'take an interest in all local activities affecting the welfare of the tenants, e.g., community centres, etc.'

Those who once were estate clerks became general clerical officers and are now assistant estate officers, have not lost in pay but, with two thirds of their superiors redundant, have virtually no prospects for a generation. Their duties have increased considerably. They are finding they must collect more and more rents and at the same time take an interest in the comfort and well-being of the tenants, iron-out troubles in the communal laundries, see that the caretakers and the porters do their work, and so on - the list is far from complete. It is a coincidence, but none the less an added burden, that they are also agents for the public utilities and a borough council in the collection of hire purchase payments on pots and pans, kettles and coppers, vacuum cleaners and furniture.

The new form of estate management has displaced many capable officers. They have been scattered over the Housing and Valuation department on work often remote from their estate experience. They too have problems of rent and fares. Though they had fair prospects of advancement in the four grades of superintendent, they can now see no more than a blank 'unclassified' future on their present scales of pay.

The estates staff have scarcely had generous treatment, whether they are in or out of the new structure. It would not be surprising if they seemed content to sit back and say 'we told you so' as the grand façade cracks and the weaknesses appear. But this is not so. Overshadowing the personal complaints, rightly voiced at the meeting, was a general tale of a desperate effort to give the Council's tenants the service they ought to have. There was genuine concern that human housing management was being limited to the bare mechanics of rent collection; that for lack of staff labourers were looking after stores. There was even the unusual plea from men on the job that the Director of Establishments should send out his Organisation and Methods experts.

What a pity that before this scheme was imposed there was no real attempt to tap the collective experience, the professional zeal of the staff, to design with them a working model. It could still be done.

Note: LCC, later GLC, estates staff were eventually (in the 1970s) converted into Estate Officers, based at District offices and so, to some extent, divorced from their "patches" on the estates. The estate service was, during the years 1975-80, bedevilled by a dispute over Estate Officers' duties: and its probably fair to say that it never fully recovered from this. The estates were transferred to the London Boroughs over the years 1980-86.

'Delayed by Fog.'

(January 1949)

The vicissitudes of those who had to make their daily journeys through the Great Fog which marked the close of November 1948 have for a brief period given rise to an exchange of minor personal anecdotes which call to mind the early days of the Blitz. Instead of the fire-bomb which didn't ignite, and the miraculous escape of the people three doors away, we are now treated to the Man Whose Feet Never Touched the Floor Until Someone Fainted At Esher, and the Man Who Was Only Three Compartments Away From The Man Who Fell Out Near Norwood. We beg to cap these experiences with the true story of the Council's servants, who, instead of being away at work for their usual ten or eleven hours, were away 114 hours 45 minutes.

They were, of course, the officers and men of the Council's sludge vessels. Extraordinarily few Londoners know anything about the essential service, maintained year in and year out by the Chief Engineer's department, of disposing of the great volume of sludge which accumulates daily after purification and sedimentation at the two sewage outfall works. But on every week-day tide you may reckon that a sludge vessel is setting out from Beckton and from Crossness loaded with 15 or 16 hundred tons of deposit, which it carries to the North Sea and dumps over a large depression in the ocean bed which is appropriately called the Black Deep area. The name, sludge vessels, is somewhat repellent, and may even suggest an open and noisome barge; but they are in effect small tankers, and the Council's Marine Superintendent, Captain J. H. Monro, will assure you that they are kept in such trim condition that they are known on the river as the L.C.C. Yachts. Of the Council's fleet of four vessels, one was mined and sunk during the late war and another is in Chatham Dockyard being converted for oil fuel. There were therefore only two ships, the *J. H. Hunter* and the *John Perring*, in operation when the fog rolled down on 22nd November.

During the first part of the week it was nothing more that seasonal fog. Both vessels left their outfall stations on Monday's afternoon tide, anchored in dense fog that evening, and did not make the outfalls again till Wednesday afternoon, but for the next two days their voyages were but little impeded by weather. It was with the evening tide of Friday, 26th November that the fun really started, when there set in the longest continuous period of dense fog that the

Marine Superintendent has known in forty years' experience.

The *John Perring* loaded at Beckton with its usual 1,620 tons of sludge, and sailed at 18.30 hours. On the way down river she encountered considerable fog in Erith Rands, where a large number of ships were anchored about the fairway, and the Master, Captain G. Norton, was himself obliged to anchor for a short time. But at 19.45 the weather cleared a little, and he weighed and proceeded, arriving at the Black Deep at 23.50, and discharging his cargo in the normal manner. On the return journey, however, he ran into dense fog off the Chapman Lighthouse, and although he was able to steam slowly as far as No. 2 Mucking Buoy, in the Lower Hope, he was compelled to drop anchor there in 30 fathoms at 02.55 on Saturday. And there, save for a brief attempt to proceed that afternoon, the *John Perring* remained until 11.30 on Wednesday, 1st December.

Throughout this period of unprecedented delay the prime anxiety was of course to keep steam up. The vessel had last coaled on the morning tide on Thursday; she had since made three and a half trips, and was due to coal again on Saturday. A steamship is not like a car, which can shut off its engine when it is immobile. The *Perring* was lying at anchor in a dense fog in a fairway crowded with shipping, and she had to be able to make an immediate move, or meet any emergency that might arise: to do that the First Engineer had to maintain at all times a sufficient head of steam. There were adequate reserves of fuel for all normal contingencies, but by Sunday morning (after 30 hours) it had become apparent there was something distinctly abnormal about this persistent fog, and it seemed prudent therefore, to begin to eke the coal out. The First Engineer therefore reduced his fires to a minimum, and warned the Master that he would not be able to have the use of the engines quickly, as it would take rather longer than usual to raise the necessary steam.

A further anxiety which now presented itself was food. Commissariat arrangements on a sludge vessel are that the crew feed themselves, and the stewards feeds the officers. Incidentally they manage remarkably well at a reasonably low cost, but rationing has greatly reduced their pre-war caches of dainties and their emergency reserves. The trouble was that they were on the return journey of their last trip before the week-end break. Stocks of food were therefore at their lowest, and, more important, although the fresh water tanks had been filled on Friday morning, Friday is always a heavy day for water consumption on a sludge vessel, because the crew all take baths in the expectation of meeting their wives again after a week away. On Sunday, then, all hands were forbidden to use fresh water for washing, and water was rationed for cooking and drinking. At the same time hard biscuits from the lifeboats were issued to the crew as their food was almost exhausted.

On Monday, 29th November, in a further effort to save coal, steam was cut off from the steering engine, steam whistle, and all steam heaters. Thereafter, except for those working in the engine-room, it was a cold ship as well as a hungry one. In County Hall, where nothing was known of the vessels except that they had not been seen since Friday, colourful fantasies were being sketched of the fortunes that were being lost and won at solo and pontoon in the mess-room, especially as the crew had been paid just before sailing. But we are assured that the men are too careful of their families to do much gambling, and that they passed the time with radio, darts, and periodicals. On Monday and on Tuesday,

7 lbs of biscuits were issued (for 24 men), and the fresh water ration successively reduced; but Captain Norton puts on record that all hands accepted their discomforts in good spirits and co-operated in every possible way.

The *J. H. Hunter*, meanwhile, was experiencing similar difficulties, as she lay anchored off the Chapman Light. Captain Bingham's log for $4^{1}/_{2}$ days is a monotonous record of 'Vessel swung to ebb, dense fog all day,' and 'Vessel swung to flood, very dense fog, variable airs.' Here also they were down to hard tack and rationed water, but the fuel situation was easier, as the *Hunter* had coaled on Friday morning.

On Tuesday evening, as Londoners were making their three or four-hour grope homeward, Captain Norton and the First Engineer of the *Perring* had a further consultation, and decided to draw the fires from the two top furnaces under each boiler. The head of steam fell dangerously low, however, and on Wednesday the fires were relighted. But the knobs of coal remaining in the bunker could now almost be counted, and on Wednesday morning Captain Norton recorded: 'The fog still remaining dense, and the further outlook "more fog," I gave orders for the deck officers and all the seamen to turn to breaking up all the wood possible, and pass same down to the stokehold.' The men who man the sludge vessels are Council's servants as well as sailors, and the First Mate therefore dutifully subjoined to the Master's report a list of items used as fuel, careless of the headaches it would cause some administrative assistant at head office, trying to devise some procedure for accounting for the discrepancies on the ship's inventory.

Wednesday morning therefore saw the crew of the *Perring* grimly (or gaily?) attacking with saw and hatchet the bunker hatches, the bosun's chairs, the pilot ladders and the staging. But, most fortunately, at 11.00 the fog showed signs of lifting and all stokers were sent to the stokehold and bunkers to assist in keeping up steam. Captain Norton hove up the anchor and made tracks slowly for home, gradually increasing his speed after an hour, until at 13.15 on 1st December, the *John Perring* arrived at Beckton, at the same minute as the *J. H. Hunter* arrived at Crossness.

The crews were released to get stores, the ships were coaled and loaded, and the sludge vessel service started off again.

Note: Fogs such as that of November 1948, referred to in this article, were for centuries a recurrent feature of London life. Dickens, in the first few pages of *Bleak House* (1853), describes one of these fogs in terms that would have been very familiar a century later. The great fog of December 1952 was one of the worst on record: it was claimed to have been the direct cause of over 4,000 deaths from respiratory complaints. It was after this episode that the Clean Air Act of 1953 set in train the process of cleansing the air which, in the course of time, made such fogs a thing of the past - the last long-lasting and serious London fog was in December 1962.

Three-Line Whip: The First Council Meeting.

O. W. H. Holmes
(May 1949)

It was thirty-nine years since such a tense Council meeting had been held, and with crowds outside and members having to ballot for places in the galleries for their friends, and the Press being denied places if their past attendance had been desultory, the scene was set for the big moment in the Council chamber on 13th April. About 2.15 a few members (Labour whips, probably) fluttered round a little anxiously, and then a cathedral hush ensued. It is usual for members of the majority and minority parties to meet in secret session separately before each Council meeting, so that it was not altogether surprising that Sir Percy Harris (the Liberal Party) was the first to enter the chamber. He marched across to his old seat, with the result that he found himself engulfed by what seemed like hordes of Conservatives, after their three-year confinement to a single block of seats in the chamber. At 2.25 the bells began to clang, the shorthand writers filed in, and the sun devoted a strictly impartial beam to the central dais. Mr. MacDonnell, with small sense of the dramatic, came in very early and gained a cheer. Mr. George Wright sat for a moment on his old front bench seat as Chairman of the Restaurants Committee, but thought better of it when he realised that this was now enemy territory. Then all in the chamber stood up as the head messenger boomed out 'The Right Honourable the Chairman of the London County Council' - one could almost feel the capital letters - and in came Mr. Walter Owen, the retiring chairman.

Mr. Owen made a few necessary announcements, and then humanised them by adding that tea would be available in room 129; the formal return of those elected (which breathes not a word of party strife) was 'laid on the table', and battle commenced. By this time there seemed to be scarcely any seats free in the chamber, save for about eleven on the Conservative front bench.

With refreshing economy of words Mr. Walter Boys (Lab) nominated Mr. J. W. Bowen for chairman for the ensuing year. He presented his case effectively, spoke of Mr. Bowen's service to the Post Office Union, of his chairmanship of the old Mental Hospitals Committee and the Establishment Committee - 'two happy committees' - summed up Mr. Bowen as the sort of man about whom no one wanted to say any nasty thing, and wound up a little incongruously with the warning that Mr. Bowen has an expert knowledge of the law of defamation of character. Mr. Sargood (Lab), seconding, spoke of still other fields in which Mr. Bowen has shown his worth.

The Hon. John Fremantle (Con) then rose to nominate Dame Barrie Lambert. He began by saying that the nomination to the chair had never been challenged before, but this of course was not the case. He spoke of why his party felt this nomination of Mr. Bowen unfair and even remembered to say (what was never in dispute) why Dame Barrie would be a good chairman. He also pertinently added she would be impartial.

At this point Sir Percy caused a minor stir by walking round to the dais and saying something to the chairman of the Council. And the sun became disturbingly partial and shone unambiguously on the Conservative front bench.

Perhaps the ever-watchful Clerk had thoughts of pulling the curtains across. In any case Mr. Fremantle wound up with a winsome analogy about England's three sovereign queens, and suggested a third woman chairman of the Council would be a good thing too.

The Conservative skipper now came in to bat. Mr. Henry Brooke spoke in trenchant terms which the papers have duly recorded and which called forth full-throated roars and counter-roars. It must be a disagreeable experience to be in the way of Mr. Brooke when he feels like that. In short, he seconded Mr. Fremantle.

Sir Percy Harris then brought the temperature down a little. He explained he had never sought to succeed Mr. Sidney Stanley in notoriety. He spoke of the Council's high traditions, and was sorry that a distinguished non-party man of the order of Lord Rosebery had not been put forward. In his dilemma, he proposed to vote for Dame Barrie. This can have disturbed but few: it was an inexpensive gesture, for on this vote the Labour party had about ten aldermen at hand to swamp him. And so they did, with help to support the steps of Mr. MacDonnell and with guidance for Mr. Chrisp, their blind member. Mr. Bowen was shortly after invested with his chain of office and Mr. Owen modestly sought a place among the rank and file.

Mr. Bowen, who had been spared hearing the bitter exchanges which preceded the election, thanked the Council for his election and the needle match began. Without speeches, members struck off from stencilled voting papers bearing the names of six Labour and eleven Conservative nominees, the names of all but eleven candidates, and filed out to ease the tension while the staff at the table counted - with care rather than speed. Then the bells rang again, and the new chairman read out eleven names which had attracted 66 votes and six which had 64. Which seemed to suggest that, when there was a serious vote, Sir Percy was a good socialist. Then the eleven new aldermen filed in (there were only two new faces) and signed the book at the table and parted to their different sides.

Then up shot Mr. Brooke, moving that the Council do now adjourn. This gave him an opening for a further onslaught about the electorate's wishes and jiggery-pokery. And much else. This entitled Mr. Hayward, as leader of the Council, to reply, and the most polished speaker would have had a hard task to deploy his arguments against such barracking as he met. He began by saying he wouldn't need his five-minute ration, but he was 'gonged' before he had finished all he had to say. Another division then followed, which Labour of course won.

When the members began to reassemble, Miss Marcousé (Lab), crystal clear of speech, proposed that Mr. Bernard Sullivan (Lab) should be elected vice-chairman. And it was gradually realised that not one Conservative was present in the benches opposite, and neither was Sir Percy. All the wiseacres deduced that some plot was afoot, but none of the wiseacres knew what plot. Then the missing members marched in and speculation grew. They heard Mr. Keen (Lab), who seconded, warn all members that Mr. Sullivan was a stern critic of women's wear, because he was a trade expert in such matters. Despite this, the speakers' advocacy, plus Mr. Sullivan's personal qualities, won for him not only an unopposed election but quite a hearty clap from the Conservatives as well as his own party. In his Yorkshire brogue Mr. Sullivan thanked the Council,

73

confessing he was short of education and inches, but he hoped his sense of humour would carry him through.

The election of the deputy chairman, the usual prerogative of the minority party, was a happy affair. Everyone seemed to like Mr. Charles Pearce, with that twinkle in his eye. But he only just managed to get to his elevated chair. First the new chairman summoned him by the name of Mr. Charles Peace, which put everyone in a good humour. Then Mr. A. W. Scott, his seconder, almost forgot to escort him to the dais, and finally the chairman almost forgot to allow him his brief speech of thanks before the invasion of 'flashy' photographers was allowed.

The photographers showed an interest in three subjects - the new 'dais', the Council as a whole, and the Conservative front bench. Perhaps the *Daily Herald* man wasn't there?

Members must have been ravenous for their tea by this time. They usually get it long before this, and one wonders if they will sustain themselves with energy tablets in the chamber in future for fear of missing a vote. But there was to be one more division, when the Conservatives fought for an equal share of the seats on the Selection Committee which is set up to decide which members shall serve on each of the regular committees. But the Labour party used their majority to refuse this and, of course, as matters by this time stood, they had made their decision to bear full responsibility for the government of London for the next three years. Having left themselves with only a margin of ten in the Council chamber, Mrs. Corbet (Chief Labour Whip), who normally doesn't have occasion to speak in the Chamber, pointed out that Labour felt they must have the whip hand in deciding how the available seats on the Housing, Education, Parks and other committees should be apportioned.

In any case margins will be precariously small, and all committee clerks will go to bed with the standing orders by their pillow to brace themselves for the conundrums which heated members will hurl at them as the committees warm to their task.

Note: The LCC elections of March 1949 resulted in a dead heat between the two main contenders: the Labour and Conservative parties each won 64 seats. What happened next is well described in this article - Labour was never again, in the lifetime of the LCC, to be in danger of losing control.

Men at Work – In Darkest County Hall.

(August 1949)

Disaster seems to be dogging the section. Lambswool - youthful, smiling Lambswool - has disappeared! It is now 4.45 of Friday the 19th and since 9.53 on Monday the 15th nothing has been seen of him. We fear the worst. A mere fledgling in Council service, he was sent by Swilbin on a mission that might have daunted a veteran.

It appears that fifty years ago (or it may have been sixty) the Batterwell Borough Council laid a sewer along the dreary stretch of marsh known since Dickens' day as Batterwell Level. It had now become necessary ('for reasons with which you need not concern yourself,' said Swilbin loftily) to enlarge the sewer, and this would involve heavy expenditure. Who was to pay? Batterwell, said the County Council, basing themselves on an exchange of correspondence with the Chief Engineer in 1939. The County Council, said the Borough Council, on the strength of a sub-paragraph in the draft statutory plan of 1936, and a verbal undertaking by the County Valuer in 1933. The County Council came back with a minute from the Chairman of the then Sewers and Watercourses Sub-Committee in 1927. Batterwell, smirking all over its municipal countenance, blandly quoted the report of the Government's Investigating Commission on Rodent infestation in Batterwell, 1911. The County Council pooh-poohed this and politely but firmly drew attention to the Council agenda of 1907. Here Batterwell lost all patience and, plunging right into the archives, emerged with a malodorous document of dubious authenticity which purported to be an agreement between the parties, circa 1897. To this the County Council had so far found no reply.

'Mr. Boxcalf wants you to drop everything,' said Swilbin, 'and get him the whole story. Every word that has ever been written about the confounded sewer. It's time we taught Batterwell a lesson.'

And Lambswool, leaving the relative security of the North Block, had plunged lightheartedly into the labyrinthine corridors of the main building.

For the first day or two we thought no more of the matter. But when Wednesday morning came and he had not returned, misgiving grew; by the afternoon alarm was general. By Thursday, the question of who was to break it to his parents was being gloomily debated. Even Swilbin, to do him justice, was looking haggard and guilt-stricken (as well he might).

At 2.15 this afternoon Chopleigh flung his pen down and said that he was going to look for him. Without a moment's hesitation Oxshott, his rival for the love of Miss Sheepish, announced his intention of accompanying him. Chopleigh wrung his hand silently. As for Miss Sheepish, she was splendid. The two men she loved best were about to be swallowed up in the unknown that had engulfed Lambswool, but the courageous little woman gave no sign. In such moments one sees one's colleagues with new eyes.

The Chopleigh-Oxshott Relief Expedition moved off from its base at about 2.25. From that moment I can best describe its progress by quoting the moving bulletins which were 'phoned back by Chopleigh.

2.40. Reached Architect's (T.P.). Lambswool left here for the Engineer's about four days ago. He was making good progress and appeared in high spirits. We are full of hope. Weather splendid.

2.50. Engineer's. Lambswool seen here three days ago, moving N.N.E. Heading for Solicitor's? He was advised to abandon his quest but insisted on pressing on. We shall follow. Morale high.

3.25. Conditions deteriorating. Trail growing weaker. We have covered three miles of rough terrain since leaving base. Oxshott's feet troubling him greatly. I fear he cannot long continue.

3.40. Public Health. No news. Oxshott weak but determined. There seems little hope.

4.20. Put in at Clerk's. Natives hostile and very primitive. Took one prisoner. He made signs to indicate that a stranger was seen this morning and was driven away by the tribesmen with shrill threatening cries. Can it have been Lambswool?

The last bulletin, an incomplete one, was received barely five minutes ago. It simply said, 'Oxshott delirious.' Then Chopleigh's voice trailed off.

Meanwhile, their afternoon tea, horrible at the best of times, grows coldly repulsive in their cups. And Miss Sheepish sobs quietly.

4.55. A wonderful moment! They have returned, bringing Lambswool with them. Oxshott looks terribly emaciated, but all three are in excellent spirits. Old Goatsby says it is the greatest day he has known since the relief of Mafeking, when Mrs. Goatsby (Miss Cantilever at she then was) so far forgot herself as to bite a policeman. Even Swilbin is deeply moved.

Best of all, Lambswool has carried out his mission! All three are staggering beneath mountains of documents, yellow with age and bitten by whole generations of rats.

'Got it,' said Lambswool, triumphantly. 'Right back to when the Council was a mother's meeting.' (It still is,' said Chopleigh, *sotto voce*.) 'The whole story of the Batterwell sewer. Exclusive!'

'Oh, that,' said Swilbin, looking somewhat embarrassed. 'As a matter of fact, we aren't bothering with that any more. Mr. B. has reached a gentleman's agreement with Batterwell. He wants you to drop everything and concentrate on finding sites for Homes for Aged Lepers with Nonconformist Leanings.'

'Carve me up in little pieces,' said Chopleigh.

Bermondsey Story.

(July 1950)

Bermondsey Story by Fenner Brockway. George Allen and Unwin, December 1949. 15s.

When the most brilliant man of his time at Guy's Hospital abandoned the opportunities and honours of Harley Street to become a poor man's doctor in Bermondsey many of his friends were puzzled and disappointed, but in doing so he made one of the greatest personal contributions to social history of our day.

Alfred Salter was born in 1873 in Greenwich. His father was an administrative officer in a gas company, and both he and his wife were intensely religious and even puritanical. The boy's grandfather had practised as an amateur 'vet' and Alfred's interest in nature study and animals inclined him towards a medical career. As a student and a research worker he toiled prodigiously. The list of his achievements becomes a remarkable recital, and he would have made a great name as a doctor and bacteriologist. But a sense of mission led him to take up residence in a settlement at Bermondsey where he met his wife Ada who was also doing social work. It was probably her influence that converted him to Christianity, though he was already a pacifist. With her full support he decided to remain in Bermondsey and set up a co-operative medical partnership with Dr. George Lowe and three friends.

Salter was the leader of a small group which in 1910 founded the West Bermondsey Labour Party, acquired a headquarters and set out to win Bermondsey for socialism. He decided that this would take twelve years. Actually in thirteen years they had won the Parliamentary seat, both L.C.C. seats and a majority on the borough council, of which Ada Salter was the first woman mayor.

The Salters' home and garden had always been bright with flowers and plants and the new council set out to change the face of Bermondsey. The Beautification Committee planted thousands of trees in the drab streets, brightened such public gardens as there were, cleared churchyards and laid them out as gardens, and encouraged the planting of front gardens and window-boxes by the residents. Patches of slums were turned into garden villages in spite of the insistence of a Tory L.C.C. and Ministry that tenements should be erected.

The story of municipal enterprise is an astonishing one. A model health centre which became world-famous was erected, a light-treatment centre and facilities for obtaining T.T. milk helped to combat tuberculosis, and baths and up-to-date wash-houses were built. A municipal orchestra was formed, library extensions undertaken, a lecture hall built and a remarkable collection of prints of old Bermondsey was acquired. Many improvements were made in the institutions and the poor law generally was humanised. Apart from their council activities members of the party helped to run a co-operative bakery with a turnover of £160,000 a year, and Salter himself provided and organised a convalescent home in Kent to which he sent his poor patients without a fee.

As a busy M.P. he eventually had to give up his practice and he played a great part, particularly after the 1931 election when only fifty Labour members were left, as he had great ability in mastering a subject at short notice. With a group of doctors which included Somerville Hastings he visited Russia to investigate medical and health organisation. Salter had suffered much during the election at the hands of Bermondsey Communists who tried to break up his meetings, (he described them as 'the worst rogues, thieves, jail-birds, scroungers and hooligans ever collected in the borough'), but he had the highest regard for the enthusiasm, self-sacrifice and devotion of those he met in Russia. He remained astounded by the Russians' development of curative medicine and their indifference to the sanitary prevention of disease, and he found intolerable the suppression of views contrary to the official party line..

He also visited America with George Lansbury on a peace mission. As a pacifist he had stoutly championed the ill-treated conscientious objectors of 1914-18 and he had never ceased to work for peace. The introduction of conscription and the outbreak of war in 1939 left him exhausted and broken, and he was profoundly dispirited by the defection of colleagues who had deserted their principles. A final blow was the death of his beloved wife and the destruction of large parts of the Bermondsey he knew so well.

Fenner Brockway's biography is a vividly written and inspiring account of one who loved and served the common people and worked unceasingly to bring about a new state of society. It gives us glimpses of many familiar figures - Mrs. Lowe, Charles Ammon, Herbert Morrison, Somerville Hastings, and the Prime Minister. But the impression which will endure is that of Alfred Salter - Socialist, Pacifist, Christian and Republican.

Cricket – A Memorable Final.

(September 1950)

Few of those who took part or were spectators will forget the final of the Inter-Departmental Cricket Competition which was played at Bexley Hospital in 26th July, 1950. To the historians it will be the match in which the Architect's department retained the trophy by beating Housing and Valuation by one run; but to those present it will be the memory of that gallant but unavailing last wicket stand of 52 runs by 'Skipper' Simpson and Moody of Housing and Valuation that will linger. One run to tie, two to win, but all lost when the umpire (strictly neutral) adjudged Simpson lbw. - everyone would have been happier had the ball been hit for four or the wicket bowled down, but it was not to be.

Winning the toss Douglas decided that his side should take first knock on a wicket that was soft on the top from overnight rain, and by lunchtime the Architect's had scored 62 for 4 wickets, mainly due to Dean (31) who had been bowled by Simpson when attempting to force the pace. After lunch, with the wicket becoming easier as it dried out, Boxall and Munro put on 56 quick runs before Boxall was unluckily out, stumped off the wicketkeeper's pads, for a well earned 44.

In spite of some steady bowling by Simpson and Benjamin, the Architect's batted consistently well down to No. 11, and with Munro and Douglas contributing 40 and 24 respectively (including many quick singles), the innings closed at 194. The Valuer's bowling honours were divided among Fenton (4 for 46), Benjamin (3 for 36) and Simpson (3 for 38).

Tea was taken between the innings and after the interval Housing made a very similar start to the Architect's, losing 4 wickets for 63, followed by a partnership of 41 by Collins and Benjamin before the former was caught and bowled by Boxall for 24. Without much support the doughty Benjamin continued to score all round the wicket and had made top score of 47 when he fell to a fine catch by Ayre in the deep field. Wickets continued to fall without any great additions to the total, and with nine down for 141 it seemed that a comfortable victory for the Architect's was in sight. Simpson however had other ideas and with Moody batting more like a No. 5 than a No. 11 the score mounted steadily to 183, when the wily Douglas made his tactical move. He took off Boxall, who had bowled 32 overs without change, and went on again himself. After his first two balls (the first a no-ball) had each been despatched for four by Moody, excitement rose to fever pitch and, to prevent any undue delay upsetting their batsmen's concentration, the nine Valuer's men, not actively engaged at the moment, moved as one across the ground to seek the ball temporarily lost in the corn adjoining the far boundary. The remainder of the over yielded only one run and Boxall was put on the other end to attack Moody who was able to take an easy single. The fifth ball of the over, however, was the undoing of Simpson, who played it with his leg with fatal results. The tactical move had been successful and the Architect's still held the Bowl!

Boxall bowling 32.5 overs took 6 wickets for 81, the other wickets being shared by Fryer, 2 for 28, and Douglas, 2 for 36.

The umpires were N. P. Bush (Parks) and D. E. Wilkinson (Supplies).
A grand day's cricket, on which all players and officials concerned are to
be heartily congratulated, was suitably rounded off in a local hostelry.

Sculpture at Battersea.

John C. Craig
(May 1951)

If you think that sculpture should merely form a pleasant detail on a
building, or something to fill an odd space, even if you think that it should be
entirely subordinate to architecture or landscaping, then this exhibition is not for
you. That is, not entirely, for even if you hold such views there are certain pieces
which may please you. You may, however, thing that an artist is free to pursue
his own ways, irrespective of public opinion. If you hold this view of the artist's
social responsibility, the exhibition in Battersea Park this summer is likely to
present you with both a challenge and a stimulant.

It is not the pieces which immediately leap to satisfy the eye, nor those
which cause an instant spring of emotion, which are best. Neither are these
always the most outwardly significant of what we assume to be the artist's
intention. When considering modern art it is a sobering thought that today's
scornful laughter may, and often does, give way to tomorrow's mature approval.
For this reason I must pass over certain exhibits such as Giacometti's 'Three
Men Walking' (No. 15), Reg Butler's 'Torso, 1950' (No. 7), or Archambault's
'Iron Bird' (No. 2) with the confession that they convey little to me, either
emotionally or by form and material. I will also take a chance, and whilst
admitting that I am not ready for them, I will say that I do not think that I shall
like them any better tomorrow.

A Challenging Show

What, then, do I want from an outdoor exhibition of sculpture? Form,
colour, material, setting and a sense of movement or stillness? These are all to
be observed in the forty-four pieces on view in Battersea Park. Although this
number appears small when set in several acres of wooded park, as against the
confines of an indoor exhibition, some of the statues almost appear to be jostling
each other. The main watchword should therefore be economy when using
sculpture in the open air. It should be welded into the landscape as part of it, not
too dominant and certainly not subordinate, always, of course, with certain
exceptions. However, the exhibition proves once again that sculpture in natural
settings comes triumphantly into its own. This second show is more varied,
more argumentative, and more challenging even than the previous one.

It also proves that there is an indoor and an outdoor brand of sculpture,
with variations within these two types. For instance some pieces are more
suitable to the small formal garden. Two examples are Gill's 'The Deposition'
(No. 16), which would be admirable against a mellow brick wall as background
to a little pool, and Thomas's 'Terpsis' (No. 41), a most suitable subject for the
centre of a rose or herb garden. On the other hand the lusty young woman

'Pomona', by Nimptsch (No. 35), Henning's 'Standing Girl' (No. 19), Despiau's 'Assia' (No. 11) and others of this type are admirably suited to a background of sturdy bushes and trees in gardens or parks of the English landscape school. 'Assia' in particular conveys a most voluptuous appreciation of the female form in this open air framing.

Romantic Melancholy

With Mailliol's 'Mediterranean' (No. 28) we enter the realms of romantic melancholy. The figure reclines sadly against a background of yew. The mood is redolent of early twentieth century romanticism linking with the music of Mahler and Bruckner. 'Mediterranean' would fit into the brooding midnight-noon atmosphere of one of Di Chiroco's deserted piazzas. Amongst the more traditional, or formally representational work, the one which pleased me most was the 'Evensong' by Charoux (No. 10). The brown terra cotta contrast heightened the effect of this against the green background, and from any viewpoint the effect is of harmony and rhythm. Soukop's 'Mother and Child' (No. 40) had the same effect though the rhythm is more subtle. One of those which, in my opinion, do not gain by the open air treatment is Wheeler's 'Adam' (No. 43), which seems too formally smooth, more like a cultivated Adam trained by Charles Atlas than the earthly father of men. I place Hardiman's 'Night' (No. 17) in this class and also Ledward's 'Caryatid Figures' (No. 24). These should be incorporated in buildings to be completely successful.

One wished that the modern Italian school might have been more fully represented. Manzu's 'Child on a Chair' is delightful. Turning from this to the work of Manzu's slightly older contemporary, Marini, it is clear that whatever Italian sculptors create in the modern idiom it is never displeasing to look at.

When we come to the abstract or non-representational works the challenge of the exhibition becomes pronounced. I disliked a piece of bronze, 'Mother and Child' (No. 26), by Lipchitz. This struck me with the force of an obscene nightmare from a future world. The imaginative world of Lipchitz is one I would not wish to inhabit. Max Bill's 'Rhythm in Space' (No. 5) is curious. In itself its smooth curves are crisply fascinating. Against a clear sky it is innocent, but seen in from of the dark yew trees it changes into menacing black holes in the dead white of a bleached skull. Marini's bronze horseman is interesting in that the surface appears to be very old. Whether this conscious creating of an ancient appearance is legitimate art cannot be argued here, but I cannot imagine this piece being so successful indoors.

Lambert and Henry Moore

One of the most triumphant of the newer pieces is the 'Pegasus and Bellerophon' of Lambert (No. 23). This dominates the whole of its surroundings. One should build a garden around this rather than put it in an existing garden. And then we have Henry Moore in a new mood; his bronze standing figure is an advance on his 'Three Women' and I approach it in the same sense of cautious intrigue as I do McWilliam's two-piece head. Standing by Moore's bronze one can see his three monumental women in their permanent position on the other side of the lake. How familiar they look to us now, and they seem to be telling themselves not to worry about the brash new boy over the water. He will no doubt find his place in time just as they have done.

The catalogue of the exhibition is one of the best publications of this sort to be issued by the Council, and is worth every bit of its five shillings. The article, 'The Sculptor's Problems,' by Nikolaus Pevsner, told me more than the exhibit by his namesake Antoine Pevsner.

Calder's Mobile

Near one of the entrances is a mobile by Alexander Calder. A mobile, in case you did not know, is a thing of bits and pieces which hangs, or is otherwise suspended, and goes with the wind. M. Pevsner calls his exhibit 'Column of Victory capable of development' (Colonne développable de la victoire). I thought, when looking at the mobile, that here is an artistic medium which is much more capable of development that the column of victory. However, not this particular one of Calder's.

It only remains to say that the whole of the arrangements connected with this exhibition are exceedingly successful and it is a most peaceful place to rest from the rigours of its fun fair neighbour.

Who is Sylvia?

C. V. Smith
(February 1953)

I'm a duffer with dates. 1066: Battle of Hastings; 1215: Magna Carta . . I know those as well as I know that Easter Day is the first Sunday after the full moon which happens upon, or next after, the twenty-first of March. But that's where we came in. Not that my history's hopeless; I just can't recall when its bit and pieces happened. Which is odd when you reflect that in all my long life I've never once forgotten a face. At least, I hadn't - till that morning last week.

It was on the bus. I looked up from my book to see that freckled nose which twenty-odd years ago had tortured my boyish world. "Sylvia!" I stammered.

Her eyes were still blue, her lashes still long; and she flashed me one of those smiles which once on a time would have spurred me, her shining St. George, to the succour of every distressed damsel in Christendom. She started to say something as I joined her, but I was so all Hallelujah Chorus that I bore down on her like a verbal flotilla. Where had she been? Where did she live? And was she - married? I didn't think she could be; she looked so - happy! 'You haven't changed a bit', I told her.

She crinkled her lips to the blush of the year's first rose. 'I —— ' she began.

'I've never forgotten you', I hurried on. 'Remember that picnic at Box Hill, and how when it rained we ate sardines under a gorse bush? And when we were cut off by the tide and had to be rescued? Margate, wasn't it?' She didn't answer, but turned her head to look out of the window. I glimpsed over one pink ear a wisp of that corn-gold hair which, I recalled, had always tickled. 'The last time I saw you', I reminded her, 'was nineteen-twenty-eight. That fancy-dress do at the

Grand. You were Queen of Hearts and I was one of King Arthur's knights'.. I moved a hand to hers. 'I hate this growing old'.

She quoted something about youth's sweet-scented manuscript having to close, and half got up from her seat. I held her back. 'You can't go yet', I protested. 'I've waited - all those years - to tell you I'm sorry. It was my fault we parted. If I hadn't lost my temper and sloshed that Napoleon guy ———. Still, he asked for it. I thought he was going to kiss you. And —— and I was jealous'. I stared down at my feet. 'After all, I did love you'.

Colour flooded her cheeks. 'Thank you for saying that', she said. 'And now I must go - really!' She clattered down the stairs before I could stop her. 'Sylvia!' I called, stampeding after her, but the conductor flourished a hairy fist an inch from my nose and said, "Ere! what's the perishin' game?' There was one of those dramatic pauses that ususally precede a murder or an earthquake. Sylvia broke it by throwing over her shoulder: 'By the way, I am married - two charming children'. Then - pouf! - just like that - she didn't exist.

That night there was a dance at the Town Hall, and the first person I barged into was - Sylvia! Her earlier disappearance had left me so depressed that I found myself jerking her arm up and down like the handle of a village pump. She, however, was staring at me as if at a ghost. 'Jiminy!' she exclaimed, 'it's Bill! - or is it?' She stepped back a pace and eyed me from head to toe. 'Fatter', she mused, 'and thinner on top. And, I dare say, just as quarrelsome. Otherwise - no change'.

An odd feeling was suffusing me. 'Did you expect any?' I asked.

She laughed. 'Well, twenty-four years is a long time'.

'Twenty-four years!' I echoed. 'What on earth - This morning! On the bus! Surely you remember? '

She goggled at me as if on the sudden I had turned into the Crystal Palace. 'Bill', she said, 'you're ill. Go and lie down. This morning I was in Gloucester. And I never ride on buses; they make me sick. I haven't seen you since that night you lost your temper and flattened old Boney!'

Rise, Sir Arthur.

(August 1953)

During this Coronation summer, when Londoners and visitors from all parts of the country and the world have thronged the heart of our city to delight in its gay decorations, County Hall itself has been not the least admired of all our famous buildings. The soft pastel effects of its green and amber floodlighting brought a faerie beauty to the river front, especially when seen through the foliage of the trees that line the Victoria Embankment.

On 6th July fairyland extended its sway to the interior of County Hall. A brilliant and distinguished assembly of more than fifteen hundred guests attended the annual Chairman's Reception, and the Council received the greatest honour the year can offer by the presence at the reception of Her Majesty the Queen and H.R.H. the Duke of Edinburgh, and other members of the royal family. The Chairman's reception every year is an occasion for special effort by all the staff who are concerned with its decorations, furnishing and lighting; with the flowers which bring grace and colour to its normally severe lobbies and corridors; with the refreshments and the music provided for the guests' delectation; and with the exhibitions and displays which seek to present in miniature something of the Council's history and work.

The Queen with Sir Arthur Middleton.

For Her Majesty and the notable company who shared with her the Chairman's hospitality this year the effort made was both greater and more successful than ever. She and the Duke joined in the dancing in the Conference Hall, and those few of our colleagues - discharging their stewards' duty of dancing-on, and keeping others dancing-on, unselfconsciously - who were privileged to share the floor with her will long treasure the memory of Her Majesty's enjoyment of a few moments' relief from the formalities of state.

Others of us saw the Queen's arrival in the Council Chamber, to be welcomed by the Chairman on behalf of the assembled members of the Council and Mayors of Metropolitan Boroughs, and heard her reply with a warm and sincere acknowledgment of her own special affection for London, as herself a Londoner born and bred. Around the principal floor, others at their posts of duty noted the genuine interest with which the Queen and the Duke of Edinburgh studied the exhibition illustrating the Council's services, and the display of modern methods of presenting architects' and planners' ideas in three dimensions, by models and anaglyphic (stereoscopic) drawings. More than one of the stewards bore witness to the keen and pertinent questions put to them, especially by the Duke of Edinburgh.

Chairman's Reception, 1953.

The final touch of fairylike romance came late in the evening when the Queen conferred upon the Chairman the honour of knighthood: not - as is usual with honours for public service - by formal announcement in a published Honours List, but by the immediate grant of the accolade upon the scene of the announcement of her royal purpose. Mr. and Mrs. Middleton were transformed to Sir Arthur and Lady Middleton in the midst of their enjoyment of one of the happiest evenings of their lives. We tender our warmest congratulations to Sir Arthur on the honour bestowed upon him, not less because (as we are sure he will be the first to recognise) in honouring him Her Majesty the Queen was giving her thanks through him to all the members and staff of the Council, in whose care are so many matters of vital concern to every Londoner.

London to Moscow — Impressions of a Young Liberal.

Eric Deal
(April 1955)

Mr. Eric Deal gives some impressions formed during a recent visit to Soviet Russia as a member of a delegation on which he represented the National League of Young Liberals.

Visitors to the Council's offices are not usually entertained with cigars, minerals and fruit in the way that I was recently when I visited the offices of a District Soviet in Moscow to talk to the Chairman of the Executive Committee and the District Education Officer. But, while we were entertained lavishly, the building itself was even more dingy than most L.C.C. offices and greatly in need of a new coat of paint. In the course of our discussions we found several similarities between local government in Moscow and London; there is a committee system much the same as here and the main point of difference is in the extent of the Russian Soviet's activities in commercial and industrial under-takings, which provide the major part of its income. This discussion, however, took only three hours in a trip lasting three weeks; these weeks were filled with numerous visits and discussions and our hosts from the Anti-Fascist Committee of Soviet Youth and our ever-willing interpreters had a hectic time arranging a programme which on several days lasted from 5 a.m. till midnight. Even so, there was still a lot more we would have liked to see and many of our questions had to remain unanswered through lack of time.

Sightseeing in Moscow
We arrived in Moscow as the first snow of the winter was falling and it was a common sight to see women, who in the Soviet Union do many jobs for which they are thought unsuitable here, clearing the snow from the streets. During our stay in Moscow our visits included the Kremlin and the Lenin-Stalin mausoleum in Red Square, where a long queue of people waiting to file past the embalmed

bodies of the two dead leaders can be seen for six hours every day; we saw some of the new, over-ornamented skyscraper buildings, the famous Metro and the massive new University building on the Lenin hills just ourside the city. A group of us went by bus to the Moscow coalfield, while another party visited the Lenin Library and talked to the Director. Each evening there was something arranged for us, usually a concert or opera or ballet at the Bolshoi Theatre.

One Sunday evening we went to a service at the Moscow Baptist Church, where five times a week a congregation of about 2,000 crams itself into a building suitable for less than half that number. Some of us also saw a mass christening service at an Orthodox Church when we were strolling round Moscow on our own. There was no restriction on our movement and we were able to wander about freely and take photographs - although the easiest way to see the inside of a Soviet police post is to take photographs in one of the older areas with its wooden houses, badly in need of paint and often lacking running water.

From Moscow we flew to Tiflis, the capital of sunny Georgia, where the people were even more hospitable than in Moscow and lavishly entertained us on the local wines and foods. Our visits included factories, a hospital, a kindergarten, the University and a Pioneer palace, and a whole day and two nights were spent on a trip to a collective farm growing citrus fruits; on the same day we visited an orphanage and the State Institute of Tea, where the beverages consumed at a welcoming breakfast bore no resemblance whatever to tea. For our entertainment in Tiflis we visited a circus and a large-scale State amateur talent competition.

On leaving Georgia we flew back to Moscow and, after a frank discussion with our hosts on East-West problems, took the 'Red Arrow' sleeping-car express to Leningrad, which seemd the most westernised of the places we saw. After two days some of us returned to Moscow for further visits including the district Soviet, the permanent building exhibition and a trip to the Troitsky Academy at Zageck, where priests for the Russian Orthodox Church are trained. We also paid a return visit to the headquarters of the trade union movement. Our delegation had already had a five-hour meeting with trade union leaders on the methods of fixing wages, which is done on a piecework basis, and the social and cultural services which are largely administered by the unions. We returned because we were concerned at the needy appearance of some of the older people we saw and wanted to know more about old-age pensions and the care of the aged.

Even after such a heavy programme as we had a visitor cannot expect to return as an expert on the Soviet Union. Nor is it easy to summarise my impressions of this land which is still one of many enigmas and contrasts. On the personal level the people we met were more than friendly and anxious to help: in shops, in the streets and on the Metro people frequently came up to talk to us. Everywhere we went we were met with expressions of goodwill and the desire for peace; there was hardly a speech which did not include the phrase 'fighting for peace'. On the material side, in spite of a housing shortage and the drab uniformity of people's dress, we gained an impression of progress and it is in this that the great appeal of Communism would seem to lie: on the other hand, some of the things we noticed, such as the building styles and an increased supply of consumer goods in the shops, were affected within a few weeks of our return by changes in Government policy. Only time can tell whether further internal changes are in store and whether this atmosphere of peaceful co-existence, which makes visits like mine possible, will continue.

There are several aspects of Soviet life which I found disquieting: the emphasis on political indoctrination in schools, the ignorance of conditions outside Russia, the artificial sense of political unity, the pride in the achievements of the Soviet system which blinds the people to the possibility that other countries have made equally outstanding progress in their own way or have views which may be right, are just some of these.

But visitors can more easily understand the background to these and how they are so often an inevitable result of the political system and processes of thought to which the Soviet people have become accustomed. We were able to put our different views to our hosts and discuss them frankly, although we usually had to agree to differ. I came back feeling more than ever that, in spite of opposing ideologies, there are many similarities and points of contact between the Soviet and British peoples and that, in spite of the difficulties, visits and exchanges between the two countries ought to be encouraged.

Note: After the death of Stalin in March 1953 and the subsequent elimination of his chief of police (and putative successor) Lavrenti Beria the first of many "thaws" in the cold war soon set in. Under first Georgi Malenkov and then, from 1954 onwards, under Marshal Bulganin and - as, increasingly, the senior partner - Nikita Khrushchev the Soviet Union seemed to be seeking peace (and even friendship) rather than confrontation. The new atmosphere of goodwill was at its peak in 1955 when the first of many "summit" conferences took place at Geneva (setting a pattern for later such conferences it agreed to go on talking, but on little else). Like so many later "thaws" it all ended in tears - the suppression of the Hungarian revolution in November 1956 brought the cold war back with a vengeance. But how pleasant the atmosphere had seemed while it lasted!

Schweitzer at the Royal Festival Hall.

(December 1955)

The girls in a London secondary modern school were recently asked to write a short paragraph about people they would like to meet. They ranged from Wilfred Pickles and Norman Hartnell to Queen Salote and Carl Dolmetsch, with occasional aspirations in the directions of conversations with Dan Archer and Dan Dare.

My own choice would have been unhesitatingly Albert Schweitzer - and it almost happened.

On 18th October the Philharmonia Orchestra under one of the greatest of the younger conductors, von Karajan, gave a farewell concert at the Royal Festival Hall before leaving for America, and Schweitzer and a few friends were present in one of the boxes. It was rumoured that he might be persuaded to try the organ after the concert, and when the hall had at last been cleared of the enthusiastic audience there remained a small, expectant group of music critics, photographers and staff.

Soon the tall, slightly bowed figure with the familiar mass of grey hair and heavy moustache appeared on the platform, wearing a black suit made long ago (and not very well made either) by some Continental tailor. He was accompanied by Ralph Downes, eager to demonstrate the new organ, and, in spite of his eighty years, Schweitzer nimbly scrambled over the partition in front of the organ and sat at the console.

There followed a string of quick-fire questions in German about the instrument, all in a strong resonant voice which easily carried halfway across the hall. Then a series of tentative minor chords, modulating, building up, exploring the great resources of the instrument. More questions followed, more chords, and the tiny audience somehow grew as attendants and stewards discreetly crept into the empty hall, and von Karajan himself tip-toed in and leaned across the console watching the master intently, and occasionally throwing in a smiling interjection in German.

At last came the glories of Bach's own most famous show-piece, the *Toccata in D minor*, obviously designed by the composer for displaying the possibilities of a large instrument. It was played simply and straightforwardly at a moderate tempo, with the player's heavy outdoor shoes occasionally bungling a pedal note by way of encouragement to lesser mortals whose toes often touch wrong notes.

Then, without a pause, the familiar notes of the short chorale prelude on the tune known to English ears as *O Sacred Head*, which Schweitzer himself has pointed out oddly started life as a secular love-song *A dainty maid disturbs my mind*.

A few more questions, a word of praise for the 'beautiful organ,' and the music was at an end. Schweitzer, who dislikes concert organs and has refused three hundred invitations to give recitals whilst in this country, had played Bach on the Festival Hall organ.

Going down in the lift afterwards, he did not seem in the least tired after his long day, and made a jocular remark about catching the last train. At the artists' entrance there was a little crowd of young people hoping for von Karajan's autograph. Schweitzer was immediately recognised and besieged instead, but he smilingly fought his way through amid a spontaneous outburst of applause to the Rolls-Royce which someone had thoughtfully and appropriately provided.

Next day he went to the Palace and Downing Street, but it is certain that he could not have had a more appreciative and sympathetic audience. Someone commented to one of the staff at the Hall on his being kept late at work. 'That's all right,' he replied, 'I'd stay here all night for him.'

Note: Dr Albert Schweitzer (1875-1965) first achieved fame as a musician, bringing a rare perception to his interpretation of Bach's music. Later, he attained even more widespread renown for his work as a mission doctor in Africa: his hospital at Lambaréné in Gabon was established in 1913 and was for long a centre of light and civilisation (albeit with somewhat authoritarian overtones) as well as of healing in a particularly deprived part of Africa. In his later years honours showered down upon Schweitzer: in the year of this article he became a member of the Order of Merit.

'Dull would he be of soul . . .'

(November 1956)

Wordsworth was, naturally, a sentimentalist. If he had spent many years working at County Hall, left it to work for another authority and then, after a lapse of eight years, found himself again marching up its steps as a visitor, I feel sure his muse would have inspired an ode, or at least a sonnet, reeking of nostalgia and tear-jerking in its emotion.

I found myself in such circumstances recently. I don't think I am imbued with an over-generous streak of sentimentality but I confess to some slight emotion akin to the wanderer's return as I resisted an impulse to fly up the stairs. What did it matter if the signing-on book was being removed? For years I had been one of the combatants in a continuous, many-cornered struggle to get to sign the book; for years I had fought adversaries in the form of the vagaries of London's transport, the inclemency of the English climate, my own disinclination to arrive early and the supererogatory zeal of various messengers; to-day it didn't matter.

The suspicious glare of the liftman was wasted on me. I stalked into the cage as if I owned the joint and demanded the required floor firmly, albeit politely. He could wait for the other imagined passengers who were only halfway across Westminster Bridge - I didn't care.

What are the ingredients of the peculiar smell of County Hall? In my days we blamed part of it on to the nearby slums but to-day's vista of over-planned gardens and promenade vitiate such a theory. Stale tobacco smoke, the fustiness of unconsulted files, the olfactory effect, real or imagained, of rows of similar offices in rows of similar corridors - all these remain. A rose by any other name - but I'm getting my poets mixed.

The aroma, the atmosphere, so well known to me and almost a part of me many years ago, flowed over me but left me unmoved. Perhaps my soul *is* dull . . .

Some of my former colleagues were seated just as I had left them years ago. One was as busy as ever, surrounded by drafts, reports, piles of in, out, pending and typing. Another, who had never been quite so busy, was washing; it was a little too early, even for him, for the pre-lunch wash and, I thought, a little to late for the post-arrival wash; perhaps he had been disturbing some files.

The wheels of County Hall were grinding, as they did of yore and as they will be when all my memories have faded. It was pleasant to sink once again for a brief spell into that aura of nonchalant impersonality. it was pleasant to meet old friends once again. But the real thrill of my visit was the greeting of a cleaner, forgotten I am afraid by me, who looked up from her work as I passed and called ''Ello, ducks, are you coming back again?' That, at least, boosted my ego even if it didn't burnish my soul.

Unto Us a Child.

(December 1956)

(A house-mother in the Children's department describes how she and the seven children whom she cares for will spend their Christmas. They live in what is known as a 'small family home' - that is, a modern, four-bedroom house, indistinguishable externally from its neighbours, which are 'higher-income group' property on an out-county housing estate.)

The spirit of Christmas begins to invade our house at the beginning of December. 'Our house' contains seven children, whose ages range from 7 to 14 - three boys and four girls. I live with them. To the Council and to the Staff Association I am known as a house-mother, but to the children I am 'Auntie'.

For five of the children this will be our fourth Christmas together. Previously they had been living in a much bigger establishment, and when they came to me it was their first experience of living as a real family - and how they love it. At first it took them quite a time to get used to the idea of calling me 'Auntie' - they would keep calling me 'Miss'.

The two younger children spent their first few years in a residential nursery for the under-fives. They came here two years ago to join their brother and sister. The Council always tries to keep a family together if it is at all possible.

It is interesting to watch their educational advancement, how well some of them can read, while others are not so quick but are clever with their hands, are good at drawing, and show plenty of imagination. Th eldest girl has passed an examination to stay at school for an extra year. She is taking an extended course in shorthand, typewriting and commercial subjects, and seems to be progressing very well.

Valerie, who is now ten years old, is a very different child from what she was when she came. Now she is full of confidence. She converses sensibly and is very fond of history. She has told me a lot about the Romans which I had quite forgotten. Brenda, almost the same age, is a dreamer, but I expect she will get on. She has very definite ideas about dress, and makes the most amazing outfits for the dolls. Brian, who is almost eleven, is now quite a good reader. I think the television has helped him a lot - the children's programmes are much enjoyed.

For weeks before Christmas the children are busy making paper chains and decorations, Christmas cards and calendars. I pretend to take no notice of the whispered consultations and collections of pennies from their weekly pocket money, which I know will result in a parcel on my plate at breakfast on Christmas Day, for myself and my family.

I should explain that I hope Christmas will be a family party for my own folk as well as my charges. I am a widow with four grown-up children (twin sons in the Royal Navy and two married daughters), and they usually manage to be here with us, so the party is complete.

We have a Christmas tree, which will bear a present for each of them, provided by me or my daughters. On Christmas Eve seven socks are carefully hung up; they will be filled with novelties of all kinds, and the odd spaces stuffed with nuts and fruit. The Council makes an allowance for me to buy each child a present. They open these at breakfast-time on Christmas Day, with other presents from my own family and friends, and any from the adopted aunties of the children. In our house four of the children have adopted aunts.

One of the children's special delights at Christmas is the wearing of new clothing. Buying their clothes is a thing I enjoy too. The girls have a new dress, and perhaps a new pretty apron; the boys have new shirts and perhaps a new tie. One of their favourites is a tie gaily patterned with Martians or cowboys.

After all the excitement of receiving presents on Christmas morning the children enjoy themselves until dinner-time, when we have the traditional Christmas dinner and cheer the pudding in and listen to the Royal broadcast. We play quiet games until tea-time, but after that we really let ourselves go. I have my own piano and one of my sons plays the songs and tunes that the children ask for. They really enjoy that. Then we have games with prizes and forfeits - always a favourite with the children. Sometimes the children act their own little Nativity play before the grown-ups.

Bed-time comes all to soon for them, but they console themselves with the thought that they have a visit to the circus in store, and perhaps a visit to the local theatre to see a pantomime during the week. Also on New Year's Eve they are all invited to a children's party, organised by a social club of which I am a member. So, although my own children are now adult, I can still re-capture the spirit of Christmas with other people's children.

Whitsun Up the River - New Style.

D. A. J. Searle brings the Harding story up to date

(January 1957)

The tradition that was started some sixty years ago by the five young gentlemen (or chaps) of the Statistical department was re-established in 1952, and every year since a group has left County Hall on the Friday night of Whitsun week-end for a similar purpose and destination. But the years have left their mark. The scope has broadened; the men, no longer gentlemen, are drawn from many departments; they bring their wives; and the wives bring their children.

On Friday 18 May 1956 eleven men, eight women, two children (one fifteen months and one three years) and a dog departed from London for four days' camping and boating on the River Thames. Single tickets to Wargrave, a distance roughly comparable with that to Reading, were 5s 3d, comparing much too favourably with the 3s paid by our fellow employees of 1898. I can only assume, and it is a reasonable assumption in view of their lavish tipping (1956 - nil) and luxurious method of transport to Paddington (1956 - rush hour tube at 8d each, plus 4d for the dog), that they travelled 'first'.

We hired four camping punts for £18 and borrowed two others from private owners. A large tent was hired beforehand for £1. Shortly before sunset on a fine night that promised a fine week-end, the six punts pushed through

Shiplake Lock and up a river quietened by the dusk to the island of Hallsmead Ait. Two hours later all was silent; the flames had left the fire and a chilly mist was fast closing over the first camp of the week-end.

The records and accounts of this week-end, although lengthy and detailed, prove beyond doubt that, although five departments were represented, Comptroller's was not. There is no trace of an auditor's pencil and not even a check on the mathematics. The documents providing evidence of expenditure are confined to three receipts and two departmental reminders requiring payment of a private trunk call to Maidenhead. This could indicate a decline in efficiency or alternatively a growing trust in one's fellow man. The grouping of expenditure however remains unchanged from that adopted in 1898.

The food section (drink absent by reason of cost, not temperance) is divided into goods purchased beforehand and those acquired on the journey downriver to Maidenhead. Over half a hundredweight of vegetables and fruit (potatoes, a bad year, 5d a lb), 57 tins of foodstuffs, a mass of dairy produce (including 4 dozen eggs 15s 6d and 20 pints of milk) and a formidable list of general food items, varying from a $2^1/2$ lb jar of salad cream to 20 kippers, were consumed. The continental tastes of the organizer at least can be inferred from such items as 6 tins of frankfurters, 2 tins of sauerkraut, 4 lb of spaghetti and 1 oz of paprika (use unknown). Luxurious good like tinned salmon and Devonshire cream, probably considered essential in 1898, do not feature in the 1956 list, and cigarette smokers, for obvious reasons, were left to fend for themselves.

The total cost of the week-end, excluding fares, was £38 15s 8$^1/2$d. Taking the fares into account the total cost per head was £2 13s 9d (children and dog thrown in), and of this 18s 9d was paid for food, an increase of only 5s 8d over the cost in 1898. Before there is a general rush by the Official Side to use this information to resist future wage claims, I should point out that, by comparison, we virtually starved. If, for instance, we had purchased 30 lb of ham (9$^1/4$ lb was purchased for 5 people in 1898) and had excluded *all* the meat that was in fact bought, the net increase in cost would have been about 10s per head. And that is only one item - imagine the cost of 10 lb of ox tongue or 8 lb of spiced beef, not to mention 4 bottles of Jameson's whiskey.

Accounts, even late Victorian ones, must inevitably seem empty and cold - solely the mechanics of a holiday. The substance and heart that make it what it is and provided the reasons why people do it are missing. We know nothing of what the five young gentlemen discussed (promotion?) or sang (Samuel Hall?) round the fires that they must have built, or who fell in the river and how many times. An incident always occurs which makes the holiday unique.

I remember the occasion when a tin labelled sauerkraut proved to be full of red plums - a fact not altogether displeasing to some. It was a mystifying circumstance, which became more mystifying two days later when a tin of plums was opened to disclose sauerkraut. On our return the mystery was explained as a practical joke by the staff of the office in which the tins had been kept. They were surprised to learn that we had only discovered the switch with the plums and sauerkraut. Other labels had been changed. In fact they had spent two or three days thinking up which changes were likely to prove the most catastrophic. It was then realised that Friday night's stew must have contained the two tins of orange juice destined for Saturday's breakfast, and that to two tins of orange juice considered bad and discarded the following morning were, in fact, soup. It was, perhaps, fortunate that the tins were of so many different sizes that the labels did not lend themselves to change, otherwise this would have been the most chaotic week-end ever spent on the river and relations in that particular office would never again have been restored to that cordiality of which chief officers are so prone to speak, to so doubting an audience on their annual Christmas visits to sections.

The river has changed a great deal in the last sixty years. The great houses still stand in the Goring Gap and high on other fringes of the Chiltern Hills but few to-day are used for what they were then. Their eighteenth-century landscapes, so carefully planned and planted, are often blotted and unbalanced by bungalow sprawl and caravan sites. Bungalows sometimes weather into the landscape but nothing is more obtrusive or ugly than caravans. The urban spread of London has swallowed Richmond and Kingston and is now filling in the pre-war framework that ran out beyond Staines. As the cab has been replaced by the taxi so the punt and the skiff are rapidly giving way to the cruiser and the launch. In 1957 the lock gates at Mapledurham and Cookham will be operated by electricity and the lock-keeper will sit in a glass cabin pressing buttons. All are aspects of progress that the five young men of the Statistical department could hardly have foreseen and would most certainly have deplored.

But in the upper reaches the river is much as it was, and there one can push into still backwaters, to break the unbroken surface of water and to linger, oblivious to the passage of time and to the roar of the traffic on the arterial Thames nearby.

As Others See Us.

An Open Letter from a Member of the Council

(April 1957)

As a member of the London County Council it is one of my (self-imposed) duties to read *London Town*.

I do this because I think that, as an employer, I ought to know what an important section of the Council's staff (about one-sixth of the total) think and say about their employers. I have studied this for some time and now (if the Editor allows) it is my turn to say what I think of the staff.

If any of my readers have the idea that what 'the Council' thinks ought not to be published, I can only say that they have the mentality of the ostrich. I know that when I am in a dispute I want to hear all about my opponent's case: otherwise how can I try to expose its fallacies and correct his errors?

Not that I have any authority to speak for 'the Council'. I am not a member of the Establishment Committee. But I have as much right as another to speak as a rank-and-file councillor. My point of view, you know, added to those of my fellow-members, has its influence in determining Council policy and its staff relationships.

We expect a clear case

It is in relationships with others, it seems to me, that most of you who write in *London Town* lack something. You do not write in way that will convince us councillors - or indeed one another. You assume that the justice of your case is obvious. Now we members are accustomed to studying detailed, closely reasoned reports by officers; we naturally expect a clear case to be made for more staff or better pay. I can assure you that questions which members raise in committee are usually enquiries whether the rise is enough: but we have to be convinced, not just told that it is so. In your *London Town* letters you seem to assume that, because you think your wages are the most essential thing in life, the Council must think so too and not worry about getting the job done. You imply that the Council must be both stupid and malicious to refuse your demands.

Have you never had demands made on you - for higher trade union contributions, for instance, or higher rates or more rent? If so, did you at once see how right it was that you should pay more or did you want a full explanation, comparisons with what other people pay, and so on? If you are wise, you certainly asked for these things before you paid up.

Not the only pebbles

And the Council needs persuasion too. You are not the only pebbles on the beach, you know. Perhaps you ought to be paid more, but so ought a lot of othe people we employ; and we ought to be spending more on many other important objects too. Councillors are elected to maintain and improve London's social services. They have a duty to the electors to see that their money is spent to the best advantage. What the Council does, too, is supervised and to some extent controlled by the national government. We know that staff ought to be treated fairly, but substantial salary claims must be weighed against the Council's over-all responsibilities. Perhaps you do not agree: perhaps you think that your personal pocket matters more than anything else on God's earth. That indeed is the impression one gets from reading the correspondence columns of *London Town*. And it is not a pleasant impression. It suggests a narrow, materialistic, egotistical approach and it fails to endear you to the ordinary Council member. This is unfortunate, for members normally have confidence in and respect for their officers. The impression made by officers in committee work and in managing departments and divisions is in sharp contradiction with the impression created by reports and letters in *London Town*.

It is not always easy to follow your reasoning - when you deign to use any. Sometimes you imply, in an indignant letter to the Editor, that because A has had a rise B ought to have one too. How simple-minded! Don't you first have to prove that B's job is as good as A's? I should have thought so. No one expects you to shout with glee at every little betterment your Association fixes up with the Council, but all I ever see is a string of complaints that what has been got is not enough: I chortle, too, when I read those fundamentalists who say they'd have no bread rather than half a loaf.

Why did you join the Council?

Why don't you write more often about your own achievements - the schools, the houses, and the host of material and cultural improvements which this Council is making for Londoners? Why did you join the London County Council? Why do members give so much time to work that brings neither prestige nor financial reward? Surely because we all care deeply for London and the contribution we can make to our great city. It's a partnership and we should all be proud of what has been accomplished but always seeking for new ideas and improvements. *London Town* is an ably produced journal; its quality could be enhanced if architects and engineers, planners and educationalists, even lawyers and accountants, contributed bright material about their work. The Council has a vast organization: few of us know much of what goes on outside our narrow ken. Let *London Town* tell London!

I write this candidly, but as a friend and an enthusiastic trade unionist of many years' standing. What odd things you quarrel about - petty economies in your union office, whether to spend a few pence a head a year on teaching your members the elements of Association affairs (which they obviously *need!*), and then you bicker among yourselves about whose fault was your recent ill-luck at arbitration. Some of you seem to revel in disunity in your own ranks. In my union we stand together.

Perhaps the funniest thing was a letter one of you wrote accusing the others of being 'yellow-bellied' in negotiations with the Council. Colleagues of mine who have experience of negotiations from our side tell me that this is the most comical perversion of the facts. What induces you, not content with abuse of your colleagues, to invent offences of which they have not been guilty?

So altogether, you see, I haven't a high opinion of you - AS YOU REVEAL YOURSELVES IN YOUR JOURNAL. I am writing in my most didactic vein; for I only want to do you good. Your collective abilities are, I know, very high and most of those I know personally deserve well of any employer. I expect my criticisms are much too general and I know that most of you are more level-headed and understanding than the writers I have castigated. All I ask is: can you not, in your publicity, show more imagination, an aptitude to understand other people's problems, and more charity with one another?

Note: This and the subsequent contribution represent an example (all too rare, perhaps) of an attempt at reasonable dialogue between employers and employees at a time when Council/staff relations had become somewhat embittered.

The Member Answered.

To a Member of the Council

(May 1957)

May I, Sir, as a rank-and-file member of the Staff Association and, I trust, one of the more 'level-headed and understanding', take the liberty of answering in equally forthright terms your thought-provoking letter in the April issue of *London Town*.

First may I say that I appreciate the protocol that requires you to preserve your anonymity, and I ask you to believe that there are equally pressing reasons why I should remain nameless.

Thank you, Sir, for the compliments you paid as well as for your criticisms. Will you excuse my quoting your phraseology in answering some of the latter.

First of all, 'we assume that the justice of our case is obvious' and 'we do not write in a way which will convince you Councillors'. You 'expect a clear case to be made'. What is our case? Why is it that it appears to you that 'our personal pocket matters more than anything on God's earth'?

We are not alone in our complaint. We are only a small part of an important section of the community who feel that they have suffered far more than their fair share from the prolonged period of currency debasement in recent years (I eschew the use of the popular and convenient euphemism 'inflation'). This financial process is now, as it has always been through the centuries, a purely fraudulent one in its effect, has hit hardest those on fixed incomes, those with pensions or money savings and those with money owed to them on long-term contracts of any kind. People in career jobs with what they thought was a guaranteed future, modest perhaps but secure, find themselves cheated of their hopes. A senior officer who has made reasonable progress over many years now finds himself with the standard of living equivalent to that of an officer before the war *three grades below* his present one. This is factual. It has occurred during the period when recovery from the effects of war has largely been made, when the national economy is expanding and when the doubling of the standard of living of the nation in the next 25 years is held out as more than a possibility.

We have lost not only our relative position in the community - we could not expect to retain that when other sections needed so much to bring them up to a proper standard - but also about 50 per cent of our absolute standard; and this in a time of increasing prosperity. Furthermore, while the 'striking classes', to use a term which connotes a broad division in the social structure, are doing more than to insist that the real value of their remuneration shall be maintained and are pressing by *force majeure* for a share in the increasing total product of the nation, the 'non-striking' classes are not even able to maintain their present much deteriorated position.

Struggling up a down escalator

It is not surprising if they are feeling bitter and despondent. What incentive is there in struggling to ascend the staircase only to find that it is a descending escalator? A continuance of this process is apparently to be our lot for ever! In these circumstances it is not be wondered at if we tend to direct our resentment to some personal object and sometimes vent our spleen unfairly on our employers. Perhaps we have sometimes yielded to the temptation to criticize the Council too harshly. After all they are not responsible for the monetary system! They have in my own view been reasonably just towards the staff in comparison with other employers in the same position, i.e. employers who have not been *forced* to make concessions to their employees. It is a truism that nobody pays more for an article than he must and no employer pays his employees more than he is obliged to. Possibly all that we can really complain of is that, whereas the Council once regarded its staff as *corps d'élite*, to be paid and treated as such, the present trend appears to be to abandon that position. If this is a fact, it is clearly the Council's own affair. But is is not surprising that the staff are aware of and feel resentful about it. We still have some *esprit de corps*.

Why has the present position come about? Surely there is one outstanding reason. It is because we are not and never have been organised for active defence of our standards. Why not? Is it because we are too reasonable, responsible and restrained, because of our gentle traditions, or is it because we have no fire in our bellies? Most likely it is something of each.

We see no end to it

I venture to say, Sir, that some of the pettiness, bickering and apparent disunity arises from the deep *malaise* which undoubtedly exists as a result of frustration from continuing injustice. We have taken serious knocks, we continue to take them and we see no end to the process. Incidentally it comes as a surprise, although I suppose it must be accepted from an 'enthusiastic trade unionist of many years' standing', that our pettiness and bickering compares unfavourably with that which is to be found in trade union affairs generally.

You ask, Sir, 'Why did you join the Council?'. The honest answer is, of course, 'To earn a living'. To many of us there may have been the incidental appeal of work connected with social service. But let us not pretend that the reason was anything but financial. Nevertheless, most of the staff who have made their way in the service are dedicated people who couldn't acquit themselves better even if they were unpaid devotees of public service for its own sake. Far from there being any falling away from their high concept of duty while their standards were being so severely reduced, in fact during that same period many additional burdens and complexities have been placed upon them, so that they are probably now giving far more to their jobs than ever before. Understandably, the staff feel they are being penalized for their virtues!

In conclusion, this thought occurs to me. I trust you will not think it discourteous of me, Sir, to express it. I cannot help wondering whether you as a trade unionist would have greater respect for us if we, the staff of the L.C.C., were more united in purpose and determined in action; if we closed our ranks and stood shoulder to shoulder (to use some of the heroic terms so beloved of trade union leaders); if, in fact, we exchanged our attitude of reasonableness, responsibility and restraint for one of rancour and marshalled our latent power as skilled organizers and administrators to join the *striking classes*.

Guildford to Gomshall.

(November 1958)

Mr V. W. A. Conn of the Architect's department submitted the winning essay in the Sir James Bird Cup Competition. Dr. L. W. H. Payling, Inspector in the Education Officer's department, who adjudicated, found it 'almost impossible' to decide whether Mr Conn or Mr David G. Moore of the Comptroller's department should receive the Cup, and we have pleasure in printing both essays.

'Hayfoot — Strawfoot'

V. W. A. Conn

On another occasion Guildford would have been a pleasant town to linger in, but now we hurried through, impatient to be on our way. There is a strong element of compulsion in these walks; the set route to be read and followed like a game played with board and counters; the distance to be covered in time for tea at the other end and the shaming possibility of not keeping up with the others without too much visible effort; the ever-present threat of the essay, half resented like a school holiday task, a token retribution for an afternoon of freedom; but also, always, there is the pull of open countryside, the recurring longing for the sight, sounds, smell, the very taste of the country.

We plugged away up the steepness of Pewley Hill between a new outcrop of suburbia, squandering our initial energies on hard pavements, to come out on to high heathland with a valley on our right. A toposcope, a sundial-like object, pointed to distant hill features, and the slight assonance in word association brought the memory that there lay the country over which H. G. Wells's Martians had stalked.

Our path now sloped downhill but gratitude was tempered by the certainty that we should soon be climbing again. The sun was pleasantly hot, the air humid above earth dank from recent rainfall. The rough track went between fields - pasture - of uncut clover thick with charlock - then the lush green of early wheat. We were busy identifying wildflowers for future mention, campion, vetch, ragged robin, veronica, speedwell and herb robert.

A short stretch of woodland, a hot half-mile uphill and we flopped down outside the pilgrims' church of St. Martha-on-the-Hill. From a booklet I learned that the compact little church had been rebuilt in 1848, the previous building having been associated with Bunyan's *Pilgrim's Progress*. Evidence pointed to a long record of pagan rites and heathen ceremonies on this hill, the site being on the ancient east-west road through southern Britain, its origin far back into pre-history.

We sank footdeep, slithering in thick sand down the further side of the hill and crossing with some trepidation a field in which a black bull herded his harem of cows, some with calves, entered a huge field where two tractors were carting cut hay. I felt very much the intruding, idling townsman as we filed somewhat sheepishly past men building a rick. Then, a tangled steep descent, a grassy path lined with elms and into Weston Wood of great beeches where we became lost among great banks of purple rhododendrons.

We did not catch up with the others until along the riverside path by the Tillingbourne which led through meadow and parkland into the village of Shere. Old colour-washed, timbered cottages, gardens full with English country flowers, the charming old bridge, the river with its line of willows, narrow streets, the White Horse Inn, the grey church with Norman tower, all add to make Shere a strong candidate for Surrey's prettiest village contest.

I was more than ready for my tea by this time, but there was another mile by footpaths to Gomshall before, by the river, in the garden of the Compasses Inn, we came to rest. Cress sandwiches, home-made jam and cakes did not linger on the tables for long, and thirst was at last assuaged by delicious cups of tea.

The Small Eye

David G. Moore

I did not count how many we were as we set out from Guildford one sunny afternoon in June, but the straggling line we formed looked uncommonly odd. For within it were experienced-looking hikers, brandishing notebooks, and others (like myself) with the air of office fugitives.

We left Guildford by turning off the High Street through an impressive portico. It seemed we wished to put the town behind us as quickly as we could. But no one, except the young, rushes headlong up steep hills, and Pewley Hill which faced us was uncomfortably steep. The climb took us past a school where children careered madly through their playtime oblivious to the heat.

Quite suddenly, after glancing behind to see the town of Guildford compact and tidily roofed so far below us. the steep climb was over and there was no sound except our own. The countryside was with us.

What was there to see from now until we stopped? Much, no doubt, for him who enjoys recognising a special variety of flower or weed, tree or shrub, soil or manure. What can a confirmed city-dweller say beyond acknowledging a particular beauty which has given him pleasure? I know what I remember most, and if the impressions are fleeting it is simply because I am a metropolitan creature who has not yet, perhaps, discovered how to stand and stare.

I recall a girl on horseback, glimpsed for a moment a quarter mile away from and below us. There was the tiring trek up a path so thick with trees that we were robbed of sun: it led to a tiny Norman church, St. Martha's, standing alone in its own little graveyard. Some of us went in. The verger intoned a potted history of the church and thought we might like to sign the visitors' book. I had strange thoughts. Do they still bury people up here? And if they do, how do they get the coffins up that hill without a road? And is Surrey all hills, and do we never walk down them?

We passed along narrow tracks where our shoes sank into sand; we passed beside a copse. Sometimes we fought the outstretched arms of bushes along our path. A field, with cows, had to be negotiated, and one of the cows turned out to be a bull. Happily he remained docile, but it was good to pass through the gate at the other end. Men were at work elsewhere with tractor and pitchfork; there was a clean smell to the air, but, more to the point, were those pitchforks friendly? We were, after all, tramping through their field. Then there was the interlude when half of us lost the others. We who strayed off course had for reward an enchanted winding path of tall, rich and stunning rhododendron trees.

We found ourselves at Shere, a charming village where at that moment the only apparent activity was centred in a 'tea shoppe'. So they do still exist: this one is even called 'Lavender Ladye'! On we went, managing to resist, unlike some of our number, the comfort of ice cream from the lavender ladye. At last, with tiredness in the muscles, sand in the shoes, and surprises in the turn-ups, we reached a welcome inn at Gomshall. Teas was spread out on tables on the lawn beside the quietly trickling waters of the Tillingbourne.

The walk was done with and I was glad. Yet I have a feeling that I shall walk again - perhaps not so far, for thirteen stone is a lot to carry, but I hope with equal pleasure.

Everyday Life in 1909.

Ian Wilson
(April 1959)

The time, May 1909; the city London. The lads in the streets were whistling *'Let's All Go Down the Strand'* and the tunes from *The Merry Widow.* The buses that wove around Eros were white, yellow, blue and green as well as red; motor cars mingled with horse-drawn traffic; a new model automobile, just shown at an exhibition, had outside seats built up on the roof and reached by a little ladder, like a stage-coach. People were talking of the 'car problem' but said it was less acute here than in America. In Brooklyn, 'because of the ever-increasing speed of public vehicles and the desire of drivers to stop as infrequently as possible' the high school authorities had their girls taught in the school gymnasium how best to board and descend from moving tramcars; the London papers carried a picture of the girls practising, apparently clad in calf-length bloomers.

The music hall was in its hey-day. It held sway at the Old Vic early in May, with a special talent competition for artists who had never played a full week in the West End. That Christmas *Peter Pan* had been revived for the fourth time; Mrs Patrick Campbell was at the New playing two short pieces, one of them *Deirdre* by W. B. Yeats; Marie Lohr, though at 18 much too young for the part, was enjoying a triumph as Lady Teazle in *School for Scandal*; Marie Dressler (already described as a 'big, kindly, clever woman') had arrived as a new actress-manager at the Aldwych to put on a musical called *Little Mena.* The ban which for over thirty years had stopped *Samson and Delilah* from being staged had at last been lifted - at the request of Queen Alexandra, so it was said - and it was mounted at Covent Garden in brilliant style.

At home they made their own amusements. Whist drives were the new craze in suburbia; 'they have taken the place in public estimation of the matrimonial agency', wrote one newspaper. The musical evening was the key to social success and if you were no pianist there was the pianola, much extolled in advertisements.

Edward VII had just come back from a rest cure at Hove, followed by a trip to the Mediterranean with his Queen in the royal yacht. He still led a glittering society in the fashionable round - the Derby, Henley, the opera - but he was 68 now and not in good health (he had little more than a year to live). At the other end of the social scale there was an extreme of poverty London no longer knows. Early in 1909 the *Illustrated London News* printed a picture of Shepherds Bush Green under the caption 'A scene of human tragedy enacted every night'. It showed groups of down-and-outs, men and women, seeking shelter there - a

A scene in London, 1909.

scene, said the paper, which could not be paralleled anywhere in the world. 'On the green huddle the flotsam and jetsam of London who have drifted from Hyde Park and elsewhere before the "move-on" of the police . . . Many - and it is believed that the L.C.C. are in sympathy with them - argue that the green should be shut after dark: others protest against the cost of this plan and the interference with ancient rights.' The cost was the cost of the extra workhouse accommodation.

The middle classes were deeply disturbed, but at a suddenly uncertain future rather than at the social conditions. Early that year revelations of the growing German naval strength had shocked the country. The Conservative-Unionist Opposition were clamouring for a bigger army, urgent military preparations, more British Dreadnoughts. The Dreadnought battle-cruiser, the first all-big-gun ship, had made all existing navies out of date and the powers were competing feverishly to assemble new fleets. The Germans reputedly had fourteen ships projected. The Admiralty wished to increase the British building programme for 1909 from four battle cruisers to six; the Opposition called this hopelessly inadequate and wanted eight laid down at once. In March they coined the famous slogan: 'We want eight and we won't wait.'

The quickly developing flying-machine was another threat, half-discerned. In December 1908 (on the same day that the L.C.C. staff held their first mass meeting - at Birkbeck College) Wilbur Wright at Le Mans had broken all previous records in mechanical flight. He remained in the air for close on two hours, 'soared to a height of 400 feet', and covered nearly a hundred miles. The *Pall Mall Gazette* wrote: 'After such a performance as that it is impossible to set any limit to the possibilities of the aeroplane in the future . . . Already Berlin and Chicago are forming passenger airship companies and there is talk of building four great airships for pleasure trips from Paris. At this rate, as Lord Wemyss said recently, "we shall all be flying soon".' A German military expert, Rudolf Martin, argued that Germany could build 50,000 flying machines and land 100,000 men on the Kent coast in half-an-hour. This was derided as 'futile' in the *I.L.N.* on the ground that it would be impossible to find landing room in Kent for so many machines. The paper added 'The lecture has been received as a welcome contribution to the gaiety of nations', but the irony was unconvincing.

There is a sense, in May 1909, of being on the eve of an explosion. A growing violence is in the air, in the threats between nations, in the class antagonisms, in the agitation and demonstrations. Patience was running thin; the Irish were tired of waiting for home rule, the suffragettes tired of waiting for the vote. Even the temperance campaign was violent. Mrs Carrie Nation, who arrived from America to conduct an agitation against the evils of drink, had won fame as a 'saloon smasher'. Her usual method was to enter a bar and smash everything within reach with a hatchet. She landed in Glasgow where she was met with a hostile crowd and had to take refuge, to her chagrin, in a hotel bar. The militant suffragettes were constantly in the news. They broke windows and tied themselves to statues in Westminster. One of them, having interrupted Lloyd George at an Albert Hall meeting, produced a horse-whip with which she belaboured the stewards until 'she was conquered and removed'. Another ascended in a dirigible balloon, armed with handbills and a megaphone, with the object of travelling above the route of the royal procession when Parliament was reopened; but it was a cloudy day and the balloon was almost invisible. The main labour disputes were in the coal-fields, where there were strikes against non-union and blackleg labour. Real wages were falling steadily. There was labour unrest in Paris too and an interesting development was noted; 'for the first time an alliance was made between workmen and lower civil servants.'

And in May 1909 yet another conflict was foreshadowed - that between Lords and Commons. At the end of April Lloyd George had introduced his Budget. It put income tax up from 1s to 1s 2d and created a super-tax for incomes over £5,000 a year; it imposed a new tax on motor cars and petrol; it increased the duty on spirits and tobacco (cigarettes remained at ten for $2^1/_2$d but the saloon bar price of a whisky went up to 6d). Above all it taxed land values and this made it certain that the Lords would oppose it. In the end, after months of debate, they rejected the Budget entirely; a long and bitter constitutional struggle followed, culminating in the Parliament Act, 1911, and severe curtailment of the Lords' power to amend legislation.

The Cabinet which fought this battle appears an outstanding one to us. It was led by Asquith (Balfour led the Opposition); Lloyd George was Chancellor, Churchill was at the Board of Trade, Sir Edward Grey Foreign Secretary, Haldane Secretary for War and John Burns President of the Local Government Board.

The forty Labour Members of Parliament supported the Liberal Government; some said the tail was wagging the dog. The young Labour Party was a growing force; it was flexing its muscles, feeling its strength. The brilliant young Victor Grayson had recently won a famous by-election for Labour. In 1909 he addressed a big May Day demonstration and prophesied a great future for the party. 'In less than twelve years we shall have a group of 100 socialists, hallmarked and tried, in the House of Commons. Then there would be no need to abolish the House of Lords. It would emigrate to Fiji.'

In those early days of May the Budget debates pushed everything off the front page - even the Cup Final. This was won by Manchester United, who beat Bristol City 1-0 at the Crystal Palace. It was a disappointing game and there was some barracking. Crowd reaction in Scotland was rather sharper. Rangers and Celtic met in the Scottish Cup Final and played a draw; the replay also ended in a draw and the crowd shouted for extra time; when this was refused they rioted and set light to a grandstand. The cricket season opened in fine weather and Surrey scored 645 (Hobbs 205) in five hours and twenty minutes against Hampshire at the Oval. This was described as 'phenomenal scoring' - even by the standards of the day.

Also buried in the inside pages was an idea which had occurred to a speaker at a municipal banquet in West Ham. This was for the creation of a great new city, a single local authority for the whole of London north of the Thames and east of the Lea, to be called Eastminster. 'From West Ham to Dagenham and Woodford to North Woolwich, the area would be under a single government and a great gain in efficiency would result.' And as we look back over half-a-century, that is what we see: that our fathers and grandfathers were groping as we grope. grappling as we do with imperfectly perceived problems, problems the same as ours and yet different, parallel with ours and yet distant. And one fears that our solutions are likely to be no more adequate than theirs.

Hail, Hardship Post!

Wynne Bartlett of Clerk's is not dazzled by Washington

Wynne Bartlett
(October 1961)

We are becoming so accustomed to criticisms of the minor irritations of life in this country, as voiced by tourists from abroad, that we tend to accept them meekly and seldom answer back. Now, after a visit to the United States (admittedly a very short one), I feel less apologetic about such matters as our climate, the licensing laws and our complicated coinage system.

Let us compare the summer climates of London and Washington. We must admit that the weather in London is frequently inclement and always changeable but it is, surely, seldom downright unbearable. In summer the weather in Washington is certainly sunnier, but seems equally changeable and frequently becomes almost insupportable. The morning in June when we landed in the American capital the temperature was 92° F and the humidity about 96 per cent. Two days later, greatly to our relief, the temperature had dropped to 64°. After my return I read an article in *The Times* which complained that the temperature in Washington was again in the nineties and the humidity near to precipitation point; the writer referred to the fact that the British Embassy in Washington used to be regarded by the Foreign Office as a hardship post because of the climatic conditions.

It is true that in America they have air conditioning to mitigate the worst horrors of the weather, but this is not always an unmixed blessing, as anyone who has caught a chill after shivering under an icy blast from an air conditioner immediately after sizzling in the open air will testify. (We were, in fact, advised to take light wraps to wear indoors.) Moreover, except in the most modern buildings, the fans create a terrible racket. Indeed, after suffering half the night from a particularly noisy fan in one hotel, I decided it would be preferable (or anyway a change) to be stifled instead of deafened, so I turned the wretched thing off to get some sleep. Incidentally, if you think that London has more than its fair share of rain in the summer months, you may be surprised to learn that the average rainfall in Washington in June is nearly $3^1/2$ inches. I think it's just over 2 inches in London.

It seems unlikely that critcisms of our licensing laws can come from *American* tourists - I should hardly think they'd have the nerve. My first experience of their liquor laws was in a bar in Washington where, having ordered an innocent lager, I was politely told that it was illegal for women to be served at the bar! It would be quite all right, they said, if I would kindly step back a couple of paces and sit at a table. Well, licensing laws vary from state to state, so I do not suggest that this anti-feminist attitude is universal, but I was told by a sympathetic bystander that the District of Columbia was by no means unique. Obviously, the ghost of Prohibition still lingers in many states. In Washington the bar at the theatre dispenses nothing more inebriating than Coco-cola, while on Sundays spirits were unobtainable anywhere in the city. Philadelphia was completely 'dry' on Sundays until this summer.

While on the subject of drinks, we all know of the American predilection for icing everything: a London wine waiter once told me that he had refused to serve an American who wanted his Burgundy well iced. Everywhere you go you can see food temptingly displayed on mountains of crushed ice. So it really was rather disillusioning to be served a bottle of white wine which had been kept at room temperature and only put in the bucket at the time we ordered it. We had the choice between lingering over our meal for a couple of hours or drinking the wine unchilled. And if Americans think that warm beer is undrinkable I can only say that warm white wine is a lot nastier.

Americans are, as we know, very gadget-conscious and many of the labour-saving devices which now make life easier for us began life across the Atlantic. But there is one useful gadget, known as an egg-cup over here, which doesn't seem to have occurred to them yet. If you order boiled eggs at a restaurant the waiter will break them up for you and scoop them out into an ordinary cup. This unappetizing mash was enough to put me off boiled eggs for the duration of my visit. I was told that in some hotels you were expected to juggle with the hot egg in you hand, which must be very profitable for the dry cleaners.

Tea-drinking is becoming almost as popular in America as over here (though I was invited to one so-called tea-party where the only beverage served was iced raspberry juice - it was absolutely delicious). Tea-pots 'imported from Britain' were on sale in New York, but they were only used as holders for the ubiquitous tea-bag. When I attempted to advocate the superiority of the brew made with proper tea-leaves I met with a cold reception. 'What a lot of trouble it must be', they said, 'to empty out the tea-leaves and wash the tea-pot.' Never mind, the coffee was excellent, though it was necessary to restrain the waiters from bringing it with the first course at lunch or dinner. They seemed to find it eccentric to drink coffee only at the end of the meal. Generally speaking, the meals were gargantuan by our standards, and I wonder that tourists from America don't suffer from starvation when faced with the more modest portions served over here.

The next time an American visitor asks plaintively how we expect people to know that a coin marked 'Half crown' is worth two shillings and sixpence, I think I shall retaliate by asking how *he* expects visitors to know that the correct coin to proffer for an item marked '10 cents' is the one called a dime. I had always thought that the *dime* and *nickel* were slang terms, and I was therefore as surprised to find them engraved on the coins as I should be if the Royal Mint started turning our coins engraved *bob* and *tanner*.

Another trap for the unwary was that all banknotes were the same size, colour and design, regardless of denomination (at least up to 50 dollars, the largest I handled). The only difference is in the particular President portrayed on the note and the figure 1, 5, 10, etc., which denoted the value. I wondered how blind or very short-sighted people managed. Incidentally, the notes were very similar in size and colour to our own pound-notes, and at least one of our party found that he had given away pound-notes instead of dollars.

Before I went to America I imagined that, out-of-doors, the people spent most of their time sitting bumper-to-bumper in traffic jams in the cities, or tearing along magnificent highways at about 120 miles an hour in those enormous cars they all seem to own. The traffic jams and the magnificent highways were there all right, but I was surprised to find that, even on the six-lane turnpike roads that link up the large cities, the speed limit was 60 m.p.h. I travelled faster on an ordinary coach on the M1 recently than ever I did in America. I asked where it was possible to drive their powerful cars at full speed and was told, 'Legally, nowhere except on certain roads in the western desert'. Illegally, of course, many drivers ignore the speed limit and there is a constant battle between frustrated drivers and the police with their radar traps which they keep hiding in different places. As soon as the driver spots a speed trap he signals to oncoming drivers to warn them - the courtesy of the road, as our coach driver put it.

Pedestrians, outside built-up areas, are practically non-existent and I saw very few cyclists. We were warned that we could be fined on the spot if we crossed the road against the traffic lights, even if there wasn't a car in sight. To the jay-walking Londoner, who has perforce to dodge between the traffic because few of our traffic signals allow him time to cross, this may seem hard, but in America the traffic lights allow a pause for pedestrians (they have lights saying WALK and DON'T WALK) and I think their system is better.

Most of the things I have mentioned are small matters but I thought they might be of interest because they are so trivial that one never sees them mentioned elsewhere. Another article could be written on the more important aspects of American life, but I do not think a twelve-day visit qualifies me to write it. I must, however, conclude by saying that the most important impression I brought back was of the friendliness and hospitality I met wherever I went.

Section 3: LCC into GLC/ILEA

Introduction

By 1962 it had become clear that the LCC was to be abolished: but the shape of the authorities which were to succeed it only gradually emerged over the next few years. In the end it was "business as usual" for many, as the new GLC inherited substantial powers and responsibilities from the LCC (and other county authorities in respect of outer London), and the ILEA took over the LCC's education responsibilities. However, there were significant differences which came to be reflected in *London Town*. It was not quite the "mixture as before" in its columns from April 1965 onwards, although the format of the journal remained unchanged: but there was a good deal of continuity with all that had gone before.

It was the "traditional" type of *London Town* article which still appealed to most readers. Contributions with a literary and/or historical interest, or with an obvious relevance to London, were still published frequently, and such regular features (dating from 1900 in some cases!) as reports of sport days, cricket finals, club activities, etc., etc., still appeared throughout these years. It is those items of general and (surprisingly often) lasting interest which are featured in the following pages. As always, one may get the very "feel" of the age from the pages of *London Town*.

Eastway Park.

David Moore
(March 1962)

Opened over three years ago, Eastway Park is the pilot of the Welfare department's most recent scheme of development in the field of care of the aged. It is perhaps common knowledge at County Hall that the Council's policy is to do away with most of the existing large residential homes - relics of a by-gone age although more comfortable inside than many would think from their ugly and uninviting outside appearance - and replace them by small homes. What is probably less well known is the experiment of Eastway Park.

At the Welfare Conference in 1961, Mr D. C. R. Munro, the Chief Officer of the Welfare department, said 'One of the problems I think we have all tried to solve is to overcome the fear which so often assails the old souls who have at last to realize that they can no longer live alone but must go into an old people's home. The abrupt change from a private, independent life to a communal life with others is something which even the stout-hearted face with some trepidation. To the weaker, frailer, more sensitive old people it can be a really frightening prospect.' Eastway Park is the first material contribution to the solution of this problem. Purpose-built on a $1^{1}/_{2}$-acre site at Hackney Wick, it consists of a light and attractively laid-out home for 78 old people together with thirty flats for those who are not in need of care and attention in the fullest sense, are able to lead reasonably independent lives of their own but require some degree of assistance. The flats are entirely separate from the home, but share its external architectural pattern and are rather like a housing estate in miniature, scaled down to two-storey size. At the root of the scheme is the belief that at some time in the future the old people in the flats may have to go permanently into the home; and when they do there will be nothing strange or alarming about the change.

Quiet independence

Old people, the matron suggested to me when I visited the home last month, are often to some extent prepared for loneliness, and quite a number of the residents of the flats retain all their quiet independence and are subject to no interference whatsoever. But those who wish to may come into the home and take part in any of the activities that are going on there. They can watch television, have their meals there (or, if they prefer, have meals sent over to them), take part in the handicrafts sessions, join in with the residents of the home when outings are arranged, or just sit and chat in any of the comfortable lounges. Matron has no control, in the conventional sense, over the flats but she is a kind of guiding eye. She is there and her staff are there if they are wanted. if, for instance, an elderly person in one of the flats falls sick or needs help, an 'H' card is placed in the window. 'Everyone', I was told, 'is conditioned to look at the windows.' And it is not long before a call for help is answered.

Personal touch

I detected during my visit a genuine family atmosphere about the place. Matron, like all the matrons I have met at Welfare homes, is a great believer in the personal touch. The people in the flats see her at least once a week, on rent-collection day, and many - particularly those who come into the home more often - will see her more regularly still. Eastway Park is in fact a community with a community life. Home helps visit the flats two or three times a week to attend to those chores which are beyond the old people, and good relations exist with the borough council and other local organizations. Arrangements are some-times made by these bodies to give the flat-dwellers holidays - 'Going away with the Town Hall', as one lady delightfully put it. Their families call when they like, and many have helped to furnish some of the flats quite elaborately.

The flat I saw was, however, a typical one. The bed-sitter, kitchen and bathroom were bright and compact and yet more spacious than I expected. Good-sized windows looked on to the wide lawn dividing the flats from the home. Each flat is centrally heated, fed from the home's own plant, and an electric wall-fire is provided in addition.

The home of course is provided under the National Assistance Act, the flats under the Housing Acts. The allocation of flats is arranged jointly between Housing and Welfare departments. Eastway Park, the Matron thought, was about the right size for this kind of welfare development. With larger schemes there was a danger that the personal touch might be lost, 'but a lot depends of course on the matron'. Looking over the home, I could see what she meant. It may be a 'small home', but it covers quite a bit of earth; and eighty old people, to someone inexperienced in these matters like myself, seems a formidable number to take care of.

Not unnaturally Eastway Park has become something of a showplace. Visitors come from far and wide to go away tremendously impressed. But, if it is a showplace, it is a showplace second. It remains first a home and, apparently, an unique one in this country. The Welfare department have similar projects under way, however. One is already under construction in West London, and not surprisingly will probably be called Westway. I caught myself, at the end of the visit, wondering about 1965 and all that. Matron was non-committal. All she would say was that at present they barely know they're being supervised from County Hall. The Royal Commission and the Government, I seem to recall, tended to spread around the idea that the L.C.C. was some vast, giant, impersonal machine, and what was wanted was something more personal, more localized. If Eastway Park, and indeed the Welfare homes as a whole, are not precisely that then my dictionary definition of 'impersonal' will need to be revised in the 1965 edition.

Note: The LCC welfare services, part of which forms the subject of this article, were all transferred to the new London Boroughs on 1 April 1965. SInce then those services have been enormously expanded, but it's doubtful whether the very high standards attained by LCC welfare have yet been surpassed.

Editorial.

(April 1962)

At the end of February, when the town halls of outer suburbia and of inner London were still ringing with the loyal cries of parish pumpmanship, the House of Commons held its first debate on London government. It displayed, as the *Local Government Chronicle* remarked, a noticeable lack of enthusiasm for the Government's proposals and 'the debate was pervaded by fear rather than hope'. Our contemporary might have added 'or than anger', for the indignation voiced in local councils and papers by local patriots of various political persuasions was not reflected to any extent in the discussion or in the voting. The party line was drawn as strait as ever and only three Conservative M.P.s voted against even 'noting' the Government's proposals. This development, taken with the monotonously predictable attitudes of the affected authorities as reported, has led some observers to assume that the battle is over.

In our view it has barely begun. It must be remembered that the debate occurred before all the observations asked for by the Ministry had been delivered, before any of the discussions arising from those observations, before in fact our own Council had held its special meeting to formulate its observations. Though there are good grounds for anxiety at the way matters are being advanced, headlong rather than step by reasoned step, we still consider it premature to regard even the main outlines of the reorganization as irrevocably decided. The attitude of the peripheral authorities, the hardening of opinion concerning the unity of the Council's education service and the value of its Architect's department, the irresistible passage of time and the constant demonstration, by those in the know, of additional areas of doubt and disruption left exposed by the Government's exiguous plans, all these increase the chances that any ultimate change in London government will differ considerably from the White Paper both in detail and in date.

The proposals which have now been noted do not include any definite pronouncements about the future of the education service for 2 million people in the centre of London; nor about main sewerage, sewage disposal, land drainage, certain parks and open spaces, rate equalization, Public Control services, Supplies department activities; nor about any of the extensive range of local government activities in London with which the Royal Commission failed to deal. Nor, of course, do they have anything to say about the staffing of the services which they distribute so confidently. *And yet already one-tenth of the time allotted for the reorganization has slipped away.*

Still no comfort

It would not be appropriate here to deal critically with the Council's special meeting. Readers who are interested in political exchanges will have read the published accounts of the debate. As staff, we have no politics. As staff, it may be reported here that we received thanks and praise from both sides. Speakers from each side also expressed dissatisfaction with the attitude to the staff displayed by speakers from the other. There is little sign yet of any feeling of great urgency among those who hope to be running local government services in London, in whatever form, after 1965, to secure a sufficiently specific assurance of fair treatment upon which the present staff of threatened authorities can rely. Bromides issued as answers to questions in the House of Commons are not enough. Expressions of admiration and affection are not enough.

What is wanted is a commission backed by Whitehall, charged with the assembly and analysis of information about the staff of affected authorities, and empowered to plan and publish, subject to official approval and to negotiation, an outline scheme of grading and conditions to be applied to the staffs of new authorities. It need not be exhaustively detailed; it will not be necessary to commit the authorities in advance to more than minimum standards, or to attempt to approach staff on behalf of any particular authority. Provided the staff can see that something has been laid down for them, that there is something which they can appraise in the way of a career in local government beyond 1965, they will be content to stay at their posts and do the work they have chosen. Let it remain otherwise, let the future remain blank and ominous as it is at present, and no-one can blame a man or woman with a living to earn, dependents to support, a career to develop, if he abandons London local government in favour of something more reliable. As we have already remarked, one-tenth of the time has already elapsed. By the time a Bill is formulated and the post-1965 authorities are finally delineated, perhaps half the time will have gone; and also perhaps half the staff and half the knowledge and experience they hold between them.

Note: This was one of many *London Town* editorials on the impending reorganisation of London government (which, of course, eventually took effect on 1 April 1965). At its meeting on 12 March 1962 the Council had come out strongly against the plans for reorganisation.

Sports Jubilee.

(May 1962)

L. C. Cooper of Clerk's (widely known as 'Jack' in sporting and social circles in County Hall) has organized the Annual Sports since 1939. This year's, fixed for 29 June at Hurlingham Park, will be his seventeenth meeting, the sequence being interrupted by the war.

The Sports is a unique event in the Council calendar. It is the biggest single activity of its kind in which the staff engages. It is the only occasion where people can gather on a casually social footing to meet old friends and talk Council gossip. It is always a rare combination of sporting competition on the track, amiable conversation on the sidelines and informal party in the Star & Garter in the evening. But this year there's a buzz in the air that says the 1962 meeting is exceptional. I had a word with Jack Cooper to find out what this was all about.

What's so special about the 1962 Sports, then?
'This is our fiftieth meeting and that's something to boast about. There are not many sports clubs who reach the half-century.'

Do we know much about earlier meetings?
'Well, I've been unable to find any report about the first meeting which almost certainly was held in 1899. But the second meeting was held at Herne Hill on 16 June 1900, and the July issue of the *Staff Gazette* reported that the meeting was held " before a large company of keenly interested spectators. The weather was deliciously fine, the arrangements worked smoothly throughout . . . The band of the Feltham School contributed largely to the success of the meeting . . ." Included in the programme were bicycle events and a Band Boys race. Following meetings were held at Herne Hill, Crystal Palace and Stamford Bridge. The early meetings were essentially all-male affairs. It was not until 1910 that two special events (egg-and-spoon and donkey races) were included "for the ladies of the staff".'

Have athletic standards risen much in your time?
'Not to any appreciable extent. The records for the 100 yds set up by R. L. Jordan (10.2 secs in 1935) and by Miss M. Brereton (12.2 secs in 1938) still stand, although Jordan's record has been equalled on two occasions. On the other hand performances in team events have improved without question.'

What is your outstanding athletics memory?
'Undoubtedly the mile event at the 1954 meeting when Beaumont (Comptroller's) won from Herbert (Public Control). Herbert had been mile champion and cross-country champion since the 'thirties and can be numbered among the outstanding Council sportsmen of all time. At the bell, the race was betwen Herbert, Beaumont and Kennedy; by the middle of the back straight Herbert led by five or six yards; at the final bend Beaumont made his challenge and amid terrific enthusiasm won convincingly, but I think we were all a little sad at Herbert's defeat. I shall never forget the tremendous ovation given to him at the

prizegiving. In another way 1954 marked the end of an epoch for that was the last meeting held at the Duke of York's Headquarters.'

And outstanding personalities?
'Many. But I would prefer not to talk about personalities but about the officials who year after year turn out and do a magnificent job. For many of them our meeting is their only athletic experience. Nevertheless I can remember some years ago a prominent A.A.A. member telling me that he would be delighted to have them all at the White City officiating at an A.A.A. championship meeting. I owe all of them a great deal and you won't mind if I use this as an occasion to say "thank you very much".'

Are there any special plans this year?
'We always have a very crowded programme and if every event is well-supported the Club will be more than satisfied. I certainly hope that every department will enter teams in the inter-departmental events, particularly in the the two Tug-of-War contests (though why anyone pulls in a tug, I shall never know!). We shall produce a rather special programme this year which I am sure everyone will want to keep as a memento of this great occasion.'

Naturally you're keen to make this a big success?
'Yes, competitively, socially, and in every possible way. If we cannot make this meeting a really outstanding success, I don't think we deserve either a sports club or a sports meeting. I hope that everyone will buy a ticket (after all, sports meetings do cost a lot of money) and that we shall have a record number of competitors. And I would like all pensioners to know that the Sports Club would be delighted to welcome them to the meeting. If they would be kind enough to drop me a line I should be very pleased to send them a ticket.'

One last question, Jack. How much longer are you soldiering on as organizer?
'A very good question. Every year I say "This is the last one - I've done my fair share." But then every night I give up smoking! Anyway with 1965 hanging over us, who am I to prophesy?'

. . . Writ in Water.

C. D. Andrews
(June 1962)

The history of London's water supply goes back many hundreds of years. Early in the seventeenth century a predecessor of mine acquired an interest - and it was a profitable one - in the New River Company which was set up to bring water to London from the springs and wells of Hertfordshire. As London grew, other water companies were set up and several local authorities established their own undertakings. At the end of the last century, however, there were outbreaks of disesase as well as accusations of malpractice and profiteering. As a result, the Metropolitan Water Board was brought into existence.

It may be true, Mr Chairman, that good cannot come out of evil, but I am sure we can all agree that in this case a good result was evolved out of an evil situation.

The above forms part of the Gracious Reply which Her Majesty Queen Elizabeth II was pleased to return on 30 March 1962 when she inaugurated a giant reservoir built by the Metropolitan Water Board at Walton. Who would have thought that within five days Her Majesty's Minister of Housing and Local Government was to pronounce sentence of death on what Her Majesty had described as a good result from an evil situation, by announcing his intention to abolish it and transfer its powers to the Greater London Council!

Tactful summary

Whatever the underlying cause of this extraordinary decision - and even the most faithful Government newspaper was constrained to suggest, even in its headline, that it was the sequel to the refusal of the M.W.B. to postpone or reduce a $7^1/_2$ per cent pay award to its staff - whatever the cause the historical paradox is acute. For the Queen's speechwriter was making a very hasty and tactful summary of the events leading to the establishment of the Metropolitan Water Board. In actual fact there was a running fight at the turn of the last century between the Progressive (i.e., Liberal and Radical) London County Council which had strong ambitions to take over the supply of London's water (amongst other things) and the Conservative Government which was determined that the powers of the L.C.C. should be diminished rather than increased. The Government won all along the line. By creating the 28 metropolitan boroughs in 1899 it torpedoed the Council's policy of 'unification', and by creating the Metropolitan Water Board in 1902 it struck off one more of the public utilities which the Council had hoped to operate. Now, 60 years later, the Government is still advancing its policy of what Lord Salisbury used to call 'tenification' as opposed to 'unification' - the building up of smaller municipalities in narrower areas within the metropolis - but to the tenuous though inflated rump of the "unificatory" body it proposes to add that water undertaking which it had previously denied.

A confused fight

The fight for the control of London's water was a stirring but a confused one. When the L.C.C. started work, in 1889, some of the water companies, particularly in the East End, were giving grossly unsatisfactory service, and the Council very soon appointed a Water Committee to make enquiries and if necessary open negotiations. In 1891 the Council found itself in the unfamiliar role of collaborating with the City Corporation in a Bill which the Corporation itself had promoted and which, after joint negotiation, provided for an L.C.C. Water Committee to be responsible for London's water, with one-eighth of its members appointed by the Corporation. This Bill was rejected by the Parliamentary Select Committee, but they clearly favoured a single water authority for London and suggested that the L.C.C. should be authorized to buy out the water companies. This, it may be added, was under a Liberal Government, though a weakly-based one.

The L.C.C., with some financial misgivings, offered to take over the eight

113

water companies 'at a fair and reasonable value'. The water companies replied that they were not interested. The Council thereupon introduced eight Bills into Parliament, for the acquisition of the eight companies. When these had passed their second reading in the Commons, however, Parliament dissolved and a Conservative administration was returned. This Government would only allow the Council's Bills to proceed if an ad hoc authority were substituted for the Council and if the water companies were paid more compensation than had been proposed. The Council refused these conditions and the Bills were rejected.

Touring the Welsh valleys

The Council had never been satisfied that the Thames Valley would provided enough water for London, and L.C.C. surveyors were sent throughout the valleys of Wales to map out more reliable resources. A scheme was prepared for supplying London with Welsh water, and another series of Bills to take over the water undertakings was promoted in 1897. The Bills were defeated, but in the light of the growing public dissatisfaction the Government promised to set up a Royal Commission on the subject (the last one had reported as recently as 1893). The evidence presented to this new Commission appeared to confirm the Council's views (which had originally been aired in yet another Royal Commission) that the Thames could not produce enough water for London, and since there had been severe shortages of water in the East End the Council again introduced a Bill, in 1898, seeking to acquire the companies and definitely scheduling its plan for bringing water from Wales. This again was rejected.

The latest Royal Commission did not publish its report till 1900. It concluded that in all normal circumstances existing sources of water were sufficient, and it recommended the creation of a water board. The Government endorsed this, despite strong representations in favour of the Welsh project. But its action was so tardy, and the further restrictions on consumption which the water companies imposed were so unpopular, that the Council had actually had its Bill rejected twice more, and had decided to deposit it yet again, before the Government gave notice of its legislative proposals.

Game to the last - it was now 1902 - the Government proposed a Water Board which differed widely from that recommended by the Royal Commission: instead of 30 members nominated by local authorities there were to be 69 members, of whom the metropolitan boroughs were to appoint 34 and the L.C.C. only 10. Equally game to the last, the L.C.C. protested vigorously and argued long. The net result was a Board of 66, with the L.C.C. having 14 representatives and the City and the boroughs 33. Once the M.W.B. was established, the L.C.C. has of course always been on cordial terms with it. The Board is now 88 strong but L.C.C. representation has not changed.

When the Conservative and Unionist Party announced in 1894 that 'we must not be shy of using all our political power and machinery for the purpose of importing sound principles into the government of London' their national leaders - Salisbury, Balfour and Chamberlain (the latter notwithstanding his great career in 'municipalizing' Birmingham) - waged strong war on the 'collectivist experiments' and 'revolutionary ideas' of the London County Council. Salisbury went so far as to invite it to commit suicide. In a speech in 1897 he flayed the Council and all its works, said that the only solution would be the devolution of most of the Council's functions to smaller authorities, foretold legislation to accomplish this, and added: 'I sincerely hope that my advice will be entertained by the County Council - though perhaps it may be a suicidal course to recommend - in a wise, patriotic and enlightened spirit.'

Suicide declined

The Council declined to be wise, patriotic and enlightened as Lord Salisbury understood those terms, so the Government proceeds to achieve its ends by legislative action. A lifetime later the situation has repeated itself in the field of Greater London. The arguments for 'unification' and what Salisbury called 'tenification' were examined by another Royal Commission - which specifically had water excluded from its terms of reference. In the result it seems that, once all the political stings are removed from the L.C.C., both it and the M.W.B will join in the same grey characterless regional authority. Both could perhaps lay claim to the epitaph that Keats chose:-

HERE LIES ONE WHOSE NAME WAS WRIT IN WATER

Note: The Metropolitan Water Board was not, in the event, abolished at this stage. Water authorities were completely reorganised in 1974 and have, of course, since been privatised.

Edward Ormond Williams.

(July 1962)

The *Penny Illustrated Paper* of 6 July 1907 carried a photograph of a neat straw-hatted figure paying out wages to L.C.C. Works department labourers on the job of remetalling Victoria Embankment. The embankment itself serves as the pay table and the figure is that of Mr Edward Williams a clerk, already in his eighth year of service. *London Town* for March 1950 carried an article on the retirement of a rent collector who had completed half a century of permanent service - Mr Williams again.

On 27 March 1962 the Council's senior night porter celebrated his 76th birthday and ended his work with the Council more than 62 years after he began it. Mr Edward Williams is once again the central figure.

On 1 February 1900 the Council itself was only coming up to the eleven plus mark (the metropolitan boroughs were less than a year old), and the Works department which took on office boy Williams looked out from Belvedere Road in riparian isolation from other departments. The office scene was Dickensian - the senior clerk in the middle of the room with his high-stooled juniors hunched over their ledgers all around. They feared to relax for one moment for the senior clerk had soft-soled shoes and a nasty habit of creeping up and looking over a man's shoulder! Mr Williams's first wage was 7s 6d less 3d superannuation, and his duties included running the tea club and purchasing snuff for his colleagues. The department had workshops of all kinds and stables, for there were thirty full-time horses on the fixed staff. One could go down at lunch-time to the wharves, where the barges delivered materials direct, and borrow a small boat. Mr Williams remembers getting into difficulties under Westminster Bridge - it had its hundredth birthday a few days before he retired but it was well under fifty when he was wont to negotiate it.

By 1908 the Works department was being dismantled and December of that year saw Mr Williams transferred to the Local Government and Statistics department. He remembers with admiration J. C. Spensley as a wizard of statistics and Sir Edgar Harper as a master at making them talk. There was as much last-minute rush on reports then as now, but the press for copying them was a far less efficient aid than the stencil machine. It had one glorious advantage to the hard-worked junior, however - a drop too much water on the paper and the unpleasant senior's duplicate and original could be 'accidentally' ruined!

The Statistics department was abolished in 1912 and once again Mr Williams changed duties. Until 1953 (a service life for most in itself) financial work claimed him. Comptroller's was his department until 1922 when, with his job of rent collecting, he came to Valuer's. He talks of the East End before and after the First World War with an admirable objectivity, free from sentiment but full of sympathy. 'The Landlord' (by which name the Councillor's collectors were always known) had to preserve a wary firmness as he set forth, with a watchman as 'knocker up' going on before. The double knock for catching the allegedly not-at-home tenant had to be perfected. He had also to be realistic - rents were sadly often not worth pursuing on a Monday morning until nine o'clock when the pawn shops opened ('Mum's round at Uncle's'). And on the other side of the coin, the 'landlord' well knew what not to see - the donkey that the coster-monger stabled in his kitchen somehow never got reported - and what to see beyond his strict collecting sphere - the cases of real distress to whom he was the first to call in the Council's Welfare services. Mr Williams, though he worked for the L.C.C. in Victorian times, was no Victorian landlord and despite the poverty and the hardship of the lives of his tenants, he remembers above all their good cheer and friendliness.

In 1953 his permanent service necessarily came to an end, but for Mr Williams the year was but the beginning of more service in Clerk's. where he has worked up through the porter grades to become the Council's senior night porter. When most of us have gone home he and his colleagues start their watch over County Hall and maintain all through the night the emergency telephone service. Some of the calls are not urgent but at any time someone may need to have some vital service brought into operation - navigation lights may have failed on one of the Thames bridges, a midwife may be asking for special help, an evicted family may be at the end of their unsuccessful search for accommodation. The night porter staff must know the best place for help. Comic relief is by no means absent however as the wheels are set in motion to aid the serious cases. Even Mr Williams's experience afforded no precedent for dealing with the distressed caller who had found a rat in his television set. (The correct and proven answer by the way is to take the set out into the garden whereupon the rat will run away. Mr Williams reports that the customer was satisfied.)

And for the future? He doesn't seem to be desperately keen on retirement even now - he had stayed on for a few months as it was to train a successor. But his home is in Chelsea and he plans to devote much time to two interests appropriate enough to the district - flowers and antiques. He will be a fairly frequent visitor to County Hall not least to keep in touch with his old friend Hector the County Hall cat who serves the Education Officer by day but is faithfully on duty with the porter staff each night.

Hector.

(September 1962)

The day after *London Town* published the profile of Mr Williams the retiring senior night porter, and mentioned the County Hall cat, we received a blood-stained pigeon's feather by ordinary post. Our crime reporter investigated.

Finding Hector was not easy. Hector is king of cats and his movements are stealthy. Making contacts took some time, but odd scraps of information laid a trail inexorably to the mysterious room in the middle of the long corridor. I knocked at a door marked G.P.I and eventually was ushered into the presence.

Considering I had not made an appointment he received me very courteously. After his night's labour he slept well. There was a long pause before he unstifled a yawn and with easy, almost feline, grace he beckoned me to sit down. He was large, lithe and black as night.

'I know your racket,' he began in his soft silken drawl. 'Tell your boss if I don't get a page with pictures all the gold in the Gold-fish Bowl won't save him. But don't get me wrong. Williams was my pal. Once he saved me from bye-byes when Estab said I'd clawed up the ceremonial carpet; they don't pay too much for witnesses. Williams was a good guy but only human. Cats were sacred in ancient Egypt. Quote that: it will give tone to your uncultured screed.

'I had a hard life. Turned on to the streets as a baby by a clearance scheme, my kittenhood was most disturbed. Never knew my father, soon lost my mother. Just to let the cat-squashers career faster round the Addington Street roundabout. It's enough to make a human weep. We'll always be superior beings while you continually invent better engines of death.' He preened a whisker.

'So then I tagged on to the North Block extension builders. The nightwatchman gave me my only real start in life. They were a rough, tough, swearing crew. I got kicks and I went hungry but I was one of them. They were soft underneath it all and they taught me about Life.

'When that job finished I got in with the white collar mob. The whole of County Hall is my territory now. Me and the members are like that and this "no canvassing" is virtually suspended in my favour. That time the Estab outfit were after my blood, Williams jugged me before the shooting started and I got clear on the parole of Himself in person. Top People understand each other.

'Mind you, I'm ambitious and I've climbed high. At the big parties in the evenings I always stand at the head of the ceremonial stairs. And the gentry don't stroke the Chief Officers on the head and tickle their white fronts. Being in the service of London they haven't got eight more lives. Me, I'll always land on my feet.' Hector dabbed at a passing moth.

'Looking back, it wasn't my smartest trick coming to the Hall. It's not exactly the affluent society. But the folks here are soft too, almost to the point of kindness. I'm an hon. member of this exclusive G.P.I tea club and for protection they dub out a slice of the extras in kittykat. I get four round meals a day and at night I really lash myself up with fish in the post room. If I'm still hungry or need adventure I knock off a rat or a spare pigeon.'

Pigeon! Of course! I sat staring helplessly into the large hypnotic green eyes and the black shining fur just flecked with white. We both sat in silence for a while - how long I do not know. Then the interview was over and he dismissed me.

As his entourage unfrisked me and showed me out they said 'He's quite a gentle person really. Very disdainful but easily managed when you understand a bit about him. He always signs any petition that goes round the office provided it is not against capital punishment. On wet day he walked over an important finance document and we got a couple of new schools without a fight.'

Earthquakes in London — Part I.

Ellis S. Hillman, B.Sc., F.G.S.
(July 1963)

Mr Hillman is the member of the Council for Hackney Central and a geologist by profession. In this article he gives some account of the history of earthquakes in London. In next month's issue he will present a theory about the possibility of another earthquake in this century.

The earliest known catalogue of earthquakes in Britain was published by a Sheffield physician, Dr Thomas Short, in 1749. The two-volume work was entitled *A General Chronological History of the Air, Weather, Seasons, Meteors, etc, in Sundry Places and different Times, more particularly for the Space of 250 years.*

This work with its cumbersome title is, unfortunately, suspect. It fails to provide references in support of its history.

However, accounts of earthquake activity in the vicinity of London cover some eight hundred years. A Mathew Paris writes of an earthquake which occurred as early as 1247 in the following terms:

'At various places in England, especially at London, and there mostly on the banks of the Thames, an earthquake was felt, which shook buildings, and was very injurious and terrible in its effects.'

How injurious and terrible this earthquake was, is not recorded. It is not known, for instance, whether any buildings of the day were damaged. The casualties are not known either. Information of this character might, at least, have given the historian or seismologist some facts upon which a reconstruction of these far distant events could be attempted.

Thomas Twynne's Discourse

The next recorded earthquake took place on 6 April 1580. The event has been extensively reported, and a certain Thomas Twynne described his experiences in a pamphlet entitled

A shorte and pithie Discourse, concerning the engendering, tokens, and effects of all Earthquakes in General:

Particularlay applyed and concerned with the most strange and terrible worke of the Lord in shaking the Earth, not only within the Citie of London, but also in most partes of all Englande:

Which hapned upon Wednesday in Easter weeke last part, which was the sixt day of April, almost at sixe a clocke in the evening, in the yeare of our Lord God, 1580.

This small work was edited by R. E. Ockenden and republished in 1936 under the title *Thomas Twynne's Discourse on the Earthquake of 1580.* In his introduction, Ockenden says of this earthquake: 'It was certainly one of the greatest ever known in London. An apprentice was killed by the fall of stone from the roof of Christ's Hospital Church; some stones were also shaken from St Paul's Cathedral and the Temple Church, and chimneys in various parts of the City were thrown down.'

'Dreadful and dangerous'

The almost apocalyptic atmosphere in which this pamphlet was written is conveyed by the introductory sentences:

'Among the manifold signs and tokens, whereby it hath pleased our most Gracious God, and merciful Father, in these the later times of the world, and very ripeness of our sins, to call us unto repentance, we may account at least this most dreadful and dangerous earthquake, which unto the greatest terror of all good consciences befell of late unto the City of London, and as I suppose to the most part of this Realm . . .'

The account is free from exaggeration and passages such as this are common:

'I am assuredly informed that as well as elsewhere as in London, the very shaking caused the Bells in some steeples to knoll a stroke or two. The tops of half a dozen chimnies in London were cast down: many stone works and buildings, for that they would not yield, are shrewdly shaken.'

The shock was felt in other part of south-east England, as far away as Saffron Walden, Norwich and Oxford. Even Paris and Brussels were slightly shaken.

The next earthquake we know of took place on 24 December 1601. It was described as 'a shock without much damage' and was clearly a very minor affair.

During the years 1634 and 1635 London was again shaken at irregular intervals by minor shocks. These were followed by a period of quiescence of some eighty years before the next tremor shook London, Dorchester and other places - on 25 October 1726.

The series of earthquakes experienced during 1750 were more serious affairs. The boundary of the disturbed area embraced some 240 square miles, their centre coinciding with London Bridge. The intensity was sufficient to overthrow ornaments and vases. A contemporary writer, the Rev. J. Wesley, described the first incidents in these words: 'There were three distinct shakes, or wavings to and fro, attended with a hoarse rumbling noise, like thunder'.

Further shocks on 19 and 20 March were also recorded. The first of these appears to have greatly disturbed animals in and around London. Cats started up, dogs howled, sheep ran about, a horse refused to drink, and the water was so much agitated that in several ponds fish leaped out of the water and 'darted away in all directions'.

Theodora shocked

An interesting sidelight to the 1750 earthquakes is provided in Newman Flowers's biography of George Frideric Handel. According to the biographer, the presentation of Handel's little-known oratorio *Theodora* was 'killed' by earthquake. He writes: 'The earthquake shocks began on 5 February, and when *Theodora* was produced five weeks later, the town was at the height of the scare. Society departed out of London in droves. Those who remained were frightened to go out after dark lest they should be killed by falling tiles from house-roofs, and equally frightened to remain at home in case their homes should collapse over their heads.'

He describes the atmosphere in which London was absorbed in these words:

'. . . the conscience of the town was smitten as with a wasting disease. A wave of licentiousness and drunkenness had risen to a height hitherto unknown. Crime was on the increase; sobriety was ebbing out as a forgotten virtue from the upper reaches of the social life. The people were pulled up rudely by the shocks. This London, then, was Babylon. They would escape from it before the vengeance of God descended. The churches were crowded with worshippers. The rich and the poor trembled sleepless in their houses by night, watched walls that seemed to move beneath the dancing shadows of the lights. Only when the sun rose in its accustomed place beyond the chimney-pots, did they believe that God had not singled out London for vengeance. With the coming of nightfall again the old fears returned, and, in the dreadful shades, frightened figures slunk past with the palsied steps of fear. London forgot all else save the earthquakes. It forgot Handel. It forgot *Theodora* . . .'

Other slight shocks took place in 1758, 1864, 1865 and 1886. *Nature* of 1886 reported that during the shock 'a door was heard to vibrate regularly for three or four seconds without any motion being felt in London'.

It has to be remembered that although many earthquakes felt in London are of external origin, there is a centre, a 'focus' to use the correct seismological term, situated within the present City. This 'focus' is responsible for the series of shocks in 1750 and possibly for others.

Note: Mr Ellis Hillman, a member of the LCC and the GLC from 1949 until 1986, gave generous and discriminating support to many staff activities, including *London Town*.

Earthquakes in London — Part II.

Ellis S. Hillman, B. Sc, F.G.S.
(August 1963)

Mr Hillman's second article offers a possible date for London's next earthquake.

To complete the story of experience of shocks in the London area it is necessary to make reference to those earthquakes whose focus was outside London, but whose shocks were nevertheless felt in London.

Records of earthquakes of unknown epicentre (that is, the part of the earth's surface immediately above the original focus of the earthquake) go back to 974 when Symeon of Durham wrote 'In this year a great earthquake took place overall England.' Shocks occurred frequently after this date, in 1060, 1067, 1081, 1089 and 1099. These were felt in London and accounts of succeeding quakes have been found covering the early and late Middle Ages.

In the seventeenth century, earthquakes were the subject of comment by diarists and writers. On 12 May 1687 we find Evelyn noting in his diary:

'This day there was such a storme of wind as had seldom happen'd, being a sort of hurricane. It kept the flood out of the Thames, so that people went on foot over severall places above bridge. Also an earthquake in severall places in England about the time of the storme.'

and again on 15 September 1692:

'There happen'd an earthquake wch tho' not so great as to do any harm in England, was universal in all these parts of Europe. It shook the house at Wooton but was not perceived by any save a servant or two, who were making up bed, and another in a garret. I and the rest, being at dinner below in the parlour, were not sensible of it.'

Evelyn was even constrained to engage in a detailed correspondence with the Bishop of London, Dr Thomas Tennison, on the cause of earthquakes in general.

A certain Edward Cooke wrote a full-length pamphlet on this 1692 earthquake with the curious title

The Earth twice shaken wonderfully
Or, An
Analogual Discourse of Earthquake; its Natural
Causes, Kinds and Manifold Effects;
Occasioned
By the last of these which happened on the Eighth
Day of September 1692, at Two of the Clock in
the Afternoon.

The catastrophic Lisbon earthquake of 1755, which killed 10,000/15,000 people in the greatest natural disaster of European history, also led to extensive comment in this country. The seismic sea-waves following the earthquake reached the Thames over 1,000 miles from the Lisbon focus. It left such a deep impression on the public mind that a Royal Proclamation was issued for a general fast day to be observed. The catastrophe also provided John Wesley with material for a pamphlet entitled *Serious Thoughts Occasioned by the late Earthquake in Lisbon*, which ran into six editions. Revivalist movements in the nineteenth century followed the Wesleyan path in their interpretation of these natural phenomena. A religious tract, entitled *The Great Earthquake*, for instance, describes the scene in London in 1843 in these words:

'. . . lately there was a deep impression upon the minds of many that an Earthquake would swallow up the Metropolis of this kingdom. Hundreds acted on this impression and left London and fled to a distance from it.'

This tract was obtainable for the modest sum of $1/2$d.

The Colchester disaster

In more recent times, earthquakes have been studied more systematically, and much more valuable information was gained from the famous Colchester earthquake, which was felt in London. This disastrous series of shocks covered an area of 150 square miles. No fewer than 1,200 buildings were damaged, including 20 churches and 11 chapels. A special Mansion House Fund was raised for the benefit of those owners of property who were unable to bear the whole cost of the necessary repairs.

The twentieth century has seen even greater shocks. The 1931 North Sea shock, for instance, some miles off the Yorkshire coast, was felt in London and has been described as the greatest earthquake recorded in British history; and as recently as 1938, an earthquake near Brussels was felt in London. London appears to be the centre of a whole group of earthquake centres such as Chichester, Canterbury, Maidstone, Reigate, Colchester and Lewes.

How they happen

The study of earthquakes is known as seismology. It is a branch of geophysics which concerns itself with the internal structure of the earth and the slow geological processes in the earth's crust which lead to the accumulation of great strains in the rocks, bringing about deformation, generally by plastic flow. In some cases the strain is released by fracture in the rock. The energy liberated is dissipated by elastic waves which travel in all directions through the earth. The resulting motion on the surface above these underground fractures may be of destructive intensity.

The shocks which south-east England has experienced during recorded history have been interpreted in terms of structural stresses in the region.

The line of the lower Thames Valley is the line of one of the major tectonic (structural) boundaries, separating Palæo-Europe (Primary Europe) from Meso-Europe (Secondary Europe). It is along this boundary that a number of shocks, including the Colchester earthquake, have taken place. The fact that the east-west folds of Meso-Europe advance 'wave-like' towards the earlier folded and compacted Palæo-Europe may account for the particular instability of south-east England.

Evidence for this regional instability is further provided by the fact that renewed folding took place during the line of the formation of the Alps, hundreds of miles to the south. This renewed folding led to structural changes in the chalk hills.

Under the ice

Perhaps the most important factor in interpreting these shocks is the coincidence of the tectonic boundary with the edge of the great ice-sheet which covered Britain in Pleistocene times. New stresses in the north Europe structures resulted from the 'unloading' of the Pleistocene ice-sheet by melting and withdrawal. The area to the north was depressed relative to the south by the weight of the ice-sheet which attained thousands of feet in thickness. The rise of the land following this unloading has yet to be completed, and is intermittent in character.

Few definite changes in the nature of seismic activity have taken place in historical time. To predict earthquakes is an altogether hazardous affair, in the present state of knowledge. It is tempting to refer to the answer which a distinguished Canadian seismologist gave to a question concerning the time of the next occurrence in a certain region:

'I was gratified to be able to answer promptly, and I did. I said that I did not know'.

Mark Twain

This temptation will be resisted.

In fact, the application of empirical formulæ and principles gleaned from past observations to anticipated events in the future provide a rough and ready guide for prediction. The element of probability must also enter into such calculations.

Earthquake frequency in Great Britain, as elsewhere, is marked by fluctuations rather than by any general increase or decrease. These fluctuations appear, however, to be subject to laws. For instance, the average interval in all earthquake centres in both England and Scotland appears to be about 27 to 30 years. Records indicate that Chichester had earthquakes at an average interval of 25 years, over the last four hundred years. Reigate, Colchester, Lewes, St Albans and Canterbury do not, unfortunately, provide a picture of regular earthquake frequency.

Taking 1580 as the first, reasonably well documented earthquake as a base line, the longest interval between shocks in London has been 125 years. It is therefore reasonable to suppose that London is 'due' for an earthquake of internal origin before 1990.

This does not exclude the probability of shocks being felt - strong or weak - from other centres of seismic activity. Although there were no reports that the Midlands (near Leicester) earthquake of 1957, the East Anglian tremor of 1960, or the Channel Islands earthquake of 1959 were felt in London, it is reasonable to assume that the south-east of England will continue to be the region of relatively severe, if infrequent earthquakes both of internal and external origin. Reference has already been made to Maidstone, Reigate, Canterbury, Colchester and St Albans - and it seems reasonable to assume that these centres will provide further shocks for those living in London and the 'commuting' area.

It would be wise to make some provision for the possibility of further earthquakes in the London region. In major earthquake countries (Britain is not one of them), a 'seismic constant' is incorporated in building codes, designed to withstand forces resulting from steady horizontal earth accelerations. High blocks of buildings are obviously more liable to this type of damage. Engineers and architects are often required to investigate features of damage caused by an earthquake to buildings, bridges, railways and embankments in regions of great earthquake activity.

Although it is highly unlikely that any future earthquake in this country will cause the widespread damage and loss of life associated with countries of great seismic activity, it would be a great mistake to underestimate the panic that can grip a town or city during these events, as our quotations from contemporary accounts of these earthquakes have indicated.

Greater London Council — the First Meeting.

O.W. Holmes
(June 1964)

One whose duty or curiosity leads him to the back files of *The Times* for 1 February 1889, to look up the account of the first meeting of the London County Council, will find a wealth of detail the official minutes lack. Atmosphere is there, too. Half a page of close print records the happening and a wide column comment extends the coverage to a full page. It is otherwise with the first meeting of the Greater London Council. This time the minutes will enable the reader to form a clear idea of how the meeting went, while the report in *The Times* is less that half a single column in all.

The meeting of 1964 was prepared for with much more thoroughness that that of 1889. This was mainly because there existed two political parties from whom which it was clear, well in advance, that the majority of the members would be drawn. The Greater London Joint Committee has been in being for some months, manned by representatives of the county councils and county borough councils contributing territory to Greater London. The Joint Committee had set up sub-committees, and the sub-committees were served by working parties of officers. In all these preparations the staff of the London and Middlesex County

Councils had much to contribute, and their work should be the basis of many future decisions.

Some weeks before the first meeting of the GLC, agreement was secured on the form of the agenda. There seems to have been no comparable agreement in 1889, when the first meeting did not even succeed in electing the aldermen, and even a decision to adjourn was the subject of a division. Even at this division a member shouted at his colleagues as they were leaving 'I think you are doing a serious thing; you are breaking the law'.

The Minister of Housing and Local Government, under statutory authority, designated a person to take the Chair and call for nominations for a Chairman. The majority party had already produced their nominee, and only the speeches remained to be made. It was the same with the post of Vice-Chairman. The minority party had announced their nominee for the Deputy Chairmanship. The contrast with 1889 was most marked, as there was no sustained dispute between the parties over how the aldermanic vacancies should be filled. Indeed, the parties agreed to a suggestion that, rather than elect only majority party members as the aldermen continuing until 1970, the minority should have six.

It was interesting, when the members took the places allotted to them for this first meeting, to see that several who had graced front seats in the L.C.C. meetings now sat at the back. There were distinguished guests sitting behind the members and it was not easy for the casual spectator to judge where members ended and guests began. But those who knew where the invisible line ran could form an initial impression of the new Council. There are 21 lady members out of 116. (The L.C.C. has 41 out of 146). Forty members are also members of the present L.C.C., 22 are members of Middlesex C.C., and eighteen others serve on one or other of the remaining county councils or county borough councils in the area.

The agenda paper included two motions standing in the names of the Leader (Mr Fiske) and the Leader of the Opposition (Sir Percy Rugg): one was of loyal duty to the Queen, and the other extended the Council's goodwill to the new London Borough Councils to be elected on 7 May to share with the G.L.C. the local government of the metropolis. In speaking on the former the Leader said:

... there are certain policies that we shall be pursuing, which I can put in quite simple and quite non-controversial terms. Firstly, we must set about the provision of housing in such a way that every family can expect to have decent home by modern standards. Secondly, with our new powers of traffic management, we must secure the orderly development of our city which, while making provision for the motor car, will still be a place in which our citizens can live full and healthy lives. Thirdly, as you, Sir, referred to partly, we have to protect the staff now working in many authorities who will be assimilated into the service of Greater London. We need to work to see that their careers are safeguarded and that they themselves are absorbed in work in which they can make their greatest contribution.

The Leader of the Opposition rejoined: 'I have listened to his three main policy points with the most profound interest, and I can promise him that we shall not argue with him as to the urgency and the priority of any one of them.'

The members then adjourned for lunch, and later most of them were to be seen on the steps of the members' entrance facing a battery of photographers.

When it resumed, the Council quickly disposed of the business on the paper. The first item was the set of 67 standing orders, either statutory in origin or devised from study of the standing orders of the present county councils and the Ministry's model. The non-statutory standing orders are a lot shorter than the corresponding L.C.C. ones and those who need to operate them will no doubt study the differences. There was a very useful summary of the new Council's powers and duties long-term and interim. This could have attracted interminable debate, but in fact received none.

Friendly offers of assistance came from the L.C.C. and the Middlesex C.C., and these were much appreciated. The Acting Clerk to the G.L.C. (it is to be 'to', not 'of' the Council in future) has had to convey to himself as Clerk of the L.C.C. the new Council's reply. The M.W.B. and one of the outer London councils also sent good wishes.

The meeting also set up a committee, comprising ten members of the majority party and five of the minority party, to advise on committee and departmental structures. Their report will have appeared on the second agenda paper.

In addition to this transaction of business there was a sense of occasion. Every member, save one temporarily in hospital and one out of the country, was in his place. The photographers' floodlights swept across the Chamber. Guests with coloured tickets in precise variety took their places. The new aldermen were introduced in two groups of eight, each conducted by the head messenger. The Clerk of the Middlesex County Council sat at Sir William Hart's right hand. Sir Isaac Hayward, the Leader of the L.C.C., and Lord Morrison and Lord Latham, his predecessors, beamed from the dais. The Chair was taken at noon precisely. The catering resources of the building were taxed to the limit. As on the day of election, the sun in its splendour graced the day. It was right that *The Times* should use the word 'benign' but it would be a poor reward for many who had striven to improve on 1889 if it were taken to mean that benignity was something less than the occasion demanded. The Greater London Council, as its first meeting, did all that needed to be done and did it without a fuss. It augurs well.

Note: The first elections to the GLC and ILEA in May 1964 were won by the Labour Party, which thus prolonged still further its long standing control at County Hall. The two new authorities did not begin to function until 1 April 1965 but both the GLC and ILEA were extremely active in the interim period, preparing for the impending local government "revolution".

Editorial.

(April 1965)

Lord Morrison of Lambeth

He has left us within a few days of the death of the great authority which he ruled during the greatest phase of his life. Last month's *London Town*, a not entirely serious mourning issue for the L.C.C., contained as its first and most prized contribution a message from him. His death was announced just as copies of that issue were reaching our readers, and the nostalgic mood of the special material was salted for us with a real sorrow.

We reprint, this time without any overtones, the words of Thomas Nashe which appeared above his contribution in March:

'London doth mourn, Lambeth is quite forlorn.'

No special features have been arranged for this, the first number of *London Town* to be published among the staff of the Greater London Council. After so many years of criticism of the origins and structure of the reorganized London, it would be somewhat unbecoming of us to greet 1 April 1965 with fanfares of trumpets. We have decided therefore to continue in the familiar form.

In doing so, we hope to reflect the feeling of the transferred staff - transferred whether from London, from Middlesex, or from elsewhere - that this occasion is merely a landmark in a continuing career in the public service. We, the staff, have taken up at some time in the past the work of supplying something to the citizen which that citizen has needed and will continue to look for. It does not matter to the citizen very much if the package he is handed is labelled L.C.C., M.C.C., G.L.C. or whatever, provided the contents are satisfactory. We work to make them so.

There comes together at this time a multitude of people to serve a new and powerful employer, a new and greater London. There should be no feeling of possession or seniority among former L.C.C. employees, nor of immigration or minority among those from other dead authorities. We are all transferred officers. The past is dead and the 'might have been' with it. The present is upon us with its problems of redirection. The future is common to us all, with its infinite prospects of achievement.

No fanfares to-day, then, but a greeting to the staff of the Greater London Council. While it can achieve your interest and support *London Town* will seek to serve you, to chronicle your doings and to further your undertakings. At present our news comes mainly from L.C.C. sources, but we shall seek to make equal contact with all in time. We look forward to hearing about everything from everybody.

Note: Editorial comment (written by David Moore) on the occasion of the first GLC/ILEA issue of *London Town*. A note on Herbert Morrison appears in Volume 1.

'The Ambassador's House.'

Ada Polak
(April 1965)

We are indebted to Miss Ada Polak, the deputy curator in Britain of the Arts and Crafts Museum of Norway, for this interesting note and photograph. Coade stone-work is well-known around County Hall. The lion from the brewery where the Royal Festival Hall now stands, which was transferred to the entrance to Waterloo and is now seeking another home, is our most celebrated example.

The Ambassador's House, Wellclose Square.

The two houses in the picture used to stand on the west side of Wellclose Square in Stepney. In 1961 they were pulled down, but the two reliefs in their façades were saved and are now resting in the basement of County Hall. They show allegorical pictures of 'the Arts' and 'Harvest' respectively. The one on the left is signed: *Coade. Lambeth. 1790.* The inscription has enabled their story to be traced in some detail.

During the 18th century Wellclose Square was the centre for a sizeable Norwegian colony. In the centre of the Square stood a pretty little church, built in 1696, where they could worship, be married and buried according to the Lutheran ritual they were used to at home, and in the houses round the Square lived prosperous Norwegian merchants, most of them agents for the import of Norwegian timber to Britain, with their families, servants and counting-house clerks.

In 1766, No. 21 (on the left of the picture) became occupied by a certain Georg Wolff from Oslo, who was just starting his own business in the timber importing line. Georg Wolff was an excellent man, intelligent, hardworking, kindly and honest. His business prospered, and in 1782 he found it necessary to take the neighbouring house, No. 22, as well. His firm had by now become the most important in the Square, and in 1787 his career reached its climax when he was appointed Danish-Norwegian Consul General in London. Norway was at this time united with Denmark under one Crown.

Georg Wolff's only son Jens was born in 1767. He was brought up to take over both firm and Consulate. Georg Wolff himself had come from modest beginnings and always remained a simple and unassuming man, but his son learned to speak French and Latin and was sent on the 'Grand Tour'. It was most probably Jens Wolff who had the Coade stone reliefs put up. By 1790, Wellclose Square was beginning to look old and shabby, and the young man, who was just taking his place in the firm, must have wanted to smarten up the premises. It would have been a natural thing to turn to the Coade factory for assistance. Situated on the river bank by Lambeth, it lay surrounded by London's biggest timber yards, all of them owned by clients and customers of the Wolffs.

By the addition of the reliefs, the pair of houses in Wellclose Square was made to look like one large house, and the neo-classical ornaments gave a rejuvenating touch of elegance and fashion. They also made the Wolff houses stand our from the other houses in the Square - the writer has herself heard Nos. 21 and 22 described as 'The Ambassador's House' by people in the neighbour-hood.

To-day, when both the Norwegian Church and the houses in Wellclose Square have been demolished, the reliefs from the Wolff houses are the only tangible memories that remain of the little world of the Norwegian timber merchants in Stepney.

Mahler's Swan-Song.

Keith Bennett
(May 1965)

There is some music to which one returns again and again for sheer enjoyment, deeper study and even spiritual benefit. Such symphonies as Mozart's *Jupiter*, Beethoven's *Choral* or Schubert's Great C major seldom reveal their greatness to even the careful listener; in fact, it is amazing just how often fresh light can be thrown on these works by the different approaches of great conductors. Too often in the past we have been persuaded to concede definitive performances by interpreters who specialize in the music of X or Y. While I agree that some artists may be more responsive - more 'in tune' if you like - to the idiom of a particular composer, I submit that the greater the music the more likely it is to have a number of differing, but equally valid, interpretations. The scientific approach towards the absolute in music can have little basis when its greatest mentor, Stravinsky, has changed his own performances over the years. Human beings are neither machines nor vegetables; the music they produce is not a stagnant pool of ideas.

The names associated with Mahler's music in the past have been Bruno Walter and Otto Klemperer. If asked who was the better interpreter, I would have to reply Walter, although I would hasten to add that I do not hold his readings in such high esteem as some. Walter was a lyricist to such an extent that he sweetened everything. The searing acid to be found in Mahler was often neutralized by Walter's warm humanity. Klemperer on the other hand is in the opposite camp, and his perfomances tend to be too unyielding, resulting in dry prosaic interpretations. Since the war, two notable Mahlerians have arisen. These are István Kertesz and Lorin Maazel, but I hope to add another to this short list after the performance of *Das Lied von der Erde* on 27 May.

Huge waves of sound

This masterpiece, a song cycle symphony for tenor, contralto and orchestra, was a summing up by Mahler of his life's experience. To do this, he chose translations of six Chinese poems which embraced his overall mood of reconciling inevitable death without fear or bitterness. The poems alternate between the false extrovert approach given to the tenor (Drinking Song of Earth's Sorrow, Youth, and Wine in Spring) and the more reflective subjects (Autumn Loneliness, Beauty, The Farewell) given to the contralto. The tenor, Richard Holm, will need the vocal power of a *Heldentenor* if he is to ride the huge waves of orchestral sound, but it is significant and in keeping with Mahler's philosophical concept that it is the contralto who has the more important rôle. And that raises a problem. In my opinion and experience, only Kathleen Ferrier had the vocal technique *and* silver quality of voice for this music; the tone must never become plummy, and this is difficult for a low-pitched voice. Thus, the only performance I have heard where all the beauty was hauntingly presented was when a baritone (allowed for in the score) sang these songs. But when I say that the baritone was Fischer-Dieskau . . . There is still a recording available in which Ferrier takes part, but the one with Fischer-Dieskau has been deleted; however, if you see a copy, snap it up. In the performance this month, the contralto soloist will be Maureen Forrester, who often worked with Bruno Walter on Mahler scores.

If I believe that the core of this work lies with the contralto or baritone I hope I have made it clear that the conductor has a difficult path to find; neither a swoon of schmaltz, nor too square and forthright. Hans Schmidt-Isserstedt is know to me primarily as a Mozartian and he will also include a performance of the Prague Symphony in the programme, but it is as a Mahlerian that I shall want to hear him. I cannot imagine that he will be as sentimental as Walter nor as severe as Klemperer, and it is in that region between these extremes that my perfect Mahler interpreter will be found.

Section 4: New departures

Introduction

The first decade of the new GLC/ILEA set-up brought increasing change to the staff and to the magazine which continued faithfully to reflect their wishes and needs. The long spell of Labour rule at County Hall, which had begun back in 1934, was broken in 1967: henceforth, the two major parties were to alternate in office. In itself, this was bound to increase the "political" content of the magazine; and at the same time other changes in content were brought about by the need actively to seek new readers now that a sizeable proportion of GLC/ILEA staff were no longer Staff Association members, and so did not automatically receive *London Town*.

So specialist columns proliferated, and although these were usually both well written and well informed they are not in general the stuff from which anthologies are made: and with the best will in the world we have been unable to find much of interest in the early seventies. The once famous (or infamous) coup of 1973 which brought in a completely new editorial team, brought a gradual return to more traditional ways - many columns were quietly phased out and there was a slow but steady increase in the number of "general interest" articles published. The "relaunch" of the magazine in February 1976 in a new and perhaps more striking format accentuated this process. So all the "new departures" of this decade served, in the end, only to bring the journal back to what might be called its roots - it was never again to stray very far from them.

The Sounds of Music.

Keith Bennett
(March 1967)

The most exciting month for concert-goers since the Festival Hall opened its doors nearly sixteen years ago: that is how March 1967 should be heralded. The muddle of reinforced concrete and Cornish granite aggregate which has been imprisoned behind a forest of scaffolding for so long has been forged into the South Bank Arts Centre.

By far the most important feature of the Centre for me - the complex comprised an exhibition gallery and two halls for music - is the larger auditorium, the Queen Elizabeth Hall, which is to be opened to the public this month.

Why a hall at all?
Why another concert hall? An over-simplified answer would be that the Festival Hall, for all its obvious merits, is simply not suitable for all types of music. It is nigh on perfect for the 'lean' orchestral music of Mozart and Stravinsky, but

can hardly be considered 'warm' enough, in the acoustic sense, for the music of Brahms, Wagner or Bruckner. However, this is not the main reason why a new hall was desirable. More important than the matter of a suitable reverberation period in a given hall is the much more subtle aesthetic of matching the hall sympathetically with the scale of the music. An ambivalent feature of the Festival Hall's 'dry' acoustic is that even the least powerful instrument can be heard clearly in any part of the hall. But you only needed to sit at the back of the Festival Hall for a Segovia recital and then to hear - as 1,100 'acoustic blotting-paper guinea pigs' experienced last November - that brilliant young guitar student in the Queen Elizabeth Hall, to know that the atmosphere created by the artist, the music, the size of the audience and the hall's acoustic quality, were all factors which contributed to the musical experience: whereas one could hear Segovia almost as a detached observer, one was involved with the student's intimate rustles of tone.

Nautical exterior

While the exterior of the complex reminds me of nothing so much as the superstructure of a Japanese battleship, my first impressions of the auditorium are of airiness, concrete, wood, leather and aluminium. The hall had a seating capacity of 1,106 and its purpose is to meet the musical requirements of soloist performers and small ensembles, so that it is desirable for some flexibility of the acoustics to be attempted. The 'coffee-bean' veneered walls have four sizes of slots which are 'Helmholtz resonators'. These slots communicate with an otherwise enclosed box behind the surface of the pannelling which, depending on the size of the slot, absorbs sound over a particular part of the low frequency range. These slots will be permanently fixed by the time the hall opens. Over the performers' platform is a canopy reflector which can be adjusted so that the direct sound (that which travels straight from the performers to the audience) is the best suited for an individual performance. As far as I am aware, this degree of flexibility in a concert hall is unique and the canopy adjustment does make a considerable difference, as those in the second guinea pig audience can testify.

There are no galleries, so that the problems of acoustic shadowing are avoided. The seats, in the form of two natural leather squabs supported by an aluminium shell, are either fixed to the stepping of the floor (rather like in the Mermaid Theatre) or to varying heights of support. I have reliable information from a long-legged lady that there is plenty of leg-room.

An overhead beam carrying spot-lights appears to me to be a little cumbersome and the bank of air diffusers on the ceiling are more obtrusive than I would have liked.

But the sole criterion, in my view is: how does the music sound? For me it was a newfound experience comparable only to discovering hi-fi after being conditioned to a commercial radiogram.

The Merry Widow.

Maurice Fulcher
(March 1968)

To this 1968 show of the Witan Opera Society, *London Town* sent as guinea pigs for the consumer an experienced opera singer (hereafter the eos) and a hack who is a bit of a nit about music.

To the nit at least it seemed that the monumental effort required to present a musical play must make the stoutest heart flutter. The casual critic may pontificate upon the ideal effects to be achieved but the sheer mechanics of getting the music right, mounting, clothing and moving the piece into elegant action make Sawford's drama crowd seem like a bunch of amateurs. But the critic must clear his head and cool his heart and say plainly whether he was or was not amused. Both the eos and the nit found some pleasant surprises.

The Merry Widow as a sound has lived in the top pop bracket these sixty years. It sugary tale of extra-marital relations and worship of a widow's fortune must shock the young generation. The Edwardians made love and the occasional war as well and did not mind the odd satirical shaft at some fatherland, foreign of course. But all can still hum the dancing romantic melodies of Franz Léhar. He is influenced, we are told by musical authority, by the southern Slav folk tune and his orchestration is piquant. How true.

The eos praised the music and wondered how part-time artistes could achieve so much. For this we must thank first Ronald Rappaport, the musical director, and the orchestra of which he was such a commanding and debonair conductor. Chairman Frank Gilbrook is to be congratulated on obtaining this excellent service to the society. I gather he has connexions with the Guildhall School of Music and Drama, who provided three lively and polished young dancers. He must be as good an ambassador as he was for Pontevedria in the show.

The society is blessed with some fine leading singers. Arthur Bryan, Josephine Davis and Joseph Beachus as Danilo, Anna and de Rosillon were outstanding and could be heard clearly in the farthest recesses of the conference hall. Indeed the power of the singing, both solo and chorus, was a feature of the evening, all the more remarkable when the nit recalled the many inaudible speeches he has heard there at staff meetings.

In the presentation there were many pitfalls. The stage is an open one with no proscenium arch. An orthodox set is impossible and there are serious obstacles to lighting without shadows. The producer, David Tonge, had taken over in midstream and it is therefore miracle enough that the show went on and moved with such verve most of the time. There were lulls, however, while the ballroom dancers queued up to retire. At such times the temperature of the scene falls and it takes a little time to warm up again. More could have been done to move the crowds off the mark quickly and to assemble them before the previous scene had finished, but a completely satisfactory solution would have taxed Tyrone Guthrie. Joan Littlewood might have put the orchestra in Pontevedrian costume at the back of the stage and used curtained alcoves in front to bring the chorus on from all points of the compass.

There was perhaps a little stiffness about the acting, Danilo and Anna excepted, but the mood was sustained by the music and the colourful presentation. The costumes were of no particular period but very becoming and in the main the work of the cast. There was certainly nothing stiff about the chorus of grisettes singing and dancing the can-can with swirling *savoir faire* and revealing with the final flounce of skirts that they were backing Britain to the last extremity. At this the nit applauded wildly.

It is never wise to let any artiste rest on his oars but altogether there were many sights and sounds to please the senses. In the memory lingers a snap view of shirt-sleeved house manager Rawlings reaching for his tail-coat after helping to serve the interval coffee before resuming his immaculate decoration of the auditorium. A fitting tailpiece to this spirited evening.

Sir William Hart, C.M.G.

O. W. Holmes
(May 1968)

The Council's minutes of 21 May will contain the permanent record of the career of Sir William Hart, the Council's first Director-General and Clerk. And with the speeches of the Leader of the Council and the Leader of the Opposition in the Council Chamber, the unprecedented compliment of a luncheon in his honour as the guest of leading members of the Council, and with the tributes at the farewell dinner given for him and Lady Hart by the staff of his own department Sir William's career will have had a fitting climax.

It was in 1955 that a member of the interviewing body came delightedly into a colleague's room and exclaimed, 'We've got Hart!' Of the 119 members that met in the Council Chamber on the day his appointment was confirmed, only sixteen will be able to attend his farewell appearance, and of these only eight will have served continuously. The Council that appointed him exists no longer. The very title on his anteroom door has twice been re-worded.

Mr Francis Bennett, who has been a Chief Whip for the greater part of Sir William's time at County Hall, recalls that when Sir William was appointed he rapidly made newly elected councillors aware that even from the back benches they were serving on a very worthwhile and important organ of government.

Coming, as he did, straight from a New Town, Sir William naturally took the whole of the L.C.C.'s town development programme under his personal supervision, and he gave an enormous boost to a programme which at that time of rising interest rates could have wilted away. It was largely due to his vigour and the confidence he inspired that so many towns could be brought in to assist with the great problems of relocating industry and population away from the centre.

Sir William was soon to be in the thick of the reorganization of London local government. There are on the files letters he had to send (as Clerk to one Council) to himself (as Clerk to the other) - the famous 'Hart to Hart' papers. As Lord Fiske has put it, when Sir Williams comes to look back on those years he may well be able to see them as the birth pains of a new form of municipal society which will probably spread over the whole country, and in that case, he will have served his country, as well as the people of London, very well.

The empire over which Sir William eventually ruled directly was remarkably wide. Someone has calculated that there are 99 different grades in the Clerk's department. There are now more scientists, more statisticians, more journalists and public relations men that there are committee clerks. The very expanse of this empire has meant that he has allowed great freedom to the rulers of the provinces, such as the Director of Research and Intelligence, the General Manager of the Royal Festival Hall and the Scientific Adviser. Yet details never irk him, and when recently he had ensured that the court rolls of the Manor of Harrow should come into the Council's possession he showed a facility in deciphering the medieval script *extempore* which astonished the archivists around him.

In addition to his role as Director-General of the whole of the Council's service, Sir William still had his clerkly responsibilities for the smooth running of the Council's business and that of the ever-increasing number of subordinate groups - advisory bodies, working parties and conferences, as well as the committees, sub-committees and panels themselves. He also lubricated inter-departmental relations through regular meetings of chief officers in his own room.

He now completes his tenure of the top position in local government with not a foe in sight but with a host of friends far and near, not least in the town halls throughout the metropolis. Perhaps the secret of his success has lain in his mastery of the art of personal encounter. Dignified and distinguished in appearance, incisive and intellectually alert, it is hard to imagine him overbearing anyone, whatever the difference in status. If given a thoroughly unsatisfactory draft, he has been known to return it with a disarming covering note, 'I was wondering whether we could say something like this?'

A brother chief officer has spoken of Sir William's calmness, courtesy and patience: 'Seldom have I seen him ruffled, and his capacity for containing himself under extreme provocation has been an example to us all.' His reaction to a mild crisis is, 'Oh, well'; to a major one, 'How tiresome!' Someone in the messenger service has well spoken for his colleagues in describing Sir William as a gentleman. He has the gift of paying attention to anyone who is speaking to him, and at social functions those with whom he has briefly chatted are left with the feeling that their brief encounter is the one he has most looked forward to.

Sir William and Lady Hart are manifestly a devoted couple, anxious to be real parents to their family of three sons and a daughter. They share wide interests, ranging from love of the countryside and their garden to music and the arts. Lady Hart undertakes much voluntary work, including some for the Marriage Guidance Council, and she has always been a welcome visitor to County Hall. For the future it is thought that they will divided their time between their new home in the country (where they say they will try vine-growing) and their London flat.

It is not possible to envisage them as idle and it will be hard to think of County Hall without them. They carry with them respect and affection, and, it is hoped, many happy memories into the years ahead.

The Unknown Underground.

John Adamson
(November 1971)

One tends to think of the London Underground network as something strictly utilitarian, lacking the romance often associated with deserted railway lines and forgotten canals. Quite apart from the interest of the little-known history of the construction of the network, however, the development of the Underground has left unused and disused tunnels and stations in profusion: evidence from the recent past which could well be as fascinating to any researcher as archaeological remains from the times of the Romans.

An example of this is the Metropolitan Line where it runs north-west from Baker Street. Work on this section of line was undertaken by the Metropolitan and St John's Wood Railway soon after it was incorporated in 1864; the service was to run to Hampstead with intermediate stations at St John's Wood Road, Marlborough Road, Swiss Cottage and Finchley Road. So what has happened to the missing stations between Baker Street and Finchley Road?

There can be no doubt of the reason for their demise, which was the construction of the Bakerloo line alongside in the 1930s, with its intermediate stations at St John's Wood and Swiss Cottage duplicating this part of the service provided by the Metropolitan. The fate of the actual structures, however, is not so immediately obvious. At Swiss Cottage, indeed, the surface buildings have been demolished, although the remains of the platforms are still visible and are indeed still lighted. One imagines that few travellers notice this ghost of a former station.

Marlborough Road Metropolitan Line station in the 1970s . . .

. . . and in its prime.

138

The next station towards town, Marlborough Road, is far from being a ghost. Most of it is in fact an Angus Steak House, and the photographs illustrate the building in both its former and present use. The décor of the restaurant is Victorian in style in keeping with the age of the building, and diners can see the trains passing along an open cutting. A hairdressing establishment (on the right of the photograph) is a sort of junior partner in the use of the building.

St John's Wood station, at the junction of St John's Wood Road and Park Road, was for a time renamed Lord's and trains called there only when important cricket matches were being played at the M.C.C. ground. This device did not, however, prevent it from sharing the fate of the other two stations, its buildings have not been put to such dramatic use as the Marlborough Road ones, but appear to have been incorporated in a garage which in spite of displaying a forlorn 'Open' sign has recently been closed down with gates firmly padlocked against closer inspection.

While disused Underground stations and workings would not, perhaps, ever become the subject of a cult, one can hope that these minor but very interesting features of the urban scene will be properly appreciated and even, where appropriate, preserved.

Passing Brompton Road.

John Adamson
(May 1972)

In an article last year I drew attention to three disused underground stations on the Metropolitan Line, and a *London Town* correspondent provided some information on such stations on the Northern Line. The Piccadilly Line provides a subject for research just as interesting as these other two lines.

The Great Northern, Piccadilly and Brompton Railway opened from Finsbury Park to Hammersmith on 15 December, 1906. Three stations on that line have now ceased to be used for their original purpose, Brompton Road, Down Street and York Road. They soon proved to be of limited use because they were so close to neighbouring ones, and a system of non-stopping trains was introduced so that the three stations were often missed.

The failure of trains to stop at Brompton Road caused some controversy, including letters to *The Times*. During the 1926 coal strike an attempt was made to close the station but questions in Parliament led to its being re-opened. The announcement by station staff 'Passing Brompton Road' became a familiar one, and a comedy with that title with Marie Tempest, opened at the Criterion Theatre in 1928. The station eventually closed in 1934; during the last war it accommodated the National Fire Service.

The illustration on the following page shows Brompton Road in 1925; the board at the front announces, hopefully, 'Frequent electric trains to all parts of London'. The dome rising above the station on the left is that of the Brompton Oratory. This station, like Down Street and York Road, was designed by Leslie W. Green. All three incorporated ruby red glazed bricks, making them immediately identifiable. Most of Brompton Road Station has recently been demolished, but part remains, as offices.

Down Street Station - also used as offices - may be found apparently intact in its quiet side street off Piccadilly, close to Hyde Park Corner. It was closed to traffic on 21 May 1932. On part of the site of the station tunnels a reversing siding was laid between the running lines, which enabled trains to be reversed if traffic from the north were heavier that from the west. There were also facilities for examining disabled trains. Down Street had an even more distinguished war record than Brompton Road. It housed the HQ of the Railway Executive Committee, which was responsible for the administration of British railways in wartime: Churchill and the War Cabinet met there often during the 1940/41 period of intensive air raids.

York Road, just north of King's Cross, had a less interesting history than the other two. It was closed in 17 September 1932 and, as in the case of Down Street, a reversing siding was subsequently built at platform level.

Brompton Road Station.

London's Villages — Beckenham.

John Parker
(April 1975)

'I live in Beckenham . . .' 'It's in Bromley' 'No not Bromley by Bow, London, but in Kent' 'Yes . . . the other tennis place before Wimbledon'. A fairly common social conversation, with non-South London acquaintances; but for us the name Beckenham conjures up an image of one of London's most prosperous and well endowed districts known by estate agents as 'A desirable and sought after area'.

No longer a village, Beckenham was a municipal borough of some 80,000 people until 1965 when it became part of the 39,000 odd acres which makes Bromley the largest of the London boroughs. Despite being part of the everlasting urban sprawl of London, Beckenham still has a strong feeling of identity, aided by a cordon of open spaces which separate it from its congested Londonward neighbours of Downham, Bellingham, Sydenham and Penge.

Between Dulwich and Sevenoaks on the outward radial migration corridor, the thousand year old Beckenham village has, for the last hundred years, been much influenced by its railways; these, constructed in the 1850's and 60's, brought the Victorian and Edwardian villas to occupy the land of encircling farms - still remembered by village elders. Railway electrification in the 1920's and 30's stimulated green-fields housing, leaving the villas untouched but causing redevelopment in the old High Street. Beckenham is now largely inhabited by middle class commuters who find it an ideal dormitory suburb.

The pervading impression of Beckenham is of leafy spaciousness, a combination of parks, trees, wide roads, and well tended gardens. A semi-rural atmosphere is fostered by its remaining unmade roads, numerous squirrels and the foxes which inhabit the railway embankments and Beckenham Place Park. Since leaving the care of the GLC, the wild plants and woodlands of this fine park are now sadly mutilated, but it still has the busiest public golf course in the country, and the white 18th century Mansion, now used as a golf clubhouse and restaurant, still dominates the landscape.

Until recently, three streams also added to this character, the Ravensbourne on Beckenham's eastern boundary, the Chaffwich on its western side and the Beck through the middle. However, the streams no longer meander, they are now corsetted in utilitarian concrete channels - virtually surface water sewers, necessary to prevent our periodic flooding, but one of the locality's most insensitively designed public works 'improvements' Dr Johnson's admonition on the Ravensbourne: 'But oh! how changes with changing years, 'Tis now the vilest stream on earth . . .' has finally been fulfilled.

As with most urban villages it is now normal to associate the name of Beckenham primarily with the main shopping street. This still retains its ancient sinuous pattern; with at one end, the older buildings grouped around the parish church of St. George's (its 13th century lych gate reputedly one of the oldest in England) and at the other end, clustered about a traffic roundabout, the cinema and main post office. There are long-standing plans to pedestrianise the High Street, but unfortunately a local consensus in favour of this will be hard to achieve.

The village that grew into a small town now boasts a cottage hospital, swimming pool, library, repertory theatre, an ex-technical institute, police station, town hall, fire station, several churches, a town park, a railway junction, supermarkets, innumerable estate agents and building society offices, and two local newspapers. The only buildings with any architectural or historic signifi-cance are three pubs, the 17th century 'George Inn', the 'Three Tuns' and just outside, in our only conservation area, the 'Jolly Woodman'. Near the parish church are the 18th century Rawlins Almshouses and Old Council Hall contain-ing part of the former manor house.

Redevelopment looms over the shopping centre, a backwash from that which in the last ten years has swept away so may of the old villas, and their forest trees. The building boom has been stimulated by Beckenham's potential, a trebling of permitted residential density and an 18 minute train journey to

St. George's Church, Beckenham.

Victoria (maybe these attractions explain all those estate agents or vice-versa). Ironically, the developers have destroyed much of the environment that their clients were seeking - not an unusual situation, either in London or outside its boundaries. In parts Beckenham can still match an eighteenth century description: 'A town as delightful as it is salubrious ... to the citizen and the courtier such a spot must be an invitation to repose from the bustling scenes of the capital . .' Recent developments are, however, obscuring its particular identity and even our once famed tennis tournament is now in decline. Still, the past will linger whilst the historic road names outnumber the 'closes' and 'courts' of the modern developer and while we all continue to put 'Kent' after our addresses even though we are in London.

It is what is left of the past that gives character to modern Beckenham and justifies its inclusion in a series on London's 'villages'. That character is, of couse, changing. Like so many other London suburbs whose heyday was between wars it cannot, surely, continue much longer uncomfortably suspended between past and future. The past was pleasantly rural, the future is likely to be decidedly urban. But for the present life in Beckenham is still relatively pleasing, still not quite as disturbing - even horrific - as is some other less favoured suburbs. It can and should remain so for a while yet.

Note: The first example in these pages of a long-running 1970s series - see also page 158.

All on a Summer's Day.

Hugh Springall
(September 1975)

The first Friday in July has become the traditional day for the greatest of the many inter-departmental competitions, Sports Day. For a few years now it has been held at the National Sports Centre at Crystal Palace and anyone keen on enjoying athletic competition has been able to sample the very real delight of running on the famous 'Tartan' track, however modest his or her prowess.

Frequently the event has been blessed with unbroken sunshine except for the famous thunderstorm in 1973 which provided a break between two bright halves, allowed two hardy competitors to demonstrate an exhibition of unlikely acquatic sports, and nearly stopped the whole show. This year, despite the summer of roasting drought, the sunshine was restricted to the early birds competing in the morning and after a wet lunch break the afternoon's show-pieces were held in damp grey weather before a cheerful rather than spirited, and disappointingly small crowd, and the 199th American Independence Day was not particularly heartily celebrated except by Mrs. King winning at Wimbledon.

388 competitors from thirteen departments had entered the individual events and more were involved in team events such as the relays and tug-of-war. As in the past two medium-sized departments, Treasurer's and Mechanical and Electrical Engineering, put all the others to shame in getting staff to enter, with

sixty and fifty-nine respectively, overshadowing the efforts of such giants as Planning and Transportation (10), Architect's (22). Throughout the afternoon interest was maintained in these two departments' clash in the Sir Frederick Menzies Trophy for the most personal points scored by competitors reaching a modest standard in each individual competition. Departments are handicapped on a simple scale based on size, and Treasurer's eventually won comfortably by 356 points to Mech. and Elec.'s 292.

With so many competitors, nineteen events took place in the morning including two finals. If this situation is repeated in the future it may be that the competitions can be spread more over the whole day with the possible inclusion of more events; at present there are only four women's events (one a 'novices' event), no hurdles, javelin, discus, pole vault , or triple jump.

Despite the day's greyness keen competition kept spectators and competitors involved throughout the afternoon. Bob Kislingbury (of D.G.'s) who was injured last year showed a welcome return to fitness and form, winning the 100 metres (equalling his own 1972 record of 11.1 sec) and the 200 metres and coming second in the shot put (which he won last year on one leg!) P. Brown (Supplies) won both the novices race and the meeting record, to beat the previous title and record-holder John Huntingford, (E.O.'s) into second place in the 800m with a time of 1m 58.5s. Huntingford who has been a leading athlete in the middle-distance races for some years now was beaten into third place in the 1500m, won by P. Holland (also E.O.'s).

Two of the girls were outstanding: Miss M. Russell (E.O.'s) who won the long jump with a record leap of 5.11 metres and the high jump, and Miss Denise Fitzgerald (D.G.'s) who took the 100 metres in the record time of 12.0 sec and came second in the long jump. She and Kislingbury found strong team-mates to beat the holders (E.O.'s) in the mixed 4 x 100 metres relay. E.O.'s, however won the women's medley relay, came second in the men's medley relay and the 1500m team race.

The men's departmental champions were Architect's making up in quality what they lacked in quantity, who won the 800 metres novices, the 1500 metres walk handicap and the veterans' 110 metres in which R. Robinson smoothly beat the meeting's organiser Monty Prouten into second place. The women's champions were E.O.'s who, with their third place in the men's championship, also won the Victor Ludorum - the Delhi Cup. Housing for the umpteenth successive year won the 72-stone tug-of-war and the Fire Brigade the catchweight.

The most remarkable award of the say was, however, that of the Andrew Blackman Cup for the Sports Personality of the Day to P. C. Hoare, the Director of Mechanical and Electrical Engineering, who was the first chief officer to compete in living memory and did so much to encourage his department's efforts. He did not win, nor in the end did his team, but they typified the attitude without which Sports Day would not exist.

Praise is due to Monty Prouten and his team of organisers for keeping up with a very tight schedule necessitated by the evening's international meeting. Even the Boroughs' relays needed heats! Brent won the men's and Croydon the women's. The only restlessness appeared when the massed choir at the start of the 1500 metre walk were delayed and gave a more effective performance of 'Why are we waiting' than they did of walking.

There must, however, remain questions about the suitability of time and place. Some of these will be treated in a later article.

Along the Downs — I.

Charles Hunneman
(February 1976)

The South Downs Way was inaugurated by the Countryside Commission in 1972, to provide a continuous right of way for walkers and riders between Eastbourne in Sussex and Buriton in Hampshire, a distance of some 80 miles. In spite of a long acquaintance with many of the more accessible stretches of the route, I could not resist the challenge to attempt at least to walk the whole length. This can be done over four to five days staying overnight at suitable places including Youth Hostels - or you can walk the whole distance in a series of suitably planned days, using public transport, as I did.

The Way officially starts at the Belle Tout lighthouse, near Beachy Head, and goes via Birling gap, the Seven Sisters and the Cuckmere valley to Alfriston: an alternative route for both walkers and riders starts at Eastbourne and reaches Alfriston via the northern escarpment of the Downs. This was the route I selected on a cloudy, blustery day just before last Easter, with Lewes the objective of my first day's walk.

Spurning the aid of a bus I walked through the Old Town of Eastbourne - which has many interesting old buildings and is a contrast to the mainly Victorian seaside resort we all know. But walking was the object: I had a tight schedule in front of me so I steeled myself against the charms of this pleasant little suburb and toiled up the Brighton road towards the golf course. Turning right from the road the signpost told me I was on the Way at last and this was downland walking at its best. The path skirts Willingdon and Coombe hills and one has a magnificent view across the historic but somewhat featureless Pevensey Bay to the sandstone ridge behind Hastings. Nor is one aware that, at the foot of the hill, is a fairly thickly populated strip of development (Willingdon): the sense of remoteness so typical of a downland walk really begins to assert itself.

After an hour's walking I had a brief rest and a snack: this turned out to be the last food I was to eat until late afternoon. The track soon swung in a westerly direction, giving views right across the Weald, before dropping down into the dry valley in which the village of Jevington is situated. My sense of solitude was absolute, until a small boy materialised from nowhere and whipped past me down the bumpy chalk road. This was the first person I had seen since leaving the Brighton road.

I have always thought of Jevington as one more straggling village that extends the suburban belt of Polegate into the Downs. But approach it from the east, from the heart of the hills, and you see it in its true setting as a typical downland village with a small flint church. St. Andrews, with its Saxon tower, has a most attractive exterior. Spare a few minutes, as I did, to look inside: there is an unusual Saxon sculpture of Christ thrusting a sword shaped cross into a beast's head, symbolising the triumph of good over evil.

It is quite a steep pull out of the village: at this point the escarpment is indented so that the now-familiar view of the Weald is frequently seen framed between two hillsides. Soon, however, I was climbing towards the long barrow at the top of Windover Hill, famous for the Long Man of Wilmington 'looking naked towards the shires' in the words of Kipling. And what a splendid view it is, out to the Wealden plain, with the meanderings of the Cuckmere at one's feet and the massif of Firle Beacon and Bostal Hill overshading the broached spire of Berwick church.

Jevington Church.

It is a steep drop from Windover Hill to the Cuckmere, and I was glad to be able to clip a bit off the journey by crossing the Cuckmere by the stone bridge and taking a track via Winton which led back to the ridge, so by-passing Alfriston. But don't miss Alfriston if you haven't seen it before, and don't try to be clever like me and miss out on your lunch. It was midday and I thought I could reach the Ouse valley before the pubs shut. But although it is ridge walking all the way with no undulations the distance from Cuckmere to Ouse is nine miles.

However, I was enjoying the views, with Newhaven and the sea to the left and later that curious detached outcrop of the Downs, Mount Caburn, on the right. Ahead of me, the red and white navigation mast on the top of Beddingham Hill: there were times when I thought that mast was running away from me. When I did finally stand on the top of Beddingham Hill, looking down on the Ouse valley, it was past two o'clock.

Yet another steep descent to the river valley, across the Newhaven road and the Lewes-Brighton railway at Rodmell station - more like the Bluebell line than one of our links to the continent. I pressed on to the village of Southease, past the charming 13th century church with its round tower (one of only three in Sussex, and all in the Ouse valley) only to find neither pub nor café. The Way here follows the main road to the next village, Rodmell, which I reached well after closing time. At this point the Way turns north-west, well away from Lewes, crossing the A27 Lewes-Brighton road at Falmer and rejoining the northern ridge at Blackcap. My train home was at 4.28, so further Downs walking was out of the question.

Now I had to slog it along that wretched road for $3^1/2$ miles, through Kingston and Southover, to Lewes. I was hungry and the rain, which had threatened since midday, was now falling in earnest. The charms of Southover - Anne of Cleves' house and all - failed to seduce me, and I made post haste for the station. The story had a happy ending: Lewes station not only had a buffet, but it was open!

Anyone who would follow my plan of tackling the Way in daily stages is strongly advised to make Alfriston the lunch stop. Also make sure you have thick soles to your shoes: not all the walk is soft downland turf - there are quite a few jagged flint paths. Also of help is a little booklet *Along the South Downs Way*, published by the Eastboune Rambling Club and obtainable at YHA bookshops or at Stanfords of Long Acre.

Along the Downs – II.

Charles Hunneman
(April 1976)

The second stage of my walk along the South Downs Way began at Lewes where I had left off in March, seven months before. This October day was cloudy but with sunny intervals, and the autumn tints were at their best. Once again a tough schedule forced me to turn my back on the architectural glories of Lewes. This town is built on a spur of the Downs, and it is only a short walk through residential streets before one reaches open county. I took the track towards the now deserted racecourse, following one of the former rides past the slope of Mount Harry and on to Blackcap, with its grove of trees. Here, the real Way joins the main ridge, on its way up from Falmer.

From here to Pyecombe, past Ditchling Beacon, it was all ridge walking, with the Weald on the right and sweeping Downs to the left. A friendly farmer on a Land Rover stopped for a chat and I pushed on to Ditchling Beacon: this hill, with its good road communications, is never entirely deserted and I saw more people here than I was to see on the Downs all day.

Westward of Ditchling one becomes aware of the tremendous growth of population that is taking place along the Brighton railway - in places like Hassocks, Burgess Hill and Haywards Heath. After about a mile I reached 'Jack and Jill', the two windmills which are such distinctive landmarks on the Downs above Clayton tunnel. Here the Way takes an unexpected turn to the left - not very clearly signposted, but there is no mistaking the right path as soon as you reach New Barn Farm, for it follows the edge of Pyecombe golf course, and you see it clearly going up Newtimber Hill, across the valley.

A short walk along the A273 brought me to Pyecombe village, past the little flint church with its squat thirteenth century pyramidical tower and nautical weathervane. Bang on the A23 is the 'Plough', a free house which has been gentrified out of all recognition, but where one can still hear the distinctive burr of Sussex amongst the voices in the bar. No mistakes about eating this time - a reasonable 'ploughman's lunch' washed down with a pint of Younger's set me up for the rest of the trail. Such was my determination to complete my stint for the day, however, that the half hour I had for lunch was my only rest all day.

Over the A23 I started the long climb over Newtimber Hill to the hamlet of Saddlescombe, getting a first glimpse of Chanctonbury Ring on the way. Pevsner (*The buildings of England - Sussex* - Penguin Books) tells us that the farm has a timber-framed south wing of the sixteenth century, but I wonder how many people have noticed the large public clock in the farmyard? The steepest climb I had encountered since Eastbourne brought me from Saddlescombe to Devil's Dyke.

From here there is a splendid view towards the North Downs, whilst down below is the lonely little village of Poynings, in a magnificent setting of trees. If you don't mind a road with the occasional car, it is almost as rewarding to follow the foot of the Downs, along Newtimber Lane, through a string of lovely villages - Poynings, Fulking and Edburton - to reach the Adur valley at Beeding.

But my route was along the heights and I passed the top of Devil's Dyke with a shudder: motor road, hotel, golf course and the inevitable rubbish do not improve the general peacefulness of the Downs. Beyond the hotel the path follows the northern edge of the Downs all the way to the Adur, past Edburton Hill to Truleigh Hill overlooking the valley. This was once more true downland walking - bare of trees, but with incomparable views towards Chanctonbury and distant Blackdown. Away to the left the Downs slope towards the coast, with a distant glimpse of the chimneys of Portslade power station. The power lines of the National Grid cross the Downs on their way northward here, but to me they don't intrude - somehow they fit into the pattern.

Here I was in West Sussex, and was soon climbing Truleigh Hill, where I was interested to see ploughing in progress, with the inevitable following of gulls. The path passes the door of the handsome new Youth Hostel and then begins a gradual descent to the Adur valley. Here, in spite of more tempting hills looming ahead across the valley, I had to desert the Way and head south for

148

Shoreham and home. However, the track above the valley keeps its downland character almost to the edge of Shoreham itself where it suddenly crosses the new A27 on an extremely high viaduct, close to the 'spaghetti' junction with the A283 Adur valley road.

For me, a fitting end to a memorable day was to see, across the valley, the romantic Victorian Gothic outline of Lancing College chapel, silhouetted against the setting sun. A short walk through residential streets brought me to the station. Unfortunately, although I had half an hour to spare before my train, I was too late to see inside the splendid Norman church of St. Mary de Haura.

Stage three followed closely, in November, but was an almost total disaster. I should have known better than to have started off, for the forecast said cloud and occasional showers. As I walked up by the banks of the Adur and over the old wooden bridge at Old Shoreham it had already begun to drizzle. My path on to the actual course of the Way - which I had left three weeks before on the other side of the Adur - was a long and gradual climb past Lancing College to the main ridge of the Downs, passing a most depressing rubbish tip in a combe of the Downs, and soon the cloud closed in and the rain started.

As I gained the ridge, all hell was let loose, and the rain seemed to have an almost personal malevolence. Chanctonbury Ring, that well-known land-mark, came on me with startling suddenness - I almost cannoned into the first of the trees. The whole effect of the rain, wind and mist somehow conjured up visions of the primaeval origins of this place. No views from here, of course, and, careful as I was on the slippery slope down to the A24 at Washington, I stretched my length in the white mud, which improved neither my temper nor my appearance.

However, the rain left off and a welcome drying wind was blowing as I regained the ridge beyond the A24. Pushing on westwards the going became very heavy, but I did get one misty view of the windings of the Arun towards Pulborough. This was on Amberley Mount, but here my time was running out and, for the first time in my wanderings, I had to retrace my steps, over Rackham Hill and down into Storrington for a bus to Worthing and home. But it had been better than slogging along the road.

The Constable Exhibition.

Jim Hickman
(April 1976)

The exhibition at the Tate Gallery commemorating the bi-centenary of the birth of John Constable does not offer any startling revelations. It confirms Constable's reputation as one of England's finest artists without providing any new ammunition for those who consider him more talented than Turner. Nevertheless, 1975 was Turner's year and it is only fair that Constable should be similarly honoured in 1976.

As with Turner, Constable has suffered greatly from the many poor reproductions of his work. It is easy to glance at the 'six footers' such as *The Hay*

Wain, The Cornfield, Stratford Mill, The Leaping Horse or *Flatford Mill* and dismiss them as chocolate box art. Yet examine any square inch of these paintings and there is a wealth of lovingly painted detail to be discovered - here, the magnificent catalogue is helpful with its carefully chosen colour illustrations. Seen together, Constable's paintings constitute a great hymn of praise to the glories of the English countryside and, in particular, to the areas he knew best - East Bergholt, Dedham, Salisbury, Hampstead and Brighton.

Constable self portrait.

The exhibition is skilfully organised since it traces Constable's activity year by year from about 1790 to his death in 1837 and separates the paintings he exhibited during his life and on which his contemporary reputation was based (these are shown against a plum-coloured background) from his more private works (against a grey background). Each year's work is preceded by biographical notes which provide a fascinating undercurrent to the paintings themselves. For those not already familiar with the details of Constable's long courtship of the beautiful Maria Bicknell, there may even be a temptation to pass quickly by the paintings between 1804 and 1816 whilst following their stuttering progress, in the teeth of parental opposition, towards a happy but all too short marriage. Maria produced seven children, yet was to die from a pulmonary thrombosis in 1828 at the age of forty-one.

During the early years, Constable made his living by portrait painting, whilst his landscapes remained unsold. It is the landscapes, however, revealing as they do his deep understanding and love of Dutch art (his London residence was known as Ruysdael House) which we now value most. He possessed such a precise eye for detail. As he said in his last lecture, 'The Art of seeing Nature is a thing almost as much to be acquired as the art of reading Egyptian hieroglyphics.' His success in acquiring this art can be seen in his study of Hadleigh Castle. Completed in 1829, this was based on a pencil sketch made whilst staying in the area in June 1814 when he told Maria, 'I walked upon the beach at South End. I was always delighted with the melancholy grandeur of a sea shore.' This comment takes on a poignant aspect in the context of Maria's death in the year before the painting was completed.

The Feast at the Royal Festival Hall.

F. G. Gough
(May 1976)

When I retired I thought to use some leisure to study the arts deeply, to penetrate meaning, to find the mystery behind the magic, but this was a grandiose ambition requiring knowledge and application beyond me. Nevertheless, as a first step, and apart from being constantly tuned to beloved Radio Three, I applied to be enrolled in the panel of honorary stewards at the Royal Festival Hall, and this has proved to be a most rewarding spare-time occupation.

First the public to whom the steward has prime responsibility. The average concert audience are well-behaved, happy to be there and needing the minimum of direction, except, perhaps, the poor dears who have forgotten the difference between Left and Right, Up and Down, but who are so grateful for being directed into the correct seat. Most delightful are the ballet fans, very young ladies in the longest of long dresses, hair in a bun, toes pointed, head held high and dying to be mistaken for Dame Margot. Once I had the stunning sight of a tiny, exquisitely pretty Japanese lady in national costume, perfect to the last formal fold, every strand of hair just right. Every woman within half a mile of her looked as if she had only recently escaped from a haunted house, hotly pursued by Messrs. Lee and Price. And there is the man who, to his own intense satisfaction, tells funny jokes to the stewards during the Interval: 'Why did the policeman climb the tree?' 'To get to the special branch!' His wife smiles sympathetically.

The stewards are a mixed collection of both retired and active teachers, nurses, students, office workers, house-wives and superannuated music lovers who work together in friendship and easy co-operation. Among them is an immense accumulation of experience which enables them, for instance, to deal tactfully with the people who arrive late and are excluded from the Hall, frustrated and fuming, until the end of the first item. Awkward customers are very, very rare.

The Senior stewards are a dedicated body of men and (a few) women with a remarkable record of honorary work in organising the stewards' service, almost every day of the year for up to six concerts or recitals on a Sunday and for three events on any normal night of the week. Many Seniors and some others have been members of the panel since the opening of the Royal Festival Hall.

And the music. The value and privilege of being on a rota with attendances at regular intervals in any of the three concert halls is a chance to hear a great variety of music performed at a standard that must be among the highest in the world. In addition to the familiar masterpieces (and some critics do complain of an over-preponderance of 'standard classics') there is the opportunity to hear the unfamiliar, to see newcomers and to discover elements of greatness in fields other than the classical. I recall the personality and power of the popular singer who stood and belted out song after song for an hour and a half, in complete control of his enthralled audience and finishing as strongly as he began. It wasn't all due to the amplifiers. There was the folk musician who inspired hundreds of his young audience to dance hand in hand round the Hall in an Irish jig, a feat not achieved by any other perfomer to my knowledge.

There is the thrill of hearing a work completely new and trying to estimate if it will last and become a classic of the future. For me, there was the new experience of Indian music, of actually seeing the creation of those complex webs of sound, comparable to an Eastern carpet, or the infinite patterns made by the waves along the side of a ship. I found most moving the accord between the players through the long improvisations. Occasionally there was a glance and the exchange of a half smile which I somehow knew meant that that had been a special bit, a challenge had been made (and answered) to add something new; love and understanding had passed between them and continually the beautiful sound poured from those peculiar instruments. It was a revelation.

So what is the greatest, to an earnest amateur, very much dazzled by magic and judging the music largely through his emotions? Here goes:

The pinnacle must be Mozart's *Symphony No. 40 in G-Minor*: unless it is Bach's *St. Matthew Passion*: unless it is Beethoven's *Third Razumovsky Quartet*: unless it is Shostakovitch's *Fifth Symphony*: unless it is the Mozart *Clarinet Quintet* - or the *String Quintet in G-Minor*, or, perhaps, an *Evening Raga* by Ravi Shankar: unless it is *Der Rosenkavalier*: unless, unless - and endless line of 'unless'. May it continue for ever. I am in favour of enchantment and so long as someone points me in the right direction for home afterwards I shall be happy.

What about the critics? Sometimes I feel quite sorry for them.

Note: This article was part of a special issue of the journal to celebrate 25 years of the Royal Festival Hall.

Guido Cantelli and
Schubert's 'Great' C Major Symphony.

Keith Bennett
(May 1976)

The music of Schubert was always part of Cantelli's repertoire. The very first symphony - indeed, the first music - which the young maestro conducted in Britain was Schubert's Second and one can imagine that this relatively neglected work received a splendid performance. Mere surmise on my part? I think not: Cantelli proved to be a superb interpreter of Haydn and you cannot get more Haydnesque than this early Schubert (we shall be able to judge more rationally when Volume Two of the Cantelli Legacy appears, for the symphony is included in the recordings being prepared for release).

The *Unfinished* was also to be found in his programmes and lest any reader considers that this correspondent relinquishes his critical responsibilities where Cantelli is concerned, let it be known that in my view the young conductor did not live up to his own exceptionally high standards in his commercial recording of this work.

The *'Great' C major* came into Cantelli's repertoire relatively late in his short career. He first conducted the symphony at a concert given by the Philharmonia in the Royal Albert Hall on 18 May 1953. There followed two further performances on 7 and 9 October in Milan with La Scala Orchestra and on 27 December 1953 he gave what was to be his final performance of the symphony in Carnegie Hall with the NBC Symphony Orchestra. It is cold facts like these which bring home ever more forcibly the tragedy of Cantelli's early death.

Schubert's last symphony holds more traps for the unwary conductor than many a modern 'difficult' composition. It is not music for every day and none but a first rate orchestra should dream of tackling it. To those thoughts, culled from Bernard Shore's 'Sixteen Symphonies', must be added another rider: a perfunctory performance means - for this listener at least - sheer purgatory and unadulterated boredom. It is one of the very few nineteenth century symphonic masterpieces which can be reduced to trivia in the hands of an unsympathetic conductor. The musician who wishes to have a successful interpretation will do well to remember Toscanini's incessant cry 'Singing, cantando, ah, cantando sempre! Always cantare'; without a singing, lyrical approach one is doomed to failure. But there's another problem to be overcome: the conductor needs to be able to build up the climaxes of this huge symphonic structure and to see the thing whole, no little achievement when one is contemplating a work of some fifty minutes in length.

This symphony is particularly associated with three conductors: Sir Adrian Boult, Arturo Toscanini and Bruno Walter and I have been comparing their most recently released recordings (that is to say Boult with the LPO; Toscanini with the Philadelphia and Walter with the Columbia Symphony Orchestra) with this actual concert performance which Cantelli gave with the NBC Symphony Orchestra. As expected, Cantelli's interpretation is nearest to

153

Toscanini's in conception. Theirs are the only recorded performances known to me which accomplish the *Andante con moto* in under thirteen minutes. However, the young conductor takes over a minute longer than his mentor in the first movement. The reason for this stopwatch talk is to help dispel the commonly held notion that a Cantelli performance was a carbon copy of Toscanini's. What is striking in this Cantelli performance is the judicious choice of tempi, the scrupulous observance of the score's dynamics, the avoidance of personal idiosyncrasy - but these are hallmarks to be found in the majority, the very high majority, of Cantelli's interpretations.

However, these very real virtues have resulted in a somewhat bland statement of the score which the twenty-two year old mono recording does little - understandably - to enhance. On the other hand, thirty-three year old Cantelli, was just gaining experience with what the American critic Harris Goldsmith has described as 'this treacherous piece' and it is a testament to his musicianship that his interpretation - with the experience of a mere four performances on which he could develop his conception - already had the basic qualities necessary for a great performance in the future. There was not to be a future . . . and that makes his loss all the greater. It is idle to speculate what might have been, but had Cantelli been given the opportunity to give as many performances of this elusive symphony as Boult, Toscanini or Walter, then I might be speaking of this record with even more enthusiasm.

The number of the record is ATS GC 1204 and is only available from the Arturo Toscanini Society as part of a boxed set.

Note: Keith Bennett's long-running series on Guido Cantelli (1920-56), a notable Italian orchestral conductor who flourished in the immediate post-World War II years until his death in an air accident, was destined never to be finished: the GLC (and with it *London Town*) came to an end before Keith Bennett ran out of likely material.

A moving story.

John Shove
(June 1976)

I was never one for letting the grass grow under my feet, literally or metaphorically. Before I retired I varied the attractions of a London flat, with ready access to the Royal Festival Hall, by those of a rural cottage with the finest view in Surrey. I had bought it for £300 and refashioned it with my own hands, so it never made the drain on my resources which my envious colleagues hinted.

War service in Italy made me long to see more of that country. This I did, making many friends there. I got permission from the church authorities at Amalfi to convert what was in effect a mountainside cave into a flat. So on retirement I divided my time between Amalfi and Surrey, with forays to South America and other exotic parts. On one of these I met and married my Japanese wife Chie Ko.

Times grew difficult in Amalfi; the sea grossly polluted; no security of tenure, for the church will not sell its property; the 150 steps to climb every time you went in or out grew steeper; and prices rose inordinately.

We knew and loved Greece and are now installed in Corfu. But the point of my tale is how we got there. I must explain that among Chie Ko's accomplishments are her skill and tirelessness as a car driver which have rendered it unnecessary for me to acquire the art.

To get our furniture from Surrey to Corfu we bought an old ambulance and found a young graduate beatnik to drive it in return for a holiday. Chie Ko drove us in our own car.

We left Dover loaded to the brim but on arrival at Zeebrugge we could not find my wallet with log books, passports, insurance papers, driving licences, petrol coupons, money and permission to import furniture into Greece. We were promptly deported from Belgium. We left the vehicles behind, went back to Dover hoping to find the missing documents but without success, so back to Zeebrugge to tell the young man to push on with the ambulance and we would meet him in Vienna. Once more to Dover where we got temporary replacements of dubious validity and yet again sailed for Zeebrugge by the night boat. Rendezvous Vienna! But with Chie Ko knocking up 70 mph we got there first. Then we made for the Greek frontier, after difficulties with the Yugoslav police because my wife had no driving licence and looked too young to drive. No difficulty on the Greek frontier even though the import permit was with the van and we had dutiable bits and pieces in the car.

At Corfu we awaited the van, but this had struck real trouble at the border and after 24 hours delay was allowed to go to Corfu at night accompanied by a Customs guard who came to see the van unloaded. We had to pay £50 import duties since the entry permit was alleged to be invalid for 'technical' reasons.

Then the beatnik and I set off for Amalfi to collect the first load of furniture down the 150 steps from flat to road. With the help of a local Hercules almost all was loaded, with the van's tail-piece down. Full to the brim with parts of a wardrobe tied on with rope, we set off.

In spite of trouble with the Italian police who said you couldn't see the rear number plate with the tail down and the furniture tied on, we got to Brindisi where I said goodbye to the young graduate and the van was driven on to the boat by one of the crew who repeated this good deed at Corfu.

Here the Customs cut up rough. They had already passed the ambulance once full of furniture and here it was again fuller than ever. Everything had to be unloaded for examination and they refused to provide a Customs officer to see this done at the house as before. However, luck was with us. Before the van was half unloaded the Customs were fed up with us and wanted to get home for lunch so they called it a day and we got away after paying another £100.

The end of this saga cannot be told till our return from Amalfi with the second and last lot of furniture. At least we shall be able to control our own destiny, for Chie Ko is practising driving the van and I shall be able to continue my favourite role of telling other people what to do. But we can't go yet because we have no passports. Townsend Ferries wrote to say the missing documents were in Belgium but when I telegraphed for them they replied 'no knowledge of any bag'.

To be continued . . . with a happy ending?

Note: John Shove was a noted Staff Association figure in the late 1930s. His retirement in Corfu was to prove a long and very active one.

Blackhurst looks back — and forward.

Len Hudson
(October 1976)

(Shortly after his retirement Derrick Blackhurst, lately an Assistant Director-General and, farther back, a distinguished Editor of *London Town*, met the Editor for what proved to be a fascinating and stimulating talk over past, present and future. What follows is a summary of that discussion).

Mr Blackhurst began by ranging back over his years in the service. Looking back, he felt that life was now more hard-driven than in the past. There was less time to indulge in staff club and other activities - including the production of this magazine: and outside the office the tremendous increase in the number of women making careers for themselves left less time for the home. These were themes he had developed more fully in his article in our 75th anniversary number in January 1975: they were, he felt, the most conspicuous changes in the way staff in the service conducted their daily lives.

More fundamentally, the most dramatic change had been the transformation of the Council from an instrument for getting things done into a political arena - a change that had been particularly rapid and marked since about 1970. In the past, Members of the Council had given their first consideration to the need to achieve something worthwhile for London: now, they tended to play to the gallery, to promise the earthly paradise rather than set about getting practicable improvements. As a result, staff morale had fallen, and much of the old satisfaction of working for London had been lost. Members were, he thought, now much more conscious of their vulnerability at the elections: but the paradox was that in fact whatever they said and did had remarkably little effect upon their political fortunes - those were determined by national issues, and the standing of the main parties nationally. But Members seemed unable or unwilling to recognise that simple fact.

The present structure of London government, he thought, could not possibly last. It was expensive and inefficient: the London Government Act 1963 had divided power in such a way that it was virtually impossible to get effective action on anything. The solution, he felt, was not to give more power to the London boroughs, as many now advocated: nor would it do to give the GLC, as presently constituted, more extensive powers. If this were done, bureaucracy would grow, and the Council would become even more of a political plaything. A Minister for London, with a much less directly elected authority covering a rather wider area than the existing Greater London, might be the answer. Any body entrusted with London government must sometimes make decisions that would be unpopular in at least part of its area: if it were run by politicians fearful of offending their constituents it would never make all the necessary decisions.

Under the set-up he envisaged, the directly elected London borough councils would have more extensive powers - but certain vital functions must be more centrally controlled. Education, for instance: and housing should be run on the lines of the Council's strategic housing plan, with allocation of dwellings on a London wide basis, strictly according to need. It was simple and economic for the GLC (or whatever central authority succeeded it) to control housing centrally. In the field of planning, the present division was about right - what was wrong was the complexity of the whole planning process. There was a confusion between social and economic planning and land use planning, which the system did nothing to resolve. At present, the boroughs tended to use their planning powers as a weapon against the GLC: and he suspected the GLC did likewise against the boroughs on occasion.

On the vexed question of public transport, Mr Blackhurst thought it impossible that public transport could ever pay its way in an area like London. Herbert Morrison's LPTB went a long way towards solving the transport problem in the capital - and it was very efficient. Now, we seemed to have lost the ability to be efficient. One thing worthy of consideration was the fact that if public transport - and housing as well - were not subsidised wages would have to rise steeply, and many employers in London could not then meet their costs. Hence, the city's economic base would shrink - this was already happening to some extent.

In the 'thirties, London had been the most prosperous area in Britain - and it had maintained its position in the immediate post-war years. Now it was in decline. The trouble had begun, he thought, in the Macmillan 'you never had it so good' era, when the country was enjoying a temporary boom, and thought this would go on for ever without the necessity to work to maintain it. At that time, London, due to the shrinkage of its economic base, was already an expensive luxury: but the country could afford it then. Now it could not. Only when the country as a whole recovered could it 'afford' London again. As long as the national economy was ailing, London would ail. Tourist income could keep the city going for a while, rather after the fashion of Rome: but in the longer term the very success of tourism would tend to drive the remaining industries out of London.

From the near sublime to the not quite (one hopes) ridiculous. Mr Blackhurst, as a former editor, owned to a continuing interest in this journal. It was now, he thought, unique - the last survival of a style and outlook once common amongst staff magazines. He very much hoped it would continue to survive in its present form, which showed remarkably little change over the years. He regretted the fact that the layout had become (in his view) less interesting and varied, and *London Town* was now much less of a campaigning journal. However, it retained the vital capacity to make people think, and even though the number actively influenced by the magazine was probably quite small it still did an important job in that respect.

In his own day, he had felt that the lively reporting of departmental events, people, staff clubs, etc., was essential. People had turned to that first, and if that was lively and interesting they went on to the other contents. The balance had gradually changed, however, and it was now more likely that readers would run through from the front of the magazine. The tradition of Editorial independence was very important, as was the ensuring of a proper Editorial succession. That had always been a problem, and it was probably more acute than ever now, when people who were really interested in staff affairs tended to become deeply involved in the Staff Association rather than in *London Town*. There was also the fact that really able people were now usually promoted more quickly than in the past - they consequently had less time for staff activities of any kind. No doubt the difficulties would be overcome: he hoped that as long as the service endured this journal would be there to record it.

Past and Present in Dulwich.

Barbara Clark
(October 1976)

Picture, if you will, kestrels hovering over a wood where Charles I once hunted the stag and Chaucer with his pilgrims wound his way towards Canterbury; foxes barking, owls hooting and bats flying between giant trees which form natural arches across the walk, and small boys with jam-jars collecting their annual supply of frog-spawn from the river. Artists can work uninterrupted for hours and the business man, leaving behind the noise, bustle and frustrations of city spent days, returns to his haven. This is the peaceful, lush-green corner of south east London called Dulwich.

In 1967 Dulwich celebrated its Millenium. Although it was probably more than a thousand years old at the time, the first written record of its existence appears in 967 A.D. when the Anglo Saxon King Eadgar granted an area called *Dylwihs* to one of his Lords. A Manor House was built and in 1127, Henry I gave the estate to the Monks of Bermondsey Abbey.

The land was pastoral with wide open meadows where sheep, cows and pigs led an undisturbed life and corn grown in the local fields was ground in the mill which stood near the present site of Dulwich College. Pond Cottages and the Mill Pond remain to this day opposite the College.

Now preserved in the College are ancient parchments called The Court Rolls. These documents date back to 1333 when local offenders against the law were tried at Dulwich Court, just punishments (usually fines) were administered and the entire proceedings were clearly recorded for posterity. One entry dated 1334 relates how Richard Rold took William Hosewode to court because he had '... carried off Edith, his wife, together with one cow worth ten shillings, clothes, jewels and other goods and chattels to the value of forty shillings . . .', the estimated loss to the plaintiff was thirty shillings. Might one assume that Edith was a born nagger and it was well worth the loss of twenty shillings to be rid of her?

Tenants were treated fairly by their landlords but those succumbing to acts of vandalism were heavily fined. One of the major offences was that of felling trees. John Colcok was fined 3d for cutting down an elm tree and John Webster paid 6s for applying his hatchet to a number of 'crabbe trees'. But Robert Bulkeley committed the worst act of all when he decided that 2,000 trees were no longer needed on his farm (all farms were leased) and for such a crime against his landlord he was taken to Guildford Assizes where he was fined the total sum of £150.0.0.

It might also be noted that the landlord took a dim view of permissiveness in those days. A Statute was passed in 1589 stating that no inmate or cohabitant was allowed and only one family per household could be resident at any one time. Surprisingly, perhaps, rent arrears were allowed to accrue for periods of up to three months. Tenants complained, not of their neighbours' dogs, as they do now, but of their hogs.

In 1536 Henry VIII dissolved the monasteries and claimed all monastic lands. Apparently the Abbot of Bermondsey was a gifted man. He foresaw the inevitability of surrendering the Monastery so he saved himself, and the Abbey, the trouble of being taken by force; volunteering it up to his King he earned himself a retirement pension of £333.6.8 per annum. That works out to something like £6.6.2$^{1}/_{2}$ per week and in 1537 that wasn't a bad pension considering that best quality ale cost 3d a *gallon*.

The Manor was sold to the Calton family who retained it until 1606 when it was bought by Edward Alleyn for the grand sum of £5,000. Fortune indeed smiled over Dulwich with that event for he was the founder of Dulwich College without which the district certainly would not be as it is today.

Edward Alleyn had been one of the foremost Shakespearean actors of his time. The Bard himself wrote '. . .one man in his time plays many parts . . .' and this could fit none better than *Ned Allen*. He had also been Chief Master, Ruler and Observer of All and Singular of His Majesty's Games, of Bears, Bulls and Mastiff Dogs. He enjoyed bear-baiting, was Churchwarden of the Clink Prison and the surrounding area of Southwark and he was the owner of the Fortune and Hope Theatres. He is also known to have been a lavish entertainer at his home although one of his guests must have suffered from a diminished appetite for an entry in his diary reads 'Mr Laurence Whittaker and his widoe dined with us . .' He had been Lord of two previous Manors and had amassed a fortune, but he remained generous and charitable.

Education being available only to the sons and daughters of the rich meant that many a potential scholar was deprived of education and remained illiterate merely because he was born to parents of lowly means. Alleyn saw poverty through compassionate eyes and decided to use his wealth for the benefit of both old and young alike. For the old he built a home to house 'six poor brothers and six poor sisters', for 'twelve poor scholars' he built a school and adjoining the almshouses he built a Chapel. Some students were fee paying but the free places were chosen by lottery, those drawing a paper bearing the words God's Gift were granted a place; hence the correct name 'The College of God's Gift in Dulwich'. The royal charter granting Alleyn license to build his College was signed on June 21, 1619 and is now preserved in the College which, due to expansion, was rebuilt in 1866 a short distance from the original site. Designed by Charles Barry the red brick buildings are of great architectural beauty. Little wonder since his father, Sir Charles Barry, was the architect of the Houses of Parliament. Among the old boys worthy of note are C. S. Forester, Sir Ernest Shackleton, and P. G. Wodehouse.

The body of Edward Alleyn was laid to rest in the Chapel in 1626; it lies in the chancel just in front of the altar step. He made a gift of Dulwich to the College in order that the income could be used for the maintenance and upkeep of his foundation. The Estates Governors continue to protect the environment and estates still with particular attention to the trees (there are some magnificent Chestnut trees in the village) and long may they be empowered to do so.

Over the entrance to the Chapel is an inscription, the last line of which reads, 'Blessed is he who has taken pity on the poor. Go thou and do likewise'. Opposite the almshouses is Dulwich Park. This beautiful area was graced each year with a visit by Queen Mary when she viewed the resplendent display of Azaleas and Rhododendrons. It also has on display a work of art sculpted by Barbara Hepworth but as a devotee to Michelangelo I must allow those with a greater understanding of Miss Hepworth's talents to judge its merits for themselves.

Dulwich College Picture Gallery should please the most discerning art lover and it was in fact the first art gallery open to the public. Edward Alleyn bequeathed his own collection of paintings to the college. Later the number was increased by William Cartwright but the most valuable paintings were bequeathed by Francis Bourgeois.

These had been collected by Noel and Margaret Desenfans at the request of King Stanislaus of Poland in order to open a National Art Gallery in Warsaw. Unfortunately Poland fell to the Prussians, Austrians and Russians, the King was deposed and Desenfans was left holding the extremely valuable and impressive baby. He bequeathed the paintings to his artist friend Bourgeois who in turn left them to the College. There is, however, one further fact which makes this gallery unique. Margaret Desenfans left sufficient money for the building of the gallery in order that the collection could be open to the public but an unusual specification went with the bequest. It was fulfilled and so, in the middle of the paintings which they loved so much, are three caskets where the remains of Margaret and Noel Desenfans together with those of Francis Bourgeois were finally laid to rest.

The list of notable artists whose works are on view in the gallery is long. Robert Browning spent many hours absorbed in the works of Poussin and a small painting of *Spanish Beggar Boys* by Murillo delighted George Eliot. There is a beautiful portrait of Princess Victoria, aged four, by Stephen Denning; not notably famous as an artist but the little picture has a most endearing charm. Gainsborough and Canaletto are well represented as are Raphael, Rembrandt, Rubens and the two Teniers. The eyes of Christ in Guernica's *Woman Taken in Adultery* are so compelling that I find them almost hypnotic, and other works by Reynolds, Van Dyke and Veronese make the collection well worth a visit.

Charles Dickens has immortalised Dulwich and the gallery for in the summing up of *Pickwick Papers* he wrote, 'Mr Pickwick is somewhat infirm just now; but he retains all his former juvenility of spirit, and may still be seen, contemplating the pictures in the Dulwich Gallery . . .' and Mr Snodgrass ' . . . sallied forth gallantly to Dulwich Church (the Chapel) to meet his bride . . .' An olde Worlde cottage stands a short distance from the gallery and is named Pickwick Cottage; it is believed that Dickens had this cottage in mind when he retired Mr Pickwick to Dulwich and although no mention is made of the old *Crown and Greyhound* in the book Dickens himself is known to have been a frequent visitor.

There are now three schools under the Alleyn Foundation, Dulwich College, Alleyn's School and James Allen's Girls School. All are public schools with a few free places and the total number of students attending these schools is about 2,700 so that the Old School Tie continues to flourish, at least in these parts.

Only one working tollgate remains in London and that too is in Dulwich. Erected in 1789 in College Road the tariff board still stands at the gate demanding a payment of $2^1/2$d for each score of hogs, sheep and lambs; but a present charge of 3p is made for cars.

In addition to the environmental pleasures of Dulwich the Steak House offers an excellent cuisine and the *Crown and Greyhound* (opposite its original site) will extend a warm (or refreshingly cold) welcome. The patisserie does nothing for the waistline but the delicious continental coffee, cakes and bread more than compensate the additional calorie intake.

The conclusion is from the pen of Charles Dickens. 'The house I have taken,' said Mr Pickwick, ' is at Dulwich. It has a large garden and is situated in one of the most pleasant spots near London.' It remains that way to this day and long may it continue to do so.

Note: Despite the encroachment of opulent housing developments (one of which temporarily attracted Margaret Thatcher a few years back) Dulwich village has changed little if at all in the 15 years since this article was written. The Dulwich College Gallery is certainly well worth a visit.

Section 5: The closing years

Introduction

From about 1977 onwards the staff of the GLC and ILEA lived under constant threat of a major upheaval. First it was the projected break-up of ILEA; when that was staved off it was the transfer of most of the GLC's housing stock - and staff - to the London Boroughs: finally, it was the abolition of the GLC itself, which of course became reality on 31 March 1986, when *London Town* in its time-honoured form came to an end with it. During those increasingly stressful years the journal continued to both devote much of its space to the impending changes, and to how they might be fought, and to continue to provide a wealth of articles and features of the "traditional" *London Town* type. Series of articles of a generally historical and/or topographical nature became a prominent feature: London's villages were succeeded by London's battles and a series on Commuter Country, while at the same time such up-to-date matters as the completion and opening of the Thames Barrier were fully recorded.

It is on this unchanging aspect of *London Town* that we have concentrated in this section, for the hard fought battles over the abolition of the Council need not be fought again in these pages. The magazine maintained its old high standards to the end, and we conclude with the letters pages in the final issue (March 1986) to show just how its readers viewed the demise of the journal and of the Council whose service it had both illuminated and reflected for so many years.

Poor Law in London: The Last Ten Years — I.

Peter Wootton
(July 1977)

My advent into the Poor Law was unpremeditated, almost involuntary. I thought I had settled down comfortably into sixth-form life at Wandsworth School until one autumn day in 1937 the senior mathematics master bore down on me with an advert for 'relief clerks' in the LCC Public Assistance department.

'What are relief clerks?', I asked.

'Don't you worry about that', he replied, 'Look at the money they pay them'. It certainly was good pay - 30s a week, rises of 4s each year to a maximum of £4. 4s with prospects of advancement even further. No examination need be taken: a School Certificate would produce an interview. At a time when the average 16 or 17 year old school leaver could expect about 25s a week, the temptation was too great. I sent off an application, still not knowing what relief clerks were or what a Public Assistance department assisted.

Came the interview - three elderly people sitting at a desk in a long room on the Principal Floor at County Hall and the inevitable messenger in morning dress and tails. I stood before the desk, terrified. Then a strange thing happened.

I was sat down and asked *What did I know about the Poor Law?* Still I did not connect the question with relief clerks. It seemed a weird question but in the 1930s all LCC Schools taught their pupils that everybody at County Hall was mad so I proceeded to answer it. I was studying Social History at the time so I had something to say. It was not until I mentioned 'outdoor relief' that the penny dropped - 'relief - relief clerks'. That was it. I stopped talking, in amazement. But it was too late. The damage was already done. Those good people must have though they had a budding chief officer before them. I was asked one more question 'Have you been swotting it up?'. Even then, I gave the wrong answer, something about it being the sort of thing one learns at school.

The medical was a formality. I started work on 10 January 1938, with 19 others. On our first day, we were addressed by the Chief Officer. It seemed that our recruitment was part of the Council's policy of humanising the Poor Law. We were urged to cultivate tact and sympathy. As time went on and we passed the professional examinations and achieved promotion, we and those who followed us would give a new look to the whole department. Looking back, I think that had we been given the chance, we might have done it.

My first job hardly required tact and sympathy. It was part of the least acceptable face of Poor Law, the 'recovery of expenses'. This consisted of appropriating any assets or income a person in hospital or an institution might have such as sick pay or friendly society money towards providing the services. In most cases, we also had to chase the husband, wife, parents, grandparents and children for contributions of a few shilllings a week. For each person who received assistance, be it in-door or out-door relief, a case-paper was compiled. My duties were fairly mechanical, making sure that each case-paper got before a senior officer at least once a year in case there was something that had been missed in the past.

However, after ten months of this, I was let loose on the Public, although under Supervision. I was sent to the office dealing with the relief of the poor of Pimlico.

The out-door relief scale of 1938 ensured that in the average case, after a family had paid the rent, about 10s a week remained to keep each adult and 3s or 4s for each child. There were exceptions. The average wage for an unskilled worker was about £3 and the maximum payment of relief was not permitted to exceed 75% of this. Normally the Council would not allow more than 15s a week for rent. If a family came for relief paying more than this, the difference had to be found out of the subsistence part of the relief. If they could not live on the money left to them, the alternative was indoor relief, that is, the workhouse. In fact the good relieving officer would either negotiate a lower rent for the existing accommodation or else find something cheaper for the family - there were cheap flats and rooms available in pre-war London. Moreover, landlords and landladies liked relief recipients as tenants - the Council would make sure they paid the rent! In addition, the parish medical officer or a local health clinic would often order extra nourishment, mostly for tuberculosis or anaemia sufferers and we would give food tickets for eggs, milk, Ovaltine, liver and sometimes even Guinness. Food tickets were cashed with local traders who sent to County Hall for repayment. Of course it meant that the shop-keeper knew the family were on relief. Often people took them to shops a long way from home.

Payment of relief had much in common with an army pay parade. Everyone was expected to be in the waiting hall by the appointed time. The usual attendance was around 250, the halls were usually large enough to seat everyone. The regulars arrived up to an hour early to sit with their friends. It was quite a social occasion and the babble of conversation deafening.

The relieving oficer and the assistant would set up a table either in the hall or right up against the open door of the office. There was a touch of Bumbledon about the proceedings. The people would wait with their rent books open - to show a payment made during the past week. The relieving officer would call our the name of the person and the sum due, at the same time entering the payment in a vast ledger called the Relief List. The entry served as indisputable proof of payment; the recipient did not have to give any receipt. In the meantime, the assistant would be looking at the rent book and handing out the money. The clerk would be taking statements from anyone whose financial position had changed over the past week. As a seventeen-year-old, I found the whole thing most impressive.

From time immemorial, each person had been called by forename and surname only - 'Edith Jones', 'Frederick Tucker', etc. but one day a Member came down to our officer and was horrified at this. A few days later, an INSTRUCTION arrrived. We must remember that people are entitled to their dignity and say 'Miss Jones' or 'Mrs Jones' or 'Mr Tucker'. Of couse, interference or advice from County Hall was never welcome in any outside office; this was no exception. In all relief districts there was a majority of old age pensioners but in Pimlico particularly, there was also a good sprinkling of unmarried mothers (posing in those days as deserted wives), unable to work because there was no one to look after the child. Suddenly, our Miss Jones (with the pretty baby all the old people adored) lost the protection of being plain Edith as the resented instruction was obeyed to the letter. The chorus of Oohs and Aahs as these girls were called was not pleasant listening. Both tact and sympathy were casualties that day and I gather that the same thing happened in other parts of the County. In a few weeks, the whole thing was forgotten and the old system returned. I never recall that anyone complained. Still the damage to the girls whose lives were laid bare that day was already done.

The relief office dealt not only with outdoor relief but also with indoor relief, admission of tramps to the workhouse, children to homes, old people to the workhouses that were then beginning to develop into old people's homes and mental patients to observation wards.

The admission of the tramps was regarded as entirely the relief clerk's province. We had a lot at Pimlico, half a dozen a say, perhaps. Then as now, the homeless congregated around Westminster and so came to me when they wanted to get under cover for a few days or weeks.

One of the regular vagrants was an arsonist, many times over. He had been expelled from a famous school for stopping an express train on the Great Western Railway by standing on the track with a red flag. His family took a poor view of the matter and he soon left home for the open road. Unfortunately he developed a mania for firing haystacks. When I asked him about it, he waxed so eloquently poetic about blazing hay that had there been a stack handy we might both have gone out to buy a box of matches. Soon after, he got a really long sentence, five or seven years and disappeared from the scene.

For every person who obtained relief, indoor or outdoor, the casepaper had to be compiled, unless one already existed. This was aimed not only at determining the need of the person concerned but also with the recovery of expenses, in the case of a tramp, this consisted of trying to find some other county or county borough which could be made responsible for his keep.

It was the twentieth century version of the mediaeval tenet that every parish should look after its own poor. This had found its way into the Statute Book in 1601 and remained until 1948. One was considered to be 'settled' in one's county of birth but three years' residence somewhere else without receiving anything from the rates would bestow a new 'settlement' which superseded the old. A vagrant may not have stayed the requisite time anywhere for decades and so much of his life history had to be recorded, particularly landmarks such as births, deaths and marriages which could be checked at Somerset House. When a settlement outside London was discovered, evidence would be presented to the county or county borough concerned, who would search their records hoping to find that the person concerned had broken the period by accepting some relief - even a visit to the Parish Doctor would serve. If nothing else were forthcoming, you would lodge depositions at the Magistrates' Court, who would make an order for the removal of the person concerned. Provided that he was still in the institution, it was a day out to deliver him back 'home'. Out-door relief cases were not physically removed, the home county reimbursed the relief being paid.

The Pimlico district was one of the most colourful in London and I am glad I worked there. I met quite well known actors down on their luck and needing a helping hand for a few weeks or months. Not many days went by without someone turning up at nearby Buckingham Palace with a personal message for the King, received from space or somewhere. It was often my lot to sit and entertain such people when the Police had deflected them from the Palace to the office and we were waiting for the relieving officer to return from his visits so that he could decided whether or not the messenger was sufficiently insane to be forcibly removed for observation.

Poor Law in London: The Last Ten Years — II.

Peter Wootton
(April 1978)

At the end of September 1940, I went to the new combined Southfields and Putney district. We worked in the gate house of the former Wandsworth Guardians Workhouse, by then used by the Council as an old people's home. The proper office had been demolished by a bomb a few nights before and so the newly formed staff had to start from scratch. It was a case of asking everybody 'How much did you get last week?' and 'Would you like the same this week?' until over the weeks I had managed to interview everybody and compiled new case records, trying to reconcile the sum being paid with the particulars they had given me.

Things were fairly straight by Christmas and in January I was given an acting promotion with an allowance of 7s 6d a week and transferred to Streatham. With the war-time cost of living bonus, I was now earning almost £3 a week and still barely twenty years of age.

I stayed in Streatham until just before my call-up for the RAF, spending most of the remainder of the War as sub-postmaster at a camp in the Outer Hebrides. I met three Council officers during this time, identifying them by the *London Towns* sent to them through the post - but the real 'London Town' and its problems seemed a world away.

On my return in 1946, I went to the area headquarters at Kennington and was placed, as a clerical officer earning £5 5s a week, in charge of two clerical assistants and ten temporary clerks. We were endeavouring to extract money owed by the parents of children evacuated during the War. Parents were charged 6s a week towards the children's keep and the Council had been the collecting agency. These were the ones who had drifted in arrear. The number of defaulters was steadily decreasing and so the staff had to be cut accordingly. It was my unpleasant job to nominate one member of my staff for redundancy each fortnight - the temporaries were all elderly people and unlikely to find another job. As the time came for redundancy number 4, I decided to recommend myself. I argued that as the work had decreased, the staff needed only minimal supervision.

My next job proved not only boring but also thoroughly unsatisfactory, demonstrating the unpleasant side of the Poor Law. The Poor Relief Act of 1601, the one which started the whole thing, laid the duty of 'relieving and maintaining' an unfit person firstly upon his parents, his children and his grandparents and only secondly upon the Community - in those days the Parish. Three and a half centuries later, this principle was being implemented by taking money from the relatives of patients in Council hospitals and institutions. Particulars were taken at the time of admission and the relatives were sent questionnaires similar to income tax forms. The amount of their contribution was then 'assessed'. As with the Inland Revenue, the assessment and the actual collection of the money were carried out by separate branches. I was sent to the collecting group.

We had authority to write off outstanding debts of up to 1s. A common assessment on the unmarried son or daughter of a hospital patient was 10s a week. If a patient stayed in hospital for eight days or fifteen days, the relative would normally pay for one or two weeks. But that would leave an outstanding 1s 5d for the odd day and I had to send out arrears notices, deservedly getting sarcastic replies.

The Poor Law for me had been helping needy people; dunning relatives of the sick seemed completely repugnant. Although the end of the Poor Law was now a matter of months away, I asked to be allowed to spend these on more congenial work and in the summer of 1947 was sent to the Balham office. I found that very little had changed in five years. The people and their needs were just the same.

There are families (the Victorians called them 'the submerged tenth' of the population) who find themselves maintained, for generation after generation, wholly or partly by the Community, through whatever vehicle or organisation it uses to dispense its funds. The child that has been brought up in such a family will live the same way as an adult and bring his children up accordingly. This became real to me in 1939. My first war-time task had been to empty the loft over the Chelsea office of the pre-1914 case records, lest they prove a fire hazard. Time and again, I found myself gazing at the records of the parents of the families coming for relief a quarter of a century later. The present generation may well be harder to link with its forebears as families are now more mobile and slum dwellers generally rehoused well away from their former homes.

Nevertheless, the ill-nourished child brought-up to see nothing unusual in living on money not earned by his parents is the one most likely to grow into the puny adult with a bad record of sickness, irregular work and the tendency to seek public funds as soon as things get hard - as for him they certainly will. We never managed to solve this problem: will we ever?

Note: See also the article on "The Master" in Volume 1. "Outdoor relief" was the normal method of giving some sort of financial support to the poor during the 1930s: it was granted subject to the hated "Means Test".

London's Battles: Brentford 1642.

John Adamson
(February 1977)

Considering the crucial position of London in English history ever since the Romans, it is not surprising that the city and its surroundings should have provided battlefields in times of political turbulence. It is true that London's battles can scarcely match in number or drama those of Paris, but it is nevertheless strange that they should have come to be so forgotten. It is intended in a new series of articles to describe some of these engagements and to related them where possible to the physical features of modern London.

The English Civil Wars, from 1642 to 1651, were a strange mixture, politically and militarily, of the mediaeval and modern. Remote doctrines like the divine right of kings came into the same debates as ideas about sovereignty and democracy which are very much alive today; militarily, mediaeval fortifications were pressed into active new service and the pike contended with the gun. These were wars in which loyalties were often confused and the rules uncertain.

The breach between Charles I and Parliament came, after a long period of conflict, at the beginning of 1642. Charles spent the bulk of that year raising forces in the Midlands. Advancing on London, he was met by the Parliamentary forces under the Earl of Essex at Edgehill near Banbury, in an inconclusive battle which left Charles free to maintain his advance on London, which he did via Oxford and Reading.

By 11 November, Charles had reached Colnbrook. There discussions took place with a delegation representing Parliament. It seems that Parliament considered that a truce was in operation; the Royalists did not. In thick mist the Royalist forces, led by Prince Rupert, advanced on Brentford. As the map which illustrates this article shows, Brentford in the seventeenth century was a larger place in relation to its neighbouring communities than is now the case; the Brent

167

itself was a more formidable barrier than now, and the bridge over it at Brentford had to be secured to make a continued advance on London along the north bank of the Thames practicable.

The mist in which the battle started was indeed symbolic, for the fog of war certainly surrounded the subsequent events, and it is by no means easy to piece together a picture of what happened on 12 November. The contemporary sources are of doubtful accuracy and, in some cases, authenticity, and the confusion natural to any participant in such a battle is compounded by the strongly propagandist nature of some of the accounts.

It is clear, however, that Brentford was strongly held by two Parliamentary regiments, those of Lord Brooke and Denzil Holles. It is also clear that although Prince Rupert's dawn attack achieved surprise from the combined effect of the breach of an apparent truce and the weather, the Parliamentary troops put up a vigorous resistance. It seems that Holles' troops fought more persistently than those of Brooke.

From the Parliamentary side, we are lucky to have the account (albeit a rather garrulous and self-congratulatory one) of John Lilburne, later prominent as a Leveller leader. He seems to have rallied some of Brooke's regiment. According to him, the Parliamentary forces were poorly equipped 'For when we had the Alarum first, we had neither provision (that I know of) of Match, Powder and Bullet, but were necessitated to ransacke the shops and houses in the town for our present supply'.

He claims that he several times escaped from Royalist custody, and takes such a high view of his military exploits that he says of them: '. . . I dare say of that peece of service, that the Parliament, the Citie, and the whole Kingdom, owes not more to any one particular number of Commanders and Soldiers, and for one particular engagement, than they doe to myself and the rest that was in Branford . . .' It seems that a substantial number of the combatants died, including some senior officers of the Parliamentary forces, and that the Royalists captured some 500 prisoners, as well as artillery and ammunition.

It was subsequently claimed that the Royalist forces had sacked the town and committed various atrocities. A committee of Members of Parliament investigated these, and came up with a report entitled *A True and Perfect relation of . . . The King's army at Old Brainceford*. The introduction is blood-curdling: 'For hear are Acts represented so far out of ken and view of humanity, yea, so voyd of humanity, that they are short of the good nature of wilde, savage and unreasonable creatures'.

The report notably fails, however, to substantiate this claim. So short of firm material did the authors find themselves that they were reduced to claiming as an atrocity 'that many of the Featherbeds, which they could not bear away, they did cut the ticks of them in pieces, and scattered the Feathers abroad in the fields and streets' Also '. . . they defaced some houses, and set fires of purpose, as is conceived, to fire the town which was afterwards quenched by an inhabitant'. This does not sound like a very systematic attempt at incendiarism! Such was the sympathy of Parliament for Brentford, that it ordered than an appeal should be made in churches for help to recompense the inhabitants for the damage caused, estimated by the citizens of Brentford in a petition as costing £4,000.

An extract from A Mapp containing the Townes, Villages, Gentlemens Houses, Roads, Rivers, Woods . . . for 20 miles Round London (1690).

It is clear that the Royalists won the day, and they confirmed their victory by sinking some Parliamentary ammunition barges on the Thames by means of guns sited in the grounds of Syon House. However, the high water mark of the Royalist attack on London had almost been reached. Next morning the line of advance was blocked by some 24,000 troops drawn up on Turnham Green; many of these were from the London Trained Bands, a local militia something like the Home Guard. After the struggle at Brentford the outnumbered Royalists had no stomach for a further battle and withdrew. Charles decided against any further attempt on London and returned to Reading.

The campaign which might have concluded the Civil War and altered the course of history had failed. Perhaps some of Lilburne's claims for the defenders of Brentford were justified: certainly they earned a place in the records of London's history.

Note: The Editors are considering using the London's Battles series, of which this was the first article, as the basis of a book.

Tranquillity at Farleigh.

Charles Hunneman
(August 1978)

The Sussex Downs are rich in remote Saxon or Norman churches which one comes upon suddenly in the course of walks along lonely paths. Yet why travel so far when the church of St Mary the Virgin, Farleigh is only a few miles outside the boundary of Greater London? The best way to approach it is to do as I did - walk straight across the Downs.

A good starting-point is Selsdon: if you have a car, there is a car park right on the edge of the green belt at Selsdon Woods, on the Old Farleigh road. If without a car there is a good bus service to Selsdon from East Croydon (No. 64) and you can either walk along the road, or cut through Selsdon Woods Bird Sanctuary until you reach the open downs. There are several tracks through the woods but they all lead soon to the open country, and you will be lucky indeed if you haven't a generous coating of chalk on your shoes before you reach the little hamlet of Farleigh. This consists solely of Farleigh Court Farm, with its barns and outbuildings - itself a listed historic building (18th century) of flint and brick - and a pair of cottages flanking the unmade road which leads to the church. Lonely indeed, and yet if you looked over your shoulder you would have seen the sprawl of New Addington, although this is mercifully hidden once you reach the hamlet.

This is a simple church, consisting of nave and chancel - the division is visible from outside - surmounted by a simple shingled bell-tower, and with a wooden porch and a vestry addition to the south. The churchyard is full of trees - two wych elms (one of which had the dreaded disease), two large beeches and nine lime trees.

You will have to obtain the church key at the farm and this will enable you to have a look at the farm which, according to the Victoria County History, has the remains of a moat about it. Enter the church and you will be rewarded by seeing one of the most impressively simple church interiors in this part of the county. It is aisleless. with a chancel arch which looks authentically Norman, but is in fact a Victorian restoration - as sensitive a work of restoration as one could wish to find anywhere. Indeed, the Victorians dealt very gently with this interior, most of which dates back to 1080. The timber roof was replaced after a fire in 1964, but otherwise the church, inside and out, is very much the same as when it was built: simple lancet windows and another lancet window at the west end. The walls of the church are unusually substantial for so small a building - no less than three feet thick.

The chancel was lengthened 10 feet to the east about 1250: this is indicated by the later style of the windows and the presence of the original Norman piscina on the south wall of the choir stalls - a piscina would only be built near the altar, so that the original east end must have been within a few feet of this. There are traces of quoins of the original East end to be seen on the outside walls. The east end has two lancets instead of the usual three, which is quite unusual: one is round-headed and the other slightly rounded. There is thus no window in the church which is earlier than the 13th century. There is a semi-circular stone over the west door which looks very much as though it had done duty as a mill-stone before incorporation in the building.

The inner doorway and the window above the porch are early Norman work, as is the priest's door on the south. This now leads to a modern vestry, built in 1965 after a fire destroyed its Victorian predecessor. The timber porch is comparatively 'modern': it is said to date from the 16th century, and the outer door may be of the same date. The church itself is built of field flints - of which there are many still lying about the nearby fields - with the original yellow plaster or mortar coat outside. The 11th and 13th century quoins remain and are of unusually small stones. There is a 29 inch bell in the turret dated 1663.

There are two interesting memorials inside. A brass, mounted on a wall tablet, commemorates John Brock, a citizen and poulterer of London, who died in 1495; his wife Ann and four sons and one daughter. He is wearing the long gown with string of beads of a typical merchant, whilst his wife wears the gabled head-dress fashionable at the time. A marble to Dr Samuel Bernard (1657) and his wife Elizabeth (1705) begins: *'Pastor fidus, vir nullo foedere foedatus . . .'* 'A faithful pastor, a man stained by no covenant': this is thought to refer to the many clergy who refused to sign the Solemn League and Covenant, which attempted to impose a uniformity on the churches of England and Scotland in 1643. Although it is not certain that he was rector of Farleigh. it is certain that he was vicar of Croydon and was dispossessed in 1643. The second window on the left is a memorial to a young organist of this church who was tragically killed in a road accident on his way to take duty here in May 1954.

Farleigh is the smallest parish in Surrey and has a well documented history going back over a thousand years. The very first record of the name appears in a Saxon charter of the 9th century when 'Aelfred, an earldorman, gave lands in Fearnlega to Eadrid his cousin charged 30 measures of corn to the monks of Rochester . . .' The modern name of Farleigh can be identified with 'Fearnlega'. Moving on to the Middle Ages, Farleigh was conveyed with Malden, Surrey, to Walter de Merton, who in 1249 obtained a grant of free warren there.

In 1264 he granted the manor for the foundation of a college at Oxford, afterwards called Merton College. The college has continued to hold the manor to this day. It is impressive to consider the great contribution this tiny parish has made to the cause of education through seven centuries.

Farleigh Church.

Farleigh has always been a small parish on account of its poor soil, yet in the Middle Ages there was quite an industry in the manufacture of oak shingles for roofs, and iron nails. The iron ore must have been brought from the Weald, the smiths being attracted by the plentiful supply of charcoal from the woods. Even so the area was never rich and so the little church remained unaltered throughout the prosperity which an economy based on wool established elsewhere. No Lavenham or Cirencester this but a simple church testifying to the soundness of its construction nearly 900 years ago. We should be grateful that there are still such peaceful places in the overcrowded south-east. And yet this lonely spot is a mere four miles from the Whitgift Centre in Croydon, seven from the Isle of Dogs . . .

The Uses of Power.

Len Hudson interviews Andrew McIntosh

(July 1980)

Andrew McIntosh, the recently elected leader of the Labour group on the Council, is very much a political animal - which does not make it easy to conduct an interview which must, for the pages of *London Town*, avoid too deep or partisan an involvement in political issues. However, as Mr McIntosh would be the first to recognise, there are large areas of the Council's work where politics must take second place - it is only on such always contentious matters as housing, planning and transport policies that political considerations invariably - and inevitably - predominate. These are the areas of his main interest, for it is here that most can be done to achieve his prime political objective, the distribution of resources in such a way as to ensure social justice.

Like most active young politicians, Andrew McIntosh became involved in local government at borough council level. Here he felt a growing sense of frustration in the field of planning (although not in other ways) and it was perhaps inevitable that he should follow Aneurin Bevan's advice and 'go where the power is'. In local government terms, that meant County Hall: although he still wonders whether he has yet found power. For the GLC, in his view, has not always used its very considerable authority wisely or to the best effect: much of its potential for good remains unrealised.

The GLC should, said Mr McIntosh, move away from the position of 'big brother' to the boroughs and should continue to devolve some of its functions. Even some relatively complex things could be run by agreement between the boroughs; and outside the area of politically contentious services such agreement was perfectly possible. On the other hand, this did not mean he supported the Roland Freeman line. He could not imagine any city where the central authority did not have wide powers, and so it should be in London.

The Council should function as a real regional authority, with considerable powers in such matters as the administration of the health service and policing, as well as the basic matters of housing, transport, planning and such major projects as the Thames Barrier. He saw the future, therefore, as one of considerable expansion of the GLC's activities in some directions, coupled with a smaller but inevitable - and desirable - contraction in other areas of work.

Returning to the highly political matter of housing, Andrew McIntosh expressed the hope that the law could be used to prevent further transfers of GLC housing stock to the boroughs. If the transfers currently envisaged went

173

forward there was a very real danger that boroughs such as Tower Hamlets or Lambeth would become ghettos. Some way must be found to combine local management of housing stock with a strong and workable central allocations policy before the process of devolution of housing powers could be resumed.

On transport, that other 'hot potato', he considered that the balance of public expenditure in the 1980's, as far as the GLC was concerned, must come back to support of public transport. This did not necessarily mean a 'no fares' policy: indeed there were enormous practical difficulties in implementing such a policy (e.g. how would BR's services fit in?) as well as the obvious difficulties in terms of social justice, with Londoners called upon to, for instance, pay for unrestricted free travel for tourists, etc. As always, he came back to the theme of social justice, a matter on which he has strong and deep feelings.

Mr McIntosh's socialism stems from such feelings. It is a socialism which is wary of bureaucracy, and he is alarmed at the way in which socialism and bureaucracy have sometimes become synonymous. He believes strongly in the concept 'small is beautiful' and is very much in favour of really small local councils - urban parishes? - at the bottom tier of the local government structure.

Talk of bureaucracy led inevitably to Mr McIntosh's opinions on the staff. He had, he said, been very often impressed by the quality and professionalism of GLC officers. (Cynics will no doubt murmur ' he would say that, wouldn't he?' but he seemed sincere enough to me). All too often, however, the individual talent and initiative of these officers was being stifled by the system, which was top heavy, and very conservative in many ways. One got the impression that even if the purpose were removed the machine would go on running - and would, alas, continue to conduct matters with defensiveness, suspicion and a plethora of internal memoranda.

This system, apart from its more obvious deficiencies, seemed to result in an increasing lack of job satisfaction for the staff. Andrew McIntosh did not, as he freely admitted, yet know the answer to this problem: neither did he know the answer to the increasing danger of compulsory redundancy for some members of staff. Existing policies in the field of housing made such redundancies inevitable, and he felt the Staff Association had not been as prompt as it might have been in recognising this fact. But he could not criticise: he could only try to face the problem without succumbing to the temptation to come in from the outside, as it were, and impose radical changes which might only make matters worse.

The ability to impose such changes implies the gaining of power, and Mr McIntosh was (naturally enough) confident that Labour would be back in office as a result of the May 1981 elections. If this were so, and power was regained, he wanted to see his party 'actually doing what it was elected to do', and moving forward on positive lines in the closest possible harmony with the boroughs. Whether or not we approve of Andrew McIntosh's politics we can surely all agree that these are worthy ideals, and hope that if and when he attains the authority he seeks he will remember that.

'The same arts that did gain
A power, must it maintain.'

Note: Mr McIntosh led his party to victory in the 1981 GLC elections, but the Labour group on the Council, at its immediate post-election meeting, proceeded to elect Mr Ken Livingstone - who had for some time been a prominent member of the Labour group - as its Leader - and therefore as Leader of the Council. Mr McIntosh later went to the House of Lords, where he is still an active member of the Labour group of Peers.

No political neutrality.

Ken Livingstone interviewed by Nick Wright

(July 1981)

Q. How do you think the working lives of GLC staff will change as a result of your administration?

A. Well, John Carr is at present putting together a package of staff proposals and I'd rather leave the details to him. In general, though, I would hope that the staff would become more political in outlook, more involved in the structure of London government. The co-option of staff on to committees is important here, so that Councillors can understand staff views at the time decisions are taken. We hope, also, that all staff, through their unions, will be kept informed. We intend general meetings to be held every six weeks or so, explaining the broad political line we are taking. If we are going to have to combat restrictions and cuts we must carry staff with us, and there can be no political neutrality when jobs are at stake. The public sector must learn to fight harder on its own behalf.

Q. On some points of detail: do you intend to dispense with 'Chairman's action'; what can you tell us of your intentions towards our superannuation fund?

A. As far as Chairman's action goes, there will continue to be certain uncontroversial, non-political issues that can be cleared by authorised members of each committee. What we have done is cut across the 40 years' tradition of conniving between the front benches. All major policy matters will have to be approved by the Labour group as a whole, and they will be able to over-ride the Chairs of the committees.

With regard to the superannuation fund, though the exact mechanism has yet to be decided, we would ensure that future pensioners would not lose out but would hopefully gain by backing job creation. Legally the fund cannot invest in anything non-profit-making. I would support Labour's proposals to make the export of capital illegal; it should be invested in home industry. I would have thought a unionised staff would have been unhappy about the nature of investments in authoritarian countries where labour movements are suppressed, and there will not be much left to enjoy in retirement here if industry is not backed by investment. But perhaps the most important element in our proposals is that we intend to bring the pension fund under a degree of staff control and examination.

Q. How do you envisage the development of your administration's relationship with the principal staff unions?

A. The fact that the staff are split between Nalgo and the Staff Association is a great pity. I would hope that amalgamation was a possibility. The Staff Association must have been weakened by the reduction of staff numbers over the years, and the transfer of estates still to take place will continue this. I'd have thought that there was no long-term future in the Association's having an interest in the housing departments of 32 London boroughs. I am sure that Nalgo would recognise the special character and institutions of the Association, and allow them to continue. The major problem goes back for years, to Morrison's day, when an especially cosy relationship existed between the LCC and the Association.

Q. Going on to more personal matters: how do you feel about the way the press have written you up since your election?

A. (*laughs*) In a sense without the Tories and their press I'd never be where I am today. With the *Standard* and the *Mail* endorsing McIntosh and telling people how to vote, it's hardly surprising there was a reaction. I think working-class people tend to ignore the overt political line of newspapers. Things like the *Mail* and the *Standard* are so Tremlettesque in their grossness that they can see it's not true. More disturbing is the subtle bias in radio and television. This can be all right, though, if you are not edited, since it gives you direct access to so many people. But really there is so much partisan rubbish in the press these days. Twenty years ago if you read the *Economist* the opinion was kept separate from the news; now the two are mixed. The whole atmosphere of the press is now more right-wing.

Q. We are all very interested in your personal motivation. Can you name any formative influences or personalities?

A. Well, I can think of my 1st year English teacher Eric Hobsbawm, eleven year olds debating Suez and things like that. He first made me think about politics. I had a great regard for Aneurin Bevan. As an example of a recent politician I think Robert Kennedy had developed enormously considering his background, and would have continued if he hadn't died. You should have read Schlesinger's book. On the other hand, you won't find I've spent much time studying Marx and Trotsky. I find more inspiration in my studies of animal behaviour. I was a natural historian before I was a politician and I can tell you the Labour group in County Hall operates in much the same way as a baboon troop.

Q. What about the Tories then?

A. Ah, with them its something different, more like the Mafia. It's all power and leadership with them. My favourite film is *Godfather II*; that shows an awful lot about how power politics operates and corrupts.

Q. To round off, how do you see the future of London as the effects of your policies begin to be felt?

A. We have four years. It seems to me that the most important thing to get right in that time is public transport. The industrial and employment policies are important, but you could call them experimental. In the public perception transport is what counts. The GLC must succeed here or it will probably cease to exist. We will win unless the government makes legislation to control rate demands. This would mean a very serious constitutional crisis since local government would then be finished. I am not a centralist. Centralised power seems to me to attract the least adequate kind of people. I am in favour of power in small parcels. This keeps administration and government close to the people. In the 'thirties there were people in central government who had strong ties and power bases in town and district politics. Since the war young, inexperienced people have gone straight from university into central government and their influence has been centralising and damaging. This has given rise to the increasing political split between central and local government. We can even see this at work between the GLC and the boroughs. There should be no need for a political difference between the LBA and the GLC; the relation is between district and region.

For myself, I think it would be too difficult to spend the rest of my life in local government. If I am to have a central parliamentary role I would hope it to be on the local government side.

Note: Mr Livingstone's subsequent career is well known. He led the GLC until the very end of its existence on 31 March 1986 (apart from a very brief period when he chose to submit himself for re-election to the Council, as a sort of personal vote of confidence) and then entered the field of national politics, being elected to Parliament as Member for Brent East in June 1987. At the time of writing he remains a Member of the House of Commons, but he lost his seat on the Labour Party's National Executive Committee in September 1990. Nevertheless, he aspired to the leadership of his Party following Neil Kinnock's resignation in the wake of Labour's defeat at the General Election of April 1992.

W. G. Grace and London County CC.

L. W. Hudson
(April 1981)

Although all the metropolitan County Cricket Clubs were formed before London became a separate county - Surrey in 1845, Middlesex in 1863, Kent in 1870 and Essex in 1876 - it's rather surprising that no London County XI has ever competed in the County Championship. But there was, for a few years, a London County Club whose matches were recognised as first class and whose moving spirit was no less a personage than 'the Doctor', 'the old man', 'the champion' (his nicknames were legion) W. G. Grace himself.

When, in 1899, Grace passed his fiftieth birthday he dominated the world of cricket more than ever before. There had been some signs of falling off in his powers in his mid forties, but the events of 1895, when he made 1,000 runs in May and sailed past his hundredth century - both hitherto undreamed of feats - had set him firmly back on his pinnacle. He had been playing first class cricket since 1864; he had virtually fashioned the game in the shape it now wore; he had captained England ever since Test Matches began; now, in his sixth decade, he was looking around for fresh fields to conquer.

In the winter of 1898-99 moves were afoot to form a new County Cricket Club under the name of London County, the obvious objective being equality with the other, older, County Clubs which dominated first class cricket. Prospects seemed bright. Cricket was the unchallenged national game, unifying all sections of society of late Victorian England by a common interest. The game had an immense though passive following in the towns as well as its host of active participants in the country. Test and county matches at Lords, the Oval, Old Trafford, Headingly and Edgbaston attracted huge crowds: it seemed likely that the new London County ground at the Crystal Palace would be just as popular.

The new club did not lack influential backers. Sir Arthur Sullivan, the more pompous half of the famous musical partnership, was on the committee. It engaged some equally prominent players, such as Billy Murdoch, who had captained Australia for ten years before taking charge of Sussex and, of course, the great 'W. G.'.

With his usual self confidence 'the Doctor' saw no real problem in taking on the job of secretary and manager of London County and at the same time continuing as captain, sole selector and Lord High Everything-Else of Gloucestershire. Like so many other eminent Victorians he had an inexhaustible appetite for the things in which he excelled, and he relished the prospect of running two county clubs instead of just one. Others, notably the Gloucestershire committee, thought otherwise. After he had begun the season for his own county that body passed a resolution demanding a statement of what matches he intended to play for Gloucestershire.

W. G.'s reaction was instant and quite predictable. On 28 May 1899 he replied as follows:

'Gentlemen, in answer to yours of the 26th, re resolution passed on the 16th and kept back from me for reasons best known to yourselves, I beg to state that I had intended to play in nearly all our matches, but in consequence of the resolution passed and other actions of some of the Committee, I send in my resignation as captain, and must ask the Committee to choose the teams for future games, as I shall not get them up.

I have always tried my very best to promote the interests of the Gloucestershire County Club, and it is with deep regret that I resign the captaincy. I have the greatest affection for the county of my birth, but for the Committee as a body, the greatest contempt.'

That was that. He never played for Gloucestershire (or England) again.

The club to which his formidable energies were henceforth to be wholly devoted won first class status in only its second season (1900). Grace was as good as ever - in the first match of the 1902 season, when he was approaching 54, he made 10 and 97 and took 3 for 56 and 5 for 33 against Surrey, arguably the strongest county side - but London County's games lacked the competitive edge of other first class games. Even though it was the golden age of amateurism in cricket the game was somehow becoming more 'professional': playing to win (or in the last resort to avoid defeat) was beginning to predominate over playing for enjoyment, and to entertain.

Nevertheless, for five full seasons London County played a full programme of first class matches, with 'the Doctor' always to the fore. In the sweltering August of 1902 London County hit the MCC bowling for 568 (W. G. made 131). Two years later, on the 'old man's 56th birthday (18 July 1904) London County again met MCC at Crystal Palace, and after putting them out for 189 made 117 for none by close of play (W. G. 61 not out). Next morning he went on to 166, driving with a power reminiscent of twenty years earlier, but it was his swan song, his 126th and last century.

It was also the swan song of London County. Despite such feasts of batting the crowds at Crystal Palace had steadily dwindled - south Londoners preferred, it seemed, the more competitive play at the Oval - and it had become more and more difficult to make a full fixture list or to make ends meet. Recognising the inevitable, W. G., who still dominated the club, decided that first class status could no longer be maintained and applied for entry to the minor counties competition. But even that was refused, so the London County experiment ended somewhat sadly with the club dropping down to ordinary cricket club level - in which, of course, W. G. went on almost until the end (he died in 1915).

Splendours of the Gonzaga.

Barbara Clark
(December 1981)

As the Medici were liberal patrons of the arts in Florence so the Gonzaga at Mantua encouraged and commissioned artistic activities in the forms of painting, sculpture, music and architecture. Had they not done so Mantua would doubtless have become one of the many ancient Etruscan towns which now simply add a picturesque aspect to the landscape of northern Italy.

And had it not been for the quest of Giovanni Francesco II to bring intellectual supremacy to his state and the near megalomanic desire of Isabella d'Este to be surrounded by objects of beauty and culture the biggest exhibition of Renaissance art that this country has staged for fifty years would not be on show now at the Victoria and Albert Museum. A fine portrait of the beautiful and accomplished Isabella by Giulio Romano, star pupil of Raphael, has been loaned by the Queen as have many other exhibits.

The exhibition spans the 200 years in which the family was most active in its pursuit of the arts. A large painting by Domenico Morone entitled *Expulsion of the Bonacolsi* is the introduction to the collection. It is impressive Quattroquento, as are the majority of the paintings on display, lacking the expression and anatomical exactitude on which far greater emphasis was placed by the artists of the Italian High Renaissance period which followed.

More in keeping with the generally accepted idea of Renaissance art is the delightful *Madonna and Child with St Catherine and a Rabbit* by Titian. By vocation Titian was a portraitist and by skilful use of light the subject figures in the foreground are illuminated against the unobtrusive landscape, darkening under the distant sunset. The collection also houses two smaller works by Titian.

The climax of the paintings on display is part of *The Adoration of the Trinity* by Rubens, Flemish School 17th century, commissioned by Duke Vincenzo I as an altar piece for the Church of the Trinitia. It shows the families of Guglielmo and Vincenzo in adoration of the Holy Trinity above. Sadly and almost unbelievably the lower part of this inspired masterpiece was later cut down and sold as fragments and individual portraits. Several of these have been traced and placed in their original position relative to the remainder of the painting in order to demonstrate the dimensions of Rubens's work.

Best represented is Andrea Mantegna, court painter from 1453 until his death in 1506 when he was succeeded by Lorenzo Costa, also well represented. The frescos which covered the walls and ceiling of the Camera Degli Sposi (1474) are among Mantegna's finest creations. Scenes from the life of Ludovico Gonzaga and his family decorate the walls while portraits of Roman emperors and mythological scenes cover the ceiling. In the centre is an illusive painting of an apparent opening through which cupids and girls gaze down from their ethereal realm.

The original room, which has survived, has been ingeniously photographed scene by scene, printed on large sheets of paper then pieced together again in the reconstructed room, half the original size. The idea is good but I felt that more care could have been taken in papering the ceiling.

Rich as ever are the scarlet, blue and gold illuminations of the collection of Italian manuscripts and illuminated books, notably two copies of Petrarch's *Conzoniere* and the *Speeches of Cicero* in Italian on vellum and 'The Gospels' in Greek.

The objective of this exhibition is not to bring together a store of works by old masters, the original collection is too scattered for that, but to recreate the culture and opulence which surrounded the Gonzaga. Marble busts fashioned in classic Roman style and an antique Roman sarcophagus are also on display together with a delightful set of bronze and gilt statuettes of Roman gods and four sculptured bronze plates depicting the Labours of Hercules.

Nearly 300 items are on display covering every aspect of art form from paint to elaborate reliquaries and music. A 20-minute film show on the history of the Gonzagas runs continuously throughout the day with suitable choral works of the age adding a final touch to recreate the atmosphere of the Gonzaga court.

Mantua, extolled by Vasari, called the home of Virgil, acclaimed by Aldous Huxley as 'the most romantic city in the world' has been reborn in London and with its incredible wealth of artistic and historical material it should not be missed. The organisers, however, rely quite heavily on copies and photographs of the original works which might prove slightly disappointing.

A Walk on the High Side.

Written and photographed by Gordon Farley

(August 1982)

Tower Bridge, with Big Ben one of the famous silhouettes which symbolise London to the world, was first opened on 30 June 1894. 88 years to the day it was opened again, this time as a tourist attraction which will enable the eager visitor to see the inside of the towers and to cross the river by the twin high-level walkways which have been closed for many years.

The occasion was marked with characteristic City of London ceremony. The Lord Mayor, Sir Christopher Leaver (escorted by six Thames waterpersons), his Lady Mayoress and a retinue of City worthies and their guests sailed majestically under the raised bascules in the Thames barge *Lady Daphne* (a lovely sight) to land at St Katharine Dock. Also in the procession were *Inca*, a two-masted brig built in 1854 and the oldest working square-rigger in the world, and *Marques*, a three-masted barque. Brought up from her south coast home, her elderly water-jets going full blast, was the LFB's old fire-float *Massey Shaw*.

The Lord Mayor proceeded to unveil a plaque and cut a tape across the roadway, thus releasing the halted traffic, which had been remarkably patient. Also released at this point were some thousand balloons, each bearing a free ticket to the bridge and thus worth £1.60: that's what it will cost the visitor. For his money he can see various exhibitions - about Tower Bridge itself and the City's other bridges (Blackfriars, London and Southwark) - and the museum, where the original boilers and the magnificent hydraulic engines are on show.

And, of course, the view from the newly-opened walkways, which on this sunny first day was quite splendid. When the bridge was first opened pedestrians had a statutory right to cross the river by this means when the bascules were raised. But with sail giving place to steam, and time taken to raise the bridge reduced to about six minutes, few people bothered and over seventy years ago the City Corporation closed them, first seeking the approval of Parliament, whose consent to their reopening was also needed. The walkways are completely enclosed by glass: I opened some little sliding windows to poke my camera through, and found later that someone had provided them for that very purpose. I squeezed through another window on to the outside gallery which the public will *not* be allowed to enter.

The bridgemaster, Lt-Commander A. Rabbitt, was resplendent in his gold-braided uniform. Meeting another beautifully turned-out officer with two gold rings I supposed that he was a lieutenant, but not so. 'No, I'm *Mr* Byward,' he said, 'the assistant bridgemaster', adding that once the ceremonies were over he was more likely to be found in the boiler-suit which was his usual garb.

The visitor will be whisked to the tops of the towers by the modern lifts which have been installed, but he may choose, as I did, to climb the stairs (hundreds of them - I lost count as well as breath). His reward will be to see the details of their internal structure: although they seem to be built of Portland stone and granite this is in fact only a cladding round the massive steel framework. A few boring details are not out of place here: at its busiest the bridge used to open thirty to forty times a day; now it's 200 times a year. Any vessel (even, it's said, a rowing-boat) requiring passage would sound three Morse Bs and fly the appropriate flags. Nowadays they have to give 24 hours' notice.

The City are confident that tourists will flock to the bridge (there's talk, I hear, of a joint Tower Bridge/Tower of London ticket) and I hope they are right. They do have a £5m investment to recover. Certainly the area round the bridge, containing as it does the Tower itself, HMS *Belfast*, the historic ships in St Katharine Dock, the delightful church of All-Hallows-by-the-Tower and even the imposing World Trade Centre, has plenty to offer the visitor.

The barque Marques: in the background the fireboat Massey Shaw.

In Dixie Land.

Len Hudson
(November 1982)

Washington in May . . . and it might have been chilly, cloudy old London except that I had left London basking in unaccustomed heat. However, the weather rapidly improved after that damp start and it was possible to see the US capital at its best in the best of all seasons of the year.

If capital cities are a reflection of national character Washington certainly reflects the early American aspiration (a little tarnished these last thirty years, but still alive) to be the 'last, best hope' of mankind. Nobility, not grandeur or splendour, is the word to describe the overall effect of White House and Capitol, Lincoln Memorial and Supreme Court building; the layout of central Washington was, like the almost contemporary US constitution, a noble and imaginative concept even if neither constitution nor city evolved quite according to plan. Buckingham Palace looks tawdry compared with the White House (which has the added attraction, of course, of being, unlike our own Palace, the place where ultimate power in the state resides), and the serenely classic elegance of the Capitol is on an altogether different plane to the fussy neo-gothic shambles of the Houses of Parliament.

Central Washington, from the John F. Kennedy Center to Union Station, is overwhelmingly impressive, but its outer accretions are much less so. The Pentagon (across the Potomac) looks even more monstrous close up than it does in the familiar photographs; Dulles airport is badly sited, and creates almost as many hazards as did the foreign policy of the man who gave it his name; and the inner residential area of the city have more than their share of dirt and decay - potential if not actual slums where the majority of the population of this overwhelmingly negro city live without much hope of seeing their own aspirations realised.

My route lay south, away from Washington's increasing sprawl. Past the Arlington National Cemetery, where America still cherishes its 'honoured dead', and into Virginia, which for mile after mile resembles stockbroker-belt Surrey on a far more opulent scale and with 'Englishness' accentuated almost to the point of absurdity. Not many people, I believe, ride to hounds in Surrey; but northern Virginia is very much hunting country, where Oscar Wilde would now find ample confirmation of his famous remark about the unspeakable pursuing the uneatable.

By the time the Greyhound bus had crossed the Rappahannock, suburban Virginia had been left behind. From Fredericksburg to Richmond is, even more than the field of Gettysburg, the 'hallowed ground' of that central fact of American history, the civil war. At Fredericksburg Robert E. Lee threw back the Federal army; at Chancellorsville 'Stonewall' Jackson triumphed and was mortally wounded; at Spottsylvania and Cold Harbor Grant battered his way past Lee's defences, at a fearful cost. The relics of those bloody conflicts are lovingly, one may say proudly, preserved, which is as it should be. The war brought, as all wars do, an appalling loss of life, needless devastation and an aftermath of bitterness and suffering; but all Americans can be proud, in retrospect, of those men who gave the 'last full measure of devotion' for what seemed to be high principles and noble ends. The conflict could and should have been avoided, but when it came it was fought, in general as honourably and decently as any war can be - at least it was here in Virginia.

It's doubtful whether there is anywhere else in the USA where the past is so carefully preserved as in Virginia. Perhaps it's because there is, relatively speaking, so much of it; it's here, on the James river, that English settlement in the New World began in 1607. Perhaps it's also due to the fact that in comparison with its present rather lowly ranking among the states Virginia was, for the first fifty years of the American republic, the 'mother of Presidents' (four out of the first five) and the nursery of statesmen and soldiers. All that is over now. Virginia has not provided a President since 1845 and the only national figures who live there at present do so because of its proximity to Washington - Senator Kennedy is a case in point. The state does not, however, live wholly in the past. Richmond, although it does not forget that it was the capital of the Confederacy and for nearly four years the prime objective of Lincoln's armies, is very much a modern city, although it is fortunately too small to suffer all the disadvantages of that status.

Richmond is pleasant enough as US cities go; Charlottesville, under the Blue Ridge, is quite delightful. Here one is very definitely in the South - life seems to go at a relaxed pace, people have more time (and perhaps inclination) to be courteous than up in Washington, both black and white folks seem closer to the land, with deeper roots in it, than at the North. There have been negroes in Virginia since 1619, but until a generation ago they were still very much second-class citizens. All the immediately obvious evidence is that this has now completely changed; there is no apparent distinction now between black and white Virginians. Perhaps appearances are deceptive, but I only wish that relations between blacks and whites in England were as free and easy, as relaxed in every way, as they now seem to be in Virginia.

From Charlottesville I made a detour to the home of the greatest Virginian of all - to Thomas Jefferson's Monticello. Here, looking out over airy prospects of farmland and blue hills in heavenly May weather, one cannot help envying the past owner of this superbly elegant mansion and one understands how, despite all the storms of his eighty-three years (1743-1826) Jefferson retained his serenely optimistic view of mankind, his overwhelming faith in the future of the republic he did so much to establish.

The language of the Declaration of Independence ('We hold these truths to be self-evident. That all men are created equal; that they are endowed by their creator with certain inalienable rights; that among these rights are life, liberty and the pursuit of happiness') is the essence of Jefferson. But Monticello has the feel of an aristocratic establishment; and the founder of the Democratic party apparently found it quite consistent with 'liberty and the pursuit of happiness' to own 150 slaves - even though, in his declining years, the issue of slavery roused him 'like a firebell in the night'. America and its past is not always readily understood; perhaps it's best just to enjoy it, and that comes easily enough at Monticello.

When Jefferson was born the area around Monticello must have been almost on the frontier of settlement; when he died that frontier had advanced beyond the Mississippi; now there is no 'frontier' as such. Through all these changes this part of Virginia has retained its beauty and peace - even the civil war passed it by. Piedmont Virginia was and is a backwater, somewhat away from the mainstream of Virginian life (Monticello and its illustrious owner notwithstanding) but it's none the worse for that.

After Charlottesville one gradually leaves the lush, greenly beautiful (and surprisingly under-cultivated) countryside of Virginia for the mountains - that Appalachian chain that runs from Pennsylvania to Georgia, effectively separating the vast interior of America from the Atlantic coast. The scenery is spectacular in the extreme, but the evidence of human occupation is rather depressing. The mountain people on the borders of Virginia, North Carolina and

Tennessee seem to have been left behind by time; their poverty is only too obvious; their ignorance and isolation from the mainstream of American life soon becomes apparent; even the language they speak is distinctly odd, although it would have sounded more familiar (without the accent) to a seventeenth-century Englishman.

I would have liked to spend more time in the mountains, but no tourist with inevitably limited time can hope to see more than a fraction of this enormous and varied country. So it was on to Chattanooga, where the Tennessee river winds down from the Appalachians on its way to the flatlands of Alabama and lower Tennessee. To anyone of my generation it's quite a shock to find that Chattanooga is no longer on the railway; no more can one 'leave the Pennsylvania station 'bout a quarter to four' and arrive, behind a hooting and snorting locomotive, in late evening. Without the railroad Chattanooga seems somehow lost with nowhere definite to go; but although man's work has proved ephemeral the mountains remain - Lookout Mountain, Missionary Ridge, all the lonely and lovely outriders of the Appalachians.

I went up Lookout Mountain the easy way and came down the hard. It would no doubt have been more satisfying and better for body and soul to have done it in the reverse order, but I would not then have felt so fully able to enjoy the stupendous view from the top. Chattanooga and the river beneath; a great tangle of mountains to the right; and the whole state of Tennessee, it seemed, unrolling in front below. A land amazingly empty, without the intense cultivation or the other signs of man's handiwork that one would see from similar viewpoints almost anywhere in Europe. I realised once again how new and relatively empty a country the USA still is. There is room enough for an even greater future here.

Time was running out and I could afford no more of Tennessee. I hope to continue these random notes to cover my further route through Georgia and Carolina in a later issue of *London Town*.

Bussing through Georgia (and beyond).

Len Hudson
(January 1983)

In the November *London Town* I described my springtime journey from Washington DC to Chattanooga. After the all too brief foray into Tennessee which I then recounted I had to turn south - my time was running out far too quickly. The Greyhound bus took me down over the Georgia state line into 'the empire state of the south' - the biggest state east of the Mississippi, bigger than England and Wales, but still relatively thinly populated.

The bus covers the road to Atlanta in about four hours - a pleasant run through delightful piedmont country in weather as near perfection as we are likely to see on this earth. The same journey cost General Sherman four months and a fifth of his army as he slogged southwards through the long hot summer of 1864. The road passes his battlefields, whose names (Resaca, Kenesaw

Mountain, etc.) lack the fame and resonance of the battlefields of Virginia but which were just as agonising for those who fought here.

So to Atlanta, a gleaming modern city about the size of Leeds but with a considerably better climate and cleaner streets, the prime symbol of the 'new south', and home of those dubious benefits, Coca Cola and cable television. Sherman's army burned the old Atlanta (as all who saw *Gone with the Wind* know) before taking off for the coast in the autumn of 1864, and the city which was rebuilt after the civil war has grown immensely. It has the typical American urban mixture of great luxury and appalling squalor, generosity and meanness, civic virtue and ever increasing violence and crime. It lacks the comfortable, relaxed atmosphere of the smaller towns in the south; maybe that's because too many of the people are recent 'incomers' from the north.

It has had a highly successful black mayor; it has given Andrew Young to the nation and the world - perhaps another rather dubious benefit. The old Georgia slave-owners must be constantly turning in their graves. Despite its size and bustle, however, and its almost cosmopolitan air, Atlanta remains essentially a provincial town with provincial attitudes. It's a long way from Peachtree Street to Pennsylvania Avenue, as Jimmy Carter very quickly found out.

From the ultra-modern splendours and miseries of Atlanta I rode down to Macon, mainly to see the Georgia countryside. It was something of a disappointment, being surprisingly barren and unkempt with dirt roads winding away to nowhere and rather decrepit shacks housing abundant families of 'poor whites' and those relatively few negroes who have remained on the land their ancestors worked as slaves.

Macon itself, however, was worthwhile. It bears absolutely no resemblance to the crooked little town of the same name in Burgundy which gives its name to a rather vinegary red wine. This Macon was named for Nathanial Macon, a sturdy Jeffersonian who probably knew little about Burgundy; but its early settlers, back in the 1820s, certainly had enlightened ideas about town planning. The streets were - still are - exceptionally wide and adorned with floral parkways; the buildings are gleaming white; the public parks are full of azaleas, camellias and glossy magnolias - all the luxuriant vegetation of the south, at its best when I was there. It's a charming little city, small-town America at its brightest and best.

After Macon I did not deviate still further to see Georgia's latest tourist attraction, Jimmy Carter's hometown of Plains; nor did I visit the much more attractive Warm Springs, so loved by Franklin Roosevelt, where he lived the life of a southern gentleman for a while each year and where he died (to our infinite loss) in April 1945. I made instead for Augusta, where the famous golf course looked deliciously green even in the by now searing Georgia sun, and then over the Savannah river into South Carolina.

The 'gallant Palmetto state', as it used to call itself, was the home of sedition and seccession during those years when the American republic was tearing itself apart over the issue of slavery. Its white population, outnumbered by the slaves, was reactionary and racist to a degree almost unbelievable now. Right up to the civil war the state was illegally importing fresh slaves newly snatched from Africa, and from the 1820s until the 1850s its senior Senator and revered spokesman was John C. Calhoun, whose attitudes are perhaps best summed up in Lowell's bitter satire *The Bigelow Papers*

'Freedom's keystone is slavery, that ther's no doubt on. It's somethin' that's - Wha'd'ye call it? - divine.

Slavery's a thing that depends on complexion.

It's God's law that fetters on black skins don't chafe.'

Those attitudes are - alas - alive still; but now very much on the wane.

All that was in the past, but it's still relevant in South Carolina, which gives an unmistakable impression of somehow not having joined the 'new south'. Strom Thurmond, its senior Senator for many years, stood for President in 1948 as an outright racialist; and the state voted enthusiastically for Barry Goldwater in 1964. The condition of the black population has certainly improved immensely over the past 30 years, but equality even to the somewhat flawed standard of the more progressive southern states has not been achieved. One senses a certain tension in the air even in Charleston, probably one of the most charming cities in the USA, where the best of the past has been cherished and modern development is still discreet and unobtrusive.

Charleston is an immensely enjoyable place if one can, for a while, forget the present tensions and the darker aspects of the past. Its streets are flower-bedecked and its harbour is serenely beautiful as are the Ashley and Cooper rivers, which flow into that harbour on either side of the old town. It was a Confederate attack on Fort Sumter (now a national monument) in that harbour that began the civil war; and when it ended four years later Charleston was still untaken and very largely undamaged, which accounts for the preservation of so much antebellum architecture and the still lingering atmosphere of the old south. The city was fortunate in that it did not lie on Sherman's direct route north from Georgia; he was under pressure from the north, where feeling against South Carolina was very strong, to treat it as the Romans treated Carthage.

However, the city survived to delight us now and I left it with reluctance for the long haul back to Washington, with no time left to see any more of North Carolina (a state surprisingly different from its southern neighbour) than could be glimpsed from the Greyhound bus. So it's at Charleston that I must end this highly selective account of a journey into Dixie which left so much still to see but which very much reinforced my long-standing pro-American attitudes.

The USA and its people are a long way off perfection (aren't we all?) but I found Americans (at least in the south) genuinely friendly and helpful, anxious to show the infinite variety and splendour of their country; and outside the big cities (which are undoubtedly ghastly) there is so much of that variety and splendour still to see. Americans tolerate corruption, inefficiency and petty-mindedness on a frightening scale, and they are not nearly so interested in or well informed on the outside world as they should be (are we, come to that?). But they really do believe in democracy (even in Dixie, nowadays) and they practise it on a scale undreamed of in this country. This belief and practice are invigorating, like so much else about America: perhaps it still is the 'last, best hope' for the world.

Note: Anyone who follows the author's route as described in these articles cannot help being constantly reminded of that central fact in American history, the Civil War of 1861-65. Any review of that conflict is, of course, quite beyond the scope of this book: but a very accessible account of the causes and course of the war is now available to readers in this country - *Battle Cry of Freedom* by James McPherson (Oxford University Press, 1988): a scholarly and well-written book despite the catchpenny title.

Here and there in Grenada, West Indies.

The Gleaner (David Moore)
(January 1983)

Fly Boy

LIAT, the Caribbean airline, has two nicknames - both very apt: 'Leave Island Any Time' and 'Luggage in Any Terminal'. At the end of October Mrs Gleaner and your scribe were, on time, ushered aboard the Grenada government's brand-new eighteen-seater, a Brazilian-built Bandeirante leased to LIAT and parked inconspicuously at Grantley Adams airport, Barbados. 'Welcome,' said the yo-ho-ho skipper, lolling by the front entrance and giving every appearance of having been at the rum: 'I'm your captain; there are only seven of you so we'll be off in a minute. Sorry the air-conditioning isn't working so how about leaving the rear door open during the trip?' 'Not if our suitcases are going to drop into the sea,' I said. 'Better have a look to see if anyone's even thought to put 'em aboard,' he replied engagingly - which was decent of him, considering that in six visits to Greneada luggage has only twice come with us! I checked: the cases *were* stowed, the rear door *was* locked, the skipper *wasn't* as tight as a tick, and small aeroplanes really *are* the best way to fly. LIAT (which actually stands for Leeward Islands Air Transport) got away on the dot and belied its reputation.

But not on the return, though. Four weeks later the company had real problems, no serviceable planes. Indeed Grenada hadn't sighted an aircraft since the previous day, although the affable staff checked us in with the vague promise that something might turn up. And something did - barely an hour before Pearls airport, which has no landing lights, closed for the day. A brightly coloured Avro 748 picked 45 of us up, left others on the tarmac hoping for a flight south to Port of Spain, and whipped us to Grantley Adams in 45 minutes flat. Mind you, there was only a fruit juice for refreshment: LIAT had had enough problems already, and you couldn't really expect it to remember to put some beers in the galley. But that's the Caribbean!

Local Radio

'This is Radio Free Grenada, the Voice of the Revolution.' The portable set we took with us gave us regular chunks of Prime Minister Maurice Bishop's fiery pro-Cuban, anti-Jamaican and very very anti-Reagan speeches, but the station still managed to keep a truly local perspective. One annoucement I liked particularly: 'The Productive Farmers' Union regrets postponing its raffle from 25 October till 29 November. Those who have put their names down for a ticket are asked to pay the money by 29 November. Everyone is reminded that the prizes are a young heifer, a goat and a pair of rabbits.' That's the Caribbean!

Baby talk

Grenada's hotels are small, sylish and quite luxurious. The biggest is Holiday Inn, but that burned down over a year ago and nothing's yet been done to rebuild and reopen it. That's the Caribbean too!

Mrs G and I prefer one of the smaller establishments. The staff are our friends. Ira the barman is just 23 and proud to tell us he's now father of four, his girl friend having presented him with twins since our visit the previous year. 'And two more coming,' he adds, carefully explaining that these will be delivered of different mothers. 'They're my "outside" girls,' he says: 'they no get jealous of "inside" girl, and she no get jealous of they!'

The Grenadian government exhorts by radio and by bill-board. '1982 - year of economic construction', read one poster. 'Produce more', instructed another. A third explained 'Our children are our future'. It was clear that Ira had got the message. That's the Caribbean!

Late show

'In honour of the 65th Anniversary of the Great October Socialist Revolution,' ran an announcement in Grenada's national newspaper *Free West Indian*, 'Embassy of the Soviet Union invites the General Public to view two films.' I half-expected such classics as *October* or even *Lenin in October*, but the films actually offered were of the 1980 Olympics and the circus. And as Grenadian time is free and easy (8 o'clock appointments are usually kept around 10), the Russian Revolution wasn't honoured in October at all but betweem 9 and 12 November. Even then, the public didn't turn up: had the movie been *Kung-Fu Commandos in Red Square*, the Regal would undoubtedly have been full. That's the Caribbean!

Won't pay

I like the way the Grenadian handles the debts of his spouse. *Free West Indian* carried, over three columns, the following bald statement: 'I, Thaddeus Lambert of Cherry Hill, St George's, hereby notify the public that I am not responsible for any debt or debts contracted by my wife, Veronica Lambert, née Clarke. She left my home two years ago.' That' s the Caribbean!

Note: This is an example of David Moore's long-running column, which was, as a regular feature, written in and about the West Indies every November/December.

Anniversary down the road.

Ian Wilson
(February 1983)

Walk down Waterloo Road now and you see a sad sight. On the corner of the Cut stands the Old Vic theatre, dark and empty and apparently neglected. Its former habitués are unlikely to be reassured by reports of its purchase by a Canadian millionaire who wants to put on musicals.

In contrast, the child of its reforming years, Morley College, prospers and expands at the other end of Westminster Bridge Road from County Hall. Moreover, it shares *London Town's* penchant for anniversaries: the Morley College magazine - a near contemporary as well as a neighbour - has celebrated its ninetieth birthday with a special edition which reprints page one of the first number, published in May 1892. The 1892 items were so diverting as to send this reader to the archives to consult the rest of that first issue - and do a little research at the same time.

First, then, the remarkable link between the theatre and college. Emma Cons, a Victorian reformer of shattering energy and zeal, took a lease of the Old Vic in 1880 with the object of freeing the place from its association with drunkenness, prostitution and third-rate entertainments. Under her regimen the theatre presented reputable plays and concerts - and in addition began puttting on 'penny popular' public lectures, usually on scientific subjects, by well-know speakers. It was the age of self-education as well as self-help. The lectures created a demand for something more systematic; regular evening classes began in various crannies of the building, even sometimes in the dressing-rooms.

Enter, centre stage, Samuel Morley, MP, rich textile manufacturer and devoted temperance worker, with financial help. This enabled the educational side of Emma Cons's enterprise to be housed in its own adapted part of the theatre. In 1889 (the year the LCC was set up) it was formally organised as Morley College. Not until 1924 did it move to its present site.

The first number of the college magazine strikes the modern eye as displaying the expected Victorian qualities of earnestness, confident optimism - and some pomposity. 'Self-help and co-operation are our two watchwords,' concludes the first editorial, 'and with these we launch our little ship into the kindly sea of college opinion, without any fear of storms or rocks ahead'. The temperance issue at once appears as a major preoccupation. The College was reported to be strongly opposing the proposed extension of an adjoining tavern (odd if it were the one in Waterloo Road that has just been repulsively refur-bished). The debating club had passed, by 29 votes to eight, a motion that every locality should have the power to suppress or control the sale of intoxicating liquors within its area.

The debating club also considered a motion that 'Thackeray as an author is superior to Dickens' - it rejected it. There were sporting diversions too. 'The billiard table cushions have been recovered. Players ought now to get up a good handicap in honour of the event. Nothing is such good practice as a competition - it quickens the eye and tries the temper.'

The gymnasium was popular and sometimes gets roguish treatment. 'The Gymnasium has become the possessor of a smart bay horse, 14-3, quiet to ride and drive, and carries a lady, rather stiff in the legs but this is no defect considering the rough riding he gets.' A correspondent complains that it is only provided with two mats and says he would appreciate the addition of two more to give him more chance of finding one between him and the asphalt floor when he falls. He is presumably not the hero of a later paragraph: 'We are very glad to hear that Mr Toleman, whose accident in the Gymnasium was so much regretted, is reported to be making most favourable progress. He is in the Albert Ward of St Thomas' Hospital and may be visited between 3 and 4.30 p.m., on Wednesdays and Sundays.'

A Pooteresque determination to rise above the perversity of life also shines through the report of the Good Friday excursion to Epping Forest (train from Fenchurch Street to Theydon station). 'Cricket and quoits were indulged in and about 3.30 p.m. an excellent meat tea was served, after which a concert was the order of the day. Mr Hughes's rendering of "Only a tiny piece of orange peel" was a decided success. After the concert, which whiled away the time occupied by a snowstorm, the party *en masse* proceeded for a two hours' ramble through the Forest . . . though the weather was not all one might desire, a very pleasant day was spent.'

The cricket club was pleased to announce that it had been successful in obtaining permission to practise in the grounds of Lambeth Palace on Wednesday evenings. Its first game was against Doulton's, at Hyde Farm in Balham. 'We were certainly over-matched and could not dispose of our opponents under 119, while the College could only respond with 30.' Outplayed the College may have been but it has outlasted the farms of Balham, as well as Doulton's as a resident of north Lambeth.

The fun-and-games do not get in the way of the College's main work. Examinations are advertised in diverse subjects: animal physiology, geometry ('Practical, Plain and Solid - mathematical instruments required'), applied mechanics, building and machine construction, magnetism and electricity ('mathematical instruments may be used'), inorganic chemistry, first aid . . . A University Extension Class in Physical Geography is announced, 'to be given by a tutor from Christ's College, Cambridge, the lectures to be illustrated by oxy-hydrogen lantern views - and other means.'

Still, it is the enthusiasm of the gymnasts that echoes most resoundingly over the years. 'The women students gave their first display, by kind permission of Miss Cons, in the theatre . . . The display began with Dumb-bell exercises performed by 17 members dressed in rational [*sic*] costume with orange trimmings and wearing flowers kindly given by the Vice-Principal. Free exercises came next, after which Vaulting the Horse by ten members some of whom are new recruits but exceedingly energetic. Next followed an Indian Club solo by the second leader, Miss Allen, to the accompaniment of the Love's Golden Dream waltz, the chorus being sung by members of the Gymnasium . . .'

There was however a disturbing incident at the conclusion of the men's display. From a letter to the editor:

'The band, as is customary, struck up the National Anthem and at the same time to my great surprise I heard a vigorous hissing in the Orchestra Stalls. Perhaps these sibilant gentlemen are some of those who call themselves republicans but if on these grounds they object to the playing of the National Anthem they should, to be logical, also object to using any money or postage stamps because they have the Queen's head stamped on them. In fact if these emulators of serpents wish to be consistent they should at once leave the country and settle in a republic.'

Sustained by such idiosyncratic logic, both Morley and the monarchy have survived and flourish ninety years later. Today the College - now under the ILEA banner - has over 10,000 students attending as wide a range of adult classes as is available anywhere in the country. It remains the 'centre of excellence' that many authorities (including Redcliffe-Maud) have found it, paramount in music and the arts. Congratulations to its magazine on nine decades of sturdy life: I look forward to its centenary.

Note: The Old Vic is now once again functioning as a theatre: long may this continue!

The twenties and the eighties.

Laurence Welsh
(Editor, 1926-37 and 1947-48)
(March 1983)

I edited *London Town* from 1928 till 1937. I was driven to resign the editorship because the departmental establishment officer told me to do so if I wished to achieve promotion to the rank of senior assistant (roughly equivalent to admin. C. today).

Since I then started an even more active honorary role in the Staff Association as Chairman of the Executive Committee, the change was not unacceptable, but I believe it is true that, whatever evils face the service now, such high-handed interference with the right of officers to undertake any form of voluntary service for their colleagues they choose would not now be tolerated. When the editors invited me to contribute to this thousandth number I wondered whether I had much to say to the present generation and whether I had not already said all I had to say to older generations. I concluded that I had best concentrate on some differences between staff conditions in my day and those as I see them today.

Both the Council itself and relations with its employees have undergone profound changes. In so far as this involves greater frankness, a tendency to call a spade a spade if not a bloody shovel, this is to be welcomed since it enables staff to get a better understanding of the differences between the Association and the councillors.

But when this degenerates into the kind of slanging match which disfigures Council proceedings and to some extent, I believe, those of Association committees I find the change distasteful and, to use a modern jargon term, counter-productive.

Too much seems to be subordinated to party consideration and the over-personalised and ill-mannered 'debate' (too urbane a word) which results generates plenty of heat and throws little light on the increasingly complex tasks which are supposed to be examined seriously at the summit of the Council's organisation.

Many of my former colleagues now of retiring age tell me that the officer/member relationship has gravely deteriorated. The proper relationship, they contend, is for Members to decide policy after studying the advice of those they employ and to leave it to the latter to put the policy into effect. This is a simple principle capable of a wide range of interpretations. Nowadays, it seems, Members too often reject advice they are given and concern themselves excessively with administrative detail.

No one wants an overmighty bureaucracy and it would be wrong to deny the right of councillors to probe into aspects of administration when they think it essential. A delicate balance has to be struck, but I have heard too much of professional advice being ignored or rejected for me to believe that due respect is always given to officers' skills and experience. The GLC no longer offers recruits a career with adequate opportunities for suitably qualified officers to enter the service, or, if they do, to stay there long enough to give London the full value of their expertise.

Relations between Council and staff in determing service conditions do not follow party lines in quite the same form. The party colour in recent years has had little effect in differences with the organised staff. For councillors the major consideration is the size of the pay-bill which both parties try to keep down to enable them to put a bold face to the electorate.

Another contrast between the twenties and the eighties is the frankness with which Council and staff conduct their affairs openly. They tell each other, and all readers of *London Town*, what they think of each other's policies and practices. No holds are barred. The two sides cross swords and argue in public on matters which hitherto would have been discussed only in the privacy of a committee room.

Sound enough, say I, with one qualification. Some of these exchanges have been couched in terms almost as offensive as those employed by politicians in dispute. Cannot we, the staff side, set an example? Or am I too much influenced by the old tag 'softly, softly catchee monkey'?

A word now to activists who want to speed up proceedings or introduce other reforms. Things don't get done quickly. A flattering article about myself in the September 1963 issue of *London Town* records that for many years I failed to win election to the General Committee. Today in too many constituencies there is no electoral competition and in others no candidates. Attempts to remedy this have been slow and the General Committee has swollen to such dimensions that it is difficult to hold a quorum.

One recent event reminds me of the old French saying *Plus ça change plus c'est la même chose.* I refer to the decision to cut the size of the General Committee and to replace annual by biennial elections. The idea came forward more than once in my own time. And now, over twenty years later, it has been achieved. So cheer up, you youngsters with other reforms in mind. But don't expect them to be achieved overnight.

One thing that has not changed is the remarkable vitality of *London Town*. An ally but not a subordinate of the Staff Association, it continues to provided a forum for the discussion of staff ideas, beside attractive articles on London and Londoners. Long may it flourish!

Note: This article proved to be Laurence Welsh's very last contribution to *London Town*.

A man and a railway.

Peter Wootton
(June 1983)

This year Brighton is to celebrate one of its most remarkable sons. In 1869, at the age of 17, Magnus Volk found himself owner of his late father's watch-making business and breadwinner for his mother and five young sisters. Yet his interest lay not in horology but in electricity. Batteries had been around since the beginning of the century and Faraday had produced a dynamo in 1831 but it still remained a laboratory plaything; Volk was eager to see it harnessed to work for mankind.

He did not invent the telegraph: the Great Western Railway was using it in 1843. He simply brought it to the ordinary citizen by his widely-sold 'Parlour Telegraph', a pair of transmitters-cum-receivers with batteries and flex to send messages round a bemused Victorian household. In contrast, the other toy he manufactured - the shocking coil - was largely of his own design. In this he was assisted by an heroic lady member of his staff who voluntarily tested each model before it left the workshop! Turning to the use of electricity for lighting, he purchased a dynamo from Siemens Brothers of Woolwich with a 2 h.p. gas engine and in 1880 lit his house from it. The next year he installed electric fire-alarms in the streets of Brighton and in 1882 he lit the King's apartments in the town's Royal Pavilion from a generator powered by a Corporation steam roller stationed outside the building.

An early picture of Volk's railway.

The next stage had to be electric traction, and on 14 June 1883 he asked the Corporation's Works committee to let him build an electric railway along the sea-front. Verbal approval came on 29 June and formal written permission on 27 July. He had not waited for the latter. The line was completed and opened by the mayor on 4 August. A quarter of a mile of track had been laid and a ten-seater car produced in five weeks and a day! The power came from the dynamo and engine that had supplied the current to light his house three years earlier. The dynamo is now on permanent display at the Brighton College of Technology. Within weeks the Corporation had authorised him to extend the line by a further half-mile on a widened gauge between the site of the present Palace Pier and the Banjo Groyne. He was also empowered to construct a lift to take his passengers from the new terminus up to the exclusive East Cliff. Here he met his first opposition: local residents feared that a stream of bag-and-bottle excursionists would pour into the quiet squares of the area. He yielded to their protests but the extended line went ahead and with two new coaches was taking traffic by April 1884.

He turned his attention to road transport and perfected a battery-operated car in 1887. In May 1888 it was described in a German illustrated magazine, a copy of which found its way to Constantinople, leading to an order from the Sultan of Turkey. By the end of October of that year he had delivered the car personally and was on his way home. The first export from Britain of a motor vehicle had been completed. The following year found him at Shepperton, building electric motors for Thames pleasure launches.

Sadly his most ambitious project never had the chance to prove itself. This was the railway on stilts from Brighton to Ovingdean and Rottingdean, where he built jetties. It was advertised as a sea voyage on wheels. The track was laid on concrete sleepers set in the chalk sea-bed just above the low-water mark and covered by the sea at most stages of the tide. The car could take up to 150 passengers and was not unlike the boats now plying from Westminster Pier, save that it stood on legs seven metres above the wheel base. Current was taken from overhead wires. Passengers could sit inside the saloon or on the open deck top or promenade around. The three-mile journey took about forty minutes. It opened in November 1896, a time of abnormal gales. The following week Brighton's Chain Pier was destroyed by a storm, and parts of the railway track, the terminal station and jetties were wrecked and the car pushed on to its side. An ordinary mortal might have given the sea best; not so Magnus Volk. Restoration took just six months.

The bad weather continued for some years and there were many more incidents of storm damage. Yet the coup de grâce came not from the elements but by way of compulsory acquisition. In 1900 Brighton Corporation resolved to build more groynes to protect the coast from erosion. Three would run across the track, cutting off the Brighton terminus from the rest of the route. A new terminus could have been built beyond the last groyne to serve a shortened track but it would have been remote from the centre of Brighton. In the event, financial support was not forthcoming and the car was left moored to Ovingdean jetty never to run again. Rudyard Kipling, who published the *Just So Stories* in 1902, used to fish from the Rottingdean jetty. In 1910 the car and all the metal parts were removed by a salvage firm. The concrete sleepers were left and after 87 years many may still be seen at low tide from the cliffs east of Black Rock and from the undercliff walk. Despite damage from the sea and in early days petty acts of sabotage from cab owners and fisherman who saw the beach railway as a threat to their livelihood, it had continued to prosper. Volk obtained permission to extend the track to Black Rock, making it a mile and a quarter long. The system of groynes that had led to the demise of the other line had the anticipated effect of building up Brighton's shingle beach and as the sea gradually moved away from the track, the storm damage became less frequent.

Although contributing in no small measure his skill and enthusiasm to the infant aviation industry, he continued to run the railway, with his eldest son, Herman, assisting more and more as time went by. In May 1937, in his 86th year, he was prominent at the opening of a new station building at Black Rock but a fortnight later came the sad news of his death. Herman carried on alone but in 1940 the Corporation decided not to renew the lease but to take it over themselves. In July of that year, the military commandeered the beach and spread barbed wire across the track. Post-war restoration was completed and the line reopened in May 1948. A critical year was 1960, when there was strong support for a scheme to introduce lightweight aluminium cars, but fortunately it was decided to preserve the old and so the character of the line was retained. Although the two 1884 cars were found after the war to be beyond repair, five of the other six cars in use in 1901 are still running. There are two aliens in the shape of 1898 former Southend Pier Railway cars purchased for £30 in 1949. The other two in the present fleet are 73 and 57 years old respectively.

Many so-called preserved railways have had their Victorian character re-created by enthusiastic amateurs who have scoured museum and scrapyard for material to embellish what had recently been a lightly-used mid-20th century branch line.

Volk's Railway is preserved in a very special sense; its character has been maintained throughout by professional operators. The atmosphere is genuine; it is not contrived. It is a living memorial to the man who created it a century ago. One can travel today in the very cars that Magnus Volk built and maintained.

This year marks the centenary of the original railway, which was the first public electric railway in Great Britain. Invited VIPs will celebrate the anniversary on 4 August by travelling on the twice-extended line from the Aquarium station past the three-year-old nudist beach to the Marina station at Black Rock. It is expected that between Easter and the end of September about half a million passengers will also make the trip. Motorists will find parking both easier and cheaper at the Black Rock, that is the eastern, end of the promenade.

Along the Wendover Canal.

John Adamson
(August 1983)

The casual visitor to the Chiltern town of Wendover is unlikely to realise that it was once served by a canal. The Wendover arm of the Grand Union Canal was constructed in the last decade of the eighteenth century, primarily to provide water to the main canal north of Tring, but also for navigation. It is difficult to believe that it ever carried much trade, but it fell victim not so much to lack of demand as to the difficulty of stopping leakage through the chalk underlying its route.

The start of the canal is to be found, appropriately enough, along Wharf Road, where a stream called the Well Head feeds into the old canal basin. A towpath follows the canal, not, initially, into open countryside but past estates of new houses, some in a harsh red brick; most new building round Chiltern towns and villages has toned in with the landscape much better than this. The prospect of a rural idyll was also interrupted by the occupation of the towpath by a pair of swans and a clutch of cygnets, requiring a clamber through a nearby hedge to make a detour. After that, it was possible to appreciate not just the peaceful flow of the canal (broadening at times into beds of reeds) but also the outlines of the hills which overlook Wendover; the misty and mysterious Wendover Woods, and the clearer line of Coombe Hill, with its Boer War memorial, commemorating those who, like Thomas Hardy's Drummer Hodge, lie under foreign constellations.

Soon the canal changes direction, and instead of hills on the near horizon there are the flat fields of the Vale of Aylesbury. I left the canal at this point to walk, accompanied by the song of larks, towards the village of Weston Turville. At first only the fifteenth century tower of the church appeared through the trees, and even when I reached the church there was little sign of the rest of the village. However, there is a great deal of new building in Weston Turville, distracting one from the village's past. Weston Turville was on the route taken by William the Conqueror as he circled London after the Battle of Hastings before receiving the Saxon surrender at Berkhamsted. The village was called Weston at the Conquest and the Turville part of the name comes from the Norman family settled there by the Conqueror, who built a castle in the village, which was demolished by Henry II as part of his campaign against excessive baronial power following the rebellion of 1173-4. The Ordnance Survey map marks a 'motte and bailey' but a good deal of imagination is needed to transform the slight mound visible from nearby footpaths into the remnants of a Norman castle.

From Weston Turville I walked back to the canal and followed it to the small village of Halton, with its light grey stone church which to me seemed a little incongruous in a Chiltern setting. There is a RAF base to the north of the canal, used for teaching gliding. At times the towpath becomes enclosed in an arch of hawthorn and other trees and shrubs. About half a mile beyond Halton, I took a footpath leading to the village of Aston Clinton. The village is dominated by the traffic on the A41 (formerly the Roman Akeman Street) and it seemed to me lacking in the attractions of its neighbour Weston Turville. There is however a nineteenth century Gothic school building, now incorporated in a modern school, with a bell which still chimes the hours as it did to summon the village children in former days.

After seeing Aston Clinton I returned to the canal, to follow it past the little hamlet of Bucklandwharf to the village of Drayton Beauchamp, where work was in progress on the attractive church, which is faced with a pattern of flint and stone blocks. The Cheyne family, who had a mansion here until 1760, are remembered in brasses and in a memorial sculpture to Lord Newhaven, the last of the line, and his wife. The Cheynes were Lords of the Manor of Chelsea, and Cheyne Walk is named after them.

Drayton Beauchamp Church.

At Drayton Beauchamp the water of the canal is diverted to the nearly Wilstone reservoir, but it is still possible to follow the dried-up bed of the canal. The reservoir and adjacent fields form a peaceful scene. Towards the end of this section of the canal it is necessary to divert to an adjacent road, but after a short walk the beginning of the navigable stretch of the canal appears, with a pumping station, at Tringford. After a short walk along the towpath it is again necessary to divert to a nearby road, which is a stretch of the Upper Icknield Way, but it is soon possible to return to the canal bank by a mill which obviously relied at one time on the canal for transport of materials.

The final section of the canal, going partly through a built-up area and attracting pollution, is a world away from some of the idyllic sections earlier on, and the last part, with the towpath overgrown with nettles and suffering a powerful smell from a sewage farm, can be considered positively sordid. Soon, however, the canal joins the main line of the Grand Union.

On the Edge of the Chilterns.

John Adamson
(October 1984)

In the August 1983 *London Town* I described a walk which started from Wendover and followed the Chiltern escarpment to the north east. From the south west of Wendover the escarpment continues towards the Thames. The next substantial town in that direction is Princes Risborough, and I recently explored that town and the country to the west.

Princes Risborough has some attractive buildings, but it is difficult to appreciate many of them because of the heavy traffic, and the town lacks the harmony of building style which marks other Chiltern towns such as Wendover and Amersham. A tranquil backwater is to be found, however, around St Mary's Church. This mediaeval church, thought to be originally thirteenth century, was much restored in the nineteenth century and has a modern tower. It is flanked on one side by a seventeenth-century manor house, and on another by a fifteenth-century timber-framed cottage which at one time served as the vicarage. The Manor House belongs to the National Trust, but can be visited only on Wednesday afternoons by arrangement with the tenant.

From the church, Manor Park Avenue leads south west, and I followed a route which, having crossed the railway line, soon reached the countryside and the hamlet of Saunderton, which has a traditional village pond. Neolithic, Iron Age and Roman remains have been found in the vicinity. The little church, like so many nowadays, was locked. The local pub was distinguished by the fact that one of the clients was serving himself behind the bar, and this was claimed to be the custom of the place; but before I had a chance to participate in this novel extension of the self-service principle mine host appeared. He seemed rather ill at ease and I had the impression he was a recent refugee from urban life.

A little beyond Saunderton a footpath was marked on my map running through a farm to the village of Bledlow. Although the existence of such a path was supported by a signpost, the exact route could be established only by a lively, although friendly, exchange of views with the farmer's wife - obviously this area is well off the beaten track for walkers. On rejoining the road, I was asked by a van driver for directions to Chalgrove. There is always something satisfying about giving directions as a stranger in a place oneself, and my map again came in useful. At Chalgrove John Hampden, that defender of English liberties and Chiltern hero, fell in battle against royalist forces in 1643. This was an unhappy event at the time, but in the long perspective of history there is the consolation that he died before the cause, which started with at least the appearance of a principled defence of freedom, came to be clouded by regicide, dictatorship and the crisis of legitimacy which led to the restoration of Charles II.

Reflecting on this, I arrived at Bledlow. This is a delightful village, with a church overlooking a ravine through which runs a stream known as the River Lyde. The ravine is very well maintained as a public garden. 'The Lions of Bledlow' is everything a village inn should be, with a magnificent hearth.

Quiet landscape

From behind the Lions a path climbs along the edge of the Chilterns, giving fine views. Whereas walking from Wendover eastwards the eye was taken north, the view is now towards middle England. Below is the valley of the Thame, with its numerous tributaries. The Thame eventually joins the Thames at Dorchester; the mind is led on to Oxford and the quiet, rather melancholy landscape of the upper Thames. Immediately below the path is a railway line which branches from another, itself no longer used for passenger traffic, from Princes Risborough to the town of Thame and on to Oxford. This little branch line, only some three miles long, runs from near Princes Risborough to Chinnor; originally it continued to Wallington. Surprisingly, there are still rails along the track and a modern sign to warn engine-drivers about a level crossing, so perhaps there is still some limited use for freight. A wayside halt, which can have seen few passengers even in the railway's happier days, now stands deserted and forlorn.

California redwoods

A short walk close to the railway line brings one to the small town of Chinnor, which is in Oxfordshire - the county boundary is crossed soon after leaving Bledlow. The most prominent feature of Chinnor from this direction is the cement works, and the town is not as interesting as many in the Chiltern area. The church, however, is a fourteenth-century building faced in a pleasing combination of stone and flint; the churchyard is host not only to traditional English trees but to California redwoods. The church has two excellent fourteenth-century stained-glass windows; the adjacent nineteenth-century window is a reminder that the colouring of comparatively modern stained glass has failed to achieve the delicacy which was the mark of the mediaeval artists. There are also some fine fourteenth- and fifteenth-century brasses.

Walking back towards Bledlow, I discovered that the signposted path ran through a sheep pen, the inhabitants of which reacted vociferously to my sudden arrival and departure. The view ahead is dominated by the Chiltern ridge. Behind Princes Risborough is the Whiteleaf Cross cut into the chalk. The origin of this cross is not known. Its position close to the Icknield Way has tempted some people to give it a pre-Roman date, but it seems likely that it is later and has a Christian symbolism. To the south the sails of the restored Lacey Green windmill can be seen, a sign, like the preservation of the Whiteleaf Cross over the centuries, of the pride which Chiltern people rightly take in their past.

After retracing my steps through Bledlow, I followed a footpath to the little hamlet of Horseden, with a few cottages, a dovecote, a church and a manor house built on the site of a house held by Sir John Denham for the King during the Civil War. A further short walk brings one to Princes Risborough station.

A British Rail backwater: the line from Princes Risborough to Chinnor.

Barrier Royal.

Gordon Farley
(June 1984)

There cannot be many Londoners who do not know that the danger of flooding in the capital is growing: it has been with us for centuries. Fourteen people died in the 1928 floods. I can remember, back in 1965, seeing the high tide lapping a few inches below the embankment wall at Vauxhall: on the north bank it even slopped over a little. There were other crises in 1976 and 1978.

There may still be some who do not know how the problem will be solved, but they will be those who do not read newspapers, watch television or listen to radio. Suffice it to say here that raising the level of the river banks is a part of it, but the keystone of the solution is the elegant barrier in Woolwich Reach, opened by the Queen on Tuesday 8 May. The story of the conception and realisation of the barrier is a fascinating and complicated one - indeed a book has been written about it, by Ray Horner of Public Health Engineering, the Council's project manager. Tide control is by the 'rising sector' gates, adopted after other systems had been considered and rejected and the brainchild of Charles Draper, a civil engineer who unhappily did not live to see its fulfilment.

It is probably well known that making the formal opening ceremony a royal occasion was not the administration's first choice. Mr Livingstone has said that he had considered having the opening performed by someone more directly connected with the construction, perhaps a relative of one of the four people who lost their lives during building. But the construction workers themselves, as well as the consortium of civil engineering contractors, had no doubts. 'We want the Queen', they said.

Nevertheless, this conceded, the occasion was not to be merely one for the top brass, Members decided, but for the people of London as well. So it was that hundreds of children, disabled people and ordinary citizens joined the many Members, officers and guests on the vast stand erected on the slope below what will be the viewing platform for the tourists who are expected to come to see 'the eighth wonder of the world'. Others gathered at viewpoints on the river, for the Queen was to arrive by royal barge. Many more waved and cheered from the fleet of boats anchored downstream of the barrier. They included two of the Woolwich ferries (true I heard one disgruntled car-owner complain about the reduced service), Thames sailing barges, what looked like a couple of corvettes, fire-boats and hired river-boats bearing the names and carrying representatives of some of the riparian boroughs at risk if floods came to London.

Fleet assembled

As the streams of children were shepherded into their places I was reminded of royal occasions in my childhood, when whole schools lined the roadside, each child with his bag of crisps and a waver. There were no crisps to-day, but a forest of blue and white paper flags with the barrier motif.

As we waited under the lowering sky and in the icy wind we were entertained by a commentary on the spectacle before us as the fleet assembled and with many facts about the structure, delivered mainly by Lord Birkett in his

Looking down on the Barrier.

own richly-flowing style, and on the progress of the royal water-borne procession, which had left the Festival Pier rather later than expected. At one pont an outburst of childish cheering, much waving of flags and the clicking of Press shutters betokened the presence of the Leader himself.

Then at last the arrival of the PLA launch *Benfleet* heralded the advent of the Queen, as her barge for the day, the *Royal Nore*, sped through the barrier and made a sailor-like landing at the erstwhile Sargents' Pier, now re-named the Barrier Gardens Pier. A pause while Messrs. Greengross and Slade were presented and then the Queen and her retinue made their way to the dais to the cheers of her loyal subjects.

'Unswerving purpose'

The Chairman of the Council, Harvey Hinds, greeted his royal guests on London's behalf: in her reply the Queen praised the wisdom of Parliament, successive governments and 'the unswerving purpose of the GLC', all of whom could be well pleased, before pressing the button that set the barrier gates upon their fifteen-minute closing sequence.

The Queen then disappeared into the workshop and the control-room, to shake some more of the 132 hands she was programmed to grasp and later to be offered refreshment. There was a general exodus in search of tea: with the other scribes I was assigned to tent A, where we enjoyed a nourishing cup of tea and a hunk of cake, recalling, for me at least, Sunday School outings of long ago. If HM had the same I hope they gave her a plate too.

After admiring the barrier, whose gates were fully closed by now, I wandered off to the visitors' centre, where an exhibition includes a working model of the barrier and there will be a souvenir shop selling key-rings, pencils and other things beloved of tourists.

Before leaving, the Queen shook some more hands and unveiled a plaque recording the occasion, receiving from Mr Hinds a gift of the specially-struck medal and from Karen Ann Lanham (aged nine and a charming grand-daughter of the local representative of the Boilermakers' branch of the General and Municipal Workers) a bouquet.

Later the Leader's mother, Mrs Ethel Livingstone, who had travelled with the Queen in the *Royal Nore*, dealt sturdily with newsmen's probing questions about this and what she thought about meeting Her Majesty. Mr Livingstone seemed a little defensive about what appeared to the outside world a reluctant choice of a royal to grace the opening, but admitted that, while somewhat understandably nervous about meeting the Queen for the first time, he had found her nice enough.

Members' declared intention of involving as many ordinary Londoners as possible in the event had been fulfilled. Everything seemed to have gone smoothly, a tribute to the months of preparation, 132 people had shaken the royal hand, hundreds more had seen the Queen at quite close range or had been in the armada and had seen what we all hope will be a rare event, the closing of the great barrier. It was a good day for the Council's image.

Note: The Thames Barrier is now a prime tourist attraction, with coach parties coming from as far away as Lincolnshire and Devon to see it - not to mention the ubiquitous Japanese tourists.

Before the speeches, the National Anthem.

Cricket with a Pinch of Salt.

Ian Wilson
(May 1985)

Here it is, late spring and the approach of another cricket season. But in County Hall circles this year the rapture is distinctly modified. The staff club is betraying signs of nerves; some reckon that preparing to take the field in the summer of '85 is like organising deck games aboard the *Titanic*. The more gnarled of the club's ancients, slumped painfully in dressing-room corners, are tending to dwell on distant, simpler, less care-worn days: on Council cricket a generation or so ago, before the luxuries of our own sports ground, pavilion'd in splendour, had taken away the unpredictability. It was lightly organised then, to the point of anarchy, and no-one had thought of league points or trophies; but viewed through the golden haze of memory it had its own weird charm.

Cricket elevens were raised from the staff of the LCC from its inception in 1889 but lack of a home ground hindered the development of a regular staff club. After the war, too, the cricket club was a late starter. Not until 1959 was it organised on a service-wide basis to make use of the Belmont sports ground.

Before then, though, many a departmental side used to flourish regularly at weekends. Architect's ran one, rather strong and upmarket, as you would expect. Several were lodged in various crannies of Housing and Valuation, then one powerful department; the biggest out-county housing estate, Becontree, had its own sports club with cricket and football sections and a well-kept ground (it was the long tube journey to the far east that sapped the strength of opponents from central London). In Chief Engineer's, cricket teams were known to emerge from various parts of the main drainage system.

But Supplies produced possibly the most endearing of the nomadic cricket tribes of those days. Clerkenwell Cricket Club originated in the Supplies depot in that submerged London village and most of the team worked there. It was not strictly a 'wandering' side; they played home matches on rented pitches in City or Council recreation grounds, in inaccessible places like Walthamstow and Hackney. Sunday games often involved walking through the echoing City of the Sabbath and catching trains to rurally-named but semi-derelict stations like London Fields or Cambridge Heath. The Walthamstow playing fields - one of the 'home' grounds - contained so many pitches that cover-point in one match would find himself chatting uneasily to square-leg in another. It was necessary to maintain constant all-round vigilance.

On Saturdays there was not much time between finishing work at 12.30 and the scheduled start of the match, especially as the troops were somewhat dilatory in assembling. Saturday travel was however sometimes assisted by a van which left the depot laden with players and gear - and pressed for time. It was rather like going on a posting in the Forces, and the driver thought so too; an Eighth Army veteran, he regarded the distant venue - Avery Hill, perhaps, or Caterham - as his Tobruk. He would shudder to a halt as if at the head of a relieving column. The club's gear was kept in a mountainous but mouldering bag that looked as if it had spend the winter in the rain. On the other hand, the kit it contained always seemed slightly on the small side (Harrow-sized bats, pads that scarcely covered the knee-cap, rather dainty gloves), an idiosyncrasy linked in some people's minds to the fact that the depot supplied sports equipment to schools.

Clerkenwell's greatest asset was the richness of the supporting characters. The legendary Charlie Bagwell (Staff Association stalwart and noted sage) was a regular at one stage. He would stand in the slips talking to his neighbour, Nick Telfer. Nick was a considerable help if you could get him out of the pub. He used to station himself at first slip and take snuff. He was never known to stop a ball but was said to take the occasional wicket with a well-timed sneeze. The conversation never flagged. Gazing tolerantly at the plantain-packed pitch and Lowryesque surroundings, they would recall opening the innings together for 1 Zingari ('Was that when you got your hundred before lunch, Charles?) and country house cricket before the war ('My word, you had to watch that butler.') Whatever it did to the batsman, it totally bemused the rest of the fielding side. Telfer went on to bowl leg-breaks once ('Wasn't that the wrong'un, Nick?' called out Bagwell as the first ball bounced twice) but he ricked his ankle on a stone and had to be helped off for a medicinal brandy. The over was never finished and he was still limping to the pub.

It all ended in 1959 when many of those concerned helped to start the staff club and establish cricket at Belmont. That's when we were introduced to plunge-baths and sight-screens. There's progress for you.

Letters to the Editor.

(March 1986)

Message from the dais

Harry Kay
(Vice-Chairman of the Council)

Sir,

It is sad that this should be the last *London Town*, at least in its present form. Whilst I have on occasions strongly disagreed with your editorials, your demise, after 86 years of service, is to be deplored. It is service that brought me to write this letter.

It is to the credit of those employed by the GLC that their service to the community and their integrity are recognised by all who have had dealings with them. It would be ridiculous to assert that harmony existed between every officer and every elected Member, but in the main elected Members have little to complain about. It is invidious to mention a few but I will chance it. Those officers who serve the Forum for the Elderly, the entertainments licensing appeals committee, Arts and Recreation and the Chairman's office (which includes all the dais members), not forgetting the messengers, are especially thanked by me.

The people of London will lose the skill and dedication of a large number of public servants; this is one of the many things this Government will have to answer for.

I am convinced that within five years a new authority will rise from the ashes. Perhaps (as the Chairman, Tony Banks, MP, stated recently at the Lord Mayor's dinner) it will combine the finance and authority of the City of London with the electorate of a Greater London.

I send to all employees of the GLC the best wishes of my wife and myself and hopes for their future.

A minor tragedy

I. W. Wilson and P. J. Bacon

Sir,

It may be said that in the wreckage of London local government the death of *London Town* is but a minor tragedy. Still, many of us will deeply mourn its passing. It has served the staff since the turn of the century, its unique constitution enabling it to maintain a freedom of comment and an independence of attitude that were in fact a source of strength to the union it supported. That the Staff Association in recent years found this occasionally difficult to grasp is another minor tragedy.

Over the years the journal has served to make the Association's member-shop more aware and informed. Perhaps an even more important function had been to give its dispersed membership a sense of identity. Its regular appearance has been a reminder of the continuing realities of Association life. When this unifying influence is removed, what will take its place?

The Association promises a journal (it is presumably a monthly) in the form of a small newspaper. It had better know what it is taking on. To what extent for the Association there is life after abolition will no doubt depend on many factors: one of them will be whether it can achieve an effective replacement for *London Town* for communication with its members. The present journal's special character has attracted over the years a stream of editorial staff and writers prepared to work in their own time and for no monetary reward to produce a quality paper. Its standards and traditions are high. It will be a hard act to follow. (Retired members will wonder sadly what they are going to get for their subscriptions in future).

It's true that the recent upheavals have been accompanied by a drying-up of the flow of editorial volunteers. One cannot conclude without paying tribute to David Moore, above all, for keeping the flag flying and the *Staff Gazette* in existence until the old world came to an end.

Truly sad

W. A. Williamson

Sir,

I am saddened to learn that this issue of *London Town* is to be the last.

Saddened because, whatever else it may or may not be, *London Town* is a genuinely democratic magazine in that its columns are open to all Members and officers to air their views. If more in both categories failed to avail themselves of the opportunities presented, so much the worse for them; contributions on virtually any subject were always welcomed. *London Town* has been the only forum for staff with something to say to be accorded wide publicity. Its loss is thus irreparable.

May I offer congratulations to a long and distinguished line of Editors; and a special word of appreciation for the present incumbent, David Moore, whose unremitting and skilful endeavours have provided an informative, entertaining and objective journal during challenging and changing times.

So the GLC goes, and *London Town*.

Truly, a sad month for London.

People who cared

'Penelope'

Sir,

Fifty years ago I joined the LCC Supplies department. The times were not unlike the present. For every vacancy for employment there were twenty or more applicants.

I was interviewed in a beautiful carpeted room overlooking the Thames. I started work in the basement on the other side of the building. I wrote orders for building materials in indelible pencil which got all over my hands and cuffs. I did the post at the end of the day and was always the last to leave, and there was no payment for overtime to add to my 28 shillings a week (less deductions). I was very disappointed.

And then I read *London Town*. Out there somewhere in the building were people who cared for the same things as I did, who thought that women should not be paid less than men, who could see no reason why they should have to give up work if they got married, who were interested in what was going on in the outside world and who thought it was a privilege to work for the citizens of London (even though we had a duty to educate our masters). It cheered me. Working for London! 'A servant with this clause makes drudgery divine . . .' and this idea did make a difference. Of course I joined the Staff Association and took part in its many campaigns - to restore the 1930 wage cuts, for equal pay and the abolition of the marriage bar, for affiliation to the TUC, to keep in touch with our colleagues who were called up during the war, and so many more issues.

But, looking back, to me the importance of *London Town* was its morality, its belief that public service was important, that rights and duties had to be balanced, and that the local government officer was not to be manipulated by his or her political masters.

Farewell

G. P. Ashelford

Sir,

To those I have met over the past thirty years, as 'A' Day fast approaches I bid a fond farewell. I intend to keep in contact with some of you, but the vast majority will have to recollect the good times and happy memories for as long as you care to retain them: in my case it will be for the rest of my life!

Sadly, standards have declined drastically over the past few years, and as far as I am concerned (and, I am sure, many other long-serving officers) County

Hall has become a sick joke. That was the main reason for my decision not to soldier on after 31 March.

I shall miss all the many activities outside my employment - the Staff Association, the Chess Club, the County Hall branch of the Royal British Legion, the Staff Benevolent Society, Social Club, Luncheon Club wines committee, the Real Ale Society, the Darts Club and the South Bank Wine Club.

To those colleagues remaining in harness, under whatever guise, go my best wishes for the future; to those already retired continued contentment, and to those, like myself, going into semi- or complete retirement a fulfilling and rewarding life.

Visionary

D. R. Allery

Sir,

In the archives at the Greater London Record and History Library at Clerkenwell my daughter came across *How Greater London is Governed* by Herbert Morrison, 1935 edition. Page 98 contains the following:

'For some curious reason Parliament has seemed to have a fear of order, dignity and cohesion in the local government of the Metropolis. Even today one hears reports - which I hesitate to take seriously - to the effect that Parliamentarians are apprehensive at the growing powers of the LCC and sometimes stories come to me that some MPs have a vision of machine guns directed at Parliament from the terrace of County Hall!'

Our Herbert was right in the end.

Finally, a letter from the Editor

Dear Readers,

This last issue of *London Town* has been put together with a feeling of immeasurable sadness. Perhaps that is hardly surprising - for no-one could have an association with the journal for more than thirty of its 86 years' existence (and be pall-bearer at its funeral) without developing genuine affection for what it represents and regard for what it has achieved. Elsewhere in this issue you will find some commentary on all that.

My purpose here, however, is not to wax nostalgic but to take the opportunity to say a personal thank you. First, to some former Editors: Pat Bacon, who first allowed me to write a regular column of film criticism; C. D. Andrews, who enticed me into the production team and urged me to tackle additional subjects of rather more pressing concern to the staff than the pleasures and the horrors of the silver screen; the late Graham Harris, who taught me the principles of editing and how to 'lay out and make up' the magazine; Len Hudson, who welcomed me back into the editorial fold after a period of inactivity in the '70s and who, even in retirement and up to this moment, has proved a staunch friend and dedicated associate; and, most of all, Laurence

Welsh (doyen of Editors - 1926-37, 1947-48 - and of the Staff Association too), simply for being an inspiration to all who succeeded him.

Next, my thanks go to a good many others (some, alas, no longer living) who, either on the technical or business side of *London Town* or in the Committee of Management, have done so much for it during my time on the gazette and aided and abetted my own efforts as well: Joyce Ansell, Reg Nidd, Ian Wilson, Maurice Fulcher, Wally Feltham, Gordon Farley, Tom Choat, Mary Cartlidge, Eric Peirson, Jeffery Brand, Gerald Oppenheim, Michael Costelloe, Nick Wright, Les Needs, Robin Oakley-Hill, Keith Bennett, Phil Popham, Tony Gillmore, David Crawford, Bill Baxter, Derek Bean and all my helpful friends at the printers and advertising agents.

From the Staff Association - notwithstanding our occasional ups-and-downs, part and parcel of a strange love-hate relationship - I single out Fred Hollocks, Charles Corcoran, Arthur Capelin and Derek Addison.

These sentences have all to easily turned into a list. No apologies for that, though, as they form the essential preamble to a mention of those to whom I am equally, if not more, indebted - the staff who are or have been *London Town's* readers. These are the people I may sometimes have pleased, from time to time angered, occasionally disappointed, but always at least tried to serve. Thank you for having me. Good-bye and good luck!

Yours sincerely,
David G. Moore

Note: The final *London Town* letters page - given in full in view of its unique nature.

Section 6: Brief Revival

Introduction

After an interval of exactly one year *London Town* appeared again in a very different guise and now available to subscribers only. How and why this came about has been recorded quite succinctly in the pages of *Almost a century*: all that need be added here is that this new "slimline" version of *London Town* was overtaken by events, in the formidable shape of the abolition of ILEA, before it could become at all firmly established or could expand its paid-up circulation beyond a modest 500 or so - though its actual readership was certainly well beyond that figure.

In this concluding section of the *Miscellany* we give a brief selection of the type to articles which appeared in this new style *London Town*. The arts and travel, both at home and abroad, were well covered; the London's Docklands series maintained the *London Town* tradition of commentary on the changing - and changeless - urban scene; the Editorials (not included here) ranged far and wide, again in the long-standing traditions of the journal. All in all it was a worthy successor to all that had gone before it.

The Museum of the Moving Image.

Andrew Bucknall
(Spetember 1987)

Beneath London's Waterloo Bridge, behind the bright yellow hoardings, a unique new museum is taking shape. The British Film Institute's Museum of the Moving Image - a highly visual, changing exhibition tracing the history of the cinema and television which began construction in June 1985 will be opening in June 1988. The Museum of the Moving Image (MOMI in its abbreviated form), the first new addition to London's South Bank buildings for years, will be one of the very few public buildings in this country built without a penny of taxpayer's money. Anthony Smith, Director of the BFI has been instrumental in this remarkable achievement, working closely with the successful Museum Fund Raising Committee chaired by Lady Howe.

The bulk of the money needed to construct the £7 million Museum has been raised from private sponsorship and public donations. The impact of the Museum's design will be seen in the building's steel and glass walls with the concrete underside of Waterloo Bridge as its roof. Indeed the lack of traditional style will be one of the main features and passers-by will be able to see the moving images projected on the external walls, and lasers and neon will give the Museum/NFT complex a remarkable profile against the otherwise drab concrete skyline of London's South Bank.

Inside the Museum the fascinating story of the evolution of moving images will be told with the emphasis on participation and direct experience - in place of the traditional museum approach of 'mahogany and brass behind glass'. Museum presenters will fulful the role of hosts, information officers and security staff combined replacing the old Museum 'guards system'.

Videodisc technology will ensure that the Museum's highly visual presentation including still, moving and multi-image projection is of the highest quality and allows a variety of programming possibilities. At regular intervals one-eighth of the exhibition will be changed and contemporary developments will be continually incorporated. This novel approach will also be appreciated in that the Museum will not be organised chronologically; it will tell the whole story, technical, social and artistic of the development of moving images from their origin in ancient cave paintings to their future in the laser and hologram technology of tomorrow. Original equipment, working models and large replicas will demonstrate the fascinating technical development which led up to the birth of cinema less than 100 years ago.

From there the story broadens to take in the early innovators, the coming of sound and colour, the 'star' system and the growth of cinema into the massive industry it remained until challenged by the advent of television. Film and TV worldwide will be examined and the enormous influence it has on our lives. However the emphasis will be on the practical experience; a simple video rostrum camera set-up will allow visitors to animate short sequences themselves and play back their creations immediately. Similarly in an operational TV control room overlooking a miniature TV studio, visitors will use controls to learn how camera angles and positions, props, lighting and vision mixing work. Above the main deck level, a mezzanine will house special (sometimes touring) exhibitions and at the rear of the building in the Moving Image Workshop there will be a continuous programme of live talks, lectures, films, magic lantern shows and other events to complement particular exhibition areas. Through a glass wall visitors will be able to watch technicians and projectionists at work in this area.

In the evenings, the Workshop will revert to being a conventional cinema where the world's classic films will be screened in rotation throughout the year. The completion of the MOMI building in June 1988 will enable Londoners and visitors to London to be justifiably proud of one of the world's great production centres for film and television with four TV channels, three film schools, a large film festival and a thriving video industry. So the distinctive art forms of the 20th century, film and television, alongside theatre, music, painting and sculpture will finally take their proper place on London's South Bank.

Eng. Lit. revisited: Beowulf – the first ripping yarn?

Peter Rowland
(May 1988)

It's amazing, really, that they've never got round to making a film of it. At Malmesbury, one is pleased to note, there is an Athelstan Cinema, and had this establishment been operating as a cinema in 988 as actively as it is operating as a bingo hall in 1988 the chances are that it would have been showing, to packed houses, *The Saga of Beowulf* - and following it up, while the Anglo-Saxon audiences were still reeling in their seats, with Beowulf II.

For *Beowulf* has all the ingredients that are required, in this day and age, for box-office success. Composed, perhaps, as early as 680, although not actually committed to Old English parchment for another three hundred years, it is a poem which had its listeners and readers perpetually agog to know what happened next. The action takes place in Denmark, where the venerable King Hrothgar presides over as amiable a court of Viking warriors as you could wish to meet. They hunt and do valiant deeds by day, with lots of feasting and revelry to round things off in the evening, and come night time settle down to their well-earnt slumbers in the King's magnificent assembly room - the Heorot, or meeting hall. Contentment, however, comes to a sudden end when a terrible monster known as the Grendel appears on the scene - a hideous creature, descended from Cain, but at least twice the size (so one gathers) of your average Viking. He is, truly, the terror that stalks by night, rather like an early Vampire, for he invades the meeting hall and seizes no fewer than thirty of the warriors, devouring some of them on the premises and taking away the rest to his lair. Time and time again this happens, with the result that Hrothgar and his diminishing band of supporters are obliged to evacuate their meeting hall as soon as the shades of night begin to descend. There are, now and then, some courageous souls who stay behind to do battle with the monster, but when the dawn comes, and Hrothgar and Co. venture to return, all that remains of these brave chaps is a small pile of bones.

At this point, and not a moment too soon, our hero arrives. News of the Vikings' plight has reached the ears of Beowulf, a doughty prince from Geatland whose fame is already pretty prestigious, and accompanied by a handful of keen supporters he speeds to the Danish court and announces that he will either rid them of the Grendel or die in the attempt. A great cheer goes up, followed by the inevitable feasting and revelry, although it may be that the court are a little disconcerted when Beowulf announces that he will do battle with the Grendel unarmed, because the Grendel isn't armed either and it would be taking an unfair advantage of the monster to make use of his sword and shield. (The first recorded example of the public school ethos in English literature - doubly remarkable, indeed, in view of the fact that the public schools had not yet been invented.) Somewhat dubiously, perhaps, the King and his colleagues with-draw, giving Beowulf and his chums a free run of the meeting hall as night and the Grendel draw near, but all turns out for the best. The Grendel, as it happens, is protected by a secret spell against swords and spears but has omitted to insure himself against brute force. Having observed (with a certain degree of scientific detachment) the manner in which the Grendel seizes and devours one of the Geats, in order to get the general idea of how the monster operates, Beowulf seizes hold of its arm and hangs on to it, ripping it off as the mortally wounded Grendel makes his getaway.

Thunderous applause all round. Unparalleled rejoicings, etc. But that certainly isn't the end of the story. Just when you thought it was safe to go back into the meeting hall for more feasting and revelry and kipping down for the night - as, indeed, the King and his nobles waste no time in doing - it turns out (hold on to your hats, folks!) *that the Grendel has a mother, ten times as terrible as himself!* Now this is something which no one has thought to mention up till now

214

- one of those little things which obviously slips the mind - but sequel time is upon us and somebody does eventually recall (rather late in the day, alas) that, yes, there *have* been recorded sightings of *two* such monsters wandering in the gloaming and that one of them is said to bear a faint and hideous resemblance to a female. The Grendel's mum, understandably annoyed at the way in which her offspring has been duffed up, is hell-bent upon revenge and wastes no time in paying a midnight visit to the Heorot. Another Viking warrior is utilised as a tasty morsel and all is consternation. Beowulf (who, for reasons not made clear by the poet, had been sleeping elsewhere on that particular night) hastens in pursuit of monster No. 2, following her to her den at the bottom of a vast lake (a descent which takes nine days), and then comes a tremendous fight and much hacking of limbs - for on *this* occasion, such is the scale of his adversary, Beowulf has no compunction about making use of a sword. And so, bearing as a trophy the head of the original Grendel, he returns to the Danish court and is hailed again as the saviour of the land.

There is more to come, including an encounter with a dragon, but the ground we have covered is quite enough to be going on with and one is dumbfounded afresh by the fact that *Beowulf* has never yet been translated into cinematographic terms by our whizzkid impresarios.

But the truth of the matter is, of course, that they *have* made a film of it - or, to be more precise, they have made *four* films. Times and places have been altered, the costumes have been up-dated and some of the names have been changes, but the fact remains that the Grendel and his mother have starred, respectively, in *Jaws* and *Jaws II* and that Beowulf (regarded at one time as a "feeble princeling", the Anglo-Saxon equivalent of Clark Kent) can be found in *Superman* and *Superman II* - for all these productions are, in effect, simply the latest manifestation of a story that is, almost literally, as old as time. There is, truly, nothing new under the sun, for the twentieth century craves larger-than-life heroes just as desperately as the tenth, and the longing to see Good triumphant and Evil vanquished - in the story books, at any rate - is as strong as ever.

London's Docklands: Wapping.

John Adamson
(July 1989)

Wapping today is a veritable hive of activity. The social and economic arguments about the renewal of Docklands have been much rehearsed; whatever view one takes of them it is difficult to avoid a feeling of exhilaration at the sheer scale of the building work which has been undertaken and is in progress.

By coincidence, Wapping has in close proximity two institutions which say a great deal about, and could indeed be considered symbolic of, the sort of society we have become. The first of these is "Fortress Wapping", the News International premises in Pennington Street, which runs close to The Highway.

"Fortress Wapping" certainly does look like a fortress, with the box-like main building as the keep, and the old walls around the site as curtain wall. Memories of the violent confrontations between demonstrators and police outside this site which used to fill our television screens have now faded, and the introduction of new printing technology is an accomplished fact. No doubt the News International move to Wapping has brought all sorts of production benefits, but one feels the isolation of journalists from the camaraderie of an environment like that of Fleet Street is a bad thing for them and the service they provide. The functionalism of "Fortress Wapping" seems to embody the contemporary corporate approach which can so easily undermine the respect for the individual which is so important for the media, as it is in other fields.

Close to "Fortress Wapping" is Tobacco Dock. This Dock was originally built between 1811 and 1814 and was used not only for tobacco but also for wool, wine, spirits, and other commodities. It is now being transformed into a massive complex of shops, restaurants and the like. Replicas of two eighteenth century tobacco ships are in place on the adjacent quay, and the first phase of the development is already open.

When I approached the Tobacco Dock building I did so with a generally favourable impression of the scheme. The adaptation of old warehousing to new requirements seems commendable in principle, and there is no doubt that Wapping needs more shops. Once inside, however, I felt increasing doubts. Partly it was the Muzak, presumably intended to induce feelings of relaxation and inclination to buy things, but likely to have the opposite effect on many. Partly it was the generally trendy nature of the shops, which made it difficult to believe that what one might call the indigenous inhabitants of Wapping would feel at home in such an environment. Mainly, however, it was the fact that there was hardly anyone there. When I visited, on a weekday morning, the "yuppies" were no doubt all hard at work. Tobacco Dock is, however, clearly aimed partly at the tourist trade, and the tourists who were present in large numbers in the Tower/St. Katharine's area were obviously not reaching it. Perhaps it will become part of the tourist trail in due course, but it lacks the attractive open aspect of St. Katharine's, indeed the converted vaults could be considered rather claustrophobic. It is perhaps unfair to make a judgement at this stage; one should wait until the whole complex is completed.

"Fortress Wapping" and Tobacco Dock are some way from the River, where the "authentic" character of Wapping may be said to lie. To discover this, one moves from St. Katharine's Dock east along St. Katharine's Way, where one sees the familiar pattern of rehabilitated warehouses and new building, which continues as the road turns into Wapping High Street and then Wapping Wall. No doubt flats in these developments have their attractions, particularly for "yuppies", in terms of novelty, views, proximity to the City and the possibility of capital appreciation. However with the lack of gardens and with busy narrow roads which often have poor visibility round corners, this accommodation is hardly ideal for bringing up children. The prices will, of course, rule out large categories of people who have an important role in maintaining a flourishing community.

A famous Docklands pub, the Prospect of Whitby, in 1950.

The atmosphere of old Wapping is perhaps best found at the Town of Ramsgate next to Wapping Old Stairs. Here one can well imagine dark deeds. Not far away was Execution Dock, where the bodies of pirates were left chained to be covered by the tide. The better known Prospect of Whitby, which claims to be London's oldest riverside inn, is more "lost" among new buildings than is the Town of Ramsgate, but the view from its balcony is particularly fine. There is not a great deal of activity on the river these days; pleasure craft take tourists to and from Greenwich, the river police patrol, but there is nothing like the scale of commercial activity once to be seen. The curve of the river reflecting the changing sky remains, however, as it has been for many centuries, and is a reminder of the comparatively transient nature of some of the issues which now seem so important to us. Close to the Prospect of Whitby is Shadwell Basin, which is now the site of watersports organised by the East London Marine Venture. The sight of young people enjoying themselves learning to canoe is indeed a cheerful one.

I had hoped to find in Wapping an old village centre similar to that in Rotherhithe. In Scandrett Street there was such a centre, with St. John's Church (built in 1756) adjoining a school erected shortly after the Church. Unhappily, most of the Church was destroyed by bombing, only the tower remaining; and more recently the school building which had painted figures of a boy and girl in niches, has fallen into a sad state of dereliction. Around the corner, however, in Green Bank, the Roman Catholic Church of St. Patrick, built in 1879, has been refurbished with the aid of a grant from the LDDC. Near this old village is the Wapping Sports Centre.

Wapping presents a fascinating mixture of old and new. For better or worse, it has been hauled firmly into the late 1980s. Its inhabitants of earlier times, making a chancy living from the River, were not perhaps all that remote in spirit from its new "yuppies" on the high wire of international currency dealing.

A not so restful journey in Peru.

Gail Elrick
(July 1989)

I was beginning to wonder if Peru, as a choice for our annual holiday, was a mistake. We had been forewarned of course, about theft, terrorism, rampant inflation and the like. We had heard good things too. That the people (not just the thieves) were very welcoming, and we had been longing for years to visit Machu Picchu, the famous lost city of the Incas.

We had even learnt that Lima was not too bad. That was untrue. It is quite awful. During the months of April to December the city is covered in a kind of fog. It feels cold and damp and even the buildings take on a permanent grey hue. We arrived in September and found a city that as well as being encased in this fog, was not very clean, its buildings were disintegrating, the roads were pot-holed and even the money changers looked hungry. Moreover the economy was on the verge of collapse, prices of staple goods having risen an average of 500% during the previous week. No wonder some of the inhabitants had turned to crime.

We were therefore very glad to make our escape to Cuzco where although the security and financial problems remained at least the sun shone and the streets were clean. Standing at about 11,000 ft, it claims to be the longest continuously inhabited city in South America. Our main interest in it was as the former capital of the Inca Empire and for its curious mix of architectural styles, where Inca stone walls blend with attractive colonial and modern buildings. We were amazed to find so many of the locals in traditional dress. One always suspects when seeing postcards that they are posed for the tourists. We got quite used to seeing women in the distinctive dress of bowler hat perched on the top of the head, hair in long plaits tied together at the back, a short flared skirt surmounting layers of petticoats, knee length wool socks and most importantly the brightly coloured shawl wound around the back, usually carrying the youngest in the family plus the shopping.

Security remained a problem. Thefts from tourists were very common although only one attempt was made against us that we were aware of. Carrying backpacks, as we were, made one vulnerable. This was countered by wrapping it in a sack (difficult if one wanted to make legitimate access) but this did make life hard for the razor/knife merchants. We preferred to adopt a fairly rapid swaying gait when carrying the backpacks, especially if one was stationary.

However, interesting as Cuzco was, we wanted to get to Machu Picchu. Fortunately for the preservation of the latter from the worst ravages of the tourist trade, travel is really only possible by train or foot. We chose a mixture of the two, following the Inca trail. This is an extract from our diary.

Thursday

Rise at 3.45 am. Walk to the station in the dusk to find a huge crowd camped on the steps outside. Vendors selling 'mate' tea doing a good trade. risk some - glasses not very clean but need something to wake us up. Doors of station open and crowd surges in. Amazed to find that the seats we had reserved actually existed and that the train left on time. Train follows seemingly unending series of switchbacks up the hill. Keep tight hold of our bags at the slow parts. This is a notorious point for thieves boarding.

Reach Kilometre 88 at 9.00 am. This is the start point for the Inca trail. Other tourists who are going to Machu Picchu by train look in amazement as we pile onto the side of the track, miles from nowhere. It starts to rain. John (my husband) helps drag my voluminous waterproof cape on to cover me and the pack. Pay entry to the trail (2,800 Inti - about £10), cross Urumbamba River on suspension bridge and begin trail.

Rain gets harder; it trickles via the gap in the cape at my neck and begin to get very wet. Start to feel effect of the unaccustomed altitude (breathlessness) and pack feels heavy (not used to carrying the camping gear). Catch up with another gringo, (Paul from Greenwich), who has given up his job to travel around South America. Recounts how he was on a long distance bus when the price rises happened. The driver had to make a whip round among the passengers to pay for petrol.

Struggle uphill to meet a group of trekkers sheltering from the rain. Consensus is that we are actually farther on than we realised. Had obviously been concentrating so hard on the climb that we missed a village. Walk on with the others until we reach 3 stones camp site. Decide to camp here although it is still early. The trail rises very steeply from now and don't want to risk having to camp too high (where it will be cold).

Put tent up quickly, (will it leak? - the only previous outing was at Swanage!), climb inside and have lunch. John complains at the lack of space and point out, for the umpteenth time, that bigger tent would be much heavier. Rain stops eventually (tent has not leaked). Bring out new stove and keep fingers crossed as we try to light it. Meal of instant soup and rehydrated chicken curry. Bed at 6.30 pm.

Friday

Wake early and wash in stream before anyone else is around. Paul and co. leave first (we are not very adept at packing up the camping gear). Trail very steep but sun comes out and we don shorts. Climb through tropical forest and onto bare mountainside. Adopt a fairly steady pace. Begin to be overtaken by some members of a group (mainly Dutch) who are only carrying light day packs. Last few hundred feet to the top of the pass (13,800 ft) are hard. The Dutch cheer when anyone gets to the top. Pass called, in Quecha (the original language), Warmiwanusa, meaning dead woman's pass. How apt. Clouds have descended so no views (again). Very steep going down; Dutch scamper down but we opt for more leisurely pace. The packs tend to unbalance one a bit.

Reach valley floor. Dutch camp being erected by the porters so carry along trail a little and find a lovely flat sheltered camp site with its own stream. Meal of rehydrated spaghetti and bed at 7.00 pm.

Saturday

Have help in packing up our tent from the cook boy attached to the Dutch group. He wears a small red poncho and a flat hat. Is fascinated by all our gear. We learn his father is a farmer but conversation ends there. Our Spanish is poor and suspect his is too (Quecha being his first tongue).

Wave him goodbye and continue up the trail. Feel smug because we are moving faster than the Dutch group (they probably overdid it yesterday). One of them needs oxygen. Reach the Inca site of Sayamarca (dominant town) just as the mist clears. Get a superb view of ruin and the surrounding area. Now walking on excellent Inca paving. Large flat stones, very well put together. Mist down again and if it was not for the paving we would be lost. Aware of very steep drop on one side. Creepers and branches overhang the trail, weird, like something from the 'Lost World'. Trail passes through two Inca tunnels, cut into the rock, about 15 ft. long and high enough to stand up in. Incredible feats of engineering. Reach ruin of Phuyapatamarca (town above clouds), now in the clouds. Could camp here but decide to carry on. Join the recently discovered stretch of Inca paving and steps, thousands of steps descending very steeply. Glad we are going down and not up! Have the trail to ourselves until it ends abruptly above the new ugly hotel/hostel. The rapid return to civilisation is not welcome. The only place to camp is the hotel grounds but the best places taken

*Detail of the very impressive ruins of Machu Picchu - the "lost city of the Incas",
discovered as recently as 1911.*

221

by a group. Squeeze in with other trekkers and pitch tent with some difficulty. Even stove begins to play up. Eventually it grudgingly lights but only long enough to rehydrate a meal. Bed at 7.00 pm feeling grumpy.

Sunday
Very early start. Want to get to Machu Picchu well before the tourist train arrives. Stove now dead but porters give us hot water boiled on their open fire. So much for modern technology. Reach Intipunku (Gate of the Sun) where the first view of Machu Picchu should be possible. Of course it is misty. Sit for a while hoping it will clear but give up. First view of the city when we are practically on top of it. It is far better preserved than we had imagined it. Thus ended the Inca trail but not our holiday. How we got out of Peru (with some difficulty) is another story.

Note: Machu Picchu, part of which is shown in the illustration on the previous page, is remarkable as the most complete surviving relic of the highly sophisticated Inca civilisation and empire which flourished during the fifteenth and early sixteenth centuries only to be destroyed by the Spanish *conquistadores* under Francisco Pizzaro in the mid 1530s. The Inca empire was established during the period c.1440-90, mainly under the emperor Pachatutec: it extended over almost 400,000 square miles of the north-western segment of the South American continent, and came to be held together, much as was the Roman empire, by a network of splendid roads and bridges, and the operations of a vast bureaucracy. The empire was ruled by a divine Emperor, descendent of the sun god, but in practice his powers were circumscribed by custom and by the ever burgeoning powers of the Imperial civil service, which operated a system similar to state socialism with a fully blown "welfare state" and state ownership of most of the resources of the empire - e.g. the ubiquitous llamas, which provided transport, fuel, meat - and sacrificial animals for the many elaborate religious rituals.

Although remarkably advanced in many ways the Inca state proved to be no match, in the end, for a mere 180 somewhat ruffianly Spaniards, for it was extremely backward in many branches of technology despite its achievements in the building of roads and bridges and of such immense cities as Machu Picchu and Cuzco, the capital of the empire and the original home of the Incas. So, in 1533, it fell irretrievably, though its bureaucracy still continued to operate for some years, though now serving Pizzaro rather than the Inca Emperor.

Section 7: The Staff Association

Introduction

The London County Council Staff Association came into being in 1909, twenty years after the establishment of the Council itself, as a result of spontaneous action by large numbers of staff who were deeply angered at the Council's stated intention to place a "bar" in its grading structure. This is not the place to go into detail on a very complex issue: suffice it to say that the matter was eventually resolved largely to the satisfaction of the staff, but by that time (the mid 1920s) the Association had become quite firmly established - and the *Staff Gazette* had become its organ, though retaining a large measure of editorial independence.

From its very beginning the main object of the Association was to negotiate with the Council on the pay and working conditions of its members and as early as 1911 the Council informally recognised the Association as a legitimate negotiating body. In 1917, the Whitley Council on the Relations of Employers and Employed recommended the establishment of joint committees on an industry-by-industry basis at national and local level to discuss not only pay and conditions but also general problems of management - a radical idea then and, indeed, even now. Hardly surprisingly, the high ideals of Whitley largely foundered on the rocks of employer and union intransigence. However, Whitleyism, as it came to be known, did take root in the public sector. The concept of Whitleyism was given its own unique variation by the Council and the Association, who established an Interim Joint Committee of Members and Staff in 1920 (made official and permanent in 1927) to negotiate all matters of pay and conditions. This was quite separate and distinct from the national Whitley machinery, and was to remain so for many years.

Until the abolition of the GLC in 1986 - an event very soon followed by the absorption of the Association into the GMB (General, Municipal and Boilermakers) trade union - the Association engaged in an unending round of negotiations on pay and conditions: by the early 1950s the "pay round" had become an annual event. The Staff Association functioned, in fact, as a trade union, although it was not registered as such until after the Second World War, and by 1956 its members had so far recognised and accepted this trade union role that they voted for affiliation to the TUC. In later years, from about 1962 onwards, the Association became very heavily involved in negotiations over the transfer of Council staff - to the new London Boroughs in 1965 and then again (on a more piecemeal basis) in 1971, 1979-80 and 1985-86.

At the same time, the Association was very much of an extended social club. It's true to say that in LCC days at least the numbers within the service were small enough for all the prominent figures in the ranks of the staff to be known to each other and to "socialise" on a regular basis. It was all rather like the House of Commons, where total membership is still small enough for Members to feel themselves in a club, and where friendships are formed across party barriers. It would be fair to say that even as late as 1970 the Association was run on what would now be called a "network" basis. After 1970 things changed: the staff grew steadily in numbers through most of the 1970s and the senior officers who had provided much of the leadership of the Association since its beginning no longer (for a variety of reasons) took such an active part. Nevertheless, some elements of the old "network" role of the Association remained until the end.

Over the years, as the Association came to be accepted by the Council as a part of the LCC way of life there was also a growth in unofficial contacts: and during the long period of Labour Party control at County Hall (1934-67) these contacts proliferated, for the majority of the Association's leaders during those years were at least supporters of (and often active members of) the Labour Party. There is, however, no really firm evidence, either written or anecdotal, that either Council Members or Staff Association personalities were unduly influenced by their political affiliations or even, in some instances, their personal friendships. In later years, say from the mid 1970s until the abolition of the GLC, relations between the Association and the Council became much cooler and more distant.

So, however it had all begun, the Association finished up as a fully fledged trade union, with all the strengths and weaknesses appertaining to that role. It had, however, always been a trade union with a difference - not least by reason of its uniquely democratic constitution, which made its General Committee, consisting of, for much of its existence, one representative for every forty members of the Association, the ruling body. The Committee has been aptly described as "an annual conference meeting monthly": and until the last few years it really did rule the Association, being ever wary of the leadership even when, as was usually the case, a majority within its ranks supported the normally moderate and cautious policies of that leadership. During the 1940s and 1950s in particular the standard of debate within the General Committee was very high, and there was some competition for membership of it: it was only in latter years that the meetings became so tedious that it was difficult to maintain a quorum.

Inaugural Entertainment.

(April 1911)

Although the Staff Association had for some time before 25th February emerged from that provisional state of existence through which all new bodies pass, having taken to itself a written constitution and such-like trappings of authority, it was not until the date named that it made its bow in the shape of an inaugural entertainment. We gather that this function was originally intended to be in the nature of an advertisement to draw into the net the indifferent and the scoffer - even such slippery fish as our hard-to-be understood individualistic colleague, with his defective sense of communal instinct and his desire to prowl on his own. So quickly, however, did the membership mount up that when the inaugural entertainment did arrive, it partook more of the nature of a proud parade of strength, rather than of an advertisement for recruits. Such at least is the impression we took away from the Birkbeck Institution (I apologise - College, for it has risen in rank since some of us imbibed wisdom under its roof). The promoters had found it necessary to fix on a Saturday because of the expense of hiring a suitable building on another evening of the week, but despite this drawback (for it is no small effort to many to drag themselves back to town on a Saturday evening), the Birkbeck was comfortably crowded with about 700 to 800 people. The fair sex appeared to be in a majority. There was no formal reception but one and all at the outset made for the college theatre, where the Musical Society and the Dramatic Society had promised good things. We append below some observations by our dramatic and musical critic on the entertainment provided.

Just before the interval the only speeches of the evening were given. By this time the company included the Chairman of the Council, who was accompanied by Mrs. Whitaker Thompson, Sir Laurence and Lady Gomme, Dr. Garnett, and Mr. B. M. Allen. The Chairman of the Council, introduced by the Clerk of the Council in a few happy words, delivered a humorous homily on the advantages and disadvantages of staff societies, and the audience then dispersed to refresh the inner man, to make the acquaintance of the wives, sweethearts, and sisters of their colleagues, and to inspect the products of the Staff's genius. And a very pleasant interval it was. Many of us, for instance, had never seen an exhibit by the Faraday House Sketch Club. The club's fine show was much admired, and we heard more than once the question asked "Are any of them for sale?" (Are they?) The Camera Club, too, had some good specimens, though one would have liked to see a much larger exhibit. The *Staff Gazette* made a big bid for publicity in the shape of an inviting poster, by W. A. Cross, and the cups and trophies of the athletes made up the complement of a good "exhibition room."

The Sub Committee which arranged the many details of the entertainment are indeed to be congratulated on the success which attended their efforts. In particular, it may not be amiss to express the sense of obligation which all members of the Association must feel they owe to the scandalously overworked Secretary, Mr. L. F. C. Maclean, for the time he has given and the services ungrudgingly offered to the Association, not merely in connection with the inaugural function but in all the hundred-and-one details attendant upon the launch of a Staff Association. If the energy displayed by members in such preliminary matters as constitution-building and inauguration is infused into all the Association's activities (and its aims and objects are stated broadly enough), we shall indeed begin to rub our eyes at seeing crystallising into reality that fond dream of our official youth - a representative Staff Association which, without regard to fear or favour, can speak, when necessary, in the name of the staff.

The Dramatic and Musical Performances

The entertainment programme consisted of a short play, *"The Conversion of Nat Sturge,"* rendered by the L.C.C. Dramatic Society, and a number of musical items which took us back at once to the Caxton Hall Smoking Concerts. *"Nat Sturge"* is a cleverly-written little piece which figured on the bill at the Haymarket a year or two since, and being very well played it was most heartily received. The "hero" is a burglar who breaks into the house of the Bishop of Minterweir in pursuit of "five 'undred golden suvrins" which inhabit the bishop's safe; he is trapped by the prelate and offered his freedom if he will marry his captor's exceedingly unprepossessing step-daughter, Julia, who has a passion for re-

225

Next Year, Perhaps.

claiming scoundrels of his type. After a mental struggle he refuses to accept his freedom on this condition, but is, however, magnanimously allowed to escape. Mr. S. Powell played admirably as the bland bishop; as the burglar Mr. H. Chesney was also very good, although in one or two passages he was difficult to hear owing to an over-elaborated hoarseness. Miss Gwladys Burkett was successful in the slight and ungrateful part of Julia, and Mr. Percy Merriman looked like a burglar's apprentice for a few minutes. Altogether the play (produced, of course, by Mr. Arthur O'Keen) was a most creditable and welcome item in the entertainment.

The various selections arranged by the Musical Society were heartily received, as they always are. We who write this have had the pleasure of sitting under Mr. Van Lennep's orchestra on so many occasions that it is difficult to say anything new about it. The selections given, which included Gounod's *"Mirella,"* *"Spanish Dance"* (Moszkowski), the *"Raymond"* overture and excerpts from *"Patience,"* were all well rendered, and there was at least one encore. Miss Ethel Bentley sang *"Fidelity,"* *"Heart's Desire,"* and *"Carmena"* pleasantly; Mr. Alexander Henderson, who has a very fine voice, gave *"Stonecracker John"* and *"My Old Shako,"* and Mr. Hading Morton was very heartily received in *"Drake goes West"* and another contribution. We again had the pleasure of hearing the violin of that clever young lady, Miss Margaret Bradfield, who repeated her success of the last smoking concert with *"Danse Hongroise"* and *"Souvenir,"* and Mr. Van Lennep controlled the proceedings in his usual able manner.

Note: It was about this time that the LCC Staff Association began to attract increasing attention from the *Gazette*, which had virtually ignored its early struggles. In those early days, as will be seen from this piece, the social side of things was of at least as much importance to members of the fledgling Association as the trade union aspect.

An Historic Debate.

C. D. Andrews
(January 1941)

The first meeting of the General Committee of the Staff Association since intensive air raids began was held on Saturday afternoon, 7th December, and, belying fears, attracted a large attendance. Though the agenda covered many topics, discussion was centred on whether or not the Association should submit the post-1930 entrants' claim to the National Arbitration Tribunal. After a lively debate the committee decided to approve the Staff Side's recommendation that, while the Council's refusal to use the arbitration procedure provided for in the Joint Committee constitution was to be deplored, it was not desirable to submit the claim to national arbitration.

Before this controversial issue came up, several speakers stressed the need for more adequate A.R.P. for the staff, particularly in outside offices. Mr. Fisher (Architect's), drawing on his personal experience of the Rescue Service, impressed upon the committee the danger of strutted basement shelters in buildings that were not steel-framed - reinforced concrete shelters of the

Haldane type were much safer. Mr. Button (Clerks of Works) asked for better protection for Rescue Service staff stationed at buildings leased from the metropolitan borough councils.

In urging the rejection of that part of Staff Side's recommendation on he post-1930 entrants' claim which opposed a resort to national arbitration, Miss Forstner (Public Assistance) initiated a debate which, still going strong when the closure had to be applied after two hours' hard discussion, was, on the whole, maintained at a high level of oratorical accomplishment. The formal character of the debate was changed during its course by the submission of an amendment to the Staff Side's recommendation in favour of an immediate reference of the claim to the Minister of Labour for consideration by the National Arbitration Tribunal. It was on this amendment that the vote was taken.

Those who urged and those who were opposed to the submission of the case to the National Arbitration Tribunal were agreed in their estimate of the tribunal as a body set up primarily to prevent strikes and resist wage claims. There the agreement between the two parties ended.

The arbitrationists were by no means convinced that a strong case, vigorously backed, would altogether fail and pointed out that even small concessions wrung from the tribunal which it would be impossible to secure in any other way until after the war would be well worth having. They did not, however, base their case for proceeding to arbitration solely on their estimate of the chances of obtaining a partial satisfaction of the post-1930 entrants' demands. Whatever the result, an appeal to the tribunal would show the Council that the Association was not prepared tamely to accept its dictates, was in fact ready for a fight. Failure to make a stand now would be to miss an opportunity of strengthening the position of the Association in the eyes of the Council on other issues; in addition it would tend to create disillusionment among the younger members of the staff, the lifeblood of the Association, many of whom were now on active service and looked to their colleagues to protect their interests while they were away. It was unlikely that the Council would in face of a resort to arbitration by the Association retaliate by destroying the Joint Committee machinery which the Council had itself found so useful, nor that there was any real danger of the Association's amenities at County Hall being withdrawn. But the arbitrationists felt that, even if the Council did adopt these drastic measures, the Association would emerge all the stronger for having taken a firm line. What was the use of keeping the Joint Committee machinery if it did not produce the goods? The Association's right, laid down in the Joint Committee's constitution, to veto proposals calculated to worsen staff conditions was not to be despised, but it could be nullified at any time if the Council chose to terminate the Joint Committee agreement. In short, though there were risks in proceeding to arbitration, they were risks that were well worth taking.

Those who opposed a resort to the tribunal stressed the extreme unlikelihood of obtaining even a small part of the post-1930 entrants' claim by this means and urged that it would, therefore, be against the post-1930 entrants' best interests for the Association to take a step which, they felt, might well seal the fate of the Post-1930 Report. It would be far better for the claim to wait over until the end of the war unprejudiced by an adverse arbitration decision. To put the report in cold storage was not to jeopardise it, but merely to preserve it until in the first flush of victory there was a reasonable chance of its recommendations being accepted. Apart altogether from this, we could not ignore the possible repercussions of defying the Council. The staff could not afford to lose the Joint Committee machinery which had achieved so much for them that could not have been achieved without it; the right to veto was a very valuable safeguard, the loss of which should not be lightheartedly risked. The Association had other tasks more important than the Post-1930 Report issue, which, after all, affected only a section of the membership. The Y.A.C.'s case was a good one (though it should be borne in mind that the Council had committed no breach of faith). It was vital that no decision should be arrived at which, while achieving nothing for the staff, might seriously weaken the Association and even lead to a split. Let us not risk any breach in the unity of the Association.

Among those who spoke in favour of arbitration were Mr. Fisher (Architect's), Mr. Judd (Public Assistance), Mr. Shove (Clerk's), Mr. C. G. Smith (Fire Brigade), Mr. Hughes (Chief Engineer's), Mr. Puddifoot (Public Assistance), Mr. Welsh (Public Health), Mr. Wright (Chief Engineer's), and Miss B. Turner (Public Assistance). Those voicing the views of those against arbitration included Mr. Leigh (Clerk's), Mr. Tilley (Architect's), Mr. Willmot (Education Officer's), and Mr. Michell (Comptroller's).

The debate concluded with a statement by the chairman of the Staff Side setting out the reasons which had actuated them in arriving at the decision to oppose arbitration. In criticising statements made in a letter sent by the Central Y.A.C. to members of the General Committee, he defended the attitude and action of the Staff Side in their negotiations with the Council. There had been a genuine desire on both sides of the Joint Committee for a reasonable wartime compromise, but both sides had realised the impossibility of achieving it. Mr. Nicholson went on to express his firm belief that the tribunal would concede not a jot or tittle of the claim. Manual workers might stand a chance of getting some small advance. Clerical workers, for example, the bank officers, had secured nothing.

It should be remembered that the main purpose of the tribunal was to prevent interruption of work through strikes and lock-outs. It was exceedingly doubtful whether the tribunal would consider this dispute as coming within its scope, but if it did the result would be that the report would be killed for all time. The Council would, he thought, welcome a reference of the claim to arbitration as a useful way of getting rid of an embarrassing nuisance. Mr. Nicholson added that he was himself very disappointed at the turn things had taken - one of the reasons he had accepted the leadership of the Staff Side was his desire to see the Post-1930 Report through. But for the war he was certain that the Council would have conceded a great deal of the claim. After the war we should achieve success. He was so convinced that to resort to arbitration would be harmful to the Association that he felt that if the committee decided in favour of it he would have no option but to give up the leadership.

Mr. Nicholson's speech made a considerable impression on the committee, and, although at one point the amendment had looked like being carried, the vote, which was then taken, resulted in a victory for the Staff Side by 52 votes to 29.

Thus ended one of the most important General Committee debates of recent years.

The rest of the proceedings were rushed through at breakneck speed (even the substantial balance shown in the accounts aroused no comment). The Executive Committee's resolution in favour of going forward for a further unspecified increase in remuneration for the staff to meet the higher cost of living drew, however, an amendment from Mr. Judd urging that a 20 per cent increase should be aimed at. A vigorous campaign could be developed much more easily around a definite figure than around a vague demand for an increase. This would not affect our unity of action with other black-coated workers.

Mr. Welsh agreed that Mr. Judd's point was valid but said that the civil service organisations had found it tactically better not to be too definite in their claims on this issue. The amendment was lost.

Mr. Judd also moved that regular meetings of the General Committee should again be resumed, to which Mr. Nicholson readily agreed, with a warning about the necessity of a good turn-out if they were to be worth while. If they are all as well attended as this one, we shall have reason to congratulate ourselves.

We tell the World . . . at Kingsway Hall.

(February 1947)

As Miss Patricia Knox said in opening the mass meeting on 6th January at the Kingsway Hall, 'The next time we must have the Albert Hall.'

In spite of the snow which fell all day, in spite of colds and the knowledge that the trains would be even more disorganised than ever, the staff rolled up in their hundreds.

They lined the back of the hall and the gallery, they packed the platform, they surged down the gangways. There were at least 2,500 inside when the doors were shut, and a crowd of about 500 collected outside to wait impatiently for John Vetch to come and speak there. Many others gave up and just went home.

It was a magnificent tribute to the interest of the staff and the solidarity of their support for their leaders in the wage claim as well as to the brilliant organising that made it all possible.

Throughout the progress of the claim, said Miss Knox, there had been the closest possible consultation between the leaders of the Association and the general membership; the meeting would give all sections of the staff the opportunity of accepting an active share of responsibility for the claim.

Mr. John Vetch then reviewed the history of the claim: there had been general dissatisfaction with rates of pay, and it was clear that the Council was thinking of revision. The Association began to prepare its claim in July, and when the Staff Side gave notice in October that they would shortly present a detailed claim they urged that the Joint Committee should, in the true spirit of Whitley-ism, examine the whole problem together and make recommendations. Instead, however, the Establishment Committee considered the matter separately without reference to the Association's case and put forward their own proposals for consolidation with minor increases.

The Association's claim was for better pay for all grades, particularly those in the lower ranges, and for better pay quickly. Higher rates were being paid elsewhere and the Council was having great difficulty in recruiting or retaining staff; the Association's plan would ensure the Council the staff it needed to translate its schemes, such as the County of London Plan, from paper to reality.

The Council's proposals, on the other hand, gave no adequate recognition of the cost-of-living increase, no immediate benefit for anyone, very little in April, and not much in the end. Its date of application was April, 1947, while the substantial increases of the higher grades dated from April and July last; it was even less favourable in the lower ranges than the existing pay, so that there would have to be supplementary allowances for existing staff; and it upset the pay relation between the 'third tier' officers and the principal assistants, which would have been preserved by the Association's plan.

The Official Side said that to quote rates of pay outside the service was inadmissible, and that any way the new entrants to banks receiving their greatly superior minimum rates compared not with the general clerical class, but with the first class (b). In that case, said Mr. Vetch, who does the routine work in the banks?

The Official Side also declared that it was improper to use the shortage of staff to get more pay for existing staff. But Mr. Vetch pointed out that the Official Side had never hesitated to rebut salary claims if it was able to recruit at the existing rates. And it had taken full advantage of the slump in the 1930's to recruit to the general grade (b) with its 90 shillings maximum. While a flow of staff between public authorities was good, at present it was a one-way flow, and some technical departments were becoming training grounds for government departments and other local authorities. The Council was well aware of the shortage, and the case could not be argued without quoting supporting evidence - that would be like going to a doctor who gets angry at the mention of the symptoms. Under-payment was the disease and shortage of staff the symptom.

As for the cost of the claim, while it would be considerable, it would not be insuperable. At the Council's estimate it might be a 3d. rate, but some authorities would have to increase the rates by far more to implement the National Charter. London ratepayers had had value for money from the staff, and he was sure that they would not begrudge the money for an efficient service.

The Official Side had declined to 'take seriously' a claim based on a formula for all staff, but said that, if the Staff Side would agree to their proposals, they would entertain separate claims grade by grade. If the Staff Side pressed the argument that staff shortage demonstrated that rates of pay were inadequate higher rates might be introduced for new entrants only; moreover, if the official proposals were unacceptable as they stood, the whole offer might be withdrawn.

'That could mean only one thing,' said Mr. Vetch, 'We were being asked to negotiate under a threat. That would be a negation of Whitleyism, and we will not respond to such threats.'

He thought, however, that the deadlock could be broken by starting from the relationship between the principal assistants and the third-tier and working downwards; and if, as the Council's press statement indicated, the Official Side were really willing to negotiate the Staff Side would be glad to resume discussions at the next meeting - freely and on equal terms. The Staff Side were confident of a really good case, and of having the whole staff behind them, and they looked to the meeting to confirm that confidence and to send an unmistakeable message to the Council.

The unanimous support of a special meeting of the L.C.C. Branch of N.A.L.G.O. was conveyed to the meeting by its secretary, Mr. J. B. McCann (Public Health). He went on to illustrate the irrelevancy of the official cost-of-living index, framed from information gathered in 1904. The items included were very restricted; and the heading 'miscellaneous,' which accounted for only 4 per cent of expenditure, covered many heavy items including household goods and fares, so that each increase in fares had little effect on the index figure. Similarly, the only means of lighting known to the framers of the index were candles and oil lamps; even if electricity charges were trebled there would be no increase in the index - provided that candles or paraffin oil cost no more! We were being mulcted all round: as taxpayers we subsidised the cost of food to stabilise a completely false index so that the staff's claim could be branded as outrageous. The L.C.C. Branch of N.A.L.G.O. were confident that unity of staff would be maintained as between grades as well as organisations, and he warned the meeting against any offer by the Council designed to divide the staff.

'An army of generals, however competent, will never win a war,' said Mr. Welsh (Public Health). 'Your generals must be supported by a united and enthusiastic body of soldiers conscious of the army's objectives and eager to share in their achievement. That is what we find to-day in this service, and for that reason we shall march to victory.'

Mr. Welsh reminded the meeting of the events of 1929 when the Council delayed twelve months before dealing with the Association's claim for a general review of salaries. There had not been wanting defeatists who would have accepted the Council's meagre counter-offer, but the strong pressure of the membership as a whole had made this impossible; the Association had stood out for better terms and had ultimately secured a favourable settlement. Co-operation between leaders and rank and file had brought this about, and would do so again to-day.

Rate for the Job

The claim had provided for new scales to apply to all members of the staff, irrespective of their date of entry or of their sex. The Official Side realised that the first part meant the abolition of dual scales, said Miss Betty Turner (Clerk's), but they astonished the Staff Side by asking whether the second really meant that they wanted equal pay! Miss Turner recalled the evidence given to the Royal Commission by Sir Eric Salmon that there was no justification for the differential rates in the Council's service on grounds of efficiency or quality of work or value to the employer, and she said that it was more than a matter of justice for the women concerned - it was one of hard cash. It was high time that the Council paid the rate for the job to whoever did the job in all grades, and made it a rate satisfactory for all members of the staff.

Mr. L. J. Macfarlane (Housing and Valuation), the chairman of the Central Youth Advisory Committee, then gave a vivid picture of the effect of the present wages for the younger members of the staff. The new entrant receiving 47s. a week gets 8s. 6d. less than if he had gone into a bank; at 21 he gets 90s., which is 10s. a week less than if he were a municipal roadsweeper or lavatory attendant; and at 25, when he might well be thinking of getting married, he is getting £1 a week less than his friend who failed to get through the general clerical class examination and went into one of the big banks. He quoted the budgets of several members of the staff, all regularly over-spending on essentials, eating into their gratuities and war savings. Many had spare-time employment and many were looking for other jobs. Several were going to become teachers, and found that they would get more even when training. 'The wonder is not that so many leave the service,' said Mr. Macfarlane, but that so many stay.' The Council could not run a first-class service on cut-price wages, and he was sure that the vigour of the staff and their campaign would win what was their right - a living wage.

Publicity Work

The last speaker from the platform was Mr. D. L. Blackhurst (Clerk's), the Association's publicity officer. He gave an account of the publicity which had been given in the press, and of the press notice issued by the Council which painted a completely incorrect picture of the Association's actions, and to which the Association had taken the strongest exception. He also spoke of the part played by the Executive's publicity section, and appealed for volunteers to assist in its work.

These speakers having dealt with the various aspects of the claim, it was thrown open to general discussion. Mr. W. A. Devereux (Education Officer's) moved a resolution, which was carried with acclamation, stating that the meeting considered that the Association's claim for a general increase in salaries and wages was just and reasonable; regarded the counter-proposals put forward by the Council as inadequate and unacceptable; and pledged whole-hearted support for any action which the Association might consider it desirable to take in order to achieve a satisfactory settlement.

He said that he would not have believed a couple of years ago that he would be better off now if he had stayed in the forces. When he started in the service his financial position was very precarious, but even now that he had reached the maximum of the scale he still found it impossible to make ends meet. London was well served by the Council's staff, and the Council would be doing great harm to the ratepayers if it endangered that service.

The resolution was seconded by Miss R. Bush (Typewriting Service) who emphasised the need for additional staff and the difficulty of recruiting at the present rates of pay and prospects. Mr. S. H. Hassell (Housing and Valuation), speaking as a member of a local authority where he was on the other side of the fence, said that he was convinced that the claim was a good one. He pointed out that the Association would be able to go to arbitration. Mr. T. C. Braybrook (estate superintendent), a member of the Staff Side, read an extract from the County of London Plan, in which the Leader of the Council called for cordial co-operation from everyone to implement the plan. The answer was that the Council should not risk disaffection among the staff by its attitude to their just claim.

A vote of thanks was given to Mr. F. Church (Social Welfare) who played the organ before and after the meeting. The meeting then wound up, after Mr.

233

R. W. Clarke (Social Welfare), the chairman of the Executive Committee and of the campaign section, had congratulated the staff on their grand attendance, and had moved a vote of thanks to the president, which was carried with loud applause. Thus ended what will undoubtedly be a historic meeting of the Council's staff.

Note: Following the meeting described in this report the Staff Association made a very favourable settlement with the Council, establishing those "1947 standards" of pay which became something of a benchmark throughout the 1950s. They were, in fact, never to be regained until, in the period 1958-61, the Council revolutionised the whole pay and grading structure of the service.

Anti-Semitism Condemned.

C. D. Andrews
(November 1947)

The Committee re-assembled on 25th September with a formidable agenda before it. Much of it, however, was accepted without discussion. The effort to break the deadlock in the equal pay controversy, by asking the Council to declare its acceptance of the principle, and proposing that women should at least receive the men's rate of increment and proceed to the men's maximum; the request for a further allocation of fifty positions in the major establishment for competition under the reconstruction scheme; the move to aid pensioners; the recommendations on public relations; the comprehensive proposals concerning the recruitment, grading, and salaries of professional and technical staff; all these the Committee agreed in silence. It interfered with the Executive's recommendation on Saturday morning leave by carrying Mr. Berstock's amendment which, in effect, welcomed the attempt to include temporary clerical assistants in the existing arrangements, but insisted that if they were to be included then so should Supplies Department warehouse supervisory staff and analogous grades. It prodded the platform on the subject of joint efficiency committees. It grumbled about the increased rail fares, but was told firmly by Mr. Karslake that no more letters would be sent to the Minister of Transport. It rose to thank the Staff Side and Joint Committee for several of the agreements reported on. And then, having completed its consideration of these internal matters which are its avowed business and interest, the Committee enlarged its gaze to include the streets and homes of London, and debated for an hour or more, in sorrow and in anger, the renascent cancer of anti-Semitism.

The debate was of a very high standard, and would have been interesting even if one were solely concerned in studying how and how not to steer a controversial motion through a suspicious assembly. The controversy and the suspicions arose, of course, not from any doubts as the the the filthiness of incitement to race hatred, but from an unwillingness to handle a subject with party-political implications. That the Committee did finally handle it, embrace it even, without cavil or misgiving, was very little due, in the event, to the chief supporters of the motion.

Mr. Fulcher (Housing and Valuation) moved the resolution, which set out to draw the Home Secretary's attention to the increasing efforts by Fascist movements to stir up anti-Semitism and civil strife in London, claimed that the existing law was not used against those responsible as it could be, and pressed for stronger action and further legislation. Mr. Fulcher was, as it appeared from a subsequent speech, acutely aware of the General Committee's allergy to topics which could excite party-political controversy, and, perhaps for this reason, he took the debatable course here of speaking as though there were no political implications at all. He presented a case for treating the provocation of race hatred as a crime, in a speech that for all its humanity and its characteristically diffident rhetoric was, at least to this correspondent, commonplace, and well below his usual rousing standard. Mr. Gough (Supplies) seconding, argued that the tolerance of this propaganda was a menace to the Jewish people, to all trade unionists, and to progressive people everywhere, but he again rarely rose above the academic level.

Mr. Hine (Supplies) was the first to bring home to the meeting the realities of anti-Semitism. Having declared that it was necessary to address this resolution to the Home Secretary because these insulting speeches were made under the full protection of the police, he cited his experience as an instructor in evening classes and said he was appalled by the anti-Semitism expressed by adolescents who must have been far too young to have been influenced by Fascist propaganda before the war. He knew of two case of Jewish women who had become mentally deranged by threats of persecution. One was the wife of a Gentile member of the Council's staff.

Here Mr. Paveley (Legal) rose to express the misgivings which were to be expected. All decent men would agree with the resolution, but was it wise for the Association to endorse it, and enter into political controversy, without at the same time protesting against such things as the murder in Palestine of innocent British victims of Semitism?

Mr. Bagwell (Supplies) dismissed this as a red herring, and went on to argue just why the resolution concerned the Staff Association. His speech, which combined close reasoning with shrewd appeals to humanitarianism and self-interest alike, could only have been improved by being delivered in a less halting and tentative manner. The Association was a protective organisation, he said, and had to preserve the rights and liberties of its members, Jews included. A Jewish member of the General Committee was among those who had received vile threatening letters. Moreover, Fascism only started with the persecution of Jews; it worked on to Freemasons, trade unionists, and Communists. Any Freemasons present could begin to feel uneasy. The Association was further concerned to defend trade unionism, and no less to preserve an honest and justly administered public service, which Fascism would destroy.

Mr. Michell (Comptroller's) was the first to protest openly about the party attachments that might be read into the motion, but he was too late, for the speeches of Messrs. Hine and Bagwell had done much to persuade the Commit-tee that this issue was irrelevant. Mr. Michell proposed to amend the resolution by omitting the reference to Fascists ('because not all anti-Semites are Fascists,' and because Fascists should not be given advertisement), by omitting the request for stronger action and further legislation, and by omitting to communicate the resolution to the Council and the Press. Now that politics was raised, Mr. Fulcher talked back in politics, passionately and not very coherently. Mr. Macfarlane (Housing and Valuation) quoted some details of the anti-Semitic ritual, and asked what were these thugs if they were not Fascist.

Mr. Tilley (Architect's) now rose to crystallize the sentiment of the body of the meeting. With dignity and eloquence he described how his initial disquiet at the introduction of politics into the Committee by such a resolution had been overcome by the facts and arguments he had heard. 'Fascism is outside politics,' he declared. Anti-Semitism was always stirred up by people with axes to grind, and instances of Jewish conduct or of terrorist activities in Palestine were irrelevant to the issue. He abhorred gangsterism, whether it was in Britain, America, or Palestine. If Fascism were crushed, anti-Semitism would die, for it was a plant engendered in the swamp of the minds of the gentry of Ridley Road.

This powerful speech ensure that Mr. Michell's amendment was lost by a large majority. In subsequent discussion, Mr. Fulcher made an unworthy attempt to smear as pro-Fascist those who had been concerned at the prospect of handling a motion with political implications, and brought Mr. Paveley to his feet to make an indignant disclaimer, but in spite of this episode the Committee carried the motion without opposition.

It was now the turn of Mr. Macfarlane, who moved a resolution condemning proposals to solve the economic crisis by cutting the social services, and calling on the Government to introduce an overall economic plan in the devising of which workers and management should participate fully. An attempt should be made to get joint action among public employees to implement this policy. In two able speeches Mr. Macfarlane and Mr. Say (Public Health) gave the Government a compact, cogent, and confident lecture on how to solve the crisis, like young angels storming the Crippsian heaven. The Committee heard them in silence, and, apart from a plea by Mr. Moverley (Architect's) for more emphasis on the positive planning side, carried the resolution without discussion.

Note: There had been an outbreak of (mainly) working-class anti-semitism in East London and in Liverpool in the autumn of 1947, provoked by the campaign of terrorism conducted in Palestine (then administered by Britain) by such Zionist activist groups as Irgun and the Stern Gang. The state of Israel was not established until the spring of the following year, following British withdrawal from Palestine, and all through 1947 Jewish anger and frustration at what they perceived to be Britain's pro-Arab policy was mounting rapidly. The murder of four British soldiers in August 1947 was the occasion for those anti-Jewish outbreaks in Britain which quite rightly alarmed and disgusted responsible opinion in this country.

The Thirty Minutes' War.

C. D. Andrews
(June 1948)

(Our correspondent, who has been reproached for his five-line dismissal, in our last number, of the proceedings of the General Committee of 22nd April, here makes full amends, with acknowledgments to Alexander Pope.)

I chronicle Committee bickerings,
The contests dire that rise from trivial things.
This verse, O Muse, to ROBERT CLARKE is due;
This ev'n BETTINA may vouchsafe to view:
Slight is the subject, but not scant the praise,
If she inspire, and he approve my lays.

On Lambeth's shores, where bombed ST. THOMAS cowers,
And Thames reflects the Parliament'ry towers,
There stands a structure of majestic frame
Which from th' encircling County takes its name.
Here London's statesmen, after long debates,
Decree the rise of houses and the rates;
Here the great HERBERT, whom four realms obey,
Did sometime counsel give - and Council sway;
Here my Lord LATHAM ruled, until the Board
Of Transport claimed him, and gave us HAYWARD.
Here, too, the Staff, their int'rests to protect,
Their departmental delegates elect,
Who monthly in Committee represent
The workings of a model Parliament.

And now, declining from the noon of day,
The sun obliquely shoots his burning ray;
The hungry principals append initials
To scripts that will be signed by high officials;
The harassed seniors push away their files;
The juniors take their towels and walk for miles;
The clerks their writing-engines lock away,
Heeding no more 'IN,' 'OUT,' or 'PENDING' tray;
And delegates of every rank are seen
Jostling for kippers in the staff canteen,
Scanning agendas as they gulp their tea,
And scampering to room one-forty-three.

Herein the heroes and the nymphs await
With various talk of the entry of the great;
One speaks the glory of the Central Yac,
And one describes a well-phrased reference back;

A third interprets motions, noes and ayes -
At every word a reputation dies.

Now portly WILLMOTT pushes to his seat,
Precursor of the office-crowned élite;
Executive JOYCE EATHERLEY appears;
Th' egregious BAGWELL enters with his peers.
And lo, with modest pomp, the Platform comes -
Treasurer MICHELL, still pond'ring weighty sums,
SAY, who must publicize what others say,
And next the President, nor grave nor gay,
Frigidly genial, to Prudence wed -
Though PUDDIFOOOT he is no Puddinghead;
The fair nymph CORBETT, and BETTINA TURNER,
Who ably champions wage and salary earner;
The Secretariat, BACON, AUSTIN, BALL,
Th' industrious clerks of clerks of County Hall;
KARSLAKE, impressive 'neath his rims of horn;
And last, with hollow eyes and features worn,
Th' Assembly's Chairman, who must regulate
The furies of the yet unleash'd debate;
See how the selfless years have graved their mark -
Aloof, alert, care-full, cadav'rous CLARKE!

The gavel knocks, an instant hush descends
On smiling foemen and back-biting friends;
The tourney opens, and the troops prepare
Triphibious war (but mostly in the air).
To agendas now all bend the agile mind;
The previous minutes are approved and signed;
Questions are called and out steps hardy FRY,
With dex'trous sword BETTINA'S guard to try:
'To ask the Chairman of Staff Side,' he pries,
'How many projects seeking salary rise
'Th' Official Side have spurned?' BETTINA parries
With a cool 'Five.' The sanguine FRY then carries
His onslaught: 'In how many of those five
'Were answers giv'n where you could not contrive
'Rebuttal?' The nymph whirls her blade on high:
'Naturally, none,' she says, and shatters Fry.
Straight in the lists the warlike HUTCHINGS leaps,
Mustachios agog, and swiftly steeps
A dart in venom, and, with aspect fierce,
Subsistence mysteries would pierce.
The nymph, unruffled, stays the fearful blow,
Catches the dart, and with unerring throw
Returns it: 'None should know as well as he
'The matter is referred to the G.P.'

238

Thus far the battle, and a brief respite
While the new members' names are called. (They might
Have been received with more than aquiescence
If they had graced the meeting with their presence).

The truce expires, the ranks re-form to thwart
Th' Executive Committee's first report,
And the first victim of their deadly wit is
The constitution of the sub-committees.
HUTCHINGS, still smarting from BETTINA'S quip,
Each hair erect on his proud quivering lip,
Enjoins his comrades they should not adopt
Committees which have powers to co-opt.
'Look in your Constitution,' he declaims,
'Does it permit them to include the names
'Of *personæ non gratæ* to our Club,
'*Non* elected, ev'n *non paid* their sub?'
He speaks, and KARSLAKE at his lightning quails,
And, as the broad oak bends before the gale,
So KARSLAKE bends, and pliantly withdraws
Sub-section (a) of the offending clause.

Exultant now, the regiments advance
To Number Two Report, and break a lance
Upon the measures it suggests be taken
To bring a little fat to comrade BACON.
Not that the troops the principle deplore:
Contrariwise - the rasher should be more!
Discretion, here be thou my guardian sprite;
How can I name the foremost in the fight,
Or pen th' encomiums which all resound,
While BACON sits outside the battleground?
Enough that KARSLAKE (now almost a stammerer)
Agrees to reconsider it in camera.

So sways the battle, and th' opposing shock
Of Platform *versus* Floor beguiles the clock,
For when a truce is called to politics
The dial shows a quarter after six.
One brief half-hour sufficed for the furor:
In truth 'twas but a Thirty Minutes' War!
The gavel raps, in lieu of Cease Fire horn,
The mountains travailed, and a mouse is born!

Note: This parody is, of course, on Pope's *Rape of the Lock*. All the characters featured in it would have been very familiar to readers of *London Town* at the time, but although readers of this volume may have little or no knowledge of them this should not detract from enjoyment of this piece. Just one note of explanation - "glories of the Central YAC" refers to that Youth Action Committee of the Staff Association which was still functioning and still considered to be a hotbed of militancy.

Cry 'Havoc' and let slip the dogs!

C. D. Andrews
(October/November 1950)

By a strange irony, the news that the Council's staff were to discuss the Council's proposed security measures against them was conveyed to the national Press by an unauthorised, unknown, but efficient informant. The result was banner headlines in the newspapers, a good deal of reasonably accurate copy and reasonably fair comment, and a clutch of reporters pacing up and down outside the guarded doors of the first-floor room where the crowded General Committee decided on its attitude.

The reporters had to wait three hours for their Press statement. This meeting of 12th October would in any case have been of the utmost importance, for the Executive Committee were presenting their recommendations on the form in which the claim for a cost-of-living bonus was to be presented to the Council. One conjectures, however, that even the manner in which they were to attempt to defend their crumbling standard of life was of less moment to the members thatn the manner in which they were to attempt to defend their crumbling civil rights. The debate on the claim was disposed of quickly, while the main security debate went on unflaggingly, without the usual seepage of home-seeking hearts, so that many were still trying to catch the Chairman's eye when it was finally resolved that the question should be put.

Cost of Living Claim
The Executive presented a sober and reasoned report explaining why they recommended a cost-of-living bonus claim of 15 per cent on the first £400 a year, and 10 per cent on any remainder. They recognised the anxiety of senior officers to preserve adequate recognition for their responsibilities, but could not undertake to press for full compensation for them. The 15 per cent on the basic £400 was consonant with the rise in the interim price index since 1947, however unsatisfactory that index might be. Meanwhile, incomes from profits and interest had increased, and the general index of rates of wages had also increased. The Council's staff, the Executive contended, could not be expected, indeed could not afford, to make disporportionate sacrifices.

Mr. Tofts (Clerk's) moved as an amendment that there should be a bonus of 15 per cent on all salaries, in order that the differentials of senior positions should not be further eroded. He pointed out that the 1947 settlement had seriously reduced these differentials; it was probably in keeping with the time then, but the process had gone far enough, and threatened to undermine incentives to promotion and to ignore the responsibilities of higher posts. The principal grades, whose 1946 settlement was based on civil service rates, could now hope for increases in line with the Chorley Report. The £400-a-year men

240

would, if the proposals were accepted, be receiving adequate compensation for the higher cost of living. Without a uniform percentage bonus it was the middle grades who would again be the depressed class. The amendment was seconded by Mr. Oates (Clerk's).

Miss Turner said that the Executive appreciated that a strong case could be made on the grounds of the rising costs for Association members of all incomes. However it was the Association's policy to present claims which were not only completely justified but which also would be backed to the hilt by the whole of the staff. Many different opinions had been expressed on the form that a bonus claim should take, but in order to obtain maximum support the Executive had formulated a claim based on the increase in the cost of the more essential items of living. Mr. Moverley (Architect's) also emphasised the need for unanimous support behind whatever claim was to be put forward.

Mr. Cameron (Public Control) and Mr. Gregory (Welfare) said that similar doubts as to the adequacy of the proposed claim had been expressed in their departments, but the committees had decided to support this minimum request in order not to split the ranks.

Mr. Tofts' amendment for a uniform percentage was lost by 16 to 83, and after thanks had been expressed to those who had put in so much work in preparing the claim the Executive's recommendation was agreed without a dissentient.

Proposed Security Investigations

Miss Turner now rose to introduce the Executive's report on the Council's proposed security investigations, which she said was one of the most important questions the Association had ever had to consider. She stated at the outset that the release of the Association's committee agenda papers to the Press had not been authorised or inspired by the Association or its officers. It was only by great good fortune that the information had not been seriously distorted - a thing which might have brought incalculable harm to the staff.

The Executive had been informed that, in order to prevent the leakage of highly secret information which would be of use to an enemy, the Council proposed to draw up a list of staff whose work required them to handle such information, and to have the police enquire into the reliability of these individuals. If the police reported unfavourably, a small sub-committee of the General Purposes Committee would decide whether to transfer the officer or to preclude him from dealing with confidential documents. An officer so affected might appear before the sub-committee and call witnesses to testify as to his character, but, contrary to the normal staff disciplinary procedure, he would not be represented by an advocate, or be told the source of the information against him, or have the right of appeal to a committee which had not already decided his guilt.

The Executive Attitude

Pending discussion in the General Committee, the Executive, said Miss Turner, had not expressed any opinion on whether the Council ought to take these steps, but it was very strongly of the opinion that, if they were taken, proper safeguards should be instituted. To prevent individual persecution, a list of jobs, not staff, should be drawn up; only persons holding the named posts should have their private lives enquired into, and if they objected on principle they should be given the chance of transferring. An accused person should be given the fullest possible opportuity to rebut the charges made, and if the source of the information were not divulged no-one would know whether it was based on malicious gossip or genuine mistakes, both of which had been acted on in the 1940 enquiries. An accused person should have the right of appeal to an independent tribunal where he could be defended by an advocate. An officer's security record should not be brought into account when he was being considered for promotion.

Miss Turner referred to the common opinion that since communists, at least in other countries, cared little for civil liberty, it was not important whether they got it here. That attitude was not good enough, she said. If the procedure were operated without safeguards it could bring grave injustices. There were frightening possibilities if it should get out of hand, like the American witch-hunt, which, having chased the communists, now chased liberals who expressed opinions distasteful to the organisers. She concluded that there was the gravest responsibility on all concerned to keep their heads and not allow a witch-hunt.

Mr. Bacon's Amendment

The Executive had been scrupulous to give no opinion on the principles behind the proposals, but this did not prevent individual members from giving theirs. Mr. Bacon (Education) therefore moved, with his usual cool eloquence, that the General Committee were opposed in principle to the Council's proposal to initiate investigations into the private affairs and political beliefs of members of its staff; they considered that the relations between the staff and the Council should be conducted solely on the basis of ability and character, and that the introduction of political tests constituted an unwarranted interference with the rights of the staff as citizens.

Mr. Bacon said no-one would deny the right of any state to take measures which it deemed necessary for its security. In Britain the Official Secrets Act was designed to prevent breaches of security and to punish those who breached it. He read a list of offences under this Act, which he said could apply to the Council as well as the State service, and claimed that there was ample provision against would-be traitors. In addition the Council could take ordinary disciplinary action for negligence or dereliction of duty, and could prosecute for breach of contract.

Dangerous Thoughts

Now, however, said Mr. Bacon, the Council proposed to step outside these legal provisions, and, obeying none of the rules of evidence, defence or judgment, arraign an officer not for what he had done but for holding unpopular political beliefs. For the first time since Catholic Emancipation it was a crime to think dangerous thoughts. It had been stated that only 60 to 70 posts would be affected, but the speaker could place little assurance in that. The Prime Minister had stated that the civil service purge would apply only to those engaged on secret work, but it had been extended to charwomen, messengers and typists, while over the river the neighbouring local authority threatened to debar from promotion teachers associated with the Communist Party. Moreover what prospects within the service remained for an officer who could not be transferred to another job - or indeed for one who could?

Mr. Bacon concluded that the Council must take full responsibility for instituting procedure contrary to the traditions of British law and freedom. It was equally the responsibility of the staff to oppose it, and his motion gave expression to an extreme distaste for what the Council proposed.

Mr. Miller (Valuer's), seconding, asked whether anybody believed that discrimination would stop where it was said that it was intended to stop. The action proposed led down a slippery slope to the point where discrimination was exercised against any person holding any ideas offensive to authority. He cited famous American scientists and humanitarians who had been accused on the flimsiest evidence of disloyalty to the State. Mr. Miller also asked whether it was a coincidence that just as the cost-of-living claim was being presented, and the importance of a united staff was paramount, a measure had been introduced which could be calculated to divide the membership of the Association.

An Opposing View

Mr. W. O. Jones (Architect's) reported that his departmental committee had resolved to accept the Council's proposals as a regrettable necessity, subject to necessary safeguards for the staff. He thought that this was an emergency measure in a time of crisis, and was as distasteful to the Council as to the Association. Communists and fascists were prepared to fight on the side of an invader and take their orders from abroad, and under the protection of civil freedom could work against the security of the State. The government and local authorities were responsible to the public that defence plans should not go abroad. No-one, said Mr. Jones. would keep a maid if it was known that she intended at midnight to open the door to her burglar-sweetheart.

Mr. Yeldham (Public Control) thought that the proposed measures would be useless. He said that the notorious breach of security at Harwell had been effected by a man who had passed safely through the most rigorous screening. The known communists would be eliminated, but those unknown could remain. Mr. Zacks (Valuer's) said that the proposed procedure was a gross violation of the liberty of the subject hitherto known only in countries living under a dictatorship. It took England back to the Star Chamber. The Association should demand a definition of disloyalty in order to know on what grounds an officer was brought before his accusers and judges. Mr. Oates (Clerk's), on the other hand, supported the Council's proposal. He said that religious and political tests had no place in the local government service because hitherto people were not obliged by their beliefs to act treasonably if so ordered. The trouble lay at the door of the Communist Party and their fifth-column activities in various countries. He pointed out that the Official Secrets Act applied to punish offenders but not to prevent sabotage. It was now a choice between communist dictatorship and protective measures such as this.

An Evil-looking Wedge

Mr. Welsh (Public Health) referred ironically to the outspoken views of those who had maintained in many previous meetings that politics ought not to be debated within the General Committee. He observed that no precise punishment was defined for those who held opinions distasteful to the secret police and to a sub-committee of the General Purposes Committee. The measures might have been pressed on Council members by other persons less concerned with the democratic decencies. It was the thin end of a very evil-looking wedge.

Mr. Welsh described the contention that no restriction was implied on freedom of thought as 'a skilful piece of hypocrisy'. The law was already strong enough to deal with wrongdoers, but now you could be arraigned because you looked as though you were the kind of person who might do wrong. There was a powerful parallel with the Inquisition in Spain, which acted on the belief that it was better that a hundred innocent should suffer that one guilty person should escape.

Mr. Welsh asked whether the cardinal democratic virtue of tolerance was to be discarded now, on the unchallengeable evidence of spies and sneaks. This measure was dictated by fear - the fear of people who could not maintain themselves in power by justice and decency and so relied on persecution. He urged that justice and decency should be given one more chance, and appealed to the Council, in the words of Cromwell: 'I beseech you, in the bowels of Christ, think it possible you may be mistaken.'

'Do as you would be done by'

Mr. Craig (Architect's) presented the dilemma of the ordinary decent non-political man who was beset by uncertainties. Was the witch-hunt worse in America than in Czechoslovakia? On the other hand, was the cure worse than the disease? 'The communists wouldn't treat you decently,' he was told, but should not one do as one would be done by? He sought additional safeguards based on the principles of British justice, unless a free fields was to be given to intolerance wearing a mask of kindly intention.

Mr. Murphy (Education) had fewer doubts. Mr. Bacon had suggested that the prospects of an accused officer, transferred or not transferred, would be poor. Mr. Murphy thought that the prospects of a politically unreliable officer ought to be poor. It seemed logical to him to suppress dangerous thoughts, because thoughts and ideas preceded action. Nor could he see anything repugnant in apprehending someone because he might do wrong. A policeman did as much when he arrested for loitering with intent. The justification for these repressive measures was that they were intended to make sure that our own side won, said Mr. Murphy, and surely we didn't want to lose.

Mr. Henry (Education) said that the proposals penalized the moral integrity of certain individuals. Those who had openly declared their association with unpopular organizations would be the ones to suffer. How could an enquiry into one's past connections be a guide to one's present beliefs, and a prophecy of one's future actions? He could see that when the witch-hunt developed, the witches would be on the other side - interpreting the shady omens presented by the police. As for punishment, nothing more than transfer would be necessary. The jungle telegraph would operate, and the officer affected - once smirched by the crystal-gazing of gossip-ridden witchdoctors - would have his career left in the hands of vicious people with long memories.

Subject to Safeguards

Mr. Barford (Architect's) thought that the security proposals were not unreasonable. Countries on the Continent had fallen because communists had secured key positions and, at a word from the Kremlin, had struck. Given adequate safeguards, these investigations were part of the eternal vigilance which was the price of our own freedom.

Mr. Braybrook (Valuer's), in a speech which drew more applause than most, commented wryly that the most liberal views were frequently expressed with the least eloquence. He thought Mr. Welsh's eloquence had had its hysterical side, and had been used to make our flesh creep. The Pharisees thanked God that they were not as other men, but in the General Committee to-night they had come dangerously near thanking God that they were not Pharisees, and were almost ready, in the name of freedom, to tear down democracy. He thought the Executive had taken a level-headed and reasonable view of a difficult matter, and expressed his confidence in their ability to see that the purge did not get out of hand.

Mr. Gregory (Welfare) cited cased of mistaken identity and worse in the notorious enquiries of 1940.

Miss Knox (Education) shared Mr, Craig's unhappiness and doubts. She agreed with most of what had been said by the supporters of the motion, and disliked most of what had been said by the opponents, but nevertheless she opposed it. She based her decision on tactical grounds. The Council would not admit that the staff had any right to oppose the principle of their measures, and would be antagonised when the staff came to discuss the application of the measures. Furthermore, staff unity was vital at this time. There was not unity on this subject, and, if the motion in opposition was carried, many members might misinterpret the motives of the General Committee. She urged that the Council should be left with full responsibility for their action, the motion should be rejected, and the Association should go all out for the necessary modification in procedure. Mrs. Eatherley (Education) thought however that the passing of the motion could have no harmful effect on subsequent negotiations. She pointed out that London was the first local authority to consider political tests, and urged the staff not to acquiesce and queer the pitch for their colleagues in other cities.

There was still plenty of life in the debate, but it was agreed by a small majority that the question should now be put. Mr. Bacon's motion (which was technically an amendment) was thereupon carried by 62 votes to 41. A further half-hour's debate was given to the substantive motion chiefly on the question of the safeguards proposed. It was generally agreed that they were all well-intentioned, but there was no great confidence that they would be very effective. Nevertheless it was imperative that the Council should be made aware of the Association's grave fears. The motion was carried.

A Good Debate

The General Committee had previously shown that it is at its best when discussing politics. In this memorable debate, where morals and politics were inextricably fused, the Committee maintained an admirable tone. Despite deep cleavages outspokenly expressed, the assembly showed itself remarkably free from rancour. Eloquence there was in plenty, but little of it seemed studied, and less still insincere. Many of the most telling phrases self-generated from the clash of the debate itself. In general the Committee seemed moved by a profound disquiet, the majority at the thought of what the Council intended to do, and almost all at the thought of the manner in which, as the Executive were informed, the Council intended to do it. The Council's proposals, however, are still under confidential consideration, and their final form has not, at the time of this report, been decided.

Note: The Council's proposal to use a political vetting system for staff whose duties were deemed to be sensitive has to be seen against the international situation at that time, when the cold war seemed likely to degenerate into a Third World War: the Berlin blockade of 1948-49 had been followed by the Communist take-over of China (1949) and then (1950) the outbreak of the Korean War. In the USA, where the influence of Senator Joseph McCarthy was now considerable, a "purge" really was going on; but in Britain opinion was a good deal calmer. By late 1951, although the international situation was still very threatening, the Council quietly abandoned its vetting scheme.

Annual General Meeting – discussion on LCC abolition.

(June 1962)

The report of the General Committee on its work in the past year was received without much ado at the Annual General Meeting of the Staff Association on 14 March. The occasion was not, however, a simple or altogether conventional one. On the agenda appeared a notice of motion on the subject of London government, concisely phrased to outline the Association's anxieties and set out its policy.

Mr Moverley (President of the Association), who moved, announced that the motion had the full backing of the Association's officers and committees and he expected it to be carried 'with acclamation'. As responsible public servants with a proper sense of public service, he said, we could speak with experience on whether the Government's proposals were good or bad. Using examples such as the housing, welfare and children's services, he maintained that the price to be paid for making local government more local was gigantic: chaos would ensue and public services be seriously impaired. By saying this we were not making incursions into the political arena, and if asked to declare our interest in the matter we could directly and honestly answer 'Our interest is public interest'. Seconding the motion, Mr Gregory (Chairman of the Executive) detailed some of the practical aspects of the charges facing the staff. We favoured the larger authority on the grounds that services would deteriorate if handed over. The interests of the staff would also suffer. We did not want to see 'a mad scramble for jobs' and urged the Government to set up a statutory commission for staff transfers. Already, he pointed out, two metropolitan boroughs had advertised positions as if the new structure was already in being. And the draft regulations on compensation were far from satisfactory.

The contributions from the floor were few but valuable. Some speakers helped to strengthen the wording of the motion; others added weight to what had already been said. Mr Timson (Education) deplored certain borough councils 'jumping the gun' regarding staff appointments; if uncontrolled it could lead to a breakdown in the public service. Mrs Ansell (Education) criticized the fragmentation of services which had been efficiently administered for a long time, and Mrs Austin (Public Control) felt that to achieve public sympathy we should have to make nuisances of ourselves in our own districts. When, finally, the motion was put to the meeting it was, as the President had hoped, carrried unanimously and with acclamation. The meeting had expressed its belief that the Government's proposals would lower the quality of the public service and injure the interests of L.C.C. staff; and it urged the Government to provide a statutory body to superintend the transfer of staff in local government in the Greater London area; to fully compensate those who could not be offered employment on terms as favourable as they enjoyed at present, and to permit staff participation in the formulation and operation of the necessary administrative machinery in these matters.

Note: Staff anxieties about the abolition of the LCC are also reflected in the Editorial on pages 109-110.

T.U.C., 1965.

C. S. Corcoran
(November 1965)

In recent years the national press has become increasingly interested in proceedings at the annual meeting of the Trades Union Congress, and this year there was a concentration of publicity media at Brighton, equalling, if not surpassing, the total for any previous occasion on which the T.U.C. had met. From the beginning one issue dominated all others - that of prices and incomes policy - for George Brown, Minister for Economic Affairs, had discussed the Government's intentions with the General Council the previous week, and a statement had been issued on 2 September indicating the Government's plan to introduce legislation in the next session of Parliament.

On Saturday morning, 4 September, I found myself at a grouping committee in the conference room of Brighton Pavilion called between representatives of a dozen unions which had submitted motions about prices, incomes and productivity; it was presided over by Sir Harry Douglas from the General Council. The aim of a grouping committee is to condense several motions into one or more 'composites' with the intention of expediting debate during Congress week: a union representative attends such a pre-meeting determined to ensure that the particular aspect of the subject with which his organization is concerned should not be submerged by the compromise needed to compress many separate drafts into one or two comprehensive ones.

How to proceed
This was certainly the case with prices and incomes. In addition to the Staff Association, woodworkers, constructional engineers, boilermakers, draughtsmen, chemical workers, technical civil servants, firemen, tugmen and bargemen, those in the health service, and others in the civil service and the private sector had tabled motions or amendments. The Civil Service Union was concerned about those on lower incomes and sought adjustments in rates and taxes; the firemen drew attention to the relevance of wage earnings in contrast to wage rates; boilermakers wanted the economy to be based on a greater degree of public ownership and D.A.T.A. declared that a 'norm' of not more than $3^{1}/_{2}$ per cent annual increase for wages and salaries was unacceptable. Another problem also faced this meeting - how to proceed in the absence of a report from the General Council on the outcome of the latest discussions with George Brown. The grouping committee started at 10.30 a.m.; at mid-day we decided to defer further discussion until the following Monday afternoon, during Congress time, by which time it was expected that union delegations would have received the expected supplementary report from the General Council and be able to instruct those attending the resumed grouping committee meeting on the attitude to take in the new situation.

In the event I was called to the Congress rostrum on the Monday afternoon to speak to our other motion - about trade union structure. The main emphasis of my speech was that structural reforms could not be based on the assumption that small, local or specialized unions were either inefficient or outdated. It was not a simple question of large-scale efficiency versus small-scale democracy, for while many large unions were models or democratic procedure they had their problems in communication and satisfactory representation at local level: Ford's works at Dagenham was an example where several unions, many of them large, were failing to meet particular circumstances. My remarks then turned to comments in the General Council report dealing with unnecessary competition between unions as one reason for a widespread reluctance to join trade unions, and Congress was told that in recent months a big national organization had been trying to encroach on the Staff Association's traditional field and had even launched a costly new publication in pursuance of that policy. For unions to promote organizational rivalries of this sort was surely to put a premium on non-membership. I concluded with a warning that undue centralization or control, whether by Government or T.U.C., is as undesirable in this sphere as it is in any other. The motion was formally seconded and was carried without difficulty.

Meanwhile, Mr Hollocks (the Association's Secretary) was engaged in discussion at the resumed grouping committee meeting, where, after over an hour's argument, the bulk of the motions involved had been composited into two distinct formulations. He was faced with the prospect of either allowing the Association's motion to be absorbed into one of these or seeing it passed over in the big pay debate on the Wednesday and deferred to Friday morning (which would effectively consign it to oblivion).

'Increased rewards . . . '
The Association's delegation, comprising Mrs Austin (Vice-Chairman,

General Committee), the Secretary and myself, had already discussed the basic lines to be followed if these circumstances should arise and, after reporting the position, Mr Hollocks agreed to the Association's name being added to those supporting that 'composite motion' which he deemed most suitable as a vehicle for our particular interest. It contained the following sentiments: 'Congress believes that continued improvements in earnings and conditions are a necessary feature of such (a planned) economy, and that collective bargaining backed by trade union organization is the most effective way to secure these improvements... Congress accordingly rejects the Government's present productivity, prices and incomes policy and supports the efforts of affiliated unions to improve the living standards of their members and to ensure increased rewards for skill, experience and technical expertise.' The other 'composite', while expressing concern for particular groups and seeking amelioration of conditions for some sections of the community, accepted the principles of the proposed governmental policy.

In the meantime, on Tuesday, during the debate on equal pay, Mrs Austin reminded the conference that that matter had been under consideration for over 100 years and, in recording the lead given by the L.C.C. and other sections of the public service, appealed for support from all trade unionists to obtain universal acceptance of the principle. She observed that the Government's pay plans would quickly founder if working women ever withdrew their labour. Also on Tuesday a motion seeking more financial support for the National Health Service was amplified by a successful Association amendment to the effect that suggestions of a charge being imposed on patients for consultation or treatment should be resisted. The amended motion was then formally carried.

On Wednesday the big debate developed thus: the General Secretary (George Woodcock) began by moving the relevant General Council report paragraphs and a supplementary report. He spoke for nearly an hour and the burden of his speech could be resolved into a plea that affiliates should allow the General Council to try to operate an 'early warning system' on wage and salary claims in the hope that successful application of this would deter the Government from introducing legislation enabling it, by Order in Council, to insist on notification of pay and similar claims and prospective terms of settlement, and direction in the National Board for Prices and Incomes if this was considered necessary. After Mr Woodcock had spoken 'composite motion 12', which had Association support, was moved; then the other 'composite'. This was followed by George Lowthian, General Council member for the building trades, moving the reference back. He considered that a special meeting of union executives would be better able to pronounce on the latter developments.

During the ensuing debate Mr Hollocks put the Association's point of view. He said that the public service sector had had previous harsh experience of wage freeze, pay pause and guiding light; and he asked three questions. How could the hundreds of pay, grading and similar claims handled by some individual unions be properly considered together with all the others by the T.U.C. machinery envisaged? What were the proposed means of enforcement? Where did bodies outside the T.U.C. (e.g. the teachers' organizations) fit into this scheme?

In addition to Mr Woodcock, spokesmen for the unions listed in support of the two 'composites' and the mover and seconder of the reference back; some other speakers participated in the debate. They included Harry Nicholas, from the powerful Transport and General Workers, opposing the platform, and Sir Harry Douglas supporting it. The wisdom of having a motion previously tabled on the subject was shown, however, when Mr Anderson of NALGO (who had not submitted a motion) reached the rostrum, but was not allowed to speak. If his organization had tabled a motion or if the delegation had been better known (it was their first year at Congress) this unfortunate incident would not have happened.

When the debate had finished and the votes were taken the General Council won the day, the reference back and the hostile 'composite no. 12' were lost, and the other 'composite' carried; but the voting was sufficiently heavy from those opposed to the platform (3,312,000 to 5,251,000 on the General Council's reports) to suggest that the operation of a voluntary T.U.C. scheme is in for a very rough passage.

Note: Reports on the annual TUC meetings were a regular feature in *London Town* right up to the end of the GLC. At this time the TUC was truly a "power in the land" with instant access (traditionally associated with "beer and sandwiches") to the Prime Minister (Labour or Conservative) and a considerable influence upon government social and economic policy.

Section 8: Staff Association
and *London Town* Notables

Introduction

Throughout its history the journal was served - as was the Staff Association with which it was closely linked, and that LCC/GLC/ILEA service which provided its *raison d'être* - by a succession of extremely able men and women. When the time came for them to leave the stage (or, in some instances, at certain junctures during their active lives) due tribute was almost invariably paid to them in the pages of the magazine: and although such tributes can hardly be said to have portrayed their subjects "warts and all" (such was not their purpose) they usually went appreciably beyond being mere eulogies. Many of those pieces are, in fact, well worthy of inclusion in any selection of the best of the *Staff Gazette/ London Town*.

All distinctions are invidious, but unfortunately they have to be made: and the exclusion of any person from this clutch of articles that "now praise famous men" (and one woman) does not imply any judgement as to their real importance. Those who do feature in this Section were, we consider, representative figures: but there were many others, of course, who not only "also served" but who had much influence on the affairs of that little world which centred upon County Hall. They, too, were "notables" in every sense of the word.

Staff Association Leaders – W. J. O. Newton.

(May 1922)

The absence of Newton from amongst the very first of the stars discovered (in the stage sense) in this constellation is almost enough in itself to have justified some of the conjectures as to the authorship of the studies.

A biographer after the modern fashion, writing of Newton, would probably choose the sub-title "Man of Culture and Man of Affairs." Newton was already establishing a reputation as a junior with an extraordinarily rapid output of work of high quality when the momentous decision of the Council to set up the famous "£200 barrier" reverberated through an astounded junior staff. Newton can have felt little personal apprehension regarding that or any other barrier, but to a chivalrous nature there was in the situation an appeal that transcended purely personal considerations, and, in addition, during the early years of the collective staff movement, just that spice of danger which gives chivalry its full flavour.

Then, as always, a man of long views, he was one of those who at once perceived that the great lesson to be learned was the vital need of a well-knit staff organisation. No one was ever less temperamentally inclined to figure in the limelight, but, from the day he heard the "call" to the present time, Newton has, by common consent, and it might be said, as of right, occupied a dominant and an exacting place in the centre of the stage. Indeed, to recite the principal offices which he has filled - some of them several times over - the suffrages of his colleagues would be merely to catalogue the most prominent positions in the Association and its main comittees.

Chairmen, unlike poets, are sometimes manufactured articles; the essential functions of the chair are to be mastered by a moderate amount of study and observation. It is, nevertheless, true that in a chairman the best title is birthright, and Newton is a born chairman. On the bench he would not be a "talking judge" but a "listening judge" - that ideal of advocates and litigants. Yet he knows just when to intervene, and although his native courtesy, readiness and quiet humour have often dissipated a gathering storm, no one senses more unerringly and decisively the very moment for the "vote," or checks more unmistakeably the eloquence that becomes irrelevance.

The armoury of debate is very varied. Some wield a heavy bludgeon; some affect a velvet paw, from which the claws scarcely peep. Others, again, resort - sometimes, it is suspected, a little involuntarily - to the up-to-date (and yet how ancient!) device of artificial fog. Willmot's resources range from the dazzling and disconcerting fireworks of raillery and ridicule to the primitive "straight left" of the knock-out, and all of them are used with a cool science which, when necessary, camouflages itself as artlessness.

Newton's weapon is the rapier, most delicately as well as most powerfully handled, and particularly formidable in defence, in which he often uses it with such a rapid and finished skill that onlookers can frequently see his opponent is transfixed before the victim himself can feel it. An accomplished elocutionist, Newton has in his delivery an admirable vehicle for the ideas of a richly-stored and original mind, and his speeches are for his colleagues among the rewards of the drudgery of committee work. He never needlessly "weighs in," but when he cares to do so his contribution is a dominant influence.

Newton would not pretend that he really loves the often haggling detail of negotiation. That is the *forte* and even the joy of others. But he has an unfailing instinct for principles, a quality which on the dark and troubled waters of discussion answers the purpose of both compass and searchlight. It is, doubt-less, this same perception of the true objective which has made the project of an Institute of Public Administration particularly attractive to him. The select group of higher Civil Service men and Local Government colleagues who have been building, and lately launching, this vessel, so full of great potentialities, soon learned to value Newton as a fellow-labourer.

Known to many as a delightful companion whether in the committee room, the conference room, the recreation room, or the ball room, Newton, with his idealism, his practicality and his astonishing versatility, also, by universal acclaim takes his rightful and eminent place in these notes on "Staff Leaders."

Note: During a long and varied career Mr Newton rendered sterling service to both the *Staff Gazette/London Town* and the Staff Association. Volume 1 of this *Miscellany* contains (pages 245-250) his account of a visit to Stockton on behalf of the Association. His official career reached its apotheosis when he took charge of the Londoner's Meals Service during the Second World War, after playing a prominent part in the formulation and execution of the Council's scheme for the evacuation of schoolchildren from London on the outbreak of war. Volume 1 includes (pages 264-265) his appeal for volunteers to assist with this evacuation. The Meals Service proved invaluable during the "Blitz", when so many

Londoners were bombed or blasted out of their homes and their own kitchens: and it continued to render a valuable service through the years of austerity and very tight rationing of food immediately after the war, and well on into the 1950s. Later still, and after Newton had retired, the Council's School Meals Service continued this valuable service in a somewhat different form.

J. W. Ellis.

(October 1928)

It is with great regret that we announce the death on 7th September, at the age of 54, of J. W. Ellis, of the Parliamentary Department. He was at his post as late as 23rd August, looking forward to a well-earned holiday in the Switzerland which he had known and loved for so long. Then he was attacked by phlebitis, from which, from one so robust, no harm was to be expected, but complications ensued and the end came with tragic suddenness.

Ellis entered the service in the Chief Engineer's Department in 1893, but, having been called to the Bar at Gray's Inn, was transferred in 1903 to the newly-formed Parliamentary Bench of the Clerk's Department, which later became a separate department. There his devotion to duty, his knowledge, experience, and acumen were invaluable. A man of his character and ability might have looked forward confidently to occupying with credit almost any position in the service. Fortune was perhaps not altogether kind to him and a natural reluctance to push himself forward prevented him from reaching quite the rank which his friends considered that he deserved.

But if diffident when his own interests were concerned, he was indefatigable in the interests of others. Older members of the staff will remember that he succeeded the late Mr. Bockett (whom he resembled in many ways) as editor of this *Gazette* and that as 'Piper' he contributed the *Spring Garden Ballads*, a clever series of humorous verses on the lighter side of official life. After acting as editor for three years, he became chairman of the *Gazette* Committee and directed the interests of the journal for many years, including the difficult period of the war. His literary abilities led him towards the Staff Dramatic Club, in which he took a close interest, at first as a member of the managing committee and, since the retirement of Mr. G. O. H. Smails in May last, as chairman.

For twenty-four years he was on the committee of the Staff Benevolent Society and for fourteen on the committee of the War Aid Fund. On both his services were much valued and frequently invoked, especially in matters needing tact, judgment and sympathy. Arising out of these duties, or, perhaps, because he was so obviously a man to be trusted, he was often consulted privately by members of the staff, and many will recall with gratitude the kindly counsel or substantial assistance which they received.

Too old for active service in the war, he enrolled as a special constable and added to this regular attendance on several nights a week at the Y.M.C.A. hut at Paddington.

He was very far from being a literary recluse, but played cricket and tennis and was an energetic member of at least one rambling club, there being few cross-country routes in the Home Counties with which he was not familiar. His favourite hobby, perhaps, was Continental travel and during his annual holidays he must have traversed most of south-eastern France, Switzerland, Tyrol and northern Italy.

It is characteristic of him that much of his labours for others should not be known, for he was ever content to do what lay before him without much concern whether he, or another, or no one, got the credit.

He was unmarried, but leaves a brother and two sisters, to whom we offer our sincere sympathy.

He was buried at Abney Park Cemetery on 12th September, in the presence of his family, several colleagues both past and present, and many friends.

Percy Merriman retires.

P. C. E. Tisdale
(January 1943)

(As announced in the November issue of *London Town*, Mr. Percy Merriman, formerly Editor of the *'L.C.C. Staff Gazette,'* retired on 8th December. The following symposium has been arranged by Mr. P. C. E. Tisdale who himself begins by recording his own memories of many years' association with Mr. Merriman. - Ed.)

The irresistible and versatile Merriman, known as a 'Rooster' to many, 'Dagobert' to his old *Staff Gazette* colleagues, and 'Merry' to his intimates, is leaving us - and it seems all too soon.

Among his contemporaries I suppose I can go back the longest with Merriman - almost to 'knickerbocker ' days. In our early office years we gaily shared the joys of the open road, and 'flaunted in faultless flannels' round the lovely coasts of Devon and Cornwall. And what days they were - those halcyon days before the last war, when with volumes of Keats or Shelley in our haversacks we roamed the countryside with carefree spirits and a joyous resolve to outdo the birds in song. The mention of country walks reminds me that Percy Merriman is an acknowledged authority on rambling and is a guide to the Ramblers' Club. He has conducted parties even so far afield as Switzerland, but don't ask me how he got over the language difficulties; his great talent for improvisation probably pulled him through.

The Entertainer
Merriman is indeed 'a fellow of infinite jest,' overflowing with verbal quips and apt quotations (from the immortal bard to Rabelais), with an impromptu eloquence - complete with gesture - all his own. He is a raconteur of repute, and one remembers many a *bon mot* of his. On one occasion when he was giving a recital at a local hall, the curtain became stuck after the interval, but our friend immediately came in front and flashed out, 'I am sorry for this unfortunate delay, but I'm afraid we don't know the ropes!'

Percy Merriman in his prime (1924).

In recording a few of his varied activities, his performances with the 'Roosters' Concert Party undoubtedly takes pride of place, and owing to broadcasting these have become widely known and have delighted thousands. For many years he has organised and appeared at countless staff dinners and concerts in many departments as well as his own, when we have often chuckled at his spoof telegrams from prominent people. His character studies and monologues were masterly ('Fagin' was a gem), and when he wrote or produced pantomimes or sketches for departmental or club dinners the foibles of his colleagues were treated with devastating effect.

The Writer

Merriman has achieved the distinction of writing for Punch, and he is also author of a useful book on camping life. In the years of peace he was a prolific contributor to many periodicals.

Turning to his work on the *L.C.C. Staff Gazette* (now *London Town*), my mind goes back to the restful years of 1910-12, when, with youthful enthusiasm, we each wrote (among other light verse) those audacious 'Playful Parodies' in alternate issues of the magazine - ranging from Omar Khayyam to W. S. Gilbert. Happy days!

I assisted him as sub-editor and secretary from 1920 to 1926, during which period his output was amazing - and here I should like to pay tribute to his influence and example which were of inestimable value to me in my literary diversions.

The Editor

I have asked Laurence Welsh to give me a note for inclusion in this article. He writes:-

'I came to know Merriman soon after the last war when I was contributing a monthly feature on the activities of civil servants and municipal officers. He was a kindly and considerate editor, and he impressed me even in my younger and less tolerant years by his broadminded attitude to controversial topics in the realm of staff politics. He was less keenly interested in these things than I was and held them to be of less importance in the corporate life of the staff than I did. But our differences on this head were of the mildest kind - it was no more than a question of emphasis - and did nothing to prevent our forming what was to me a happy and educative friendship.

'Our main common ground was our interest in London, and especially in the London of history and literature. We spent many enjoyable hours visiting the scenes of Dickens' stories - especially the pubs! - and Merriman always made those visits a lively and fascinating experience.'

I have also received the following interesting contribution from W. J. O. Newton, known to many as a writer of distinction and a frequent contributor to the old *Staff Gazette*:-

'Dagobert' the Jester

'Percy Merriman is held in esteem and will always be affectionately remembered by those who have preceded him in retirement and by the older members of the present staff who were readers of the *L.C.C. Staff Gazette*, as *London Town* was called up to and including the period of his editorship, 1912-26, which followed two years as sub-editor. The magazine in those days had an appeal different from that which it has to-day, for changing times have influenced the outlook of those responsible for its production. During Merriman's period in the chair, the staff was a much smaller one than now, and staff politics not so much to the fore. Indeed, during the first part of the period the Staff Association was only in its infancy. The pages of the staff magazine had more of a literary and social character than they have now. The contributors were well known to the smaller number of readers, and the literary articles, light verse, and sketches, which with personal news and club reports made up the paper, were anticipated and received with the friendly interest of a family.

'Merriman saw to it that the work of his contributors was on a high level, and everything printed had to pass his test of being definitely interesting or amusing. Only one occasion, indeed, comes to memory when some of his readers thought he had fallen below his own standard, and that he will probably recall with amusement as the time when he printed an article on bee-keeping in which the subject was treated with more solemnity than some readers considered to be its due. He ensured than the subsequent discussion did not lack interest and if the article itself was not amusing the incident certainly was.

'It was a pleasure to be a contributor under Merriman's editorship, for writers had the benefit of his proposals as to promising themes and their treatment, and his criticism, always so pleasantly made, for cuttings and improvements. His precepts were pointed by example, for his own occasional contributions were models of good style, the prose (over his initials) being marked by sound taste and comeliness of expression, and the light verse (signed with his pseudonym 'Dagobert') by charm and joyful spontaneity.

'He was a friendly editor, and his friendliness embraced readers and writers alike. Both benefited. Readers looked forward to publication day, sure beforehand that they would find something good. They were not disappointed, for the contributors were glad to let the editor print for nothing in the *Staff Gazette* material similar to that for which many of them were receiving fees from the editors of other papers. There was trouble if the local agents were a day late in their deliveries - and it must be remembered that in those days the magazine was not issued automatically to Staff Association members but had to pay its own way by being sufficiently interesting to attract and retain subscribers.

'The gifted man who is retiring from our now much larger company has perceived a lot of fun in life, and he has shared the fun with those around him in work and play. They are grateful to him. They are confident that he will always find life amusing and hope that he will never lack good neighbours with whom to share his joys.

'Dagobert, your former readers and contributors salute you. They will not forget the twinkle in your eye.'

Mercutio

The Actor
This chronicle would not be complete without reference to Percy Merriman's performances for the L.C.C. Dramatic Club, and Spencer Leeming has sent me the following appreciation:-

'Percy Merriman was an original member of the Staff Dramatic Club, founded in 1903, and, until some time after the last war when other calls upon his time made continuance impossible, he was one of the most prominent and accomplished actor members. Merriman excelled in character acting, and he provided some brilliant studies. The writer first played with him in Pinero's 'The Squire,' in 1907, when he was old Gunnion. His subsequent gallery of portraits ranged from grave to gay, but all were marked with an amazingly subtle insight into character. One remembers particularly his Ambrose Pinning in 'My Friend the Prince,' his grand old Lively in 'Sunday,' but perhaps most of all his Corporal Brewster in 'Waterloo.' But there were many others. Merriman was able to make a small part stand out and be long remembered. He played an Italian waiter in 'The Bear-Leaders' with little to say, but his cameo was perfect in characterisation and humour. The younger generation will know Percy Merriman only as a pillar of the 'Roosters' Concert Party. But those of us who saw his work in the earlier days of the Dramatic Club remember him for that, affectionately and with joy. As an impersonator of humorous or tragic old age there was no amateur to touch him. *Bonne chance*, old trouper!'

The Londoner
Lewis W. Butler, who retired in July, 1940, and who was closely associated with Merriman on the *Staff Gazette* as business manager, writes to us as follows:-
'When men grow old together they forget their advance along the road of life. And now Percy Merriman is "going." I did not suspect thy years! Apart from his great work as Editor of the *Staff Gazette*, his charm to me is his unrivalled knowledge and love of London. To hear him as he took us round Shoreditch and Hoxton, Southwark and Deptford, Hampstead and the rest, re-incarnating those Victorian days of beauty and peace, of dirt and poverty, was to know the master of his subject. It was not only the vivid description as he unfolded another cameo, but the apt quotation that went with it - sparkling with life. His buoyancy has always been the attraction to those who had the pleasure of contact with him, as well as his untiring energy to serve his brother officers whether from the editorial chair or the concert platform. One cannot write of Percy retiring - the word is foreign to his whole outlook. Rather let us say he has caught sight of a new field for adventure, and so "as one of the members of the old management" I join in wishing him all happiness and good comradeship in his new life.'

Envoi
In conclusion I feel I cannot do better than reiterate the wishes so well expressed by the other writers in this symposium, and this I do with my hand on my heart.

You've given us the air, gay comrade;
Impatiently you've fled
From dull routine,
To joys unseen
And all that lies ahead.

You've given us the air, old timer;
We'll miss each joke and crack
You'd lightly toss,
Or put across
With glittering attack.

You've given us the air, proud Rooster;

*   *   *

The air will bring you back!

(Mr. Merriman, who did not desire a public presentation, wished to express his warmest thanks to his many friends for their parting gift of a cheque. - Ed)

Charles Moverley: the Chairman of the General Committee.

(August 1958)

On the first occasion that the Sir James Bird Cup was awarded for an essay on a cross-country walk, Sir James himself, the Clerk of the Council, attended the Association's General Committee to present the cup in person. This was in 1921. The youthful recipient was a Mr. Charles Victor Moverley.

At that same meeting, the Chairman of the *Staff Gazette* Committee (as Witan Publications Ltd. was called in those uncomplicated days) handed over to the Staff Associaiton the custody of the Bockett Chair. This dignified piece of furniture had been purchased by subscription in tribute to Mr. F. W. Bockett, who died in 1912. Mr. Bockett was the distinguished Founder-editor of the *Staff Gazette* who did so much to promote comradeship among the staff, and the memorial has for 47 years been the throne of the chairmen of committees and sub-committees in the room at County Hall allotted to the Staff Association.

It was not for 32 years that Mr Charles Victor Moverley was to occupy that seat in B.73, when he became Chairman of the Executive. Indeed it was not for 25 years that he was even a member of the General Committee.

True he did reappear in that assembly early in 1923, to receive the Sir James Cup for the second year running. Under the conditions then obtaining he won the Cup outright. Sir James, generous but perhaps a little less genial, had another cup fashioned, but altered the condition to ensure that this one remained in circulation. Moverley was welcome to compete, he said, but he could not be allowed to make a 'corner' in these goblets. It is not given to many young men with two years' service to come so sharply to the notice of the Clerk of the Council.

However, Moverley was in the Architect's, and has remained there throughout his 38 years with the Council, except for secondment during the last war to the London Civil Defence Headquarters. He did come to the notice of the Architect (Topham Forrest) and had an exhausting period as his personal assistant, to which he attributes his promotion to senior assistant at what was then considered the early age of 36. He is now a principal (b) in the housing division.

Asked why he was so long in coming into Staff Association affairs, Moverley replies that he determined many years ago, on deductions from what

259

he admits is inadequate evidence, that he would not seek office until he was no longer in a position to be accused of trying to further his personal ambitions in other spheres. This may seem strange to a younger generation, which assumes (perhaps on equally inadequate grounds) that prominence in the Staff Association is a natural impediment to official advancement.

The Staff Association's delegation to the TUC in 1962 included (left to right) Paul Rose, Colin Watson, Charles Corcoran and Charles Moverley.

So for many years Moverley was an enthusiastic party man only in the non-political sense, entertaining at socials with songs, parodies and sketches of his own composition, and voicing hearty partisanship on sporting occasions. During the war, indeed, as chairman of the Rescue Service sports and recreation committee, he graduated from attending sporting occasions to organizing them. Having promoted boxing at the Albert Hall, football at Wembley, athletics at the

White City, billiards at Thurston's and a concert at the Coliseum, he almost qualifies for the title of the civil defence Jack Solomons.

Venturing at last on to his departmental committee in 1945, Moverley was secretary until 1947, vice-chairman until 1952, and chairman the following year. (He was in fact the first administrative type the Architect's d.c. put in the chair.) He was elected to the General Committee in 1946, has served on the Executive with only one year's break from 1949, and was its Chairman in 1953/4 and 1957/ 8. He was Chairman of the General Committee in 1954/5 and President of the Association next year. As this year's Chairman he is repeating the cycle. He served on the Staff Side for the last five years' life of the Joint Committee and has been a member of three arbitration teams at the Industrial Court. In the wider trade union field he has represented the Association on the executive of the N.F.P.W. (National Federation of Professional Workers) for a number of years, attended the Trades Union Congress at Blackpool, and was observer at the NALGO conference at Bournemouth.

In his private life Moverley (who is four times a grandfather) finds time to sit on the board of governors of his old school (St. Ignatius College), has been active in Catholic circles, and was recently made President of the newly-formed L.C.C. Staff Catholic Guild.

Where does Mr Moverley stand on policy? One would begin to answer by suggesting that of all the Staff Association leaders he is the most intuitive, the least given to theorizing. Moverley is not merely genial by nature, he is genial by conviction; he sincerely believes in the brotherhood of men and the need to extend a helping hand and a smile. He believes in the value and dignity of working for the people of London and equally in the value and dignity of the people who do that work. One feels that the Staff Association is to him therefore simply a fellowship, both in the personal sense of friendly intercourse and in the organizational sense of a union for mutual aid. This determines that he can never be an extremist - or even an adventurer - because he organically needs the assurance of friendly backing from as many people as possible. He is, therefore, the democratic delegate *par excellence*.

The conviction that Moverley is a 'moderate' has won him the backing of many members who have had to reconcile themselves to the thought that a safe man can also be a firm champion of T.U.C. affiliation and can, on returning from a NALGO conference, go on record that good could come from talking to NALGO on linking efforts and machinery. But there is not necessarily inconsistency here. If fellowship is the criterion, a larger fellowship is obviously more desirable than a smaller fellowship, provided that the fellow-feeling of the smaller fellowship can be maintained unimpaired.

The guiding principle that government must be on the broadest possible basis of consent has not made Moverley a pliant chairman. He can be very firm in the Chair, particularly if the dignity of his office is challenged. He can also be most severely and self-effacingly just. At the recent debate on aid to the London Busmen, when speaker after speaker was trouncing the Executive for daring to favour such impious thoughts, Moverley more than once called for members to put the opposite point of view. Most General Committeemen probably concluded that here was the Establishment trying to come to the help of the harassed dais. They did not know that in the Executive Mr Moverley had been the first to raise his voice on the subject: his preference had been for a vote of censure on the busmen for inconveniencing their fellow-workers!

Note: Charles Moverley's first winning essay for the Sir James Bird Cup appears in Volume 1 (pages 196-198). Mr Moverley continued, after his retirement from the Council's service, to play an active part in Staff Association affairs almost to the time of his regrettably early death in August 1973.

Laurence Welsh: the Organization Man.

C. D. Andrews
(September 1963)

In the early 1920s competition to get on to the Staff Association's General Committee was exceptionally fierce. One aspirant who failed year after year to get elected to that rumbustious forum was L. Welsh, then of Education. In other departments young firebrands were being elected, and indeed they formed the first Ginger Group within the Association in 1922. But Welsh had solid respected old-timers in the Association to contend against in his constituency, and it was not until the end of 1927 that he won an election - one doubts whether he has ever lost one since.

By 1927 Welsh was editor of *London Town*, or the *Staff Gazette* as it was still called, but he had during the early post-war years already established himself as a fluent and compendious commentator on trade union affairs in the public services. His knowledge in this field was not accidentally acquired: very little in all the multiform activities of Laurence Welsh is the fruit of chance: rather was it the result of a deliberate decision and careful cultivation.

With the giants

A schoolmaster had first interested the youthful Welsh in the Fabian Research Department. Very soon he was engrossed in the Labour Movement (which is far from saying the Labour Party). He mixed with the Webbs, G. D. H. Cole, and other giants of the period, and recalls a Fabian Executive Committee meeting at which he and Bernard Shaw both attended but neither said a word - which is probably a record for each of them. In his service during the first World War Welsh was stationed near London, and was able when off duty to do a lot of devilling for the Fabians' production of the Labour Year Book of 1916, being particularly concerned with an examination of the position of trade unionism. This led him to speculate, as a municipal servant of some five years' standing, on the necessity for union organization in the public services. He resolved to find out more about it. After the war was over, with typical assiduity, he wrote to every black-coated staff association he could unearth and arranged to be supplied regularly with their journals. He was an early propagandist for Whitleyism. He was concerned in the foundation in 1920 of the National Federation of Professional Workers (of which organization he is now President). From 1920 also he was the regular columnist in the *Staff Gazette* of 'Public Service Notes'.

So it was no tyro who gained entry to the General Committee of the L.C.C. Staff Association in November 1927. (For accuracy's sake it should be recorded that he had served a year in 1924/5, when by some fluke there were unopposed nominations.) It was a man with a wide knowledge of black-coated employees' organizations, a man with a penetrating appraisal of their weaknesses, and a man with very clear ideas on the measures necessary to strengthen his own association.

Transformation

What were those measures? If we must inadequately summarize the aims of forty years' activity, they might best be expressed as unionization in unity - the transformation of an amateur association into a trade union without alienating the enthusiasm of the constituent members. So he has advocated the improvement of conditions, but with priority for the grievances of those most strongly organized - on an empirical basis: those grievances might or might not be the worst, but if they were strongly ventilated they were the worst current threat to unity. He has advocated the establishment of a strong secretariat on which the voluntary Officers of the Association could rely. Younger members may be amazed that until seventeen years ago there was no full-time secretary of the Association. In the last eight years of course Welsh himself has been chief executive of what has become a 'civil service' which the Association has found increasingly indispensable. He has advocated alliance with other organizations - again, empirically: alliance, even merger, could, he has argued, mean more effective pressure, and the measure of a trade union's value is its power to exert pressure. He has advocated, and practised, the rationalization of policy-making within the General Committee itself, almost to the extent of party organization. He has advocated links with all black-coated workers, and links with many progressive centres of information and action.

Here a sobering word must be inserted. Laurence Welsh has been so long identified with the L.C.C. Staff Association, and in later years has been assumed by many (and feared by some) almost to personalize it, that it is salutary to reflect on how little actual power he has wielded. We may break his long Association career into five stages. 1927-37 a critical back-bencher - influential in representing the conscience of the Association but never more than a minority spokesman. 1937-41 responsibility without power - Chairman of the Executive Committee but head of a group which failed to carry the Association with them on some of their salient and declared policies (the long campaign for unity in some form or other with NALGO being the most prominent fiasco), and failed to carry the Council with them on others (though much useful spadework was done on many grievances, from dual scales to the abolition of the marriage bar). 1941-6 at the centre of power - a leader of the 'New Policy Campaign' which swept his friends into office, though they were still hampered by the wartime impediments to achievement. (Nevertheless their achievements were real enough - the establishment of a domestic arbitration tribunal, payment for the additional hours the Council had imposed on the staff, an appreciable measure of success on the Post-1930 Report.) 1946-55 an influential statesman, a powerful back-bencher after he left the Executive in 1948, but one with many contacts in the Association's 'establishment'. 1955-63 - the Association's shrewd advisor and dedicated chief executive.

Laurence Welsh's retirement portrait, 1963. As befitted a man who played many parts in a long and active life he bears, in this study, a remarkable resemblance to Laurence Olivier.

Influence
Welsh therefore has been mostly an influence, not a directing force. This is because the Association has always been what it is called, an *association*. Government has usually been effected by ad hoc agreements reached from month to month, and only rarely by the orderly execution of a pre-announced policy. In fact only in the years when the 'New Policy Campaign' came to power can there be said to have been real *government* at all. And Welsh himself has come to acknowledge in later years that the 'ginger group', however estimable its programme, carries the same danger as party politics in local government, in that every proposal made by the group is accepted by those who adhere to it and uniformly resisted by those outside, so that an artificial disunity is created and the merits of proposals become irrelevant.

Steadying rock
The achievements which can be laid to Welsh's door in Staff Association affairs are substantial, but they must be shared among his like-minded colleagues, and they do not represent a tithe of his contribution to Staff Association history. Welsh has been the lasting influence, the predictable pressure, the steadying rock in a shifting dune of other pressures; a steadier, stronger influence than most, a permanent force for the best part of forty years, but always a force whose effect was modified by the strength or weakness of the supporters he found, the strength or weakness of his opponents, and the degree of diversity among those opponents as compared with the consistency of his own policies.

The amazing thing is that the talent and energy with which Laurence Welsh has so unstintingly served the Staff Association in what might be held to be an all-absorbing devotion - talent which would have been wholly absorbed by the volume and intensity of Staff Association affairs if Welsh was in the normal run of talented and energetic men - have been just as freely given to a host of other activities. The acute intellect, the facility to write rapid and lucid prose, the jewel-like precision of speech, the negotiating skill, the moral toughness, the ironic wit and the scintillating personal charm have served him as editor, as wide-ranging journalist, as propagandist and researcher, as a national figure in black-coated organization, and not least as a distinguished Council officer, at one and the same time as he has been an Association leader. Now that he is released in the seventieth year of his youth what further territories will his restless genius seek?

Over Fifty Years.

I. W. Wilson
(September 1963)

In 1911 suffragette agitation filled the headlines, cigarettes were ten for $2^1/_2$d and the Staff Association was considering affiliating to NALGO. In the same year Laurence Welsh joined the Council's service, having obtained a clerkship on the minor establishment. He resigned from it eighteen months later. He had taken both the major establishment and the Customs and Excise examinations, Results of the latter were announced first; he was successful and left for an intensive initiation into brewing and distilling processes in East London.

When I spoke to him of those early days he recalled above all that the great precept of the Customs and Excise office was 'Never accept a favour from a trader' - lest, presumably, one should be persuaded into disregarding a few thousand barrels. But he did not travel along these promising paths for long. When the major establishment result was published, young Welsh was placed second in order of merit; number one, however, had been involved in some dubious transaction with postal orders and was not appointed; so it was as the top man of the year that Welsh was allotted to the vigorous young Education department and sent to a divisional office at Bow. This time he was to stay in the service of the Council or its staff for fifty years.

East End

Office life in the East End, 1913: what was it like? Welsh's memories of it are vivid. A purpose-built office, modern and hygienic; yet, because of some economy drive, so grotesquely cramped that people sat side-by-side sharing the same desk. Unimpressive duties, sorting cards and the like - 'jobs that to-day would not be done at all or be done by a machine'. Memorable staff - the officer-in-charge and old School Board man (its functions had been taken over by the Council only nine years before) and a source of amusement to the youngsters because he always wore a tail-coat to the office, which was going a bit far even then; he added a fashionable straw boater in the summer, making a singularly odd combination.

There were no women in Education but there was a lady typist, a pretty and vivacious girl whom Laurence has no difficulty at all in recalling to mind. He says 'The progressive younger men in the office vacillated between exerting their best endeavours to exploit her physical attractions and advocating votes for women.' He has the impression that officer manners were rather stiffer then than now; first names were not used and people tended to be peremptory on the telephone. Men dressed more formally, especially at 'head office' (a place of tremendous authority for those out at divisions), and a hot day was no excuse for shirt-sleeves. The sordidness and poverty of the East End of those days were a shattering experience for a young man from the politer suburbs - the stench from the overcrowded tenements in the summer, the steamy workshops, the sad Chinese drinking tea in gloomy cafés. Lansbury and other reconstructions have transformed it all; no part of London, Welsh thinks, presents a greater contrast between then and now.

After four years in the Army and spells at divisional offices in the more salubrious districts of Greenwich and Shepherds Bush, there came a move in 1924 to the Special Schools division at County Hall. This dealt with an aspect of the education service then developing with great rapidity and subtlety. The Committee members exercised a close concern; they included several formidable personalities, one of them Susan Lawrence, a prominent Fabian and a member of the Webbs' coterie. When in one discussion about furniture for the children a member questioned the need for comfortably cushioned chairs when the children had not been used to them at home, Susan Lawrence acidly suggested that the soft seat might be regarded as some small compensation for other hardships. The exchange epitomized the age-long tussle between financial and service considerations. This was Welsh's first contact with Council members. With a Conservative administration firmly in office they were dignified, aristocratic, paternalistic and deeply and compassionately concerned with the handicapped children for whom they were responsible.

They were rewarding years in many ways, but not materially. The rate of promotion was to modern eyes incredibly slow. Able, even exceptional, officers were kept on their grade maximum for years. Eventually - and this has a contemporary echo - certain first class (b) officers were allowed, following Association pressure, to advance up the I (a) scale without waiting for a substantive vacancy. In 1930 Welsh was promoted I (a) but had to change departments to get it. London's hospitals had just become the Council's responsibility; he was transferred to Public Health where a new organization was being built up to administer them. Plans were made which would have revolutionized the service. Welsh calls it a disaster that the war came so soon after; there was just not enough time to rebuild or co-ordinate. The Council in fact was never to have that opportunity.

Coping with the blitz

With the war in 1939 Welsh was appointed to what he thinks of as his most satisfying and exciting job of all - assistant officer-in-charge of the London Ambulance Service. Pre-war preparations had been crude and inadequate. In the first year of war, mercifully raid-free, an auxiliary service was fashioned by a combination of improvisation, flair and hard work - and it proved able when the test came to cope with bombing and the blitz. Some 8,000 staff were hastily engaged and organized in 112 auxiliary stations all over London; Welsh with special responsibility for staff had to co-ordinate their efforts, weld them into a service and handle the human problems. Many were prominent personalities: they included writers, actors, sprigs of the nobility, the wife of the then leader of the Council, music-hall artists. Not surprisingly, considering the speed with which they were assembled, some turned out less than exemplary characters. One poor lady station officer had to be disciplined because she panicked, closed her station down in the middle of a raid and sent everyone home. Most of them proved gallant and devoted workers, capable of outstanding feats of bravery and endurance, and they served London well.

After the exhausting, adventurous years of war came the long, slow wind-down of the war-time ambulance service - punctuated, for Welsh, by lecture tours addressed to sceptical German town clerks about the democratic virtues of British local government. In 1948 with the creation of the National Health Service he was appointed one of the nine divisional administrative officers and remained in the West London division until he exchanged the Council's service for the Staff Association at the end of 1954. The means adopted for administering the personal health services after 1948, he told me, are particularly apposite to current controversies. It was the Council's imaginative policy to create a localized administration in which Borough Council representatives shared: it thus secured the twin advantages of local knowledge and a centrally organized pool of common experience and expertise.

Laurence Welsh's extraordinarily youthful vigour prompted a last question: for his unquenchable interest in the human condition, his intellectual resilience and energy, his astringent wit, his enjoyment of an elegant mastery over the English language, all these clearly render a cloistered retirement as unthinkable as ever. What then, I asked, of the future? Writing figures largely in his plans. For many years, as an accepted expert on public administration and public service employment, he has contributed widely to the journals specializing in such subjects. This he hopes to continue and, with greater leisure, develop. He already gets invited to report a strange variety of meetings and conferences. I left him deciding between reformed superannuation and refined refuse collection.

Note: Laurence Welsh had already been through one set of retirement celebrations and commemorations when he retired from the LCC service (after 44 years) in 1955. He had immediately afterwards, thrown himself into the work of Secretary of the Staff Association, in which post all the characteristic Welsh verve and energy were fully displayed. His 1963 retirement did not remove him entirely from the *London Town* scene: as can be seen on pages 192-193, he was still contributing over twenty years later. The contributions set out above were two of four tributes to Laurence Welsh, covering different aspects of his life and work.

Patricia Knox.

Joyce Ansell
(November 1972)

A remarkable person retired from the service of the ILEA on 31 August 1972. Patricia Knox was a social worker for nearly 43 years and an influential member of Staff Association committees for 37 of them. No one person did more to improve the pay and status of social workers in the service of the LCC/GLC and no one person did more for the cause of equality of opportunity for men and women in that service.

Miss Knox joined the LCC education service in October 1929 as an assistant organizer of children's care and worked in divisions 1, 2, 3, 5, 8, 9 and 10. She rose to become divisional school care organizer in Lambeth in 1959. When in 1970 the school care service and school inquiry service were combined to form the new education welfare service she became divisional education welfare officer.

Miss Knox was on the General Committee of the Staff Association from 1934-71, a member of its Executive Committee from 1936-70, chairman of the General Committee from 1944-46 and President in 1946-7. From 1943-70 she served on the comittees responsible for negotiating service conditions and was chairman of the Whitley Council in 1969-70. She played a leading part in the subcommittee which advised the Association on all the problems connected with the formation of the new Education Welfare Service. She led the Association's team which gave evidence before the Royal Commission on Equal Pay in 1945 and on six occasions led for the Association in arbitration cases on behalf of social workers.

On 4 October Miss Knox entertained to tea at County Hall a large number of colleagues and friends who came to bid her farewell.

Mr Crawley, assistant divisional education welfare officer, who had been on Miss Knox's staff since 1969 and previously in the school inquiry service, spoke with admiration of her qualities as a senior officer, her tireless self-giving to her official and Staff Association work, and her total dedication to the concept of the combined service, which had achieved a career and salary structure which was the envy of the education welfare service throughout the country.

Miss Mavis Watts, President of the Staff Association, summarized Patricia's long unbroken Association career and spoke of her ever-gracious manner, her cool and logical wisdom and her kindness to those who were learning the ways of Association committees. It gave her special pleasure that the first member of the staff to be Chairman of the Whitley Council should have been a woman who had done so much to achieve and maintain equaliy. (Hitherto the chairman had always been a member of the Council.) Miss Betty Turner, now one of the Association's 'elder statesmen', who had worked closely with Patricia for many years, said that equal pay in 1952 was her great achievement - she had always fought for equality of opportunity and the opening of all grades to men and women. She had also won the permanent removal of the marriage bar in 1945.

In presenting Miss Knox with a cheque, Miss Harrison paid tribute to her courage, determination and integrity, her negotiating and manipulative skills and her devotion to the work - she was the only person who had ever sent her a Christmas card with a PS about staff matters.

As was to be expected, Miss Knox's speech in reply was carefully composed and beautifully delivered. This was the third farewell party she had attended - the voluntary workers had entertained her in July, there had been a party at the divisional office in August and there was to be a Staff Association dinner later in October.

She had often been asked why she had not been a politician, a member of the legal profession, an administrator, a statistician, or even an architect in view of her recent efforts in planning accommodation for her staff. She thought this was perhaps another way of asking why she was a social worker. She felt, however, that she had done the job she was engaged to do - the organization of social work - and was gratified by the number of appreciative letters she had received from heads of schools. She had never ceased to emphasize that the new education welfare service was area based/school orientated. It was a creature with two legs which must work together in rhythm - if one atrophied the balance would be lost.

All the speakers in wishing her well had spoken of her departure not so much as a retirement as an opportunity to campaign with even greater vigour for the causes which she had already made her own. She confirmed that it was her intention to work on behalf of equal pay and equality of opportunity in the national field. She proposed to buy a colour television set with the cheques she had been given. Some of the programmes she sees on it will surely spur her on!

Charles Bagwell.

F. G. Gough
(October 1973)

No-one who worked with Charlie Bagwell, served with him on a committee, played cricket, or accompanied him on one of his many activities will ever
forget his great breadth of interest, his wide knowledge of a host of subjects
acquired through a lifetime of reading and enquiry.

Most people can read a lot of books, but his study was backed by a most
agile mind and lively intelligence and his conversation was leavened with a wit
and imagination none could resist. His memory was phenomenal and his fund
of likely and unlikely stories was apparently unlimited. To get him in a nostalgic
mood was to visit Clerkenwell Supplies Depot in the early thirties, to have
adventures in Spain in 1934, to endure incredible hardships with the Home
Guard, to enjoy a front stall to see Phyllis Dixey in the flesh, to see Denis
Compton bat in 1947. To him, no human activity was alien.

A classical education had endowed him with a love of language and world
literature. The history of Ireland he knew in detail. He could discuss the views
of Aristotle and it was typical that he could proceed to explain why, in his youth,
it was foolhardy to mention the name of the eminent philosopher in the bar of a
Bermondsey pub, where it had been known to lead to physical assault. To
Charlie, my uncle Toby was a blood relation; he preferred the Miller's Tale to
the Reeve's; *'The Charterhouse of Parma'* was the greatest novel. All his friends
would testify as to his debt of inspiration to François Rabelais; in hospital he was
re-reading *'The Last Chronicle of Barset'*.

The list of jobs he held in Supplies was a long one. Starting in 1930 in
printing followed by stationery, books and sports goods, he went during the war
years to medical supplies and a fire messing depot, after the war to civilian
clothing and uniforms. As one of the senior managers at Southfields Depot he
was lately engaged in marketing to the Greater London boroughs and, as a side-
line, lecturing to new entrants.

His presence in committee was vital; he breathed life into the dullest
proceedings. He was probably at his best in small meetings, but he was never
a spectator in a large one. When Charlie spoke in the General Committee of
which he had been a member continuously for thirty-eight years, there was
always laughter but the wit, not unmixed with acid, had a background of long
experience and knowledge. He knew what trade unionism was about, and there
was no mistaking where his sympathies lay. He was not brought up in dockland
for nothing.

From a lifetime of union activity it is hard to pick the most fruitful period,
but it was probably during the war when he was one of a group that, amid great
difficulties, managed to keep the Association's activities going at the highest
level. Member of the Executive and Staff Side, holder, in turn, of all the offices
in the Supplies Departmental Committee, he was a source of strength to his
colleagues. His most notable achievement was the part he played in the
assimilation of Supplies clerical and executive staff into the general structure on
most favourable terms from which a generation of the department's officers

benefited.

He was unique, he is irreplaceable. He was the most entertaining company in the world. Those who knew him might like to remember that a few days before he died he was complaining about a fellow-patient who would not stop talking.

To his wife Win we offer the deepest sympathy. Our loss is of a dear friend, a champion and colleague; hers is the loss of a life's companion of the rarest quality.

Maurice Fulcher.

(June 1978)

The news of Maurice Fulcher's sudden death from a heart attack shortly after leaving the office on 14 April stunned his friends and colleagues throughout the service. There can have been few better-known characters round and about County Hall, few more familiar figures than that large, amiable, not very tidy, lately somewhat stooping figure looming genially down from Westminster Bridge, navigating the difficult shallows of the Island Block underpass or cruising gently along York Road in search of conversation, contemplation and refreshment.

His circle of friends took in the mighty and the lowly; they were all Very Important People to Maurice. He for his part had the knack of arousing and retaining affection through all his vicissitudes and the longueurs when the mien of melancholy replaced that of merriment. For none of them will old acquaintance be forgot: yet with Maurice this range of relationships was extensive rather than intensive and perhaps he often knew others better than they knew him. For there was a deeply complex character beneath the bonhomie.

He entered the service of the London County Council as a general grade clerk in 1934 and at once joined the Staff Association. He spent all his official life in Valuation and Estates department or in the Valuation half of organizational amalgamations with Housing. The oft-remembered pre-war years in Old County Hall were crowded with intense Association activity, somehow fitted in with study for the major establishment examinations in which he was successful in 1939.

It was in this period that his reputation in Staff Association history was founded. With Jim Gregory, Pat Bacon, Betty Turner and other like-minded young officers - and some older colleagues - he set about revivifying the Association in the torpid mid-thirties. The youngest-ever member of the Executive Committee in 1938 he addressed meeting after meeting in support of his contention that the Association should provide a constitutional means for the youth of the service to express themselves; and despite some hostility the General Committee in October 1938 agreed that a Central Youth Advisory Committee and departmental YACs should be set up. A few months later *YAC News* started publication and Maurice was a member of its first editorial board.

Came the war and six years in the Army, with service in North Africa, the Middle East, Greece and France. On his return in 1946 he was plunged

271

immediately back into staff affairs and was an active and vocal member of his departmental committee to the end. Never a seeker after office, it was not until 1955 that he became chairman of the Association's Executive Committee. He was President in 1958 and by a happy coincidence was partnered on the dais by Jim Gregory and Laurence Welsh, both allies in the campaigns of the 1930s.

His official career continued in what in the immediate post-war years was the Housing and Valuation department. Though he served in several of the department's divisions, it was on the housing programme that he spent most of his time and certainly where he was happiest. Through shifting policies and a changing social scene he continued to feel a personal involvement and sense of satisfaction that he was helping in a worthwhile task. He was a patriotic Londoner, with a fierce affection for the Bermondsey of his childhood. He hated injustice, intolerance and privilege.

Few can have matched Maurice in the diversity of his enthusiasms - or in his pleasure in sharing them with his friends. The theatre, Shakespeare, wine and good food, music, music hall, the cinema, cricket, both codes of football, France, Greece, Scotland, Robert Burns, Lewis Carroll, cycling, youth hostelling, photography - these were among his interests. Perhaps two should be singled out - the Cricket Club and *London Town*. He was no great cricketer but he loved the game - its lore and literature, its subtleties and technicalities, its beer and badinage, its humour and stories - and in 1958 he called the meeting which re-established the staff Cricket Club after virtual extinction and was secretary from 1958 to 1965.

London Town he regarded almost reverently; he had a deep respect for its traditions and admiration for its standards. He contributed often, especially reviews of Dramatic Club productions, was a ready backroom helper with scissors and paste for many years, and did his share as editor when the journal was produced by a consortium between 1971 and 1973.

In some ways Maurice was the archetypal uncle. A bachelor, he was immensely proud of his own nephew and niece: in addition, he was the adoptive uncle of the children and grandchildren of many of his friends; he remembered their birthdays, treated them to the joys of the pantomime, introduced them to cricket at the Oval, football at Highbury. He was never happier that when organizing a gathering of friends (sometimes ill-assorted) at the Players' Theatre, Bertorelli's, the staff sports ground, Lord's: if the mood were right, any occasion would serve. He would have relished the large and diverse assembly at his funeral servie at Woking.

A complex, generous, contradictory man, then, who placed his energies and gifts at the service of his colleagues. He lived a jubilant and sombre, sad and happy life. He would be surprised how deeply he will be missed.

C. D. Andrews.

If Laurence Welsh was *sans pareil* as an Editor of the *Staff Gazette/London Town* it was C. D. Andrews who stood supreme as a contributor: and he also made his own very distinctive mark upon the journal as Editor, not least by taking the lead in formulating those "Spreadeagle rules" - named after a long vanished pub where they were hammered out -

which guided all succeeding Editors on good *London Town* practice.

It may seem odd, therefore, that the pages of the magazine may be searched in vain for the sort of tribute that was so prominently - and rightly - paid to Laurence Welsh. Unfortunately, when Andrews came to retire from the GLC service, in May 1974, the sort of writers who could have done him justice (Ian Wilson and David Moore spring readily to mind) were temporarily estranged from *London Town* as a result of the notorious "coup" of a year previous: and although the journal carried, in its June 1974 issue, a two page spread recounting an interview which CDA had given to the then Editor and Deputy Editor this was far from being a Laurence Welsh type eulogy and it would not fit in at all well with the other items in this section of the *Miscellany*. It is for that reason that we have sought to give Andrews his meed of praise in the form of this note.

Such praise is certainly well deserved. Andrews joined the staff of the LCC, in the Chief Engineer's Department, in 1932 (something of a vintage year for new entrants) and within a year had made his first contribution (a short poem) to *London Town*. Thenceforward, few months passed without something from his pen enlivening the pages of the journal, and his wide ranging output is well represented in this *Miscellany*. He invariably wrote cogently and clearly - and he always had something worthwhile to say. After his war service he became *London Town's* reporter of Staff Association General Committee meetings (1946-55) and then Editor (1956-61), Assistant Editor (1961-62) and finally contributor (under the pen name "Scorpius") of the influential "Wider Scene" column (1963-73).

It was an unparalleled record: and it was coupled with a steady rise through the ranks of the LCC/GLC service, including eleven years (1962-73) as Chief Admin. Officer of Chief Engineer's - a Department which was transformed (and expanded) into successively Highways and Transportation (1965) and Planning and Transportation (1969). He finished his GLC career as Leader of the Docklands Consultation Team, but his services to *London Town* by no means ended at his formal retirement: he was contributing to its pages as late as 1989. Sadly, he was not to live to see this *Miscellany*, a work in which he took a typically lively interest, for he died on 7 March 1992, a loss that truly diminishes all who knew him.

Throughout this long and fruitful career he was, behind his formidable exterior, the kindliest of men: but he never suffered foolishness gladly (suffering fools was a different matter - often enough he had no option). This shows through in almost all his work, official as well as "extra-mural", as does his never failing irreverence and his deep commitment to those democratic, liberal values that inspired the journal through almost all its life. Laurence Welsh set the *Staff Gazette* firmly on the course that was to make it *London Town* as it will always be remembered: but it was CDA who kept it firmly on that course and ensured that it would be (as he said in that farewell interview in 1974) "not just a trade union paper" but more - much more.

F. T. Hollocks.

Arthur Turner
(February 1984)

It was with particular delight that I received an invitation from the Staff Association to write a piece for *London Town* on the retirement of Fred Hollocks. My pleasure was caused not simply because Fred and I had been close colleagues on the Whitley Council Staff Side for over four years, but because my knowledge of him goes back over thirty years to 1952 when we both worked in the Treasurer's department of the Middlesex County Council. We were not close acquaintances in those days but I knew enough about his views on political and trade union matters to realise that we had much in common. When our paths later diverged neither of us could guess that the vagaries of life would eventually bring us together again in circumstances where that identity of viewpoint was to be crucial.

Fred joined the London County Council Staff Association as Deputy Secretary in 1956. His appointment was an inspired choice. By this time Fred had abandoned his professional career in local government despite the view of the then Middlesex Treasurer that he was destined for the highest office; indeed he had been working with the parliamentary staff of the Labour Party of the House of Commons. The esteem in which he was held by the leaders of the party is illustrated by a presentation book which they gave him when he left, signed by Hugh Gaitskell, Harold Wilson, James Callaghan, Herbert Morrison (no doubt amused at Fred's joining the 'goose club'), Anthony Greenwood, Antony Crosland, Alf Robens and others.

He was also by then a considerable politician in his own right, having exchanged the treasurer's baton for the leader's and embarked on a career in local politics which was to bring him to the chairmanship of the Finance committee and eventually the leadership of Hounslow Borough Council. He is remembered by many of his former Hounslow staff, as I can testify from personal knowledge, with much respect and affection. The fact that many of them were former Middlesex employees, who worked alongside Fred in his 'officer' days, speaks volumes for his character and sense of fairness.

His introduction to the sharp end of trade unionism was, to say the least, lively and a forerunner of the years to come. In July 1957 the Association affiliated to the TUC, one of the first white-collar unions to do so, and immediately ran headlong into a major dispute with the then Labour administration led by Ike Hayward. In a decision utterly offensive to trade union principles, the Council attempted to use affiliation to destroy the local joint negotiating machinery and to force the Staff Side into the national machinery. Not for the first or the last time the Association resisted. Eventually, but only after some years, Council Members came to their senses and the present Whitley machinery was formed. Fred, of course, played a major part in this period and demonstrated his abilities as a negotiator of skill, tenacity and, above all, patience.

Fred's appointment as Secretary in 1963 came just a year or so before the formation of the GLC and the wisdom of the Association's choice was again soon apparent. His experience as a former local government officer alerted him to the need from everyone's point of view of uniting the staff of the new authority. Without going into details of the whole affair, it was Fred's understanding, not shared at the time by all of his members, that measures taken in the short-term interests of former Middlesex staff were in the long-term interests of all which led to that valuable unity being achieved. It will be vital in the testing months ahead.

By the time the next crisis arose I was in a position to witness at first-hand the abilities of Fred Hollocks. My term as Leader of the Staff Side started with the election of the last Tory Council and the raising of Cutler's axe. That the

274

successive blows of that axe over the following four years did not decimate the Council was very largely due to Fred. Regrettably, a large proportion of the staff are hardly aware of the work that goes on in their interests. They complacently think that such things as annual increases in pay and London weighting, agreements on staff numbers and the avoidance of compulsory redundancies are arranged by a couple of telephone calls. The reality is of almost daily meetings, constant negotiations and much burning of the midnight oil.

This photograph was taken when Fred Hollocks was at the very beginning (1963) of his long and distinguished career as the Staff Association Secretary.

The Association is not, of course, a one-man band and the Secretary is the adviser to a team of both professional and lay officers, all of whom have an important contribution to make. Professionally, however, the man at the top carries enormous responsibility, and a lay officer can always walk away when he has done his stint. In addition, there are the day-to-day demands on the Secretary's time with many members assuming that their subscription buys his personal attention to even their smallest problems; but that is the nature of trade unionism. Such was Fred's total dedication to his job that without doubt the strain has had a telling effect upon his health.

Reference had already been made in *London Town* to his great skill as a negotiator. To this I can testify from the experience of many tough sessions at the table alongside Fred. I am quite convinced that he was one of the best negotiators among that rather select band of trade union general secretaries. Certainly he was considerably better than many, with far greater reputations, who happily went to the table backed by much heavier guns than ever Fred had. This was not the result of any lack of determination among our members. Rather it was because non-industrial workers generally expect their leaders to achieve success by negotiation rather than muscle, and at this Fred was highly skilled. With an ever-alert sharp mind and a fund of statistical information seemingly on tap inside his head, Fred was the type of trade unionist who is now coming into his inheritance on the TUC General Council. The new election rules, had they been agreed some years earlier, could have given Fred a General Council seat for which he was so well qualified. As it was, within the movement he was a well-respected man. To attend the TUC conference with Fred was an education. He knew everyone and everyone knew him, from the current Chairman of the Congress and Len Murray downwards. Len, I know, holds him in high esteem, as did his predecessor, the late Vic Feather.

I am also happy that the years of co-operation between us were years when we became close personal friends. Together with our wives we spent more than one stimulating and enjoyable week at the TUC conference, not the least of them Fred's last at Blackpool in 1981. The Saturday before that conference, which we spent with Fred and his wife Iris in a dramatic and stormy Lake District, will always be an enduring memory of one of the best men I have known. It is with great personal regard, therefore, that I send to Fred and Iris the best wishes of all trade unionists at County Hall for a long, happy and healthy retirement. From the evidence of a recent visit to them in their new home in the Cotswolds, and the way in which Iris is looking after him, there should be little doubt of that.

Note: Unfortunately, Fred Hollocks did not live to enjoy a long and peaceful retirement after such an active life: he died in 1985. The reference in the second paragraph of this article to Fred's joining the 'goose club' relates to Herbert Morrison's notorious dismissal of the (then) LCC Staff Association as "a bloody goose club" soon after he had become Leader of the Council in 1934: he was to live to revise that opinion.

M. J. Brand.

(July 1985)

31 May marked the retirement of Jeffery Brand after just over 38 years' service.

He had come to the London County Council on 1 January 1947, after some six years in the army, where he attained the rank of captain, serving first in the then Housing and Valuation department and later, when it was separated, Housing. Promotions came steadily.

Personnel work in what was at that time known as the Establishments department claimed him in 1969, and in 1974 he achieved senior officer rank, returning to Housing to work with distinction in the department's policy branch. Only two years were to pass, however, before he was back in Personnel where, in 1979, he was appointed administrative and establishment officer, the post he held until his departure.

The farewell gathering itself, on 30 May, was especially notable. It may well have been unique in nature. In the first place Mr Brand had managed to secure room 131 and the Members' terrace as the venue, and he had clearly organised the weather as well for it was a gloriously sunny afternoon. Secondly, he had arranged superb catering from the Council's special catering staff. Next, there were the guests - a vast gathering of them, representative of all those with whom he had worked, officially and extra-murally, over the years. Finally there were the speeches - from Bryan Watson (Director of Management and Central Services), Arthur Capelin (the Staff Association's Secretary) and Jenny Fletcher (Jeffery's successor as departmental personnel officer).

No stone - if the phrase is entirely apt - was left unturned: his career, his character, his interests, particularly the Staff Association and *London Town*. Much play was made of his chairmanship of the Association's Service Conditions Committee in early GLC days and of the Staff Side of the Whitley Council. And there were many present for whom the recital of the 'Brand versus GLC' court case must have come as news, for they could not have been in the service when this famous fight (ultimately for an increase not just in Jeffery Brand's pay but in all the staff's) was won.

Witty (indeed sometimes sharply witty), courteous, tenacious, hardworking and dedicated - all these things were said of the man, in one way or another, and the qualities shone through too in his own speech of thanks for his parting gift, for what had been said of him and for the friendship and loyalty so many had given him. He deserves, and all wish him, a long and happy retirement.

C. S. Corcoran.

(March 1986)

Word has it that Charles Corcoran of Architect's will not be continuing in service with any successor authority after 31 March. Even if this were not the case, this last issue of *London Town* would be absurdly incomplete without tribute being paid to his unswerving dedication to the Staff Association over so many years and, though it, to the many causes of the staff at large.

Charles Corcoran addressing the TUC, 1979.

Charles Corcoran 'won his spurs' in a period of sound service as a member of the Association's governing body, the General Committee, where his grasp of the important issues of the day attracted the notice as well as the admiration of his peers. He thus came to high office by the well-established, traditional route - by earning it. He was first elected Chairman of the Executive Committee in 1965; and, defying the adage that no-one is indispensable, he was to prove, year by year, that no other candidate for this demanding office - the key lay post in the Association's hierarchy - could match him for breadth of knowledge, enthusiasm, influence and an insatiable appetite for sheer hard work.

He has, of course, had his critics, and certainly *London Town* and he have not always, behind the scenes, hit it off too well. There are some who might argue that he has assumed too dominant a role, that his concern for the unity of the staff has sometimes made him over-cautious (particularly when a more militant stance might have seemed productive), and that he has been over-sensitive to criticism, however helpful that has been intended. A few might even accuse him of ruthlessness.

As time has gone by, however, Charles Corcoran has mellowed: yet there has at no time been anything soft about his negotiating tactics, and his absolute regard for the interests of every member of the Association has manifested itself in innumerable ways. Much of the credit for the establishment, late in 1966, of proper Whitley machinery within the GLC/ILEA is due to him personally; and it could well be that this alone stands as his greatest single achievement.

There is, though, much else to the man: tenacity, level-headedness and firm adherence to his principles; constant advocacy of the white-collar cause at the TUC's annual congresses and elsewhere; fearlessness in the face of the often openly unsympathetic, hostile and hypocritical attitude of some of those with whom he has had to negotiate in the Council; leadership; and, especially during the long and bitter abolition saga, dogged persistence in seeking to achieve objectives for the maximum benefit of the staff as a whole.

A wealth of detailed knowledge always seems to be at his fingertips. He marshals his facts adroitly and argues persuasively and sometimes with passion. And very few ever get the better of him. Charles Corcoran's will be a hard act to follow.

LIST OF ILLUSTRATIONS

Note: All illustrations are photographs unless otherwise stated. Photo credits are given for all illustrations obtained from outside institutions, whose kind permission to reproduce such illustrations in this book is gratefully acknowledged. Such institutions hold the copyright in these illustrations. Where credits are not given the illustrations have been taken from the records or files of *London Town*: copyright for most of this material is held by The Alexius Press Ltd.

The publishers wish to point out that because many of the photographs used in this book are very old, the quality of reproduction has in some instances been below recognised standards.

SELECT BIBLIOGRAPHY

It would clearly not be practicable to provide a bibliography for all the subjects touched on in this book. We think, however, that the following list of books dealir g with London-wide local government and those who worked for it, some of which have been mentioned earlier, would be of interest to our readers.

Progress Report 1909-1959, the first fifty years in the history of the London County Council Staff Association, C. D. Andrews and G. C. Burge, 1959.

Achievement, A Short History of the LCC, W. Eric Jackson, Longmans, 1965.

One Hundred Years of London Education 1870-1970, Stuart Maclure, Allen Lane, The Penguin Press, 1970.

Adult Education in Inner London 1870-1980, W. A. Devereux, Shepheard-Walwyn with ILEA, 1982.

Politics and the People of London: The London County Council 1889-1965, Ed. Andrew Saint, The Hambledon Press, 1989.

Almost a Century, A History of London Town Magazine, Len Hudson, The Alexius Press, 1991.

County Hall, Survey of London Monograph 17, published by the Athlone Press for the Royal Commission on the Historical Monuments of England, 1991.

The London Town Miscellany Volume 1 1900-1939, John Adamson and Len Hudson, The Alexius Press, 1992.

NOTES ON THE EDITORS

JOHN ADAMSON is a history graduate and a former administrative officer of the LCC/GLC/ILEA. He was associated with *London Town* as a contributor, as a Trustee of Witan Publications Ltd., and as Chairman of the London Town Club during the final phase of the magazine. Now a writer and publisher, he is currently working on a book on the Arun valley in West Sussex.

LEN HUDSON joined the staff of the LCC in 1948 and from the mid 1950s onwards held a variety of administrative posts in the service of the Council and its successor the GLC. He was active in Staff Association affairs from 1954 until 1985 and was an Editor of *London Town* from 1973 until 1990. His history of *London Town* magazine (*Almost a century*) was published by The Alexius Press early in 1991: he is currently researching a book on the Medway valley, and is actively concerned in the affairs of The Alexius Press.